THE ROYSTON CAVE

USED BY SAINTS OR SINNERS?

Local historical influences of the Templar and Hospitaller movements

by Sylvia P Beamon MA (Cantab)

Published by The Temple Publications 2009

The Temple Publications

PO Box 47

Watchet

Somerset

TA23 0WT

United Kingdom

ISBN 978-0-9557400-0-8

First published by Cortney Publications,

57 Ashwell Street, Baldock, Herts, 1992.

Cover design by Lee Yarlett. Knight logo by M. Curtis
Original typesetting by the author and Dave Sewart
Page set up and preparation by Tony Biggs
Printed in the UK by CPI William Clowes Beccles NR34 7TL

... For sincerity is a jewel which is pure and transparent,
eternal and inestimable.
For my hands and my feet are perfect as the
sublimity of Naphtali and the felicity of Asher.
For the names and number of animals are as the names and
number of the stars.
For I pray the Lord Jesus to translate my MAGNIFICAT into
verse and represent it.
For I bless the Lord Jesus from the bottom of Royston Cave
to the top of King's Chapel ...

Extract from *Jubilate Agno* by Christopher Smart written between 1749 and 1753. The poet was at Cambridge between 1739 and 1749, therefore could have had the opportunity of visiting the Cave shortly after its discovery. Alternatively, he could have read the published works by Stukeley and Parkin between 1743-6.

(I am indebted to Lucy Bright for locating this passage)

To Dave Sewart, Trevor Pitt; my husband Alan Beamon
and our family Kevin, Ivor, Murray and Stacey

Royston Cave - Used by Saints or Sinners?

(Local historical influences of the Templar and Hospitaller movements)

CONTENTS

ACKNOWLEDGEMENTS

A high proportion of my research and the writing-up of this book was carried out in the 1970s. I am particularly indebted to Professor Raymond Mauny who, at that time, was at the Faculty of Letters at the Sorbonne University, Paris and to the late Dr. R. C. Smail, former Fellow of Sidney Sussex College, University of Cambridge because, without their genuine kindness and assistance, I could not have managed to further my work. Nor without the help, patience and constancy of David I. Sewart, BSc., then of the Department of Geodesy and Geophysics who taught me how to use the computer, and, together with the support of Trevor Pitt, helped in my endeavours with the practicalities - erecting free-standing scaffolding, carrying heavy equipment etc. - which always seemed to occur on the most unsuitable of days, in a snow storm, torrential rain, or blowing a gale to you all, my grateful thanks.

I wish also to thank the following for their assistance and co-operation, the late Dr. T. S. R. Boase, a former Director of the Courtauld Institute of Art and of Magdalen College, Oxford. Members of Cambridge University: H. A. Allerton, MSc., Dept. of Geodesy and Geophysics; members and staff of the Department of Archaeology and Anthropology, especially Pat Smith, Conservation Technician; Dr. C. L. Forbes, Department of Geology; the late Prof. Glyn Daniel, Prof. D. E. Luscombe, MA, PhD, Churchill College; Mrs. D. M. Owen, MA, FSA, Manuscripts Department, University Library; Dr. J. Riley-Smith, Queens' College and now Professor of History at Royal Holloway and Bedford New College, University of London; Dr. F. Stubbings, Emmanuel College; the staff at the University Library. The Bibliothèque Nationale, Cabinet des Manuscrits, Paris; British Museum, Peter H. T. Shorer, their former Senior Conservation Officer; Dr. P. Christie, FSA; Colchester Museum; Courtauld Institute of Art; Sir Bernard Feilden, CBE, D.Univ., FSA, FRSA, FRIBA, AA Dipl(hons); Harlow Museum; Hertford Record Office and Local Studies Library; Public Record Office; Michael Rice; Royston and District History Society; Jeremy Haslam and staff of Royston Library; Emma Bond, Curator and her assistant Carol Kaszak, Royston Museum; Library and Museum of the Grand Priory ofthe British Realm of the Most Venerable Order of St. John of Jerusalem, Clerkenwell; staff of the Warburg Institute, London. Susan Ames, Caroline Brent (for reading the final draft), the late Mrs. Kay de Brisay, C. W. Cooper, C. Dale, former Newsells Estate Manager, Olive Davis, Tom Doig, W. H. Fordham, FGS (deceased), Mrs. Nina Freebody, Frances and John Garrood, H. J. Gray, Daam Wijnand Hoogendijk, Adey Horton, H. J. Lovegrove, Phil Marshall, Mrs. Violet Pritchard, FSA (Scot), Anne Rayner, Hilary Roberts and her late husband Tony, Iris Sher, J. C. Wilkerson, Mrs. Rosa Young, and to end this section, Royston and District Councillors.

My appreciation goes to those who carried out the translations - Cliff and Mary Atkins and Miss Hilary White (Greneway School, Royston), Anne Cooper and Michael Farrar Cambridgeshire Co. Record Office, J. Monk (Hitchin Grammar School), Maeta Mackenzie and Edward O. Furber.

My very very special thanks go once more to Dave Sewart for the hours of his time and expertise in setting the text in preparation for the final publication of this work (1991-2).

Finally, sincere thanks are reserved for, my husband Alan and the children, Kevin, Ivor, Murray and Stacey, who stoically tramped around churches and museums for my benefit with forbearance usually! Or, to put it another way, they tolerated my long term interest.

2009. The author would like to thank The Temple Publications, Oddvar Olsen and Stephen Andrews, for their help and interest in this new publication.

A CAVE

Esoterically speaking a cave can be 'a symbol of the universe' (Porphyry); an omphalos; the world centre; the heart; the place of union of the Self and the Ego. It can be the meeting place of the divine and the human, hence all dying gods and saviours are born in caves. A place of initiation and the second birth, of inner esoteric knowledge and for that which is hidden. The cave is also the feminine principle, the womb of Mother Earth and her sheltering aspect. It is both a place of burial and. rebirth, of mystery, increase and renewal, from which man emerges and to which he returns at death in the stone sepulchre. This emergence associates the cave with the Cosmic Egg. The cave is closely related to the symbolism of the heart as the spiritual and initiatory centre of both the macrocosm and the microcosm. Both the cave and the heart are symbolised by the feminine, downward pointing triangle.

Initiation ceremonies were most frequently held in a cave as symbolic of the underworld and the sepulchre where death occurred prior to rebirth and illumination. As a place of initiation it was also secret, the entrance to which was hidden from the profane by a labyrinth or dangerous passage, often guarded by some monster or supernatural person. Entry could only be gained by overcoming the opposing force. Entering the cave is also re-entry into the womb of Mother Earth, as with cave burials. Passing through the cave represents a change of state, also achieved by overcoming dangerous powers. The cave is often the place of the sacred marriage or union between heaven and earth, king and queen etc. the *hieros gamos.*

In Celtic thought a cave was the entrance way to the other world.

There was also the popular Mithraic belief of the Roman armies brought from Persia. Worship and initiation took place in a cave in which there were flowers and springs in honour of Mithras, Father and Creator of All; the cave reproduced in miniature the universe he had created. (Cooper, J. C. (1978) *An Illustrated Encyclopaedia of Traditional Symbols,* Thames & Hudson, London, p. 31)

LIST OF ILLUSTRATIONS WITH ACKNOWLEDGEMENTS

FIGURES:

Fig. 1. The Royston Cave: The dome was not penetrated, the eastern shaft unopened and the podium is shown as circular. A little rectangular recess inset over the 'grave area', and also part of this depression itself would seem to have been destroyed when the 'new' passage was cut in 1790. This identical drawing appears in both of Revd. William Stukeley's books dated 1743 and 1746.

INTRODUCTION

The Royston Cave is situated 13 miles [20.8 km] south of Cambridge in the County of Hertfordshire adjacent to the former crossing of two major routes across Britain. These crossroads were altered in the late 1960s to form a 'T-junction' to close off the High Street (north-south) to through traffic, except for access. A bottle-shaped 'cave', which is man-made, was hollowed out of the chalk at some unknown time in the past (Fig. 1). The walls are decorated with engraved religious figures, together with unusual signs and symbols. Today, the only way into this structure is through the 'new' passageway cut in 1790 on the east side of Melbourn Street. As to the cavern's origin or purpose, this has been a source of much interest and conjecture during the last two centuries since its discovery in the middle of the 18th century. The general consensus of opinion maintains it was used, at sometime at least, as a small oratory. But, the main question raised is, by whom? From the writer's own research, the most likely candidates would seem to be the Knights Templar.

The Knights Templar were a Crusading order in the Medieval period (1118-1308). A good description of them is that they were 'monks of war', they lived according to their religious *Rule* as monks, yet fought as soldiers in various battles throughout the Holy War in Palestine. Tracts of land, historically documented, were given to the brethren by several local families. Baldock, 9 miles [14.4 km] away from Royston, was a Templar created town. Their lands around supported them economically during peaceful times and regularly members of this fraternity travelled to the Royston market where they sold, butter, cheese, wine and leather goods.

Some Templar Churches were peculiar in shape, circular without and a few, octagonal within. It is said that they were copied from the Church of the Holy Sepulchre in Jerusalem. Although the Royston Cave does not exactly conform, it is circular without and does have a raised octagonal ledge within, although the latter's shape is not obvious now since time and wear has given it an appearance of being almost circular. (The resistivity test of 1972 indicated that the floor area was originally cut in a square, then cut again to form the octagon.) This ledge or podium may have been used as a seat, except it is rather low. Another explanation could be that it was used to kneel upon for prayers.

It would not be too surprising to find a Templar Chapel at the Royston crossroads because the Knights Templar Order initially undertook to help the pilgrims on their way to Jerusalem, and the two roads (the Roman Ashwell Street/or Icknield Way and Roman Ermine Street) were well used. The Templars also became bankers, introducing the word *cheque* into our language. They were responsible for moving large sums of money throughout this country and abroad. At Baldock and Cambridge there were Templar houses, also preceptories at Hitchin, Duxford and Shingay cum Wendy. All these places are only a few miles away from Royston and are on the route to London and Dover.

The following chapters are an attempt to put Royston into the context of the middle ages by time, its position in the district (Fig. 2), and to consider the influences exerted by both the Knights Templar Order and that of their contemporary rivals, the Knights Hospitallers. Finally, was Royston Cave a truly Christian oratory? Was it ever used by the Templars, if so, were they saints or sinners?

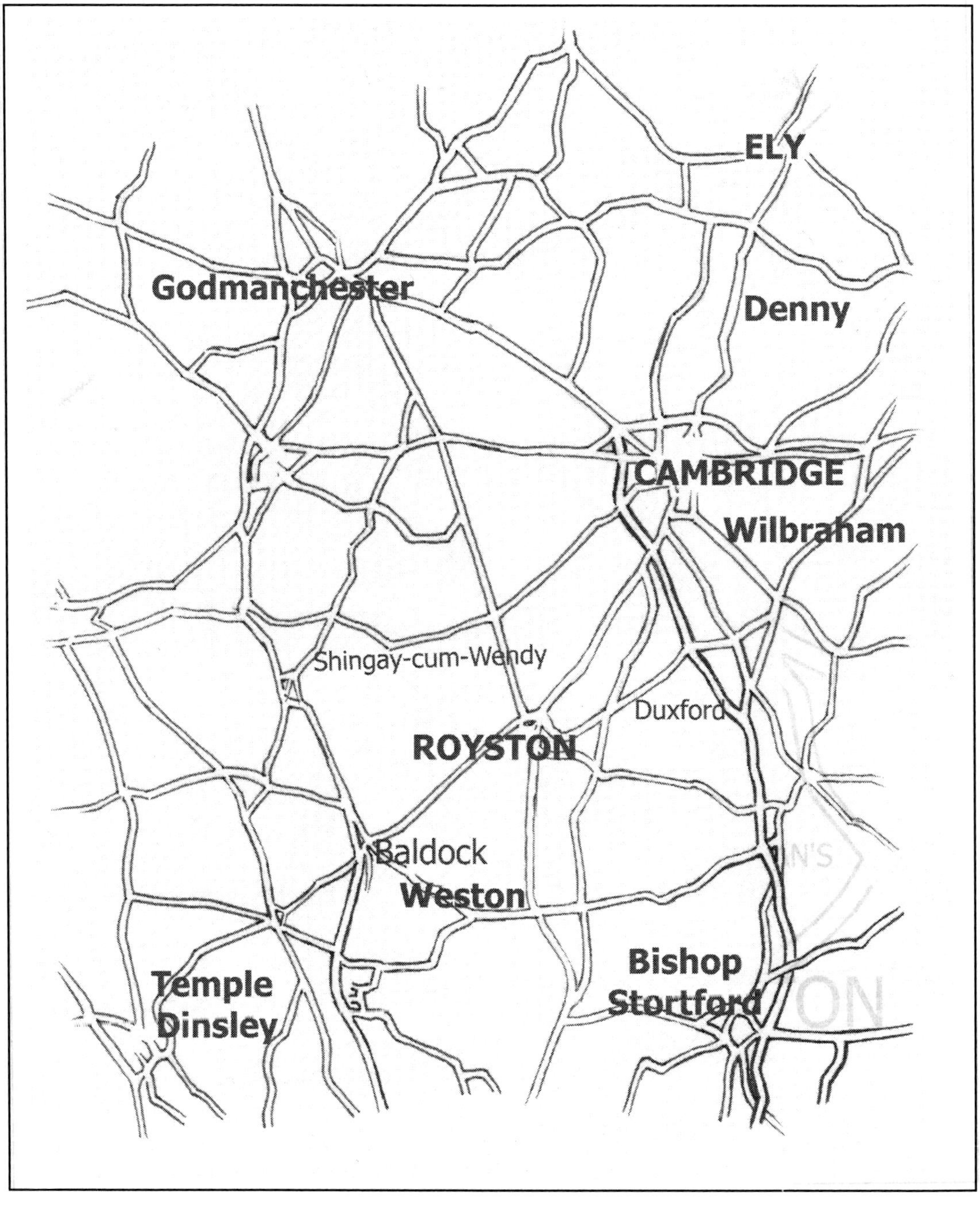

Fig. 2. Location map. Line drawing by Yuri Leitch

1. THE CROSS AT ROYSTON

At the junction of the two ancient roads Icknield Way cum Ashwell Street and Ermine Street, often referred to as 'military roads' because they were prepared or improved upon by the Roman military forces to forge their way into Britain's hinterland, formerly stood the old cross. The exact position of this venerable monument is not known, but it may be presumed to have stood in the south-east angle of the roads, somewhere between the dome of the Cave and the line of the Ermine (Ermen) Street being in the parish of Barkway, and in the fee of the Lordship of Newsells of which Eudo Dapifer, William the Conqueror's Seward, was the first recorded owner. However, it may have occupied the site of an earlier monument, even as far back as Roman times. It was not less common among the Saxons to erect a cross at a crossroads, but, the previous existence of a monument in this place cannot be carried beyond speculation. Unfortunately, neither its Saxon or Norman origin, nor the actual form the historical cross took can be determined, the upper part having been destroyed long ago. Nevertheless, the footstone, which still exists, is described by the Rev. William Stukeley (1743) in his first book, as:

'a flattish stone, of very great bulk, with a square hole or mortaise, in the centre, wherein was let the foot of the upright stone, or tenon, which was properly the cross'.

This interesting relic has had several moves, in fact, has been moved all around the town. First, to the opposite corner of the street, where it was seen by Stukeley. On 3rd June 1786 it was removed from the crossroads and placed in the yard of the Bull Inn on Market Hill until 1856; then off to rest in the garden of the Mechanics Institute (now the Town Hall). Later, it was removed to the grounds of the Crown Hotel in Melbourn Street until the Hotel was demolished in 1923, following which, it resided near to the crossroads once again between Kneesworth Street and Lower King Street, set on a plinth in front of the public toilets (Fig. 3). It languished here for quite some time before being placed in its present resting place, on the opposite side on the road (bottom of the High Street forming the T-junction) surrounded by flower beds in 1987. Various plaques have come and gone, removed by unauthorised persons, or to use the terminology of the day 'vandals'.

Joseph Beldam (1852) relates that Camden (1586), who was a great authority on most historical questions, contented himself with local tradition, and ascribed the erection of this cross to:

> "...a famous Lady Rosia, by some supposed to have been Countess of Norfolk, about the time of the Norman Conquest, which Cross, was called after her name Royse's Cross, till Eustace de Marc founded, just by it, a Priory, dedicated to St. Thomas à Becket, the Martyr of Canterbury; upon which occasion inns came to be built, and by degrees it became a town which instead of Royse's Cross, took the name of Royse's Town, afterwards contracted to Royston."

A great probability undoubtedly exists, that the earliest proprietors of the fee of Newsells, the local Manor House, had something to do with either its erection or its restoration. Not only that, but it is helped by the fact that among the members and nearest connections of the ennobled family, shortly after the Conquest, there were actually several ladies who bore the name of' Rosia'. However, Camden's statement by no means identifies the lady to whom it could be ascribed.

Other suggestions as to the reason for the name of this cross have been put forward. Rev. Charles Parkin (1746) argued that the style and title of the Priory, founded in the lifetime of the second Lady Roisia, and called after the name of the cross, *De Cruce Roaesie,* certainly implied the cross itself was at that time of considerable fame, and probably of considerable antiquity. This inference seems strengthened by the local and vernacular name of the spot, frequently occurring in the earliest Priory deeds, and latinised into *Roaesie,* which is variously spelt *Roys, Roes, Rous,* and *Roheys:* words which certainly have much of a Scandinavian character, and are not so easily derived from a female Christian name. Except, attention should be drawn to the Lady Roisia wife of Geoffrey de Mandeville, first Earl of Essex, whose Christian name is spelt several ways as *Rohese, Rohesia, Rahese* as evidenced in charters contained in *Cartularium Prioratus de Colne.* [Stukeley and Parkin spell her name 'Roisia' but Beldam uses 'Rosia'].

In the view of the historian Nathaniel Salmon (1728) he cites the learned Dane, Olaus Wormius to prove, that amongst the northern nations, the practice of burning the dead, and heaping a mound over their ashes, was known by the name of *Roiser,* and the tumulus itself, by the name of *Roise.* And various Saxon words, almost identical in sound, and of similar significance, such as *Hreaws,* pronounced 'raws', meaning a funeral; *Reowes,* pronounced 'roes', signifying sorrow or mourning, and *Rowes,* or *Rous,* implying rest or repose, all appear to confirm the Scandinavian origin of the name, and raises a strong presumption that the original cross was so-named, either from some remarkable funereal mound erected on the site, or from those numerous tumuli in the neighbourhood on Therfield Heath. (Beldam, 1884, 7-8; Stukeley, 1746, 1)

What is actually known? That there was a cross set up here, at a very early date, is undoubted. There is also this traditional association with the name of a lady. The first Lady Roisia, who as the wife of such a man as Eudo Dapifer, was a considerable personage: and possibly, through some act of restoring an existing cross, the name of this woman, or of the later Lady Roisia, may have become associated with this monument and with the town which was growing up around. Furthermore, the town is named as *Croyroys* (1262) (Ekwall, 1985, 395); *Croiroys* and *Crosroys* (1275) (Lees, 1935, 270); *Reyston* (1280); *Roiston* (1286); the later name of Royston may be *tun by Crux Roys* when the *Crux* has been dropped. (Ekwall, op.cit.)

I also mention here an extract from the *Survey Book of the Late Dissolved Priory* taken 4th May 1610 (560):

> 'Note that in the myddest of Icknell Streate, aforesaid, and at the West end of the same streate there is a fayer howse, or crosse bwylded up by the Lorde of ye sayd manor and the whole Towneshipp for a clock-house, and a Prison-howse for the use and benefitt of the whole parish, on both sydes, as well for Cambridgeshire syde as for Hertfordshire syde and standing in both the sayd Counties by the side of it is wrote:

"THE CLOCKHOWSE, CROSSE AND PRYSON-HOWSE IN ICKNELL STREATE, FOR THE WHOLE PARISHE."

In Stukeley's second book published in 1746 *Palaeographia Britannica* No. II he states:

> 'In the year 1742 they accidentally discovered a subterraneous crypt in the very centre of the town of Roiston in Hertfordshire: under the very market cross, close by the stump of an ancient cross...'

Fig. 3. The stone was moved from its siting above, between Kneeswoth Street and Lower King Street, in 1987. It now rests on the opposite side of the main road. The anonymous and unrelated photograph was probably taken in the 1970s.

A further development as to the exact whereabouts of the cross occurred when there appeared in the local paper *Herts and Cambs Reporter and Royston Crow* dated Friday, January 26th, 1973 the following report:

‘DOES ROYSE’S CROSS LIE BURIED NEAR THE STONE?

Does the stone cross which once marked Royston’s central crossroad lie buried near that very spot - within a few yards of the Roys Stone which formed its base? It does, claims Cyril Cooper, a well-known local personality, who told the *Crow* this ,week that he remembers partly unearthing the cross about 40 years ago.

It was mention of a similar find in another part of the country which recalled the occasion to Cyril’s memory. It also served as a reminder of the complete change in working conditions over the past 40 years Cyril and the workmate who came across the old relic simply dared not stop work to investigate further.

At the time - Cyril reckons it was in the early 1930’s - there was a slump in the building trade, and Cyril got a job as a casual labourer with a London firm who were laying telephone cables in Royston. He was working with another local personality, the late Bill Maling, digging out trenches at The Cross.

About three feet [1m] below the road surface and ‘just to the right of the pipes facing Baldock Street - opposite the right-hand door post of Beale’s Corner Cafe, they found the cross, or possibly a portion of it, which Cyril recalls as being about 2 feet [0.6 m] long and about a foot [0.32 m] across.

But those were not the days when a workman could show enlightened interest, ‘You must remember, we had no mechanical aids,’ said Cyril. ‘It was just pick and shovel. Work was difficult to get at that time, and if you were thought to be wasting time you simply got the sack. So the cross was covered over and we moved on.’

Cyril has lived in Melbourn for some years, but he was living at Mount Terrace, Royston, at the time in question and knew every inch of the town - that is why he remembers the position of the cross by ‘landmarks,’ Beale’s Corner Cafe was pulled down nearly a decade ago, when the actual crossroad was sealed off at the bottom of the High Street, but Cyril is still pretty sure about the spot...’

The article goes on to explain about the Roys Stone, and the final paragraph states that:

‘Whatever the truth of this ascription, it has always been believed that the stone cross which obviously stood here was lost or destroyed centuries ago. Has the personal memory of a local man brought to light - or nearly to light a most valuable relic of Royston’s past.’

Accompanying the report was a photograph of Mr. Cooper, during a lull in the traffic, standing on the spot where he believes the town's ancient stone cross lies buried.

Eagerly we awaited next week's edition only to find that the credibility was doubted, and the following was recorded:

FURTHER TO THE 'BURIED CROSS'

> 'Much local interest was aroused by last week's unique *Crow* story 'Does Royse's Cross lie buried near the Stone.' Cyril Cooper's account of how he unearthed what may have been the long-lost cross, so near its original site, won the attention of the local History Society in particular.
>
> Mr. Philip Smith (Chairman) and his brother, Mr. F. John Smith, who are well versed in the town's general history and can therefore consider the probabilities of more ancient links, have given thought to Mr. Cooper's claim, which raises many points of speculation.
>
> 'It is obviously going to be some time before the road (at The Cross) is up again,' Mr. F. John Smith commented this week, 'but we feel it would be well worth while having a look at that spot when this does happen.'
>
> But his opinion has always been that the Royse's Cross was much more likely to have been made of wood, rather than stone. There is no source of suitable stone in this area, and the Roys Stone which provided the base of the cross is not (apart from a rough mortise hole) 'dressed' at all - as it would have been if it had supported a formal stone cross.
>
> Further, the brothers have been reminded by their mother, Mrs. Frank Smith - and other Roystonians will recall - that the narrow pavement which skirted the old Crown Inn at The Cross had rather large kerbstones. Could one of these buried at the time the Crown was demolished, have been what Cyril Cooper found while he was digging there.
>
> There are of course many possibilities, and it is a very long time since Mr. Cooper had to cover up what he believed to be the Roys Cross. 'We certainly don't want to discourage anyone from having theories about these things,' says Mr. Smith, 'but we shall not be able to prove anything until such time as another trench is dug in the road.'
>
> He points out, incidentally, that the Roys Stone itself is an 'odd' stone for the area - it may well have been carried down from the north of the country by a glacial action. Any cross fashioned in the district would have to be of a different material - hence, he feels, the greater likelihood of a wooden cross.'

On the 9th February, Mr. Cooper replied through another article,

'I'M SURE IT IS A CROSS,' SAYS CYRIL COOPER

> Cyril Cooper, who told the *Crow* about the possibility of the long-lost Roys Cross being under the road near its original spot, does not agree with the alternative explanations quoted in last week's issue. 'I'm quite sure I know the difference between a cross and a kerbstone,' he declared on Monday.
>
> He described the stone he partly unearthed some 40 years ago as being 'green-grey' - and added something of additional interest.
>
> 'Under the surface of the present road at the Cross there is an old cobbled roadway,' he said. 'At the time we were digging the trench for the cables, we were below that, moving earth which had not been touched for hundreds of years. That's where we found the cross.'
>
> Cyril said also that while he was working on the cable-laying he picked up a number of coins, one of them dated 1721.
>
> He reckons too, that the Roys Stone 'could have been dug up near North Hall. When ploughing was going on behind Bridgefoot Farm several years ago, a very big stone was dug up. This stone, though not quite as big as the Roys Stone, is now at Grange Farm.'
>
> All of which is extremely interesting - it could almost be wished that the present mains-laying was to be carried out over that portion of road, so that further investigation could be made.'

I had reason to contact the local photographer Mr. R. Clark, and during our conversation then he asked me what I thought about the Cross. I said I believed it to be quite possible in view of the fact I had discovered that Cambridgeshire land had included the butter market on the other side of where the road runs today, immediately in front of the Westminster Bank, therefore the old road must have been well over on that side hence the cobblestones. Mr. Clark said, 'He had known Mr. Cooper for a great many years and if he said it was a cross he had found, it was a cross, and if I had the opportunity I should speak to him.'

I telephoned Mr. Cooper a week later and he explained he had worked in the building trade all his life and certainly knew the difference between kerbstones and a cross. I asked whether it had been in two pieces and he said, 'No, it was a cross and he had rubbed the dust off it with his own hands and it laid facing Baldock Street.' He had also sent an illustration to the *Crow,* I thought it a pity this had been omitted.

Mr. Cooper very kindly sent me a cardboard cut-out shape of the cross he found (Fig. 4). No doubt there have been several crosses and possibly this is one of them.

HOT CROSS BUNS

The Rev. Ditchfield in his book on *Old English Customs,* remarks when alluding to the origin of Hot Cross Buns that the Romans made these sacred cakes in honour of Diana whose festival was observed soon after the vernal equinox. The original home of the custom of making these buns or cakes (with their cross) is chiefly observed in Cambridgeshire and Hertfordshire and at Royston is the spot where the Roman roads called the Icknield Way crossed the Ermine Street or Way. Here stood in Roman times the altar dedicated to Diana to whom the Romans offered their sacred cakes. Here too the custom of eating hot cross buns is chiefly observed, whereas in many parts of England they are quite unknown. This is a curious survival of the Roman times which have been handed down to our day by the agency of Hot Cross Buns (see vol. I p. 48). *

Note: The cross upon these cakes may refer to the crossing of these two ancient roads at Royston. *(Personal notes of N. Maynard of Whittlesford,* c. 1870 held in the Cambridge Record Office R58/5/5)

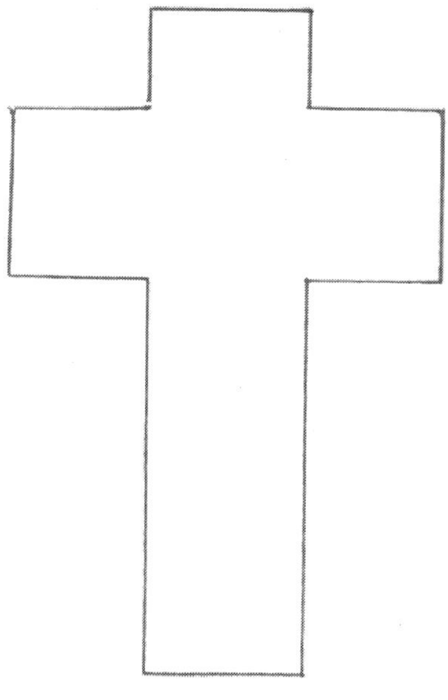

Fig. 4. Shape of a cross uncovered in the early 1930s – Cyril Cooper, 1973.

* The first evidence of Roman activity in Royston was unearthed by excavation in Green Drift, off Kneesworth Street [Ermine Street] in July 2008 under direction of Richard Mortimer of CAMARC. A copy of the report is held in the Royston and District Museum – SPB 2009.

2. DISCOVERY OF THE CAVE

THE MERCAT HOUSE, AUGUST 1742

The Cave was discovered by accident, in the August of 1742, when a bench was being erected in the Mercat House for the women who sold their wares in the cheese and butter market held there. As workmen were digging a hole for a post they struck through the eye, or central hole, of a millstone lying beneath the ground, and found a cavity approximately 16 ft [4.8 m] deep; as appeared by letting down a plumb-line. These workmen took up the millstone and removed some chalk rubble which then revealed a well-like descent of about 2 ft [0.6 m] in diameter. The shaft was quite circular and perpendicular. There were holes cut into the chalk, at equal distances apart and opposite to each other almost like the steps of a ladder. A boy was first let down into it [by force or otherwise is not noted!], and afterwards 'a thin man', with a lighted candle, who ascertained that it passed through an opening about 4 ft [1.2 m] in height into another cavity:

'This was filled with loose earth, yet not touching the wall, which he saw to the right and left. The people of the town now entertained a notion of great treasure being hidden here, and some workmen enlarged the descent.' [Hence the destruction of the footholds] 'Then with buckets and a well-kirb, they set to work in earnest to draw up the earth and rubbish. The vast concourse of people now becoming very troublesome, they were obliged to work by night, till, at length, by unwearied diligence, after raising two hundred loads of earth they quite exhausted it. Mr. George Lettis and Mr. William Lilly, tailor and salesman, who lived in the house over it, were the chief movers in opening and emptying the place.' (Stukeley, No.1, 1743, 6)

REV. GEORGE NORTH

Almost immediately after the Cave was discovered, it was visited by the Rev. George North, of Caldecot *(sic)* [Codicote, Herts.], a member of the Society of Antiquaries. Its position has been already indicated as being in the southeast angle of the two main roads, and nearly below the Cross. In a letter, addressed to the learned Society in the following month of September, Mr. North states, that on examination, he had found the Cave, not only different from what he had apprehended, but from anything he ever saw before. The workmen however, had not then reached the bottom by 8 ft [2.5 m], for which reason he could give but an imperfect account of it. But by way of illustration; he enclosed a rough drawing of its appearance at that stage (Fig. 5). Rev. North, after giving a brief description of the place and the circumstances of the discovery, expressed his conviction that:

> 'the whole work was the work of remote ages, and certainly anterior to the existence of a town on the spot...'

He added, that there was no tradition in the town to lead to the design of the excavation.

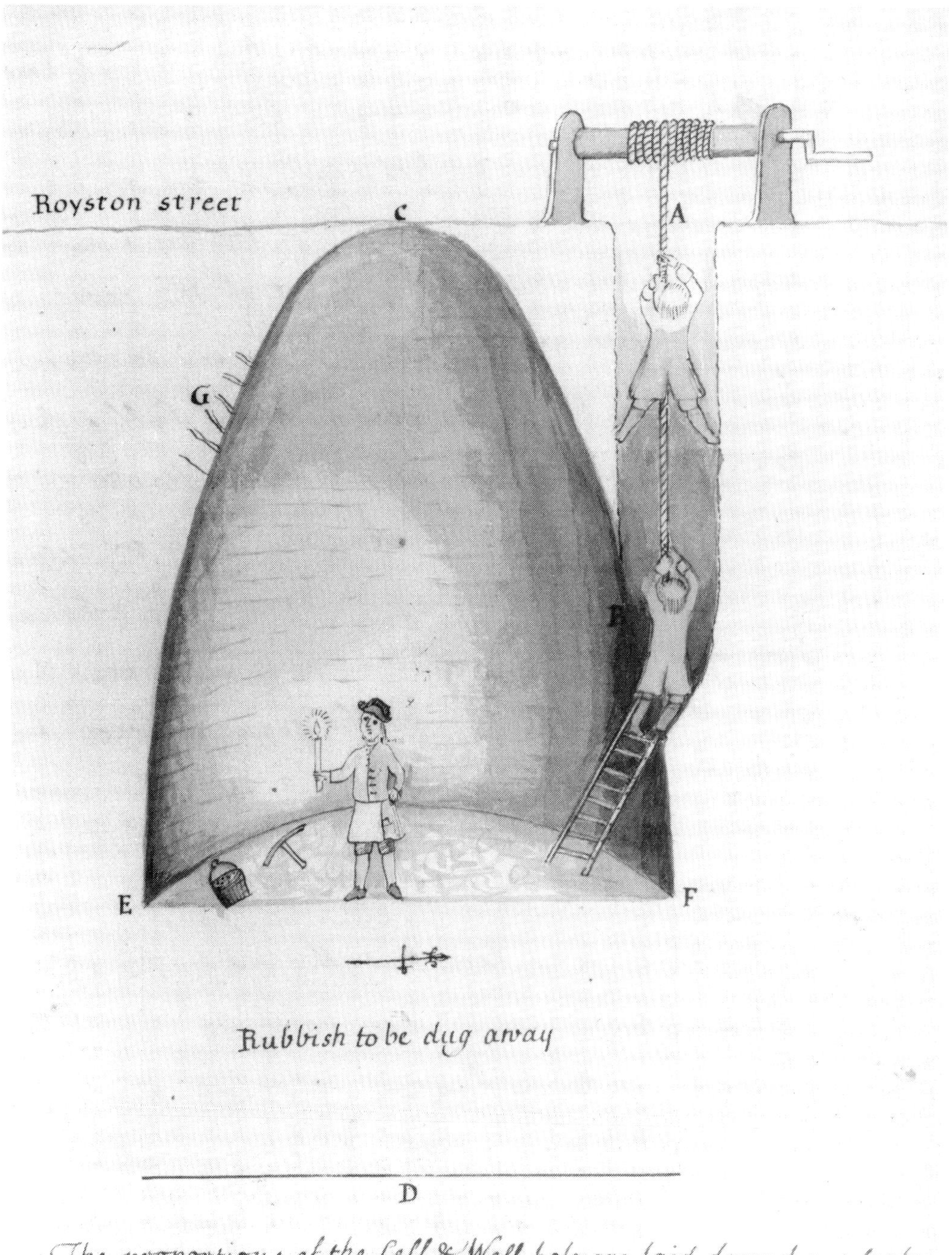

Fig. 5. 'Society of Antiquaries of London Minutes vol. 4', 1742 *and drawn by J. Ames. (Permission granted from the Society for its reproduction.)*

A letter dated 15th October 1742, badly written and illspelt, was written by the member of Parliament, Mr. William Goodhall to the Rev. William Stukeley, a former Secretary of the Society of Antiquaries (to be re-elected again in 1754):

> "... You being a Person very Curious in Things of Antiquity, I thought it would Oblige you to give you a short Account of a Place thought to be a very Grate Curiosity Latly discovered in this Town..." '...in removing a stone the workmen "found it was Hollor" and that there was in fact a large "Cavaty" beneath the street. "So they then emadgind that som very Grate Trashur was hid in that Place", but only found a "Scull and som Hewman bones..." "...som think it was for a place of Worship in the Earliest times of Chrestyanaty ... but all think it a Grate Curiosity."

Stukeley was one of this country's first field archaeologists. He visited many sites, reported on them and drew what he saw. It would seem that on arrival of the above letter, Stukeley in his normal impetuous manner, rode at once to Royston, because he was at the Cave on the 19th, examining and drawing the discovery. (Piggott, 1985, 120)

FINDS FROM THE CAVE

The only finds from the Cave reported by the Rev. North, were a human skull, a few decayed bones, fragments of a small drinking cup of "common brown earth, marked with yellow spots", and a piece of brass without any figure or inscription on it.

WHAT WAS THE CAVE'S FUNCTION? WHO WAS RESPONSIBLE FOR ITS DECORATION?

Dr. Stukeley, with the genuine enthusiasm of an antiquary, wrote in 1743:

> 'Then fully appeared this agreeable subterranean recess, hewn out of pure chalk, of about thirty foot [9 m] high, and nearly twenty foot [6 m] diameter. 'Tis of an elegant bell-like, or rather mitral form; well turned and exactly circular' [an observation which is not quite correct.] 'The effect of it is very pleasing. The light of the candles scarce reaches the top, and that gloominess overhead increases the solemnity of the place. All around the martyrs and historical pieces ...' [He refers here to Lady Roysia which I will give attention to under a different chapter.] ' ... They are cut with a design and rudeness suitable to the time and manner wherein she lived; which was soon after the conquest. I have given a plate which is a section of this grot, together with the manner of the descent. The cut is supposed to be made on the meridian line, and presents the eastern half of the place. A kind of broad bench goes quite round the floor, next the wall; broader than a step, and not so high as a seat ... 'This bench is cut off in the eastern point, by what I call the grave, which is dug deeper into the chalk.'

Parkin (1744,19) suggests that the place called by Stukeley as the "Bed or Grave" was the foundation of a brick stair-case. Stukeley had observed that brickwork was found there of a "very fine red sort, brought from some distance, People took away Pieces of it, as a Curiosity". Parkin continued:

> 'This Brick Stair-case was (as I take it) as high as those Cavities or Holes which we see in the Wall of this Section; many such Holes may be seen round the Walls of the Oratory, in which several Beams or Rafters were placed, and where was a Staging, or Landing-place, and from thence there might be, and no doubt was, some gentle easy Steppings or Stairs formed; so as to go up and down, from the said Arch with safety. And I wonder much, that the Masonry here has not been broke through, which might give more Light into this Affair. It is not to be credited, that Any Hermit should have no better Conveniency of descending and ascending near twenty five Feet, than that of a Ladder...'

Beldam (1852) states that respecting the dome, this does not seem to have undergone any close examination previously. Dr. Stukeley who saw it only from the bottom and by candle-light, merely refers to a piece of masonry visible near the top, which 'they who viewed it near,' he says, told him, 'was made of brick, tile, and stone laid in good mortar'. Beldam thought it might have been done to mend a defective part in the chalk, while Stukeley himself conjectured that it might be the original descent, afterwards walled up when the second shaft [north shaft] was made. Rev. North, who made his observations before the Cave was emptied, and therefore from a higher level, remarks that a portion of the dome had been either repaired or strengthened with free-stone and tiles, placed edgeways; and that almost opposite. the shaft through which he entered, there appeared the top of an arch, which the workmen imagined might lead to the ancient way into it. He concluded from the narrowness of this shaft [known as the east shaft] that it was designed only for a vent or air-hole. North also mentions, that the top or crown-work of the dome was curiously composed of tile work, and within a foot of the street above; and further, that some persons thought a passage ran from the Cave to the Priory, an idea which was discredited however, by Stukeley. [None of the tile work remains today.]

The subsequent discovery of a date by Beldam in this part of the Cave gives rise to regret that a more careful inspection and a fuller report had not been made by the first two visitors. All that can now be gathered from their statements is, that no inscription was then perceived; that the masonry concealing the supposed passage was at that time entire [as noted on Stukeley's first drawing in his book, No.1]; and also that the domc had not then been opened to the surface (Fig. 1).

CHANGES IN THE CAVE

Since the time of Stukeley and North, several changes have occurred, considerably altering the appearance of the place. In their day, it will be borne in mind, the entrance was by a narrow shaft in the northern side of the Cave. The 'new' passage was non-existent. The crown of the dome had not then been penetrated, and the place could only be seen by candle or lantern. The masonry concealing the opening of the shaft on the eastern side had not been disturbed.

And, the part which Stukeley called 'the grave', had not been made up to the level of the podium or broad step which encircies the floor.

A 19TH CENTURY REVIEW OF THE EVIDENCE

In the year 1852, a fresh and more careful examination of the Cave was made by Mr. Joseph Beldam, assisted by his friend, Mr. Edmund Nunn, the honorary curator of the Royston Museum: and from a manuscript report, afterwards presented to the Antiquarian Society, the following particulars have been selected:

> 'The height of the Cave from the floor to the top of the dome, is about 25 ft 6 ins [7.7 m]; the length of the aperture leading up to the surface is about 2 ft [0.6 m]; making together, with the thickness of the crown-work at the top of the dome, then pierced to the pavement above and covered by a grid, about 29 ft [9 m], The bottom is not quite circular. The diameter from north to south is about 17 ft [5.2 m], and from east to west about 17 ft 6 ins [5.3 m], the difference being occasioned by the groove of the eastern shaft, which descends this side, and had not been accurately worked into the circle.' (See resistivity test map of 26th June, 1972 - H. A. Allerton.)

OCTAGONAL PODIUM

> 'The broad step, or podium, which surrounds the floor, is octagonal and is about 8 ins [0.21 m] in height, by 3 ft [1 m] in width, being now carried over part which Stukeley called "the grave"; upon which is now likewise placed an ancient millstone, probably the same that closed the shaft discovered in 1742.' (Beldam, op.cit. - see comments on p. 24)

THE CORNICE/FRIEZE

> 'Some 8 ft [2.5 m] above the floor a cornice runs round the walls, cut in a reticulated or diamond pattern, about 2 ft [0.6 m] in breadth, and receding, as it rises, about 6 ins [0.15 m]; making the diameter of the lower part of the dome, which springs from it, approximately 18 ft [5.5 m], The cornice is not, however, continued over the grave, but descends with a curve on one side, leaving the space above it unornamented and in its original rude condition.'

Almost thc whole. circle between the podium and the cornice had been sculptured in low relief, as described by Stukeley, with crucifixes, saints and martyrs, and historical pieces; and many of these, if not all, had been coloured. Beldam specifically mentions:

> 'vestiges of red, blue, and yellow are visible in various places; and the relief of the figures has been assisted by a darker pigment.' (See report from the National Gallery, London, p. 251)

The two examiners observed above the cornice, crude figures and heraldic devices cut or scratched into the chalk, but none in relief.

RECESSES

In different parts of the Cave, both above and below the cornice, deep cavities, or recesses of various forms and sizes can be seen. Some of them oblong and others oven-shaped. They are irregularly cut into the wall, closely resembling olla-holes, niches, and recesses, usually seen in Roman, Etruscan and Phoenician tombs. (Baring-Gould in his book *Cliff Castles and Cave Dwellings of Europe,* 1911, on p. 224 suggests they are of much the same character as those found in the French caves and which the author fully endorses from her own extensive study including numerous underground visits into 'souterrains amenages' in France). One of these cavities above the cornice is about 4 ft 6 ins [1.35 m] in length, by about 2 ft 6 ins [0.76 m] in height; and another in a similar position, about 2 ft 6 ins [0.76 m] in length, with a corresponding height. These measurements are those recorded by Beldam. Besides the niches, there are innumerable small crosses, perforations, and unintelligible devices discernible in all directions.

THE EASTERN SHAFT

Beldam went on to say:

> 'immediately above 'the grave', at the height of approximately 17 ft [5.2 m], appears the masonry, supposed by Stukeley and North to have concealed the original entrance. The two lower courses only [three actually in parts, see photographic plate from a drawing, Fig. 6a] of this masonry now remain, formed of blocks of chalk [clunch - see p.116] neatly chiselled, and coloured red, giving them the appearance of brickwork. The shaft is seen above them, here impinging on the dome, and still partially filled with earth, which on examination, was found to be mixed with small fragments of the bones of animals, and a few pieces of medieval pottery, but no human bones. The perpendicular course of the shaft, proved that it formed no portion of a passage leading to the Priory.'

Exactly when the shaft was opened is unclear. Parkin (1744, 19) remarks that 'the masonry here had not been broke through .. ', however, from Beldam's comments above, perhaps it was he who was responsible for its opening.

[In March 1989, there was a small collapse of material from this shaft. Dr. Caroline Malone from English Heritage maintained the fill was gault clay, but I think it is local crushed chalk mixed with earth and was used to backfill, similar to the 'wall' examined in the cellar of Haywood's shop nearby before their new building was erected in 1975. Contained in the shaft fill was a red tile, a horse tooth and a sheep metacarpal bone. This fall was one of many which occurred in the country and was probably due to the extremes in climate during the previous two years (1987-89).]

NUMERICAL FIGURES

The inspection of this part of the Cave, by the two 19th century antiquaries, was accomplished by means of ladders and torch-light; and led to the discovery of certain numerical figures carefully and artistically cut into the end block of the upper course, giving the date of 1347.

These figures, if genuine as their appearance certainly indicated, was thought by both these gentlemen, that they might assist in tracing the transition through which Arabic numerals have passed in this country, and what was more, furnish evidence of the continued use of the Cave. (See further comments on p. 116)

Below this 'masonry', the shaft evidently expanded as it descended to 'the grave'; and the chalk in this part of the Cave never having been dressed to correspond with the surrounding surface.

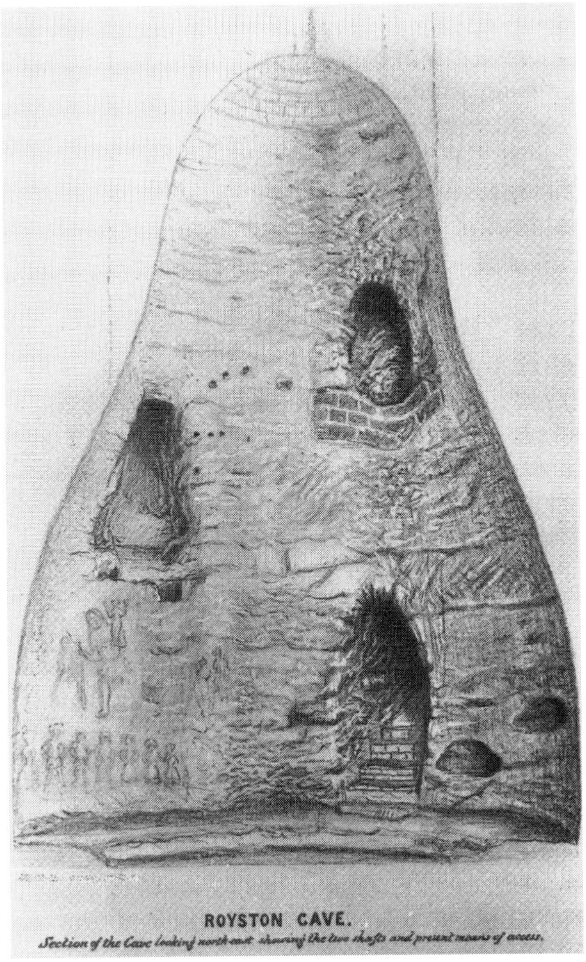

Fig. 6a. A postcard (R.H. Clark) c. 1911 illustrating a drawing which shows the dome has been penetrated, the eastern shaft opened and the 'new' passage cut.

EXCAVATION OF 'THE GRAVE'

Beldam reported that one portion of the Cave which was called 'the grave' by Stukeley, measuring 7 ft 6 ins long by 3 ft wide [2.3 m x 1m] was excavated by him and found to contain a variety of objects:

> Brick fragments, some of which bore marks of cremation, fragments of oak of great thickness and studded with clout headed nails and pieces of iron,

apparently the mountings of a small oblong chest [which perhaps contained a religious relic]. Also a rude iron instrument was found, possibly used for holding a lamp, a large lump of charcoal powdered with sulphur. Mixed with the above were a large number of non-human bones (including ox, hog, hare, and goat or sheep). There were many spherical stones of the class called *aetite* or *eagle stone* and previously known as *lapis pregnans,* which were supposed to be endowed with medicinal and magical properties. Also found were fragments of glass, leather, wood and some other articles of doubtful character. (See report on archaeological material examined in 1973-4, Appendix IX).

Unfortunately, the designation of this feature as 'the grave' continued to be reinforced, not only by Beldam, but by the majority of guides during the last two centuries. A nondescript term would have been considerably better.

BONE SHAFT?

In a paper on 'The Icenhilde Road' written by Joseph Beldam and contained in the *Archaeological Journal* vol. XXV p. 26 [Beldam died at Royston, 1866 in the 71st year of his life and this paper was published after his death] he maintains that:

> '...the Cave appears to have been originally a bone shaft enlarged by degrees to its present dimensions, and the place of the lady's grave [assumed by Stukeley] being nothing more than a continuation of the shaft [east] below the floor of the oratory, and the bones and other refuse there such as are usually found in depositories. I think this is a reasonable assumption as he states: ' ... that other bone-shafts (probably many) exist in the town, several of which were partially opened, along the sides of both the Icknield and Ermine Streets. They all apparently exhibited the same peculiarity of rough workmanship, the diameter extremely small, and footholes down the shafts on either side. One of these was in a garden in the Ermine Street, now called Kneesworth Street, I found to be a depth of nearly 100 ft [30.5 m] terminating in a fine spring of water, but like the others it had been filled up at some remote period with the bones of a great variety of animals, some of them of species now extinct...'

ROMAN COLUMBARIUM?

Beldam goes on to say, concerning the Cave:

> 'that the upper part of this shaft was no doubt first shaped into a dome and bears almost unmistakable evidence of having been designed for a Roman columbarium, the lower part being probably of a much later date, and beyond all controversy used as a subterranean chapel in the 13th and 14th centuries.'

I agree with his latter statement here, but not the former. From information in *Everyman's Encyclopaedia* vol. III, 1971 mentioned below, I personally feel it was unlikely to be a 'columbarium' because there certainly are not enough niches which were normally in rows.

> *Columbarium* (Lat. 'dovecote'):
> Name given by the Romans to a kind of sepulchral chamber, usually a rectangular structure built around an open court and lined with niches in which the urns containing the ashes of cremated bodies were laid up. Particularly common under the early empire, columbaria were developed from the ancient Etruscan and republican Roman house-tomb; they were so called from a fancied resemblance, to the larger type of dovecote, specimens of which can still be seen in France.
>
> The columbarium was ordinarily used for the interment of the slaves and freedmen of great families, who built and maintained it at their own expense; but it often belonged to funeral associations, which thus guaranteed their members honourable burial, and sometimes even to speculators. Notable examples have been found on the Via Appia. Columbaria became obsolete in the reign of Hadrian (A.D. 117-38) when inhumation gradually superseded cremation.

The Romans were certainly in the area, as exampled by the villa at Litlington, but there is no firm evidence of a settlement in the vicinity of the crossroads and it would seem rather unlikely that urns would be transported for the purpose of disposing in the Cave. (*see p. 9)

Beldam also mentions that in another garden along Icknield Street, now called Baldock Street was found a circular cavern beneath a low mound, the floor being grooved in order to carry off water, and evidently designed as a habitation or place of refuge. [I thought for posterity I should refer to another small circular cavern found at the Warren in January, 1965 (*The Royston Crow* 29th January 1965). It was considered to be a lime kiln initially but this has since been disproved. Its origin to date is unknown and it lies beside the new car park.]

Kingston (1906) states on p. 168:

> '...At as late a period as 1853 the bottom of the Cave was thoroughly examined by the late Mr. Joseph Beldam and the late Mr. E. B. Nunn, curator of the Royston Institute Museum, when beneath the surface a number of relics were found, suggesting its occupation in much earlier times than Dr. Stukeley claimed for it.'

The inference by this phrasing is that ALL the floor of the Cave was thoroughly examined, although in Beldam's book on pages 16 and 17, mention is only made to the examination of one portion, namely 'the grave' area.

CUTTING OF THE 'NEW' PASSAGE IN 1790

The property in Melbourn Street, Royston, Cambridgeshire, which generally became known as the Cave House and Estate in the 18th and 19th centuries, had really nothing whatsoever to do with the Cave as a property, except through an 'accidental circumstance'. In 1790 the then occupier of the Town House, as it was called, Thomas Watson a bricklayer, set his men to work during the hard winter of that year cutting the present passage, 72 foot [22 m] in length, down through the solid chalk into the Cave leading from the building by which it is now entered (Figs. 6b & 6c). The house is today a Video Shop. [The Royston Cave, Arts & Bookshop – 2009]

Fig. 6b. Entering the Cave by the 'new' passage. Photo Rodney Tibbs 1976

OPENING OF THE CAVE TO THE GENERAL PUBLIC

An interesting advertisement of this event bearing the date of 1794 is given below:-

ROYSTON CAVE OPENED

> 'T. Watson respectfully informs the public in general and the antiquarians in particular, that he has opened (for their inspection) a very commodious entrance into that ancient Subterraneous cavern in Royston, Herts. which has ever been esteemed by all lovers of antiquity as the greatest curiosity of the kind in Europe. T. Watson hopes that all those who may think proper to visit the above Cave will have their curiosity gratified to the full extent. The passage leading to it is of itself extremely curious, being hewn out of the solid rock.
> 'N.B. -It may be seen any hour of the day.'

Watson levied a charge of 6d. [old money - pre-decimal coinage] on his visitors - an expensive trip - he was evidently a shrewd man and intended to recoup his costs.

Many learned societies and individuals of distinction, have at various times visited the Cave. Amongst them was the French King, Louis XVIII who, during his exile in England from 1808 - 1814, occupied Gosfield Hall, near Braintree, Essex, and whilst in residence there came to see the Royston Cave.

Fig. 6c. The 'new' passage heading upwards to ground level. Photo Rodney Tibbs, 1975

It is not possible to ascertain exactly how often the Cave really was open to the public. Whether it was on a daily, weekly, monthly basis, or even a period of several months a year is not recorded. Presumptions alone can only be assessed from the availability of literary sources or pamphlets. Once the 'new' passage had been created it simplified visits. In 1825, a booklet illustrating the Priory Seal on the front cover was produced [author unknown], published by J. Warren of Royston, and sold by Longman, Hurst & Co. London, therefore expectations of a steady number of visitors no doubt warranted the cost of producing it. The Preface relates:

> 'It may be thought by some, that the present edition is quite superfluous, yet when they consider that there has not been a single copy to be purchased with plates, for the last twenty years, and not a perfect copy without for the last five years (notwithstanding the repeated enquiry after it) and added to this, the probability of so valuable an account sinking into oblivion, the Publisher has no doubt, but that they will see with him, the propriety of preserving the memory of so antiquitous and curious a relict of monkish superstition, as the Cave described in the following pages.'

The plates are copies of Stukeley's but the text has a marked preference to Parkin's account.

In a short passage from *Professional excursions, by An Auctioneer, Part I Hertfordshire* p. 83, 1843, the author Alfred Greenland remarks:

> 'At Royston, dwell no longer than to visit Lady Rose's Cave, crypt, oratory, cell, or whatever your own imagination can devise, for upon the authority of Leland, Dugdale, and a host of authors, you may call it anything you please but what it is; and do not fail to look at the Swedish Crows on the chalk downs, which are blue black like the present fashionable crapes, and web-footed.'

A passing reference published in 1859:

> '...There is an old cave, at Royston in Herefordshire [sic], which you are permitted, for a trifle, to descend, by a private entrance, there being no other, through a house...'

But here its author is referring to a visit he took as a lad! (Fitzball, Edward (1859) *Thirty-five Years of a Dramatic Author's Life,* T. C. Newby, London) Probably in the 1820s.

There have been numerous keyholders - one resident of Royston remembers going to a Chemist shop in the High Street for the key - going down the Cave was not the highlight - this was looking with admiration and awe at the Chemist's extraordinary long beard. Lily Poole was the last private keyholder and guide (1950s). She and her husband owned the shoe shop above, and before her husband died, it was he who mainly took visitors down, and apparently regaled them with his own version of history.

THE WILL OF WILLIAM LEE OF RADWELL

The so-called 'Cave' property, left for the benefit of the inhabitants of Royston in Cambridgeshire, dates back about ten years before the dissolution of the Monastery. It was originally the Old Ram's Head Inn. William Lee, of Radwell, Hertfordshire, who presumably did not know of the Cave's existence, was the owner of the house in the time of Henry VIII. By his will, bearing the date 8th day of October 1527, he, among other bequests and directions of a local character, made the special bequest which follows:-

> 'And as to the disposition of all my Lands and Tenements which I have within the counties of Hertford and Cambridge, ffirst I will that such persons as be ffeoffees to my use imediately after my Decease shall deliver estate in fee of and in my Tenement in Royston called the Ramm's head, to certain honest persons as shall be named and appointed by mine executors to the performance of this my last Will and Testament. I will that the yearly profitts of the said Tenement, the Lord Rent, reparcons, and other charges deducted and allowed, then the rent thereof comeing nere every year to be taken and retained by two

of the Antient of the said ffeoffees and putt in a Box Locked, and so to remaine in the safe custody of the said ffeoffees unto such time as any manner of Tax, Subsidie, and whatsoever any manner of other charges shall be granted unto the King or his heirs. Kings of England by Act of Parliament, and then the Money so coming of the Rent of the said Tenement to discharge and acquit all such Persons as then shall dwell in the said Towne of Royston, that is to mean within the side of Cambridge, every man and person after their porcon, and I will the said two ffeoffees, or their heirs, shall at the end of every three years make a true and faithfull accompat of 'the revenues of the said Tenement to the Prior of the said Monastery, or to his successors Priors, and when it shall happen any great sume to remaine in the said Box then I will that part of the said sume, that is to witt, all that is more than four Pounds, shall be disposed in deeds of charity amongst the poor Inhabitants within the said Towne of Royston by the good Discretion of the said Prior and successors' (see comments under Chapter 10).

Little thought William Lee that within less than a dozen years the Monastery and Prior would be no more, and still less that the time would come when no tax or subsidy to the King should be levied directly upon the inhabitants of the town. The beneficial interest of the townspeople in the trust, however, remained, and the question arose how, in the absence of any such levies and charges upon the townspeople by King and Parliament, as were common enough in his day, the provision of the benefactor's Will were to be interpreted.

During nearly the whole of the reign of George III, and also during a part of that of George II, the Parochial Parliament for Royston, Cambs., made short work of that 'knotty point'. They simply treated the Estate as parish property; the houses were let and rents collected by the Overseers, and the revenue was duly entered in the year's parochial balance sheet, with the names of the tenants, while the feoffees seem to have stood by and tacitly approved of so simple an arrangement. (Kingston, 1893, 37-8)

This house in 1694 appears to have been used as two tenements, but the premises by 1886 consisted of two small houses fronting onto Melbourn Street, and four cottages to the rear, with a barn and a small yard. The yearly surplus from the property, after the repairs had been done as provided for, was paid in aid of the poor rates for that part of the parish in Cambridgeshire. (Milbourn, 1886, 49)

ROYSTON

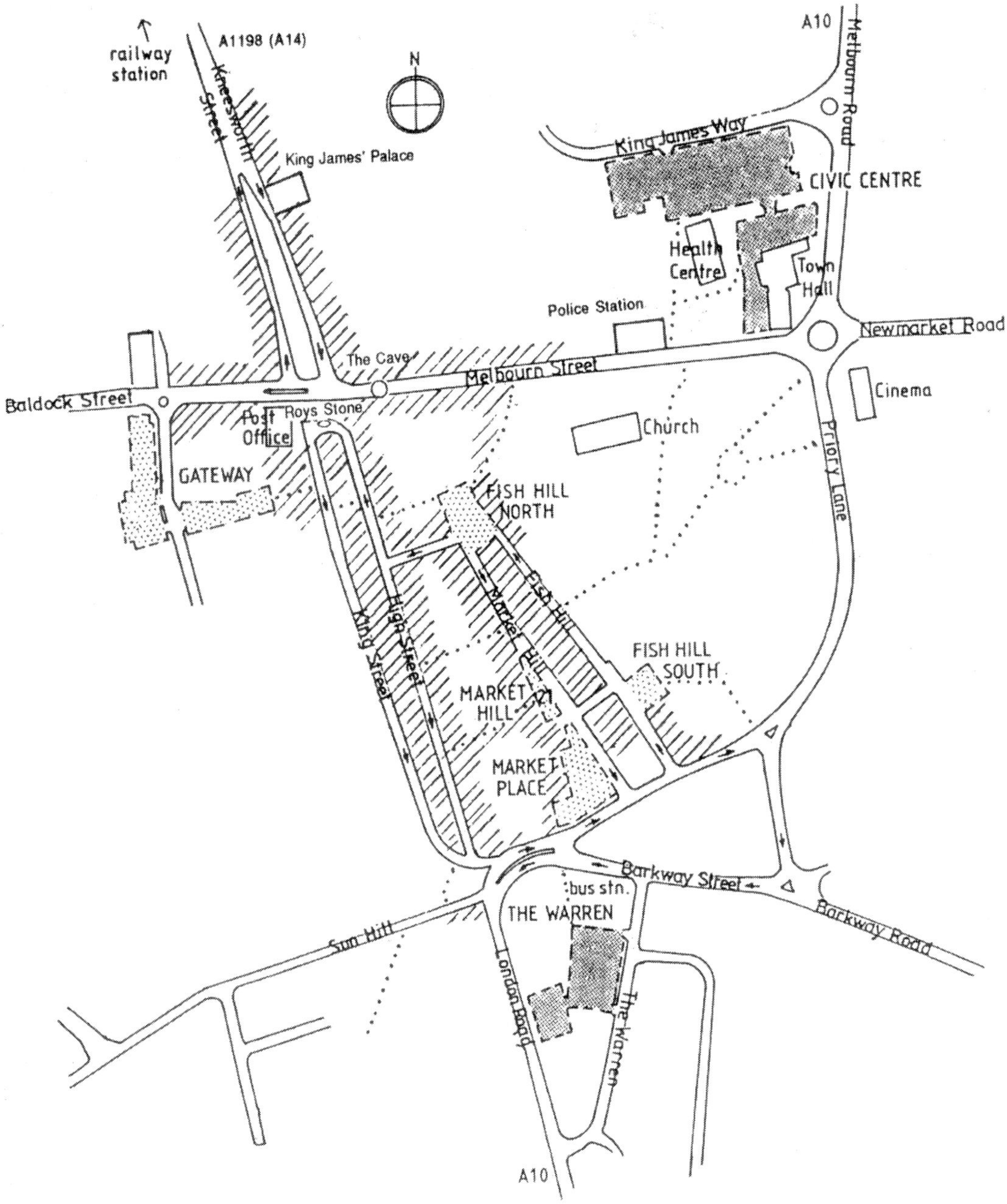

Fig. 7. Royston in the 20th century. (After the Royston Chamber of Commerce plan of 1989)

3. THE CAVE TODAY

The Cave is the responsibility of English Heritage, formerly the Department of the Environment, and Scheduled as Grade 1. The scheduling appears to have been carried out in August 1923, according to a letter to the Trustees of the William Lee's Charity, who were then the owners. There is no trace of the actual scheduling description, however, it is assumed to have included the passage. The Cave is administered by the Town Council (* see p. 37), and with aid from members of the Royston and District History Society who act as guides, open the monument for visitors during the summer months.

Half a 'bedser' mill-stone rests lopsided on the floor of the Cave. This part was exposed during the winter of 1966/7 when Mr. Philip Smith of the then newly formed History Society, and Mr. John Moss-Eccardt from the Letchworth Museum, a Ministry of the Environment representative, dug out the 'grave' area. The other half is buried at the foot of the steps of the 'new' entrance. Beldam also referred to the mill-stone but not that it was in two halves. Whether the mill-stone is the original one which covered the north entrance is in dispute. The late Mr. Arthur Thair, former hairdresser in the High Street, informed the author that he had the original mill-stone in his garden which his grandfather had obtained!

DETERIORATION OF THE CARVINGS

The carvings on the walls have deteriorated considerably during the last 80 years, as can be seen from the photographs taken by R. Clark at that time (Figs. 8a, b & c). The ever-growing volume of heavy traffic passing overhead, even though some was diverted when the new by-pass was opened in the 1980s, causes continual vibration and gradual flaking of the chalk. Rain water running down the wall from above on the left hand side of the 'new' entrance [as viewed from standing inside the Cave] and, in particular, from the damaged area where the vault of the National Westminster Bank** broke into the Cave at a point high up on its side, has in a sense dissolved some of the surface. [These water courses were more clearly visible under ultra-violet light, in December 1971, during a preliminary examination by members of Cambridge University, Geodesy and Geophysics Department]. Rain passing through the atmosphere mixes with carbon dioxide and forms a weak form of carbonic acid. As the carbonic acid mixes with the calcium carbonate present in chalk and limestone, the two chemicals form calcium bicarbonate, which as a liquid causes damage to chalk or limestone surfaces. Hydrogen, which is also present in water, is harmful too. [** Thought to have been a former post office - 2009]

The problem is not just a recent one. *The Annual Report of the East Herts Archaeological Society for 1905* expresses their alarm at the condition of the Cave. They state:

> 'The sculptured figures are, and have been for some time past, suffering from the moisture which percolates through, particularly after heavy rains.'

Herbert George Fordham of Odsey, wrote to Mr. Gerish (East Herts. Arch. Soc.) 29 November, 1905:

'... I find that Mr. N. T. Rowley of Royston, is the Secretary of the Trustees of the Charity which has, (quite incidentally), the custody of the Royston Cave. He tells me he thinks the Trustees would be very glad to be relieved of the responsibility of the preservation of the cave especially as the figures on the walls are decaying away under the influence of moisture. On the other hand, the Trustees would be willing to spend some money they have in hand on the preservation of the figures etc., if they could obtain satisfactory expert advice as to the method to be adopted.

No doubt you will communicate with Mr. Rowley.'
(*Gerish Collection,* Hertford Record Office)

I visited Mr. Fordham, several years ago, when he was in his 92nd year - two years before he died - but apparently nothing ever came of these aforementioned discussions.

Fig. 8a. This photograph was taken c.1911 and proves that many of the engravings have deteriorated since the beginning of this century - see p. 247. It will be noted that the array of figures (disciples ?) above the sword are complete and the cross on the chest of the main figure is visible.

Fig. 8b. The second photograph shows that most of the figure over the niche (piscine) has fallen away. This occurred at some time in the 1960s.

Fig. 8c. In the third picture, the head on the left of the two figures to the right of the photograph, fell off and was repaired by the Ministry of Works prior to the 1960s. The new body, English Heritage, is unable to ascertain the exact dates of the repairs.

It is true to say, that the Cave should be damp to a certain degree, for the sake of the carvings, but not as it often is, wet. Neither has its conservation been helped by the numerous occasions it has been flooded in storms, prolonged rain, melting snow, and when it became filled with sewage a couple of times from a broken pipe. Consequently, there are now no visible signs of the colouring mentioned by Stukeley and Beldam, unless the grey area on the north wall close to St. Christopher is original - see Appendix II)

From time to time small pieces break off and some repairs have been carried out but not very satisfactorily - it is most difficult to get materials to adhere to the soft chalk surface. The Town Council (formerly the Urban District Council), under the North Herts District Council, make structural repairs occasionally overhead to ensure the Cave's safety for visitors.

In the mid 1960s, an octagonal banister and railings were added, a few inches away from the step or ledge, to help dissuade enthusiastic visitors from adding their own monograms to the many already scratched on the walls through the years. This rail also supports strip lighting which illuminates the walls clearly and enables everyone to see the carvings at their best. When the Cave floods badly, the lights fuse and have to be left to dry out. Candles are used then instead, just as they were for many years beforehand. Apart from giving a poor light, candles also create soot and discolouration around the niches where they are placed.

In one of the deep recesses cut into the side (W) higher up the wall, possibly in the upper storey area, were several bits of wood. One or two pieces were crumbling and rotten. A bat was found clinging to one piece, the first time a bat had ever been recorded here (1971). The wood was examined and replaced as too modern to be dated; the bat was also carefully returned to its niche. (** See p. 37)

RESISTIVITY SURVEY

On Monday 26th June, 1972 when Mr. H.A. Allerton, M.Sc. and Mr. David I. Sewart, B.Sc., from the Department of Geodesy and Geophysics in Cambridge, carried out a Resistivity test on the Cave. It came to light that the structure might not be completely at bedrock, in some areas, as previously thought!

The purpose of the Resistivity survey was to indicate by remote sensing techniques whether or not there were any inhomogenities within the floor of the Cave. The results of this survey showed anomalous resistivity areas, some of which were directly related to known features on the floor of the cave, e.g. the polygonal step in the centre and the 'pit' near the entrance. The remaining anomalous zones could not be explained by surface features, and were therefore of considerable interest. These were marked as high-priority areas on the survey map. Mr. Allerton also remarked that the floor area had originally been cut in a square, then another square cut to form an octagon.

It was also noticed that the cross-section through the floor of the cave as exposed in the 'grave' or 'pit' near the entrance showed that the top four inches [10 cm] or so of chalk appeared to overlay 'dirt'. Thus indicating that the floor (at least in this area) is possibly man-made. (Figs. 9a & b)

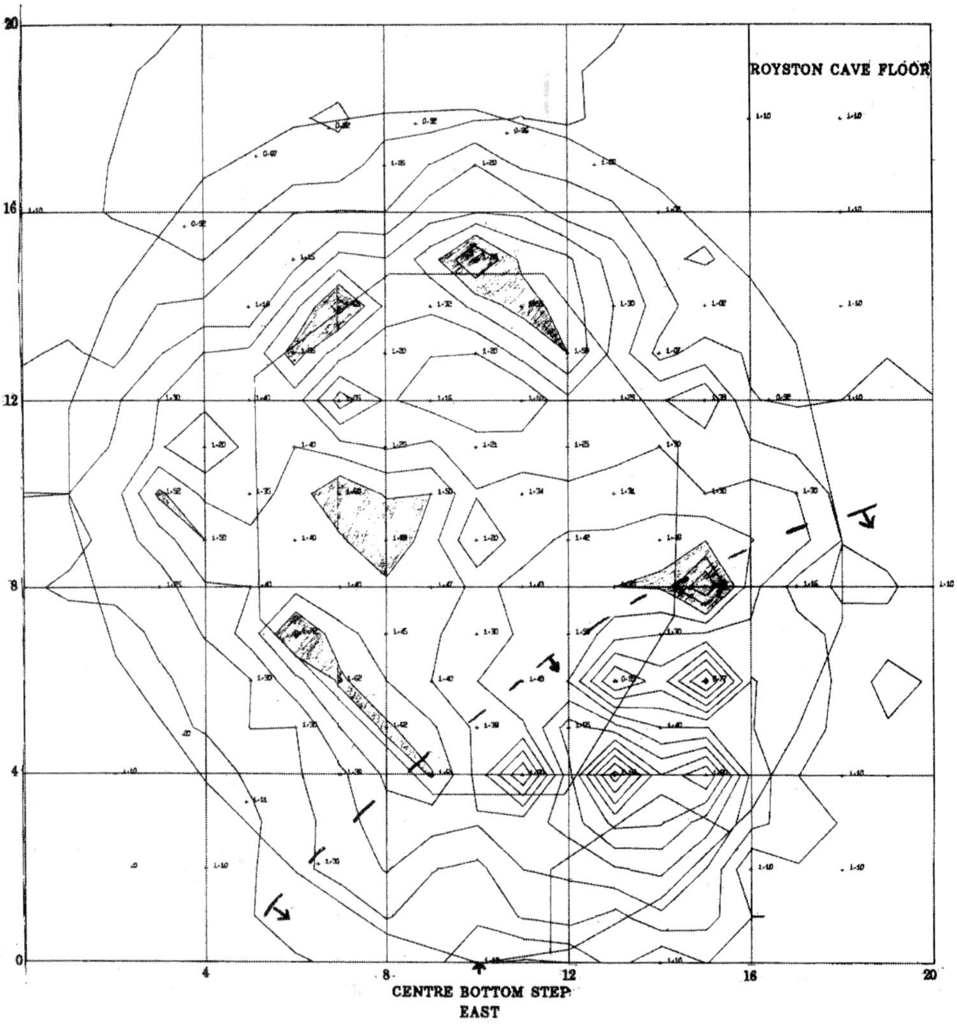

Fig. 9a. Royston Cave resistivity survey map of the floor, drawn by computer on 26th June 1972. The values shown are plotted at the centre of each spread (Wenner Array)

C		P		P		C	
|	2 ft	|	2 ft	|	2 ft	|	*C = current electrode* *P = potential electrode*

Scale: 1 square = 4 ft

Values to be multiplied by 4π giving results in Ohms/foot (mostly of the order of 12 ohms/foot). This is fairly typical of clagey chalks. Maximum variation about 100%.

The results reflect all the known surface features of the cave floor, the dashed line being an approximate interpreted position (from the results above) of the step. Data on the arrowed side of the dashed line reflects the presence of the 'grave' and steps, and therefore can be ignored. Near the walls the values are generally smooth, except at (3.5, 9.5), which is apparently a continuation of the 'high' feature from (9,4) to (6,8). The bottom of the cave is predominantly 'low', and the only anomalous portion is that centred on (8, 9.5) which is shown shaded.

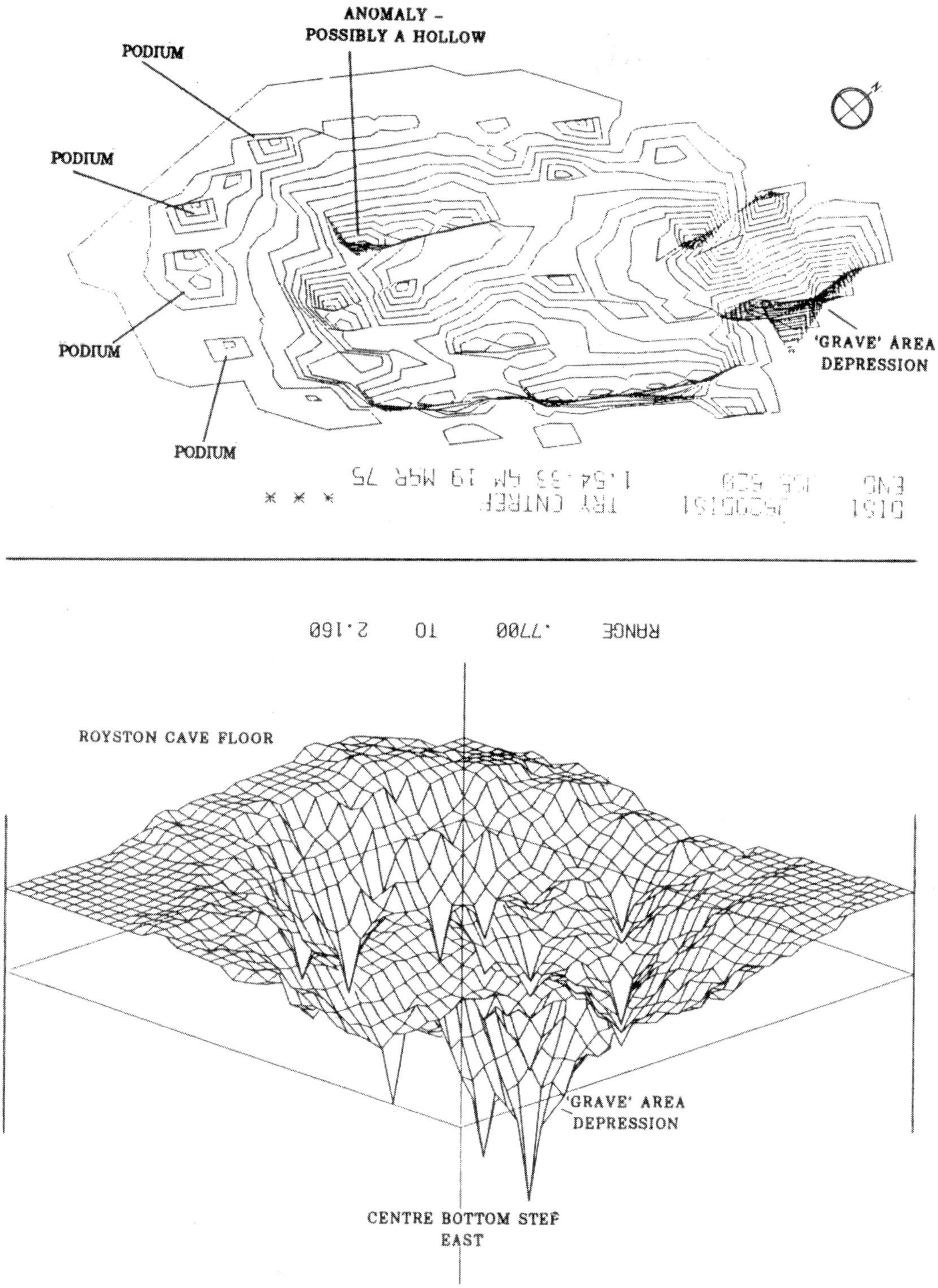

Fig. 9b. These two diagrams were early attempts in 3-D contouring software. They show the relative 'highs' and 'lows' of the resistivity co-ordinates of the Cave floor.

PRIMARY ARCHAEOLOGICAL EXAMINATION

On May 30th 1973, again with permission from the U.D.C. and reference to the Department of Environment, as it is a scheduled building, a small test was carried out on the floor of the cave by Dr. Colin Forbes from the Department of Geology, Cambridge, and Curator of the Sedgwick Museum, and an archaeologist Miss Susan Ames. Two areas of moderately high resistivity were investigated by striking with a small mattock. In each case, solid undisturbed white chalk was found an inch or two below the floor. Excavation had to be minimal owing to the chance of there being depressions containing archaeological material demanding deliberate excavation. However, the sizes of the 'lows' and their relationship to the proved solid chalk indicated that such depressions would not be more than a foot or two deep. It may be that some resistivity features are not indications of depressions, but only of local fissures emphasised by, for instance, salt derived from seepage of road runoff. A small excavation with the mattock at the foot of the peripheral step, directly opposite the usual entrance to the cave, demonstrated that the solid chalk of the step is continuous with solid chalk close below floor surface.

Striking the floor with the head of the mattock handle gave different sounds in different places; the resistivity 'high' co-ordinates 7, 9 on the plan emitted a hollow sound when struck as did a few other parts of the floor whereas elsewhere a hard ringing sound was obtained indicating the presence of solid chalk.

The depression to the right of the 'new entrance' (as if entering the Cave) which Stukeley called the 'grave' is believed by the writer to have been used as a sump for water when the chapel was in current use, for as mentioned water still naturally seeps down the wall above, and the surface is worn. It is to be noted that frog bones were found in the excavated material of 1966/7 - see Appendix IX.

From the size of some of the holes, assumed to have held cross beams to support the upper storey, they do not appear to go back deep enough into the walls and Mr. Sewart and Mr. Allerton suggested that square indentations on the step/podium were probably caused by the weight of the flooring being supported on struts underneath.

EXCAVATION

Under the direction of archaeologist Lisa G. Donel, assisted by Frieda Stewart, Christopher Montague and the writer, an excavation was undertaken for five days at the end of March 1976. It was hoped that various questions might be answered archaeologically. These were:

1) whether any features existed below the layer of compacted dirt or whether the floor was undisturbed
2) whether any dating material existed
3) to determine the nature of the podium/step around the main part of the cave floor.

Two diagonally opposed quadrants were excavated in order to identify as many features as possible indicated on the Resistivity survey, and to accommodate a very cramped excavation.

Due to restrictions by the DoE, it was not possible to examine the podium area as originally proposed. The excavation report is published under the title of *An Investigation of Royston Cave,* by Sylvia P. Beamon and Lisa G. Donel in the *Proceedings of the Cambridge Antiquarian Society,* vol. LXVII, 1978. Extracts of Miss Donel's report are as follows:

> '...A large feature (Fig. 10a) was exposed in Quadrant I. This had been filled initially by a fine silt followed by chalk rubble. The feature itself extended into the two unexcavated quadrants but did not appear to- extend into Quadrant III. Its depth increased at the centre of the Cave (0) becoming quite shallow near the outer edge, at the juncture of the podium and floor (A.A1) - see plan (Fig. 10b). Eighteenth century pottery was found near the surface of the chalk rubble fill.
>
> Because there are no records of the modern excavation of the 'grave' at the time of its being cleaned out in 1966, it is hard to discuss it with any real meaning. However, if it was really a sump then one must view the 'grave' as a successful cutting after the initial sump (F4) proved unsatisfactory. It has been noticed at times of flooding in the cave that the 'grave' acts as a highly successful container and method of drainage, whereas Feature 4 and the central area tend to retain water. This was further emphasized after the excavation when a return trip to the Cave showed the feature to be entirely incapable of draining, whereas the 'grave' was working quite well. The placement of Feature 4 is also questionable when one views it in association with the possible structure that may have stood in the cave. This, however, will be discussed later.'

Fig. 10a. Quadrant I showing 'sump' (F4). Photo Rodney Tibbs, 1976

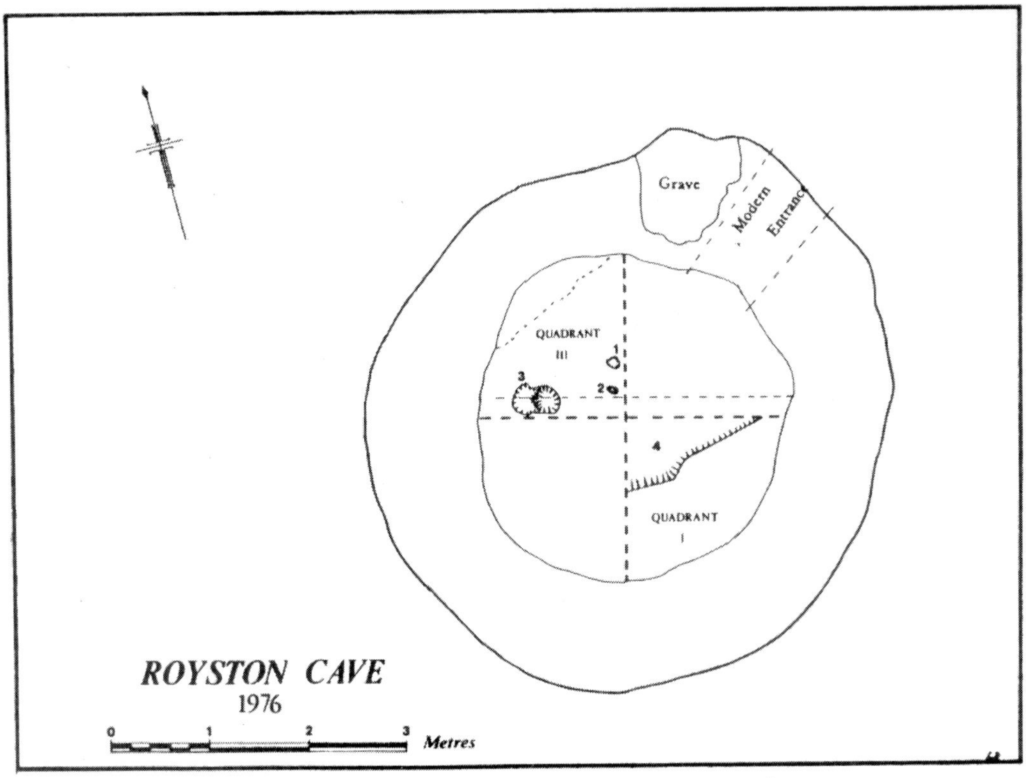

Fig. 10b. Plan of Royston Cave floor. Lisa Donel.

> 'Three features were identified in Quadrant III (Fig. 10c). These were under a layer of chalk rubble but did not have the same fill as F4. In contrast, all three were filled with a reddish/brown soil, the largest feature also containing small chalk pieces ... The third feature [largest] was a large deep hole, cut with precision into the chalk, showing a smoothed, flat bottom. Associated with the smoothed hole was a slightly deeper cutting that cut into the first but showed no flattening of the bottom, rather a very rough surface. This feature was filled with a layer of chalk rubble. It is possible that this second rougher feature was used as a hole for packing-support for F.3...'

There was no dating material found to give an answer for the initial use of the Cave. Sampling was undertaken but the laboratory was not prepared to undertake examination since the samples were considered to have been contaminated with sewage.

> 'Finds ranged from modern nails and silver paper washed in by the periodic flooding of the Cave, to clay pipe, pieces of brick and tile, and some small sherds of pottery. The physical size of the material as well as the small size of the sample have not been of great aid to the investigator. However, the pottery has been dated to the 18th century. As the material tended to lie below the modern compacted dirt and rubbish but did not appear in the lowest levels of the excavation, the material apparently found it way into the cave when it was discovered in the 18th century.'

Fig. 10c. Beam slot uncovered in Quadrant III (Frieda Stewart) Photo Rodney Tibbs, 1976

'...as the 18th century material was found above the fill of the features in Quadrant III and in the upper layer of the fill in F4, the possibility that those features had already been filled and covered before the opening of the Cave in the 18th century must be considered. There was no evidence that the features in Quadrant III had been disturbed since they were originally filled in, whether on purpose or through natural causes. Possibly the only 'treasure hunting' done in the 18th and 19th centuries took place at the 'grave' area.'

[In hindsight, the writer (SPB), thinks it is more likely that the infill occurred in 1790 when the Cave was about to be opened to the public and perhaps the floor was 'made good' to prevent the stumbling of visitors. She presumes comparatively few people would have 'plumbed the depths' until the 'new passage' was constructed.]

'The evidence of the features found in Quandrant III and the anomaly identified through resistivity and sounding tests in Quadrant IV seem to suggest the existence in the past of some structure. On examination of the walls, one is struck by the level of the original shafts which terminate some 17 foot [5.2 m] above the Cave floor. Associated with this terminal point and running at the same level are a series of niches. The larger of these niches have been suggested as storage areas. The smaller appear to have been some sort of support for a floor. If the original users of the Cave had been constantly using ladders both for getting down from the shafts as well as moving them around for use of the 'storage' niches, then the writer feels that the chalk walls with their sculpture would have shown more damage. It seems much more appropriate that a structure existed to act as a halfway platform between the end of the shafts and the Cave below. Because of lighting difficulties, the writer would like to suggest that the structure was not a complete flooring over the cave space but possibly a walkway that ran only part of the way round the Cave. The presence of features in Quadrants III and IV and the placing of the sump and the 'grave' well to either side of any supporting posts, and the apparent lack of any large features in Quadrant II tend to lend support to the idea of a partial structure or semi-circular walkway in the Cave. However, until the whole Cave floor is examined in conjunction with an investigation of the Cave it can only remain as interesting conjecture.'

OTHER KNOWN STRUCTURES WITH SOME SIMILARITIES:

Israel

Beldam, also drew attention to other structures in Palestine (Israel), and comparison should be made of the Cave with the following information:

At the village of Deir Dubban in Palestine, a few miles from Gaza, in the soft limestone or chalky rock, which the soil there scarcely covers are several irregular pits, some nearly square and all about 15 or 20 feet [4.5 m or 6 m] deep with perpendicular sides. Whether these pits are natural or artificial it might at first be difficult to say. In the sides are irregular doors or low arched passages, much obstructed by rubbish, leading to large excavations in the adjacent rock in the form of tall domes or bell-shaped apartments, varying in height from 20 feet - 30 feet [6 m - 9 m] and in diameter from 12 feet - 20 feet [3.65 m - 6 m] or more. The top of the dome usually terminates in a small circular opening at the surface of the ground above admitting light into the cavern. These apartments are mostly in clusters of three or four together communicating with each other. Some of the apartments are ornamented, either near the bottom or higher up, or both, with small holes or niches. In one apartment are several crosses cut in the wall and in another are several very old Cufic inscriptions. Similar excavations are to be seen at Beit Jibrin but being in a low situation, the water of a small wadi is in winter turned into them, and they are used as cisterns.

The Knights Templar had estates at Gaza and also a fortress to cut off the approach to Ascalon. At that time the pilgrims were accustomed to travel from Jerusalem to Mount Sinai by way of Gaza. (Robinson and Smith, 1841, 353)

From Conder and Kitchener's Vol. III (1881-3) of the *Survey of Western Palestine,* p. 266, we have more information concerning - Beit Jibrin where the principal antiquities of the place are the great caverns surrounding the village. There are about 14 caverns in all and a general description does for all of them. They consist of interconnected chambers roughly circular, from 20-60 foot [6-18.3 m] diameter; and 20-40 feet [6-12.3 m] high with domed roofs having openings to the surface of the rock above. Many of the domes have fallen in. The walls are roughly cut, but sometimes dressed coarsely with a pick used diagonally. In at least two places springs are found in the caverns. Many of the rounded chambers resemble chapels with apses to the East. Crosses and Cufic inscriptions occur in all caves at a low level. The crosses are of various kinds. The Jerusalem cross is amongst them. There is also a very curious design in Bas-relief and may perhaps be a crude representation of the crucifixion cut high up on the wall in the inner part of 'Arak el Ma,' where there is a spring. Niches for lamps are found in many of the caves.

Various indications to the dating of these caverns all seem to point to a late origin, for example:

1. The destruction of Jewish tombs in the course of cutting out the caves.
2. The various Cufic inscriptions testifying to the caverns being made.
3. The various Cufic and Christian inscriptions on the walls.
4. The medieval character of the sculpture in 'Arak el Kheil.'
5. The diagonal dressing on the walls in parts.

This list does not prove anything more than that the caves were the work of medieval excavators: but what it does show is that there were some busy people hewing away rock to specific plans as again illustrated below:

On the side of the mountain Jebel Kurintul (Or) there are two chapels. The lower one is reached through a hole in the roof of an excavated chamber about 12-15 feet [3.65 m-4.5 m] wide. Two large reservoirs exist at the Cave below. The chapel above is covered with medieval fresco on the cemented walls, also having inscriptions and graffiti of numerous pilgrims on the frescoes. The frescoes represent the Saviour enthroned, the Virgin, St. John the Baptist. In a niche is painted in red paint the letters *IC* and *XC* either side. They form a Latin cross. The rest of the frescoes are indistinguishable but the colour of the roof is rich and dark and, no doubt, when the frescoes were new, very effective. The second chapel higher up the mountain is still in use as a hermitage. This chapel is of masonry built in front of a cave of irregular shape, the walls of the chapel are also covered with fresco which are much defaced. Angel Gabriel is distinguishable as also the figure of the Virgin on the roof of the apse. The following saints are known by their titles - The Holy Gregory, the Theologian; The Holy Basil the Great; The Holy John Chrysostom; The Holy Athanasius, Martyr for the Truth. There can be little hesitation in ascribing the frescoes to the crusading period.

On the summit are the foundations of the Fortress and chapel of Tahunet el Hawa (On) There is no doubt the buildings are medieval, though the site may have been occupied earlier. This fortress is probably Duk mentioned as a fortress of the Templars between Jericho and Bethel in the thirteenth century. (Conder and Kitchener, 1881-3, III, 201, 205)

Czechoslovakia

The only other known structures to bear some resemblance to the Cave are some in the Ceska Lipa region in Czechoslovakia. The area is geologically formed of soft Mesozoic sandstone, and was densely populated in the 12-13th centuries by Czech and German colonists. The sandstone enabled the cutting of at least eight castles (13-14th century) and many artificial underground cavities including cellars, chapels etc. Most of these cavities are small, usually less than 10 m in diameter, but some other underground chambers, considerably larger, occur near Lindava.

There is a bottle-shaped cave in the Burgstein, an outcrop of rock, by the village of Svojkov. It was described by the German researcher E. Gebauer in the ancient mysteries journal *Germanien* in 1935. The dimensions of this structure are slightly smaller than the Royston example, being 21 feet [6.4 m] deep by 10 feet [3 m] wide, but it does exhibit many carvings including a crucifixion on the walls. Gebauer makes no mention of Royston Cave and was probably unaware of its existence. Svojkov, some 8 km NNE from Ceska Lipa is just one of several small, originally wooden, castles.***

Just some 2 km from Svojkov is situated the most important 'underground' castle in Bohemia called Sloup, which has a bottle-shaped cave with strange inscriptions which could be compared with Royston Cave. The castle lies in isolation 30 m high and 100 m long in the sandstone rock. This rock has had a long history of habitation since Neolithic, Bronze Age and Halstatt times. The castle was established during the end of the 13th century, its history is complex, it was several times defeated, robbers lived there etc. During the 16th century the castle was abandoned. In 1639 the Swedish soldiers burnt the castle. Between 1690-1785 hermits lived in several of its underground rooms. They even had an underground washroom.***

The bottle-shaped cave is a former prison built in the 13th century - beginning of the 14th century. In Britain we would call this an 'oubliette'. In 1699 a new 'surface entrance' was made, before that the only way in was through the 'neck of the bottle'. The walls of this former prison, 'then probably hermit house' are covered by many various symbols: small heads, crucifix, sun. symbols (?) etc. In another underground room of the castle there are stone reliefs depicting a lion, lioness, frog etc, calvary, some of them are thought to have been made by Templars. (Pers. comm. Vasek Cilek, 20/10/89)

So, who or what was the Templar movement?

*Note: The Cave belongs to the Bedwell family. On the 19 October 1964 a Lease was drawn up between George Edward Clark Bedwell of 37 Old North Road, Royston and the Urban District Council when

> *'The Landlord demises unto the Council insofar as lies within his power so do so ALL THAT excavation situated beneath Melbourn Street, Royston in the Co. of Hertford and known as "The Cave" and the passage or tunnel connecting the same with the premises known as No.8 Melbourn Street Royston aforesaid ...'*
> *'...TO HOLD the same unto the Council from the nineteenth day of October One thousand nine hundred and sixty-four for the term of ninety-nine years Paying Therefore the net yearly rent of One shilling the first of such payments to be made on the nineteenth day of October...' (The lease is held in the Royston Town Council's records).*

** In the 1980s it became an offence to enter *a* cave or disturb bats during the hibernating period October to March and a fine of £1000 was introduced. [£3000 in 2009]

*** Following the opening up of the Eastern Block countries, it has been possible to establish the facts relating to the sites quoted in these paragraphs from the 1992 edition. Both paragraphs relate to the same site that is situated on and within the 'Sloup' rock outcrop. Sloup (pronounced 'schlope') is 7 km North of Ceska Lipa and is an isolated, almost vertical-sided pillar of sandstone about 30 metres high. It has been fortified from Neolithic times and (according to *Subterranea Britannica Bulletin* 1993) a labyrinth of staircases, tunnels and rooms have been formed in the body of the Sloup rock; including the bottle shaped chamber with a circular hole in its roof and carvings on the wall that has some resemblance to the Royston Cave.

4. AN HISTORICAL OUTLINE OF THE RISE AND FALL OF THE KNIGHTS TEMPLAR ORDER

PILGRIMAGES TO THE HOLY LAND

The events which led to the institution of the Knights Templar were the alleged discovery of the Holy Sepulchre by the Empress Helena, the mother of Constantine, about 298 years after the death of Christ, and the subsequent building of the magnificent Church of the Holy Sepulchre, over the revered monument. This led to a tide of pilgrimage towards Jerusalem. Eager multitudes of people surged ever onwards to see the spot where their Lord lay. That which at first originated as ardour in devout minds, was at length converted into a necessary and meritorious act. Many were so far misled, as to believe that a pilgrimage to the sacred sepulchre was sufficient to atone for an evil life, and to establish an entitlement to heaven. Yet it cannot be doubted, that a lot of the early Christians were really prompted by feelings of the purest devotion to visit those places which had been consecrated by the death and passion of the Redeemer.

Pilgrimage became all the rage, and it went on increasing, even when Jerusalem was surrendered to the victorious Arabians, in A.D. 637, for the Caliph Omar gave the following guarantee to the Christian patriarch:

> 'From Omar Ebno'l Alchitab, to the inhabitants of Ælia.' 'They shall be protected and secured both in their lives and fortunes, and their churches shall neither be pulled down nor made use of by any but themselves.'

In the year 1064, the Holy Sepulchre was visited by a band of seven thousand pilgrims, headed by the Archbishop of Metz and the Bishops of Utrecht, Bamberg, and Ratisbon. The year following, Jerusalem fell into the hands of the Turcomans, and the pilgrims began to be fearfully oppressed. They were plundered, imprisoned, and frequently massacred; a tax was exacted from them for admission into the Holy Sepulchre, and many, unable to pay it, returned to their distant homes in sorrow and dismay, without having attained the object of their long toilsome pilgrimage. This state of affairs aroused the sympathy of the Christian world, and accordingly:

> 'a nerve was touched of exquisite feeling, and the sensation vibrated to the heart of Europe.'

When the Christians recovered possession of Jerusalem itself, the first Crusade being led by Godefroi de Bouillon (1096-9), they had not been able to rout the 'heathens' from the surrounding countryside. On arrival, the pilgrims found the mountains on the sea coast infested by bold and warlike bands, and whether they approached Jerusalem by land or sea, all were equally exposed to hostility, plunder, or death (Figs. 11 & 12) - see also Appendix III.

FORMATION OF THE 'POOR FELLOW-SOLDIERS OF JESUS CHRIST'

It was at this critical juncture in time, c.1114, that nine noble knights formed themselves into a sacred brotherhood, calling themselves the 'Poor fellow-soldiers of Jesus Christ,' for the purpose of defending the crowds of helpless women, pious old men, and others who were bearing the pilgrim's staff in the land of Palestine. They agreed in a solemn pact to aid one another, by protecting the pilgrims through the passes and defiles of the mountains, and in clearing the highway of infidels and robbers. There was in the character of these knights a romantic union of the attributes of the monk and the soldier - a good description being - 'monks of war'. They took the vows of perpetual chastity, obedience, and poverty, as are taken by monks; also solemnly renounced the world and its pleasures in the presence of the Patriarch of Jerusalem, and within the walls of the church of the Holy Sepulchre.

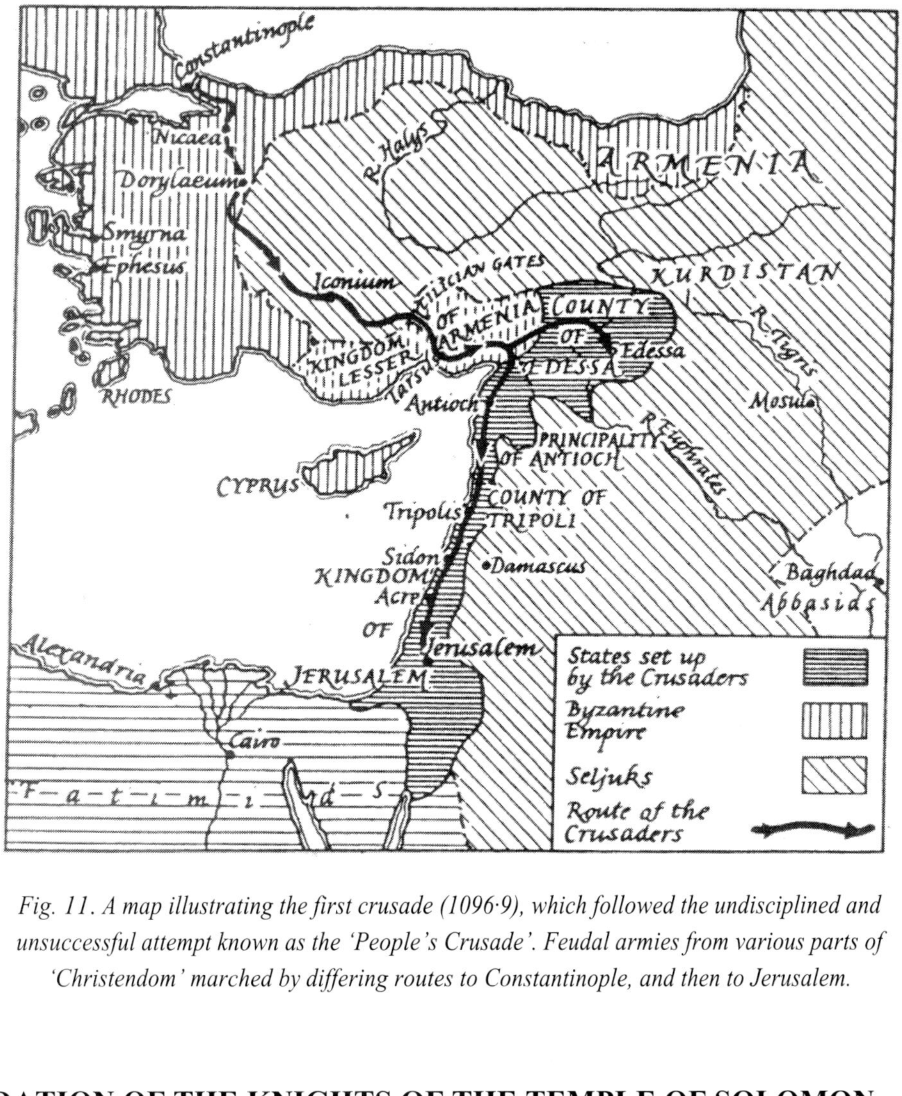

Fig. 11. A map illustrating the first crusade (1096·9), which followed the undisciplined and unsuccessful attempt known as the 'People's Crusade'. Feudal armies from various parts of 'Christendom' marched by differing routes to Constantinople, and then to Jerusalem.

FOUNDATION OF THE KNIGIITS OF THE TEMPLE OF SOLOMON

These knights had at first no church and no settled place of abode. Their symbol of poverty was two men sitting on a horse. In the year 1118 (nineteen years after the conquest of Jerusalem by the Crusaders), since they had rendered so much service already to the Christian cause by their zealous defence of the Christians, Baldwin, king of Jerusalem, bestowed on them the al-Aksa mosque building formerly called the 'Temple of Solomon,' thus, the knights obtained the appellation of the 'Knights of the Temple of Solomon.' Various gifts and revenues were given to them. The canons of the Temple of the Lord, or church of the Holy Sepulchre, conceded a large court extending between that building and the Temple of Solomon, to the 'Poor fellow-soldiers of Jesus Christ.'

The knights now extended the aims of their institution, and in addition to the defence of pilgrims, undertook the protection of the Christian kingdom of Jerusalem, the Eastern church, and all the Holy places. Their power and numbers rapidly increased: two of their most distinguished members were Hugh de Payens and Geoffry de St. Aldemar, or St. Omar, and the former, having been chosen by the knights as the superior of their new religious and military society, has been called the 'Founder of the Order of Templars.'

Ten years after their inception a group arrived in England and the principal house for the Order as the Temple in Holborn, London. Temple Cowley in Oxfordshire was the next foundation followed by Cressing Temple, Essex. Within fifty years the Templars acquired vast financial resources, particularly land. By then it is estimated that they held some 7000 manors in Europe.

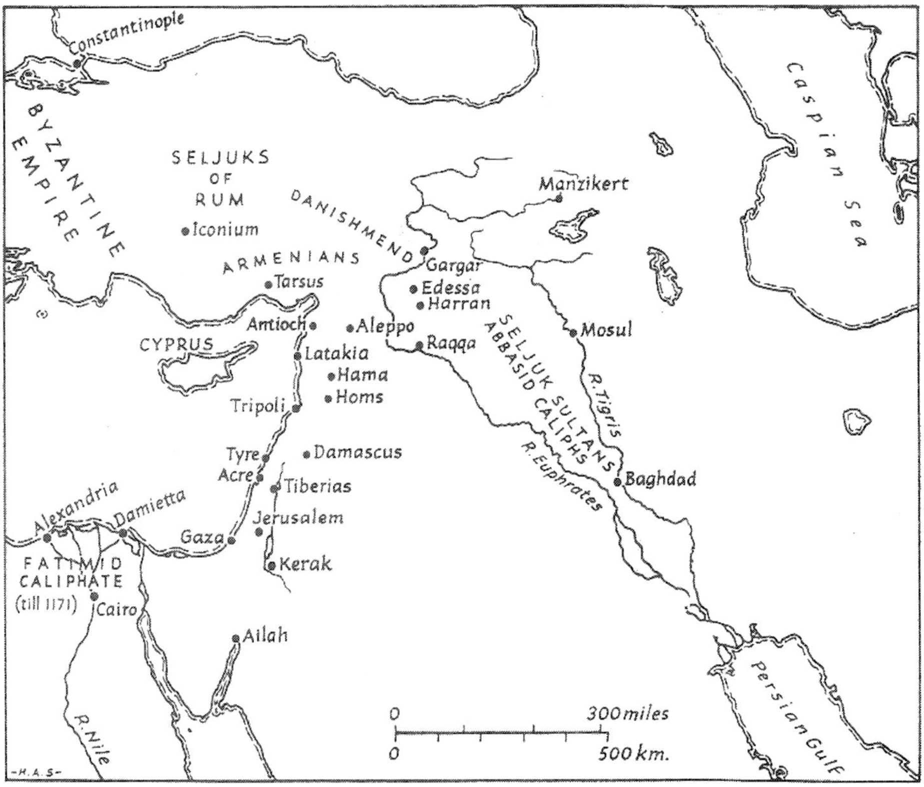

Fig. 12. The Middle East in the 12th century (Smail, 1973, 11)

THE RULE

It had become necessary to draw up a regular code of laws for the guidance of the new society. For this purpose an application was made to a most powerful ecclesiastic, known as St. Bernard, the holy abbot of Clairvaux. This learned prelate was a great admirer of the Templars, and understood their cause with all the zeal for which he was to be so remarkably remembered. He obtained the convocation of a great ecclesiastical council in their .favour, at Troyes, and to him was eventually given the task of framing a code of statutes, fit and proper for the governance of the religious and military fraternity, which became known as *The Rule.* (*Saturday Magazine* No. 646 July 1842, 99)

There were at least five main classes of brothers recognised by the Templars in their *Rule.* They served under the Grand Master. His badge was the equi-armed cross surrounded with a circle to make it the wheel cross, sometimes called the rose cross (Fig. 13). (Valiente, 1973, 357)

Fig. 13. A Templar, whether British or a Templar in general, is not known. The illustration is from Dugdale's 'Monasticon' (1718) vol. VI, part II. The octagonal insignia on the staff is interesting. Does he represent the Grand Master? A circular disc with the cross pattée engraved on it was uncovered from Denny Abbey, Cambridgeshire, perhaps the disc was an insignia of office? *(See p. 193, Fig.57d)*

The first and highest class was that of the knights who could be distinguished by their garments: a white skull cap, white mantle with a red pattée cross on chest and shoulder (the privilege of the red cross was awarded to them by Pope Eugenius III in 1147 - (Burman, 1986, 55)), and their swords were kept drawn. They were allowed three horses and an esquire. When joining the Order the knight surrendered his property, took the monastic vows and agreed never to leave unless to join another religious order having a stricter rule (the Benedictine and Augustinian Orders are specifically mentioned as religious houses which former Templars might join). Normally, the only persons to leave the Order were those who had been expelled for some serious offence. (Ibid Arts 429). Few in number were admitted and necessarily had to be of noble and legitimate lineage. These men served as mounted warriors and officials of the Order.

Second class was the sergeants or esquires who wore black or brown and were required to be of free birth. Some served as light-armed troops, and the younger ones were often assigned as squires to the older knights. They could become minor officials, supervisors of local administration, and attendants or assistants of the great dignitaries of the Order.

A third class was composed of chaplains who were wholly independent of diocesan authority and were full members of the Order, but this was not the case in the early days of the Order when they relied upon outside priests to give spiritual services especially for confession and mass. (It was their independence or autonomy in religious matters, that was to be one of the charges brought against the Order in the trials of the early fourteenth century.)

The fourth was made up of manual labourers, including carpenters, masons, smiths, engineers, armourers, tent-makers, rope-makers, shepherds, gardeners, millers, dairymen, laundry workers, vintners, grooms, domestic servants etc. All these were dressed in black stuff or brown, with the red cross on the breast and shoulder. The Templars also had book-keepers and translators. It is unclear whether they specifically belonged to this group, education being more available to the higher orders.

The fifth group of persons, known as 'confrère knights' were those of associates or temporary members, for example married men were permitted to join under certain conditions - King Richard I, came under this category; crusaders in the Holy Land were allowed to join for a time, and men might 'for the salvation of their souls' be received into the Order at the point of death, exampled by Geoffrey de Mandeville and Peter de Roucestria. (Ibid., Arts. 22, 65, 66, 69, 623 Et passim). Others, accepted for the duration of just one single crusade, were called *ad terminum* (frères à terminé), (Burman, 1986, 44)

A more complex category consisted of those who paid a yearly fee *pro fraternitate* as lay or associate members in order to secure the spiritual benefits, prayers, and intercessions with which the Templars were privileged. (Burman, 1986, 44).
Women, needless to say, were denied membership although they might be associated with the Order as wives of associate members. But, there appears to have been at least one exception, and a married woman seems to have been admitted in England. A certificate of reception of a

sister dating from the period 1189-93 is addressed to Geoffrey Fitz Stephen, then master of the Temple of England (Lees, p. 210, Chapter 5). There is also a remarkable document entered amongst the Saddlescombe, Sussex, deeds and therefore possibly relating to that particular preceptory, which is a letter from a certain Archbishop Azo requesting the Master of the Temple in England to receive Joan, the aged wife of Sir Richard Chaldese, who had taken the oath of chastity and wished to submit herself to the *Rule* of the Temple. (*V.C.H. History of Sussex,* 92)

The Templars' first banner, called *Beausant* [variously spelt *Beauséant, Baussant* and *Bausséant*], was partly white and partly black, and was superseded by the red cross on white in the reign of King Stephen of England (1135-54). Their battle-cry *'Non nobis, Dominum, non nobis, sed nomine tuo da gloriam'* [Not unto us Lord, not unto us, but to Thy name give glory] was to be heard ringing through the ranks as warring waged in the Holy Land.

ENGLISH BENEFACTORS

The principal benefactors to the Order in England were sovereigns, Henry II to Edward I; Roger de Mowbray, Geoffrey de Mandeville, William de Warenne, Ralph and Walter de Hastings, William Mareschal and two of his sons William and Gilbert, Earls of Pembroke; Bohun, Earl of Hereford, Robert Lord de Ros; William, Archbishop of York; Simon de Senlis, Earl of Northants; Simon de Montford, Earl of Leicester; Robert de Harecourt, Lord of Rosewarden; William de Vernon, Earl of Devon. During two centuries, vast tracts of land were to come into the ownership of the crusading brethren.

From the first, the Templars were favoured by Henry II and King Stephen; but charters and privileges were also conferred upon them by Richard I, John, Henry III, and Edward 1. These grants included exemption from both local and national taxation; freedom from toll and passage dues; freedom from attending local courts; the right to hold their own courts and receive the profits; and freedom from exactions of money and supplies under the pretext of scutage, forest laws or the temporary needs of the King. However, their role was by no means generally accepted, and the Templars often found it difficult to obtain these exemptions in practice [see p. 199 re Royston stallage] - hence the need for successive kings to repeat the privileges so frequently. (Burman, 1986,89)

TEMPLAR ORGANISATION

At the head of each province was a provincial master, also called Grand Preceptor or Grand Prior - who was to the province what the Grand Master was to the whole Order. Though apparently appointed technically by the Grand Master - at least in the early years - the provincial master was probably to a large degree free of his actual or direct control. In turn, the provincial master was responsible for the appointment and supervision of subordinate officials in his province and was expected to consult with his provincial council before deciding important matters or undertaking major activities. Each province was divided into preceptories which served as the basic administrative units and as the recruiting stations of the Order. The individual preceptories were often local manors, for example Strood in Kent, which had come into the hands of the Templars and thereby had been transformed into religious houses. (Parker, 1963, 6 et seq.)

Alongside the officials of the Order were the Chapters which shared in the administration of the Order and in the determination of policy. A general chapter, or chapter for business, was held apparently at least once each year, usually at Jerusalem, except after the capture of that city by the Moslems in 1187 and the withdrawal of the Christians from the Holy Land. This chapter, over which the Grand Master presided, served as the supreme assembly of the Order and it was expected that its advice and counsel would be followed by the Grand Master (*Le Règle du Temple,* Curzon (ed) Art 96). This general chapter was concerned with admitting new brothers; the grant, confirmation, and sale of Templar land; decisions on matters of war and military activities; dispatching of envoys to foreign powers; requesting aid for the Order and for the Holy Land. It was also responsible for administration during the absence of the Grand Master, plus the discussion of matters of general interest and importance to the Order. (Ibid., Arts. 36, 85, 87, 92, 106, 125)

There was another type of chapter, concerned primarily with discipline, which met frequently, probably weekly, to which all Templars in a given preceptory were to attend (Ibid., p. XXVIII). At these meetings the brothers were expected to confess their sins voluntarily, but if they did not, the other brothers were expected to denounce them, following which the proper penance for offences was to be assigned. Initially, the penance seems to have been largely left to the discretion of the Master, but in time the most usual offences, together with their penalties, were listed in the *Rule.* (Ibid., Arts. 406, 416-656)

In addition to the general and disciplinary chapters meeting in Jerusalem, there were provincial chapters and local chapters. The former dealing with the business of the Order in the province, and the latter dealing with local matters in each preceptory and especially with matters of discipline. Unfortunately, very little is known about these provincial and local chapters. (Ibid., Arts. 87, 586, 661)

As mentioned, the life of the Templars was both religious and military. Realising the danger of immoderate abstinence for the needs of military life, the Templar *Rule* permitted two regular meals daily and a third at the discretion of the Master. Meat was to be included three times a week, and wine. Fasting was not emphasized to the degree it was in many another religious orders. Special care and consideration was given to the old and sick. (Ibid. Arts. 33, 60, 61, 190-97). Their chief concern was to wage war against the infidel but as time passed they assumed other interests, possession of large estates, accumulation of wealth, participation in trade and rivalry with the Knights Hospitaller, a contemporary order; and the Patriarch of Jerusalem. For many years their bravery, tenacity, and achievements were a constant example to their fellow Christians and a terror to their enemies. (See also Appendix IV)

WRITINGS

The Crusading brethren were not without writers - the fact that they were not intellectuals and could not read Latin did not mean that brother knights were illiterate. The Templars produced several poets, troubadours and trouveurs, including one Grand Master, Robert de Sablé. Towards 1180 'the Templar of Temple Bruer' was writing Norman French verse translations of

Thais, and of Latin poems on Anti-Christ and on St. Paul's descent into Hell; one is dedicated to his superior, Henri d'Arci, frère del Temple Salemun. This unknown English poet of the Order also produced a prose translation of the *Vitae Patrum.* (Seward, 1972)

RECORDED TEMPLAR HOLDINGS

The earliest comprehensive material on the Templars is to be found from *The Inquest of 1185* which Geoffrey Fitz Stephen, then Master of the Temple in England, wisely had made. The *Inquest,* a collection of ownership documentary records, is not complete as it lacks data on holdings in and around London and in Cambridgeshire. To some extent these two omissions can be compensated by references in the Public Records and by the *Sandford Cartulary for Cambridgeshire* drawn up between 1265 and 1274 which deals in detail with Templar holdings in Cambridgeshire.

The Templars held numerous estates in Cambridgeshire which for the most part were subordinate to the three preceptories of the county, Denny, Duxford and Great Wilbraham. Some of the individual grants go back to the twelfth century, but most of them appear to have been made in the thirteenth.

Templar properties in Hertfordshire, amongst the oldest holdings of the Order in England, seem to have been about the same in number and value as those in Cambridgeshire. Lands, churches, mills, and markets at Hitchin, Preston, Dinsley, Weston and Baldock date back to 1147-48 when they were given to the Templars by such great lords as Gilbert de Clare, William Marshall, and Bernard de Baliol and were confirmed by King Stephen (Dugdale, VII, 817, 819-20, 832-33; Lees, 1935, 211-18; *V.C.H. Hertfordshire* III, 10, 18, 66, 68, 174, 176, IV, 445-46). These initial grants, and subsequent additions to them were consolidated under Temple Dinsley by the end of the reign of Henry II. Templar holdings varied in size from a plot of a few acres to huge estates like Cressing in Essex.

In the eastern and south-eastern counties, Templar holdings were greatest in Essex, Kent and Sussex. The earliest grant of land to the Templars here was that of Cressing Temple in Essex made in 1137 by Matilda, King Stephen's wife, in a charter issued at Evreux in Northern France, and was the preceptory in that area. From this time on grants and confirmation of grants of land and privileges to the Templars appear with increasing frequency. Stephen as well as Matilda, was generous to the Templars.

Closely associated with Cressing was Witham, the manor, market, church and pasture lands, which similarly received royal favour being granted by Stephen and confirmed by Henry II (Lees, 1935, 141, 149-53; D'Albon op. cit. Nos. 482-84; Dugdale, VII, 821, 838, *V.C.H. Essex* II, 177). Reyndon, Sutton, Uphall, and Rivenhall [conjoined property with Newsells, HertfordshireJ were additional Templar centres in this county.

Rivals of Stephen were also generous in the contest for the control of England following the death of Henry I. Stephen was a member of a distinguished crusading family, being the son of Stephen of Blois who had been an important leader of the first crusade. Matilda was a member of a Boulogne family closely associated with the crusading movement. Hugh de Payens the first

Grand Master also came from Champagne, an area controlled by Stephen's family. Also Godfrey of St. Omer, another of the original founders of the Templars was a vassal of the Count of Boulogne [Bouillon].

In Sussex, although no information was returned in the *Inquest,* the Templars already held an estate at Shipley and soon were to hold Saddlescombe and minor estates elsewhere. Shipley was definitely a preceptory. [Founded by de Say and Fitzwarren].

Unfortunately demesne land, which was not always rented out and which may have amounted to about one half of the arable land, was not reported in the *Inquest.* (Cf. Ibid, pp. LXXXIII). There are other difficulties too. It may seem that the convenient use of acreage is used in some cases, but even acres may vary in size from area to area, therefore it is very hard to make sense out of the land units. Messuages are repeatedly referred to, evidently meaning a house and the small plot of land on which it was located. Especially troublesome are the units which vary in size from region to region. For example, carucates may be 120, 160 or 240 acres in size; hides 64, 96 or 120; virgates 15, 24, or 30; and bovates 20, 24 or 30. (Cf. Ibid., pp. LXXIX, LXXXIII, CVIII, CLXXII). Probably the commonest sizes were 240 acres for a carucate, 120 for a hide, 30 for a virgate and 24 for a bovate. (Cf Ashley, op. cit., Part 1, pp. 7-8; Kosminsky, op. cit., pp. 35-36). Tofts however, appear to be regularly units of 12 acres. In addition, indefinite units such as crofts, cotlands, meadows, gardens, woodlands, vills and pastures are widely used. To add further to the confusion, it is sometimes unclear whether or not certain areas are being counted twice in the returns from the counties. Despite these deficiencies and difficulties, the *Inquest* is a most useful and revealing document.

KNIGHTS HOSPITALLER REPORT

The Order of the Knights of St. John of Jerusalem known as the Knights Hospitallers originated in 1092 with the building of a Hospice in Jerusalem for the accommodation of pilgrims visiting the Holy sites. The dress worn was black with a superimposed white cross and *The Rule of St. Augustine* followed. Around 1144, the Order was first introduced into England when their important house at Clerkenwell, London was founded, to which later some 65 dependent Commanderies in various parts of England, often founded on manors, were given to the Order. A certain amount of rivalry sprang up between the two main military orders, and their function was not dissimilar, both having fought in the crusading wars, except the Hospitallers went on to perform more doctoring and health care for the pilgrims. The head official, known as the Grand Prior was eventually to become the chief lay baron in England. (See also Appendix V)

Again similar to the Knights Templar, the Hospitallers' houses were small consisting of from one to three professed Knights, of which one was the preceptor or head, plus two or three secular chaplains and a number of lesser officials and servants. Little Maplestead, Essex, like other houses of the Order was at first used as a recruiting centre for the surrounding area. In the latter years of its existence, when this object ceased to be effective, the manor was let and the lands farmed at an agreed annual rent. The income was then employed for the general purposes of the Order.

Equally as important as a source for Templar possessions in England is the *Hospitaller Report of 1338*, one section of which deals with former Templar land currently in the hands of the Knights of the Hospital of St. John of Jerusalem. (Larking, 1857, 133-99)

This report to the Grand Prior, Elyan de Villanova, of the Order was drawn up by Prior Philip de Thame, an efficient manager and supervisor, who had been sent from Italy to straighten out the financial difficulties which the English Hospitallers had fallen into under the Priorship of Thomas Larcher. Like the Templar *Inquest,* the *Hospitaller Report* records the lands, possessions, and income of the Order. In some respects, it is clearer than the *Inquest* - for example, the lands are carefully listed by county; and the areas (many of which are expressed in acres) are given. But the *Report* is much less detailed than the *Inquest,* and like the *Inquest* is also incomplete. Though certain Templar lands which the Hospitallers claimed but had not obtained are specifically indicated, there are still additional holdings known to have been in their possession at this date which were omitted (cf. Ibid., 212-13). Nevertheless, the survey of 1338 was reasonably complete and accurate except for lands in the counties of Surrey, Hertfordshire, Suffolk, Berkshire and Nottinghamshire are omitted. (Parker, 1963, 15, 32, 36, 38)

Letters and Papers of King Henry VIII, at the time of the Reformation, are also helpful as they list property being removed from Hospitaller ownership but mentioning former Templar lands.

TEMPLAR ECONOMY

Grain - wheat, oats, rye and barley - was raised throughout the areas held by the Templars, but especially in the Midlands and Essex. (Lees, 1935, p. LXXI)

The medieval timber framed barn had a very specific place in the agricultural process. Storage of the crop after harvesting was the primary concern and great doors were designed so a loaded cart could enter through the 'midstrey', be unloaded, and then leave through the lower rear doors. Once gathered in the crop had to be threshed and winnowed which was done on the threshing floor between the doors (Fig. 14c), the cross draught through the opposing doors being important to separate the wheat from the chaff. When completed the grain would be stored in separate granaries.

It was only through Cecil Hewett's recognition of the specific carpentry details (Fig. 14d), in the Cressing Temple, Essex great aisled barns, just over a decade ago, that both were fully examined and confirmed to be of Templar origin. They are the best preserved examples of their age in the country and are now open to the public.

The Barley barn is the earliest, and had been of larger dimensions than as it stands today (Fig. 14a). It is dated between 1200-1220, whereas the Wheat barn was built, slightly later, c.1260 (Fig. 14b). Radio carbon dating and dendrochronology has closely verified this dating. (Hewett, C. A. (1980) *English Historic Carpentry,* Phillimores, Chichester)

The Great Barns at Cressing Temple, Essex

Fig. 14a. The Barley Barn. Photo Sylvia Beamon 1991

Fig. 14b. The Wheat Barn. Photo Gillian Rushworth 1991

Fig. 14c. The Threshing Floor of the Wheat Barn. Photo Sylvia Beamon 1991

Fig. 14d. A carpentry detail from the Wheat Barn: a notched lap joint which is only found in archaic buildings. By the end of the 13th century it was obsolete. Photo Sylvia Beamon 1991

Associated with agriculture were the Templar mills which proved highly profitable. Exactly how many there were cannot be determined, although the *Inquest* lists 81. Most of these were grain mills to which the Templar tenants, and many others in the area, brought their crops to be ground. The Templars themselves seem to have run many of them, whilst others were rented out at annual rates, usually ranging from five shillings to five marks, depending upon the size and value of the mill. (Lees, 1935, 80, 81, 131 Ex passim, Cf. CRR, 9-10 Hen. III (1225-26) No. 2376)

Wool, wine, dairy products, grain, fish, hides, salt, timber, and metals were among the standard items of medieval trade. In varying degrees, all the great English estates of the 12th and 13th centuries grew food and produced goods for purposes of sale and exchange as well as consumption. (Nielson, 1941, 465)

The Templar estates certainly were not self-sufficient; not only basic commodities such as wine, fish, and timber, but also luxury items such as fine cloth, special horses, leather, and metal ware were needed. For the Templars, as for most others, practically all of these goods were obtained through exchange and purchase at local or regional markets and fairs, or by trade with foreign merchants. In payment for these goods, the Templars could offer wool, grain, and cash to the foreign merchants, and grain, fish and livestock to the local merchants.

Wool, the chief commodity the Templars could offer for sale and exchange, was sold by grade. It is recorded that Cambridgeshire amongst other counties contracted to sell wool and included the Templars at Wilbraham. [Therfield Heath, near Royston, has always been known as good sheep grazing land. Temple Bruer, Lincolnshire, also sold wool and was situated on similar terrain.]

Wine was the second major item in the foreign trade of the Templars, it was often an import as wool was an export. The Templars were granted freedom from custom duties both for the exports and imports. It is to be noted that Baldock Templars (Hertfordshire) owned their own vineyards at Weston, nearby the town.

As previously stated, markets and fairs were a regular medium for the exchange of goods in the middle ages and were a convenient source of profit to the owner. It is not surprising, therefore, to find that the Templars obtained from the kings, who claimed exclusive jurisdiction over the issuance of such franchises, the grant of markets and fairs on certain of their properties. The first such grant to the Templars, made by King Stephen, was a weekly market (on Sunday, later changed to Tuesday) at Witham (Essex). This was followed by John's grant in 1199 of a weekly market (on Wednesday) at Baldock and an annual fair.

MARKETS

The Templars were active creators of markets and market towns, as typified by Temple Bruer and Baldock, and showed a willingness to call one into existence if no settlement was already there, however, they were not always successful. It is noted that in 1227 they obtained a charter for a weekly market and fair at Walshford Bridge on the Great North Road, but within thirteen years found it more advantageous to transfer the place of trading to the town of Wetherby, Yorks three and a half miles [5.6 km] further south at the Wharfe crossing. (Beresford & St. Joseph, 1958, 165)

FINANCIAL ACTIVITIES OF TEMPLARS

Burman (1986) maintains that while other monastic estates in the twelfth century were farmed for the provisions of their inhabitants, the Templar estates "were administrated primarily with a view to the money revenue which they yielded, rather than to the sustenance which could be derived from them",

The Templars acted as bankers and lending money was another of their financial activities. They assisted in the international transfer and transportation of funds. Carrying money over long distances was a precarious operation in the middle ages, especially before the widespread use of gold coins. Often ransoms had to be paid. Until credit facilities came into existence, only persons who were reliable and capable of defending themselves could be used. During the era of the crusades there was probably no group safer or more reliable than the Templars. In 1241 the king ordered that money which had been raised in England for the Holy Land should be delivered to a Templar and a Hospitaller to be taken at first passage to Richard Earl of Cornwall, in the Holy Land. (CPatR, 25 Hen. III (1241) p. 25; Burman, 1986, 75) Of course, the Arabic word *checque* was first introduced into this country by the Templars: it would appear that they were responsible for the great improvements in credit and payment techniques which took place in the twelfth and thirteenth centuries, particularly when the volume of money in circulation was increasing rapidly.

Templar houses became ideal places for depositing valuables, not just money or precious metals. The London Temple was used for deposits of the royal treasure as early as 1185. The vault may have been in the cellar, which can still be seen under the south entrance door of the Temple Church, an architectural feature that does not readily suggest any other specific function. The Temple in Jerusalem was also used as a safe-deposit from the beginning. The Paris Temple was used likewise. In 1204-5 King John of England left the crown jewels at the London Temple for safekeeping, practically as soon as he came into possession of them. His successor Henry III used the Temple widely, and he too deposited the crown jewels in the London vault during the Barons' revolt of 1261. Two years later King Edward forced the Templars to give him the sum of 10,000 esterlin livres which had been deposited by various barons and merchants. Smaller local commanderies were also used for safe-deposits throughout the thirteenth century. (Burman, 1986, 80-1)

SHIPS

To provision their own forces in the Holy Land, for both commercial purposes and for the passage of pilgrims, the Order maintained their own fleet. They were expert in maritime trade and later maintained houses in the key ports of southern Europe, and in England to name but two, they were at Dover and Bristol.

DOWNFALL OF THE ORDER

The Order of the Temple was perhaps doomed to ultimate failure and suppression, irrespective of the merits of its knights in battle. A possible interpretation is that their decline in the latter part of the thirteenth century was an inevitable consequence of the fading of the crusading ideal, with the diminishing of the Latin Kingdom itself, so that their *raison d'être* had gone, in fact, they had lost their way, as you might say.

The actual downfall of the Templars was due to several factors. The secrecy of the Order aroused a considerable amount of curiosity, suspicion, and distrust from which the they certainly did not profit.

The pride of the Templars, which was proverbial, aroused great antagonism and assuredly did not help them in their hour of trouble. Pope Innocent III in 1208 sternly denounced their short-comings, wrote to the brethren that their unbridled pride had led them to abuse their enormous privileges. (Du Puy, no. 29)

Insolence, closely akin to pride, was not unknown to the Templars and was manifest in a variety of ways. Royal domain and jurisdiction were infringed upon and violated by them, as a Bull of Honorius III (1222), in reference to the situation in the French possessions of the English King, indicates. In this Bull the Templars are called upon, amongst other things, to cease doing the following: usurping royal domain by erecting their crosses on houses not belonging to them; preventing customary dues from being paid to the crown; disregarding the customs of the king's manors, and involving the king's officials in troublesome law suits (Rymer, I, 258: Du Puy, no. 32). A Bull of Innocent III (1208) complained that the Templars, upon receipt of a gift or contribution, were so bold as to bury in their Churchyards even persons under excommunication. (Ibid no. 30)

The Templars were often accused of treachery, sometimes with reason and sometimes without. Certain of the economic exemptions from royal tolls, and sometimes from local toll as well, aroused resentment and hostility towards the Templars. They must have been hated and opposed, by those merchants whom they could undersell at the different markets and fairs. (CChR, 9 Ed.I (1280), 237 no. 404, *Sandford Cartulary,* op. cit., 267-68. Cf. Rot. Hund., I, 131). The fact that the Templars were generally exempted from a variety of fees, fines, aids, services etc. associated with the land, must have caused considerable envy too on the part of the populace, particularly with the neighbouring landowners. (Cf. Rot. Hund., I)

Neither did the wealth of the Templars add to their popularity, although in England, at least, the extent of this wealth was grossly exaggerated.

By the end of the thirteenth century, the Templars had become suspect, not only in the eyes of the clergy, but in those of the general public as well. 'Amongst the common people,' one of their latest apologists admits, 'vague rumours circulated. They talked of the covetousness and want of scruple of the Knight, of their passion for aggrandizement and their rapacity. Drinking habits were attributed to them: the saying was already in use 'to drink like a Templar' indicated a house of ill-fame.' (Mollat, G., *Les Papes d'Avignon (1305-78),* 233; Webster, 1955, 50 et seq.)

The same rumours had reached Clement V even before his accession to the papal throne in 1305, and in this same year, he summoned the Grand Master of the Order, Jacques de Molay, to return to France from the island of Cyprus, where he was assembling fresh forces to avenge the recent reverses of the Christian armies. De Molay arrived in France with 60 other Knights Templar and 150,000 gold florins, as well as a large quantity of silver that the Order had amassed in the East. (Raynouard, F.J.M. (1813) *Monuments historiques relatifs à la condamnation des Chevaliers du Temple et à l'abolition de leur Ordre,* Paris)

To some extent, it seems more than providential, that Pope Clement V was placed in office in 1305. Not only was he a weak and ailing man but a Frenchman too, exiled from Rome, who had fixed his residence at Avignon. He lived for much of the time in Poitiers, being the territory of the King of France. In some instances history certainly intimates that he was a 'useful tool' for Philippe le Bel, and collusion took place between them, for he the Pope, could be leant upon to support the king's bidding. Greed - being the primary goal - the king wanted to try and obtain the Templars' treasure and lands for himself and the Crown. To do so, the discrediting of the Order had to be accomplished.

The Pope now set himself to make enquiries concerning the charges of 'unspeakable apostasy against God, detestable idolatry, execrable vice, and many heresies' that had been 'secretly intimated' to him. But, to quote his own words:

> "Because it did not seem likely nor credible that men of such religion who were believed often to shed their blood and frequently expose their persons to the peril of death for Christ's name, and who showed such great and many signs of devotion both in divine offices as well as in fasts, as in other devotional observances, should be so forgetful of their salvation as to do these things, we were unwilling ... to give ear to this kind of insinuation...(*hujusmodi insinuacioni ac delacioni ipsorum...aurem noluimus inclinare*)" (Michelet, J. (1841) *Procès des Templiers I.2*)

The King of France, Philippe le Bel, who had been thought of, up to this time, as a friend of the Templars, now became supposedly alarmed and urged the Pope to take action against them: but before the Pope was able to find out more about the matter, the King took the law into his own hands and had all the Templars in France arrested on the same day, Friday October 13th, 1307. The Order consisted of 15,500 Knights, a vast number of squires and a host of lay brethren - who were all responsible to the Grand Master, Jacques de Molay. The Order also possessed more than 10,000 manors and several fortresses, including that of the Temple in Paris.

THE CHARGES

In the first few years of the 14th century, magical charges became one of the standard methods of aggression among jealous and competitive servants of the French king. From his court the fashion of denouncing other courtiers for the practice of witchcraft or sorcery spread to the English and Papal courts. And it was within this historical climate that the following main charges were brought against the Templars by the Inquisitor for France, Guillaume de Nogaret, before whom they were examined:

> The ceremony of initiation into their Order was accompanied by insults to the cross (spitting on the cross), the denial of Christ, and gross obscenities.
>
> Christ, God, the Virgin, or the saints were denied during a secret ceremony.
>
> The adoration of an idol which was said to be the image of the true God.
>
> Members practised obscene kisses.
>
> Members encouraged and permitted the practice of sodomy.
>
> Their chaplains did not consecrate the Host.
>
> Members did not believe in the Sacraments.
>
> The Grand Master, or other dignitaries, absolved brethren from their sins.
>
> The final list of charges was 127, a lot of them being repetitive.

To all those infamies a great number of the Knights, including Jacques de Molay the Grand Master, confessed in almost precisely the same terms: since however, a number of these confessions were made under torture, it is more important to consider the evidence provided by the trial of the Knights at the hands of the Pope where this method was NOT employed.

At the time the Templars were arrested, Clement V, deeply resented the King's interference with an Order which existed entirely under papal jurisdiction. He wrote in the strongest terms of remonstration to Philippe le Bel urging their release, and even after their trial, neither the confessions of the Knights nor the angry expostulations of the King could persuade him to believe in their guilt (Mollat). But, as the scandal concerning the Templars grew, he consented to receive in private audience 'a certain Knight of the Order, of great nobility and held by the said Order in no slight esteem,' who testified to the abominations that took place on the reception of the Brethren, the spitting on the cross, and other such things which were not lawful nor, humanly speaking, decent. (Michelet I, 3: Castle, E. J.)

The Pope then decided to hold an examination of 72 French Knights at Poitiers in order to discover whether the confessions made by them before the Inquisitor at Paris could be substantiated. At this examination, conducted without torture or pressure of any kind in the presence of the Pope himself, the witnesses declared on oath that they would tell 'the full and pure truth'. They then made confessions which were committed to writing in their presence; and these afterwards, being read aloud to them, were expressly and willingly approved by them (*perseverantes in illis eas expresse et sponte, prout recitate fuerunt approbarunt*) (Ibid I, 4)

Even after these events, the Pope still refused to take action against the whole Order merely because the Master, and Brethren around him, had 'gravely sinned'. A decision was made to hold a Papal Commission in Paris. The first sitting took place in November 1309, when the Grand Master and 231 Knights were summoned before the pontifical commissioners, 'This enquiry,' says Michelet, 'was conducted slowly, with much consideration and gentleness (*avec beaucoup de ménagement et de douceur*) by high ecclesiastical dignitaries, an archbishop, several bishops, etc.' (Michelet in the Preface to vol. I of *Procès des Templiers*). Although a number of the Knights, including the Grand Master, now retracted their admissions, some damning confessions were again forthcoming.

TRIALS

Many trials of the Templars took place in different countries, in Italy at Ravenna, Pisa, Bologna, and Florence, where torture was not employed and blasphemies were admitted (Loiseleur, Jules (1872), *La Doctrine Secrète des Templiers*). In contrast, in Germany, where torture was employed, no confessions were made and a verdict was given in favour of the Order. A few details of the trial in England may be of interest to the reader.

It has generally been accepted that torture was not applied in England owing to the humanity of King Edward II, who at first absolutely refused to listen to any accusations against the Order. On December 10th 1307, he had written to the Pope in these terms:

> 'And because the said Master or Brethren constant in the purity of the Catholic faith have been frequently commended by us, and by all our kingdom, both in their life and morals, we are unable to believe in suspicious stories of this kind until we know with greater certainty about these things.
>
> 'We, therefore, pity from our souls the suffering and losses of the Sd. Master and brethren, which they suffer in consequence of such infamy, and we supplicate most affectionately your Sanctity if it please you, that considering

> with favour suited to the good character of the Master and Brethren, you may deem fit to meet with more indulgence the detractions, calumnies and charges by certain envious and evil disposed persons, who endeavour to turn their good deeds into works of perverseness opposed to divine teaching; until the said charges attributed to them shall have been brought legally before you or your representatives here and more fully proved.' (Castle, Part I, 16, quoting Rymer, vol. III)

It is possible that Jacques de Molay was quite well known to Edward, even on a personal level, when Molay was a Grand Preceptor of the Order in England (see Appendix IV).

Edward II also wrote, in the same terms as above, to the Kings of Portugal, Castile, Aragon, and Sicily. After Clement V had himself heard the confessions of the Order, and a Papal Bull had been issued declaring that 'the unspeakable wickednesses and abominable crimes of notorious heresy' had now 'come to the knowledge of almost everyone,' Edward II was persuaded to arrest the Templars and signed the order for the Templars' arrest on 15th December 1307. In emulation of Nogaret's methods the Templars of England were taken at one swoop on 7th January 1308 and their property confiscated, those of Wales, Ireland and Scotland on the 10th of that month. The net was not drawn tight, and the haul was incomplete. Unpopular as the Templars were, the measure aroused no enthusiasm and the order was executed as a matter of duty. According to the author, E. J. Castle, the King would not allow torture with the result that the Knights denied all charges: but later, it is said, he allowed himself to be overpersuaded, and 'torture appears to have been applied on one or two occasions (Ibid, Part II, 1) with the result that three Knights confessed to all and were given absolution (Ibid, Part II, 25-7). At Southwark, however, 'a considerable number of brethren' admitted that 'they had been strongly accused of the crimes of negation and spitting, they did not say they were guilty but that they could not purge themselves ...' and therefore they abjured these and all other heresies. (Ibid, Part II, 30)

Evidence was also given against the Order by outside witnesses and the same stories of intimidation at the ceremony of reception were told.

In England and France the trials dragged on. On May 10, 1310 it was intimated to the Papal Commissioners that the Provincial Council, which was sitting in Paris not far from the Papal Commission, was about to proceed to final judgement against a number of French Templars as relapsed heretics. The grounds for condemnation were simply that these Templars were going back on their earlier confessions which had been obtained under duress. Church law rules decreed that a heretic, who admitted his guilt and subsequently denied it, was 'relapsed'. Since most of the intending 'defenders' of the Order had made some kind of an admission at earlier stages of the investigations, the implications of the judgement of recalcitrant Templars as 'relapsed' heretics were fatal for any kind of defence. Alas, two days later, fifty-four Templars were burned alive. (Partner, 1987, 77)

Webster (1955) remarks that the first line of argument usually adopted by those who defend the Order contend that the confessions of the Knights were made under torture, therefore they must be regarded as null and void. Secondly, that the whole affair was a plot hatched between the King and Pope to obtain possession of the Templars' riches. But all the confessions were not made under torture, and those that were do not necessarily invalidate the evidence. Torture, however much we may condemn it, has frequently proved the only method for overcoming the intimidation exercised over the mind of a conspirator: a man bound by the terrible obligations of a confederacy and fearing vengeance of his fellow-conspirators will not readily yield to persuasion, but only to force. If some of the Templars were terrorised by torture, or even by the very fear of torture, it must not be forgotten that terrorism was exercised by both sides. Few will deny that the Knights were bound by oaths of secrecy, so that on the one hand they were threatened with the vengeance of the Order if they betrayed its secrets, and on the other hand faced with torture if they refused to confess. They therefore found themselves between 'the devil and the deep blue sea'. It was not a case of a mild and unoffending Order meeting with brutal treatment at the hands of authority, but of the victims of a terrible autocracy being delivered into the hands of yet another autocracy.

Moreover, do the confessions of the Knights appear to be the outcome of pure imagination such as men under the influence of torture might devise, questions Webster. It is certainly difficult to believe that the accounts of the ceremony of initiation given in detail by men in different countries, all closely resembling each other, yet related in different phraseology, could be pure inventions. Had the victims been driven to invent them, surely they would have contradicted each other - to have cried out in their agony that all kinds of wild and fantastic rites had taken place - just to satisfy the demands of their persecutors. But no, each man appeared to have been describing a similar ceremony with characteristic touches that indicated the personality of the speaker: and most importantly of all, in the main the stories tallied.

It is difficult to discover whether Philippe le Bel did aim specifically to obtain the Templar 'booty' - he certainly needed it - and was this truly his sole reason for ridding the country of the Templars. There seems to have been a contradiction in terms. Politics being what they are, was it only a public relations exercise and to mollify the King that in November, 1309 Clement V had stated:

> 'Philippe the Illustrious King of France,' to whom the facts concerning the Templars had been told, was 'not prompted by avarice since he desired to keep or appropriate for himself no part of the property of the Templars, but liberally and devotedly left them to us and the Church to be administered,' etc... (Castle, vol. XX Part III, 3)

Who knows?

The other probable reason why the French King would have moved for the suppression of the Order was fear of the immense power their wealth had given them - not the envy of the wealth itself. The Templars dared even to defy the King and to refuse to pay taxes. The Temple, in fact, constituted a real threat, not only to royal authority but to the whole social system of the period.

SUPPRESSION OF THE ORDER IN ENGLAND

After the lengthy correspondence with Philippe Ie Bel, it had taken Edward II, the English king, some months before he took action against the Order and had them rounded up, as mentioned, on similar lines to the French in the January of 1308. The result of the English investigation was not altogether satisfactory, but the Templars were finally suppressed in England as elsewhere by the Council of Vienne in 1312. Surprisingly, Edward had drawn on Templar resources within a month of their arrest and continued to do so until the final suppression by selling their wool, using stores of grain for his war against Scotland, and even drawing Templar reserves of meat and fish for his coronation feast. He used their funds to pay arrears to his clerks and provide alms for religious houses etc... (Burman, 1986, 173)

DISPOSAL OF TEMPLAR PROPERTY: WHAT HAPPENED TO THE REMAINING TEMPLARS?

Once the Order was suppressed there were two main remaining problems: firstly, how to dispose of Templar property and secondly, what to do with those leaders still in custody. Pope Clement V managed to assert his own decision, against many members of the Council, and in his Bull of 2 May 1312 ordered that all Templar property should be transferred to the Knights Hospitallers with a single exception of property on the Iberian peninsular which was to go to local military orders in Portugal and Spain. It was also agreed that Philippe le Bel should deduct expenses from the Templars' total property and pay it into the French crown. This was for both the continued custody of the Templar brothers and for the administration of their property from the moment of their arrest in 1307.

Officially, the Order of the Temple had been dissolved by Papal decree on 22 March 1312. Contrary to the opinions of church historians, Clement V demonstrated over the next few weeks that he was not under the total domination of Philippe of France. The Pope's goal was the merger of the Templars and the Hospitallers into a single order, and he was not eager to brand a holy order, responsible only to him, as heretical. Philippe's ambition, as expressed to the council, was a new military order to be headed by himself or one of his sons, with complete access to the wealth and property of the present orders. The Pope prevailed, in his own way. On 3 April 1312, he proclaimed the Papal Bull *Vox in Excelso,* which disbanded the Templar Order without actually proclaiming it guilty of the charges brought against it. The Order was simply 'dissolved' in the parliamentary sense, and not as punishment for proven crimes against the church (Robinson, 1989, 139). However, as far as the monarchy was concerned, it was not until Jacques de Molay, Grand Master of the Order, together with his colleague, Geoffroi de Charnay, were burnt at the stake on the Isle in Paris on 18 March 1314 for heresy [retracting confessions], that the Order was seen to be finally defunct.

The process of the Hospitallers taking possession of Templar property both in France and England was by no means straightforward, even with the backing of a Papal Bull, *Ad Providum.* Yet another problem was that quite a few of the Templar properties had been donated to the Order with various bonds and agreements under the prevailing feudal system. Many of the original owners seized back the properties on the basis that their gifts were not transferable. Many a legal battle for the Hospitallers ensued, but they did succeed over the next decade in enforcing the Pope's desire by acquiring the bulk of the Templar holdings. (Burman, 1986, 172-2; Robinson, 1989, 140)

And, what happened to the Templars themselves? Templars subsequently released were free to seek membership in the Hospitallers, and a few of them did so. It should be remembered that only a percentage of them were the fighting men - the knights - most were in the lower categories, the workers on the land and servants but they still came under the Templar banner. It seems many of them simply appeared to fade away, some even married, others kept a low profile, or joined other religious houses, such as the Benedictine and the Augustine Orders. In their recent book, *The Temple and the Lodge,* authors Baigent and Leigh (1989) argue in the belief that Scotland became a haven for the scattered brethren of this suppressed medieval institution.

In a more recent article McKerracher (1991) has suggested that Robert the Bruce's most remarkable victory at Bannockburn in 1314 was orchestrated by Templars and that the battle was fought according to this Order's crusading military strategy. What is questionable, is how the soldiers were so well equipped, which was strange as economically times were stringent, and from where was the weaponry obtained?

The Templars held vast lands, in fact, more than 500 properties in Scotland. The principal preceptory was at Balantrodoch, now Temple in Midlothian. King David had invited the brethren into his kingdom as early as 1128. In the January of 1309, England's Edward II ordered his appointed Guardian of Scotland, Sir John de Segrave, to arrest all Templars still at large in the country and report them to the Inquisitor's Deputy, Bishop William Lamberton of St. Andrews. This Deputy had only been released from Winchester Castle the previous year, after taking a new oath of allegiance to Edward: he then made a visit to the Pope, to whom no doubt, lip-service was paid. McKerracher hypothesises that Lamberton's supposed interrogation of two leading Templars did not result in their arrest but an arrangement for funds, the supplying of arms possibly from their estates in Ireland too, as well as their expertise. Because of the conditions which prevailed in Scotland at the time, the Papal Bulls were never proclaimed, therefore legally the Templars were never dissolved, which in turn gave them comparative safety. What history does ascertain is that Robert the Bruce's fortunes took a considerable turn for the better. (McKerracher, A. (June 1991) *Bruce's Secret Weapon* in *The Scots Magazine* pp. 261-268)

Robinson (1989) has some original thoughts and suggests that Freemasonry has its roots in Knights Templar orthodoxy. He reveals, in his opinion, the true meaning of masonic language, secret signs, symbols, clothes and mythology in his book *Born in Blood.* He has examined certain unexplained aspects of the Peasants' Revolt of 1381 and discovered that far from being a spontaneous uprising in England it was in all probability secretly organised by Knights Templar. Because Edward II had been reluctant to enforce the Papal Bull for rounding up members of the Order in 1307, his delay of three months allowed the Templars to go underground and become a secret society. Robinson also thinks masonic oaths originated in the dreadful tortures the Templars suffered if caught; that masonic vocabulary could be explained by reference to the Norman French spoken by the Templars, and the architecture of masonic lodges could be understood by studying the former temples of the Order.

What is more, the masonic injunction to worship one Supreme Being, is the most pertinent, and can be related back to the Templars continuing religious beliefs in the face of excommunications by the Pope. The suspicion has always lingered on, that the brethren, rather than medieval stone-masons, held the true origins of Freemasonry. (See also p. 120 ff, 139 and 148)

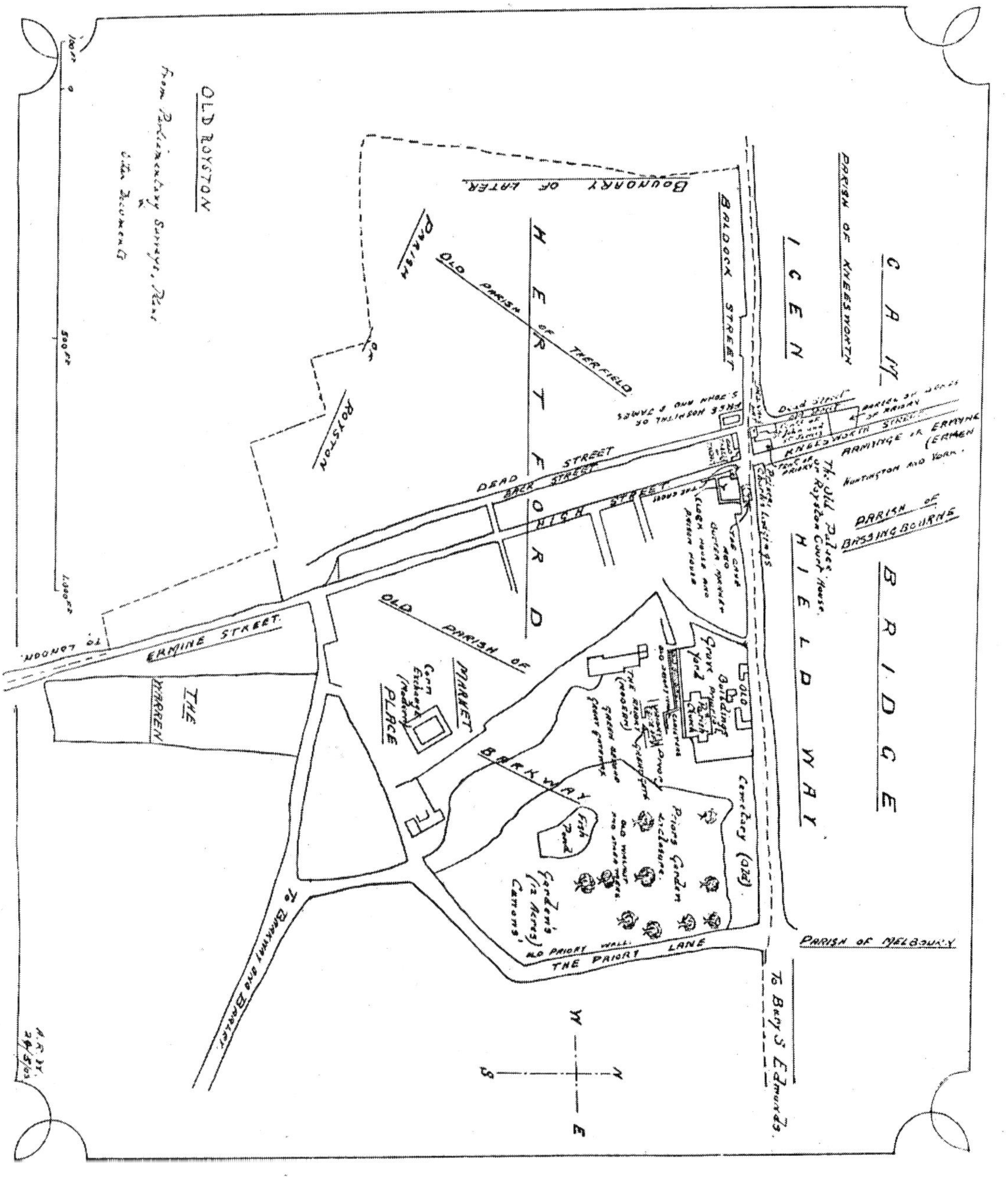

Fig. 15. Plan of 1902, made up from Parliamentary Surveys, plans and other documents
(held by J. Wilkerson, Barley)

5. RECORDED HISTORY OF ROYSTON

THE CROSS-ROADS

Ermine Street, heading north on its way from London to York, climbs the long dip slope of the chalk hills then descends to the upper tributaries of the Cam, turning a little to take in the steeper scarp slope. Before it reaches the plain it is crossed by the Icknield way which follows the foot of the escarpment and here forms the boundary between Hertfordshire on the hills and Cambridgeshire on the plain.

An intersection of such roads sounds like a geographer's ideal for a market-town of time-honoured antiquity. In fact, Royston is a comparative newcomer, with its legal and administrative status set in the later middle ages indicating unmistakably its position as post Domesday (Fig. 15). Although the town was compact, encompassing the four arms of the cross-roads, it straddled the territory of five parishes, Barkway, Therfield, Melbourn, Bassingbourn and Kneesworth, and the two aforementioned counties. In the earliest *Lay Subsidies,* held in the Hertford Record Office, they show that the number of persons assessed here shortly after the establishment of the monastery was comparatively small but had increased in later returns. It required the Act of Parliament of 1540 to give Royston its independent status:

> 'forasmuche as the Towne of Royston is a markett Towne situate and bilded to gither and extendeth itself into Fyve severall parishes whereof never a Parrisshe Churche of them is within two myles of the said towne and somme of them be three myles...'
>
> '...forasmuche as the Towne of Roiston is a greate and a comon thorowefare for the Kinges subjectis and leige people travayling from many and sundry parties of this Realme and in the said Towne is also wekely a great m'ket whereunto greate and frequent resorte is of all thinhabituantis of the Countrey therunto adioyning...' (Kingston, 1912, 70)

THE PRIORY

It is clear that in 1540 Royston was far from being a no-man's-land. It seems that when people first gathered there it was no more than just a place where four roads met in open country. Anyone working in the fields near the cross-roads went home in the evening to one of the five villages adjacent to the crossing. In the late twelfth century there is the first mention of *Crux Roys,* a wayside cross near which a house of Austin Canons had been founded (1163-84). The Priory lay within Newsells Manor in Barkway Parish and acquired the manorial rights in its foundation charter. (*V.C.H. Herts.* III (1912), 253; act, 32 Henry VIII, c.44; Beresford & St. Joseph, 169)

In founding the Priory, Ralph de Rochester conferred upon it the place in which he had built the church, the soil of the precincts within the walled close, the green space [*placea*] which was of his fee of Neuselles before the gate and front of the wall there as far as 'Holewey' and 'Cawden'. Forty acres of arable land in 'Eldefeld', pasture for sheep in the remaining part of

'Eldefeld' throughout his manor and all his land with the homage and service of his men and tenants there and in Royston. (Hertford Record Office - *Royston Notes*)

The Priory originated from a chapel for three chaplains, which was soon enlarged for seven regular canons. The number of canons was probably increased to thirteen, and the income in 1291 being about £61, but there were only six canons in 1381. The sub-prior and eight other canons in 1534 subscribed to the act of supremacy, the prior apparently being absent; and at the Dissolution (1540) *, the convent consisted of the prior and six canons. The dependency was Coddenham in Suffolk. (Knowles & Hadcock, 1953)

Richard (Dominus Ricardus) was Prior de Cruce Roys in 1292, Thomas was Prior between 1294 - 1304, and Gilbert was named as a Prior in the 13th century, exactly which part of the century is unknown. (Palmer, 1935, 35, 46)

In Royston there were two hospitals or free chapels in addition to the monastery. These two were founded at a very early date and known to have been in existence within a short time of the foundation of the Priory. One stood on the Hertfordshire side of the town, and the other on the Cambridgeshire side. Both were in a sense ecclesiastical institutions, although their object varied from the monastic functions. In some records St. Mary is joined to the dedication of both hospitals. Leper hospitals were frequently established along the great highways in the middle ages, and through them the church exercised a salutary influence as the 'sanitary authority', for these free chapels were isolation hospitals for the lepers and protected the health of the rest of the people. At the same time they were like the monastery in administration; each was under a master, and besides the leper inmates a certain number of priests and a chaplain were attached to them. The inmates lived in a little world of their own, attended daily services in the chapel, but were allowed out only with permission from the master. This was where poor wayfarers came for relief.

ST. JOHN AND ST. JAMES HOSPITAL

The Hospital, or free church, dedicated to St. John and St. James founded for lepers was situated near the cross on the south side of Baldock street, where the post office is now, which at that time was in the parish of Therfield. For the spiritual relief of poor people coming and going through the town Richard Argentine, [believed to have been a Templar - see p. 230] Sheriff of Cambridgeshire, in 1224 founded the chapel. And it was for this Hospital, in the reign of King Henry III, that Walter de Gray, Archbishop of York, on the 5th ides of July 1227 granted 13 days indulgence to such as should contribute to the support of the weak and sick brethren of the Hospital. (Tanner, John (1744) *Notitia Monastica,* pub. J. Tanner, London, p. 189)

Another early reference occurs in a *Patent Letter* dated 1st April 1251 (Membrane 9) at Westminster. Simple protection without term for the Hospital of St. James at Royston and the Master and brethren thereof. (Cal. Pat. Rolls 32 Henry III A.D. 1247-1258 p. 92)

> 'Reginaldus de Argenten in the xxth year of the raigne of King Edward... granted to God and the blessed Mary and to the Hospital of the Holy Apostells John and James of Cruce Roys a messuage of his fee with the appurtenances which I had of the grant of John Litlington chaplain, to hold to the brethren to the said Hospital and their successors for ever in pure and perpetual almes to the susteyning of poore people and the brethren ther etc. according to the grant of Richard de Argenten his grandfather...'

Dominus Ricardus Prior de Cruce Roys was one of the witnesses [1292]. This Reginald de Argentein gave other gifts of land and rents to the Hospital between 1292-1307. (Palmer, 1935, 45)

There are two more entries recorded by John Layer (1586-1640) taken from the *Chartulary of Royston Hospital* which should certainly be mentioned:

> '9. John son of Jeffrey de Merdele granted to the Hospital of St. John and St. James in Cruce Roys and to Mathew the sune of Godfrey Chaplain ther and minister of the said Hospital the yearlie rents of 5s. which I was wont to have and receive by the hands of Robert Vintner for that hermitage in Royston.'

Believed to have been dated prior to 1250. (Palmer, 1935, 45)

> '55. The prior of the church of St. John the Baptist and St. Thomas the Martyr of Royston, and John Alyngton Esq. and Sir John Byk master of the Hospital of St. John and St. James, **concerning the hermitage in Roiston** and the presentation and the saying of masse in the chapel of St. Nicholas in the feilds in Royston and other variances and controversies between them, submitted themselves to the award of Sir John Cheyne Kt., William Frevyle and Thomas Lokton squires and Thomas Pygott gentleman, who aware that each of them and their successors should hold and enyoye all jurisdiction liberties, franchises and privileges in Roiston as they and there predecessors lawfully before time occupied, and thereupon all suits to be with drawn and releases made between them and the Prior to pay to the said John Alyngton eight pounds. 7th Edw. 4th. (1467)' (Palmer, 1935, 50)

Local historian William Palmer, in 1935, assumes the hermitage is definitely Royston Cave (p. 35). It is highly possible of course, (see further comments under Hermitage pp. 68-70) but what does puzzle the writer is that neither the original entries, nor Layer himself, when he was compiling his history, qualified the existence of 'the hermitage' in anyway. Hermitages were not that common and a subterranean one, even less so. The assumption has always been that the Cave was filled-in at the time of the Dissolution of the Monasteries. If that was so, it is also strange that Layer did not mention it in passing or give a margin note - he was not averse to giving margin notes on other issues; and if the Cave was still open, again, why no comment?

In the 14th century St. Nicholas Hospital in the Cambridgeshire side of the town came under the jurisdiction of St. John and St. James. The whole was suppressed in 1547... (Page, 1912, *Odsey Hundred,* p. 255)

Stukeley also comments on this Hospital of St. John and St. James:

> 'For the most part it remains situate on the south-side of the Ikning Street, a little westward of the cross. It was a long building, upon arches, like Pythagoras's school at Cambridge. Above was the chapel. Beneath, the cells of the poor people there maintained. There were kitchen and lodgings for the warden. The new house at the east end of it, was part of the same building...'

In the early spring of 1982 an excavation of the site was undertaken by the East Herts. Archaeological Group, and it is understood that nothing of any importance was found. Unfortunately, shortly afterwards, the Director of the excavation was killed in a motorbike accident and the formal report to date has not been published.

ST. NICHOLAS' HOSPITAL

The Hospital of St. Nicholas, which was the more important of the two hospitals, was founded in that part of Royston which lay in the County of Cambridge and diocese of Ely. It seems probable that it was founded by Amphelise, wife of Theobald, son of Fulk and one of the daughters of Robert the Chamberlain; she gave two acres of land in Kneesworth in the parish of Wendy to the Hospital of St. Nicholas, and her gift was confirmed by her husband. Amable or Mabel de Cormeilles, who seems to have been a sister of Amphelise also made a grant with the assent of her husband Osbert L'Evesque (*Episcopus*). As Osbert was dead by 1203 and Theobald before 1206, while Niel the last surviving son of Robert de Chamberlain, died in 1191, the date of the foundation must have been about 1200.

Numerous small grants of land in Melboum and Kneesworth were made by more than a score of donors. Most of these were made to the brethren which, in several instances, were described as 'whole and sick'; and, in two deeds specified as 'brethren and sisters.' There appears to have been a small religious community who received lepers and possibly other sick persons. According to the statement made in 1359, the original foundation had been of a chapel and house for the lodging of lepers, plus the maintenance of a Chaplain who should celebrate in the chapel in the presence of the lepers three times a week. It is not clear whether the chaplain was head of the community; and it is curious that a grant of one half acre in Kneesworth by Thomas de Waddon Kt. (c. 1230-40) to 'the master of and brethren', is the only allusion to such a Head.

On January 1st, 1213 King John took the house and brethren under his protection, and the next day he granted the brethren of the Hospital a fair on the eve and day of the Translation of St. Nicholas [8th, 9th May]. Henry III, in 1236, extended the fair to the 'morrow and the feast'.

The patronage of the Hospital descended from Fulk son of Theobald to his grandson Ralph, son of Ralph son of Fulk, who sold two acres in Melbourn with the advowson of the Hospital and chapel of St. Nicholas to Sir Giles Argentein who already held the patronage of the Hospital of St. James at Royston (in Hertfordshire) probably founded by his father.

Towards the end of the thirteenth century the chapel of the Hospital contained a set of vestments, a silver chalice, a chrismatory, a missal and a breviary. Just about a century later, the ornaments included seven bronze crosses, sixteen banners, three censers and an incense boat. This suggests that at the later date the chapel was used by one or more of the Royston gilds [guilds], most probably only as a store for their processional gear.

Even at an earlier date it is doubtful if the Hospital was functioning, and by 1359 it was certainly a sinecure free chapel or chantry. In that year John de Norwych, nominal warden of St. Nicholas, stated that the advowson of the chapel was held by Agnes widow of John de Argentein: that for a great while past lepers had not dwelt there, and that the chantry of three celebrations weekly was then performed at the Hospital of St. James. The 30 acres of land which constituted its endowment were held of the Earl of Richmond and John de Argentein by service of maintaining a lamp in the church of Wendy. For another hundred years, services seem to have been held at least occasionally in the chapel as, in 1467, one of the points of dispute between the Prior of Royston and the Master of St. James Hospital was the saying of Mass in the chapel of St. Nicholas in the fields of Royston, as noted above under St. John and St. James Hospital. (*V.C.H. Cambridge and Isle of Ely,* 1948, 310). The site of its burial ground was uncovered, according to Kingston, at the beginning of this century, when the remains of a stone slab was removed for preservation in the Town Hall garden. Some Saxon relics were said to have been found also.

Various chapels were built to serve the resident lay communities and travellers during the medieval period. In Lincolnshire, for example, the Hospitallers founded chapels on their reclaimed land at Swinderby Moor (1378) and Eagle (1407) and the Templars had set up a Chapel of St. John in Aslackby which was still served in 1514. Many of these chapels left little trace in the records unless they so expanded as to become a threat to nearby parishes. (D. M. Owen (1971) *Church and Society in Medieval Lincolnshire,* vol. V. p. 18). Perhaps Royston Cave, if not the hermitage, was such a chapel, insignificant and not worthy of recording, the Mother Church of the area being St. Mary Magdalene at Barkway, some distance away.

* **NOTE:** *The Dissolution of the Monasteries started in 1536 with the dissolution of the smaller ones. Pope Paul III excommunicated Henry VIII in 1538 and the king instigated the general dissolution of all the monasteries the following year, therefore there is an anomaly in dates in some cases. The date of 1540 is often given as a general date for the final suppression.*

ANTIQUARIAN THOUGHT

It may be convenient here to give some account of the three main authors, and to briefly outline their respective theories on the Cave.

Dr. William Stukeley (Fig. 16a), who was Rector of All Saints in Stamford, Lincolnshire wrote, besides his two books on the Royston Cave between 1743-46, many literary works on various antiquities in the 18th century, including Stonehenge. He formed the opinion that the Cave was an oratory and that the mural carvings were done in order to depict episodes of her family history, by no less a person than Lady Roisia de Vere, wife of Geoffrey de Mandeville, whom he claimed lived at Newsells the local Manor House. He also believed that the skull and bones, found in the infill, were those of Lady Roisia and that she had been buried in the Cave. (See p. 127)

Fig. 16a. The Rev. William Stukeley (painter unknown). The portrait is held by the Society of Antiquaries in London from which permission was granted for its reproduction.

Rev. Charles Parkin, A.M., Rector of Oxburgh in Norfolk wrote an answer to Dr. Stukeley's first book in 1744 and used the former author's plates to illustrate his own work. [The writer has been able to prove this statement, as evidenced by the original drawings made by Stukeley held in the Bodleian Library, Oxford - see Appendix X].

Extract of a letter from Stukeley, January, 1744-5 at Stamford, to Mr. H. F. St. J. Theobald:

> '...I diverted myself one of these holydays in looking over part of Parkin the pretender's book against me, which I find to be a piece, malicious, rude, and insolent, and no less weak and trifling. I do really believe, when long summer days come, and we have a great deal of idle time upon our hands, I shall make myself laugh with roasting this goose in his feathers, and examin him quite through.
>
> His title is an impudent parade of words without meaning. One would judg by it that I had wrote against him, that I had personally affronted him, or been guilty of some most atrocious crime against the publick. He has pyrated my plates, and to hide the felony, erased my name underneath as the designer. He has transcribed my whole book, and then stuffing it with his impertinent remarks, turns himself out for an author, and grubstreet like, thinks he make his book sell by scandal and effrontery...' (*Surtees Society* (1883 1) *Stukeley's Diaries and Letters,* edited by W. C. Lukis, vol.II pp. 204-5)

Parkin occasioned yet another derogatory *Reply* four years later, to Stukeley's second book which today, no doubt, would be classed as libellous. There is some doubt as to whether in actual fact, he himself, ever visited the Cave. Even though Royston is not mentioned in Domesday Book, the Rev. Parkin considered the town was a lot older than it is generally accepted to be. He concluded the Cave was a Hermit's cell and oratory and, because there was a cross at Royston, maintained a Hundred Court had been held here since King Alfred the Great. There is no firm evidence of the latter theory.

Joseph Beldam, F.R.G.S., F.S.A. (Fig. 16b) was born at Royston in 1795, became a scholar of St. Peter's College, Cambridge and on leaving University entered as a student at the Middle Temple. In due course he was called to the Bar. His interests were more inclined to literary work, and the legal aspects of certain public questions such as the movement for the abolition of slavery, in which he rendered good service. In other directions his activities included antiquarian research and contributed various papers to learned Societies. It is by his book *The Origin and Use of Royston Cave,* of which several editions were called for, that Beldam is now best remembered.

Beldam on the results of his enquiry into the Cave drew the following conclusions:

1. That the Cave was first formed by means of shafts, either of British or Romano-British construction, and at a period anterior to Christianity.

2. That at a somewhat later period, the Cave was used as a Roman Sepulchre.

3. That about the period of the Crusades, it received the greater part of its present decorations, and was then, if not before converted into a Christian oratory to which a hermitage was probably attached. [It is interesting to note that Beldam did not quote Layer's documentation in evidence.]

4. That it remained open until the Reformation, when it was finally filled up, closed and forgotten.

Fig. 16b. Joseph Beldam (photographer unknown)

THE HERMITAGE?

The question of the Cave being a Hermitage was hotly disputed between Stukeley and Parkin, the latter supporting his opinion that it was by a deed which conveyed the Priory property to the Chester family. Parkin appears to have mistaken a later grant from Edward VI, which notices a hermitage, for an earlier grant of Henry VIII (in which no hermitage is mentioned). The hermitage mentioned in Edward's grant, being described as in the manor of Hedley, and in the parish of Barkway, could not have meant a hermitage at Royston, which was in the manor of Newsells and in Edward's reign had become an independent parish.

Parkin also thought the name of the manor Newcells, Neucells, or Newsells derived its name from the cell and station of a hermit (p. 14). However, we find in *Place-Names of Hertfordshire* by Allen, Mawer and F. M. Stenton that Newsells is mentioned on p. 173 as follows:

An estate map of 1791 shows the Hermitage in the area 'Green House to North Gate'.

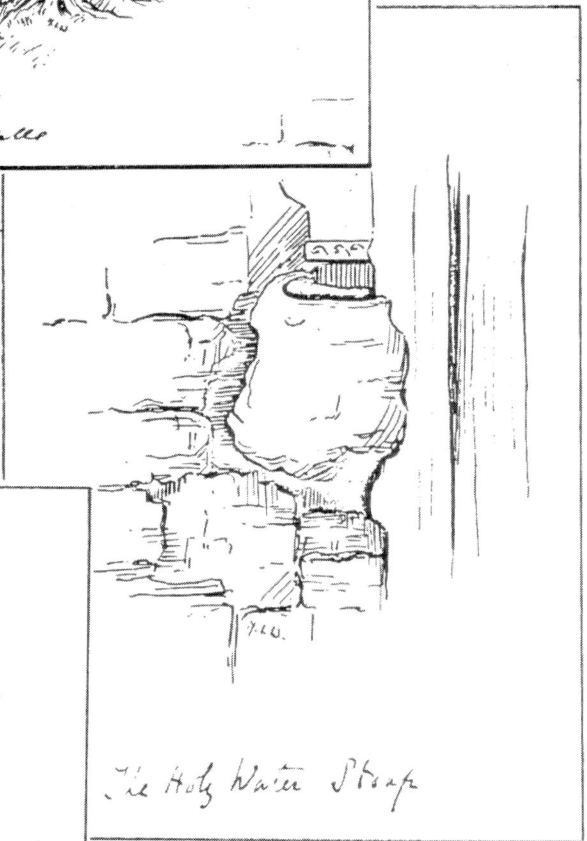

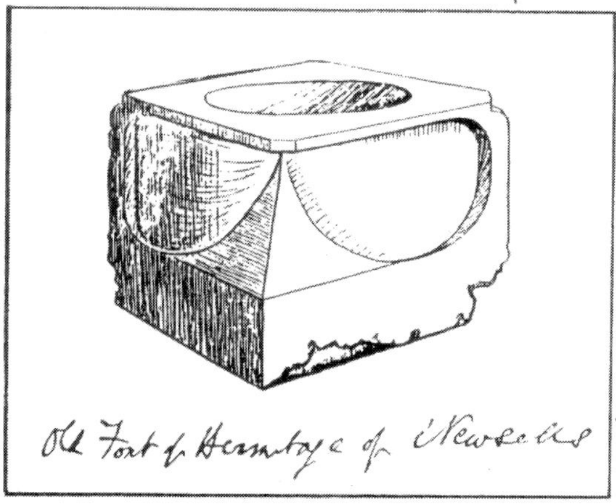

Figs. 17a, b, c. The three sketches (not to scale) are held with the 'Newsells Estate Deeds'. Although held with the hermitage sketch, it is possible that the font and stoup originally belonged to Barkway Church. In 1862 rebuilding work on the church was carried out under the patronage of the Hon. Caroline Vernon-Harcourt and she may have removed them to her home at Newsells.

NEWSELLS:
Neusela, Neuesselle 1086 DB, Newesele t. Ric. I (1301) Ch, 1212 Fees, Niewesele 12th Colch, Neusele, Niuesele 1210-12 RBE, Newsill 1637 FF. Neiselles 1087-93 France, Niweseles 12th Colch, Neweseles 1251 Ch. 1290 Pat., 1303 FA, Neuseles 1299 Pat, Newselles 1428 FA

'New building(s)', v. *sele.*

Beldam feels that the Rev. Parkin was right in his notion of an hermit actually living at Royston by reason of an entry in the old *Churchwarden's book of the parish of Bassingbourne.* This book extended back to the reign of Henry VII, and amongst other most curious details, contains a record under the date of AD. 1506, of the

'Gyft of 20d' recd 'Off an Hermytt depting at Roiston i ys pysh'

He goes on to say that it is true that this entry does not absolutely fix the residence of this hermit at the Cave. But beside the improbability of there being two hermitages in so small a town; the position of the Cave being exactly across the line which, in that reign separated the parish of Barkway from the parish of Bassingboum, shows that a hermit dying on that spot, would be correctly described as 'Departing' within the limits of the latter parish; and the existence of a cell above the Cave, moreover seems almost a necessary consequence of its close proximity to the road.

I visited the Record Office at Shire Hall, Cambridge on May 22nd 1974, to examine the afore-mentioned entry. Whilst asking for assistance in locating the record two of the archivists agreed that should the hermit have resided permanently in Royston, he would be more likely to have been referred to as 'the hermit' and not 'an hermit' because of the manner in which the other entries were consistently recorded on the same page.

Although the Cave may have been used at some time as a hermitage, I also do not think the record of AD.1506 necessarily refers to the Cave, for held with the *Newsells Deeds* is a sketch of a Hermitage situated at Newsells together with a sketch of the old Hermitage Font (Figs. 17a, b, & c). On one of the earliest maps of Newsells Park dated 1791 (reference D1ERy P5) held in the Hertford Record Office, the Hermitage is shown in the area which states, 'Green House to North Gate.' It is of course, possible that there were two hermitages in the same parish.

THE 'PIPE-CLAY' SEAL

As mentioned before, The Rev. George North of Caldecot, visited the Cave within a very short time of its discovery and stated that no relics had been found, except a human skull and a few decayed bones, fragments of a small drinking cup of common brown earth, marked with yellow spots, (similar to Denny Abbey pottery) and a piece of brass without any figure or inscription on it.

Stukeley, shortly afterwards went down and found the place completely cleared.

He records the finding of no additional relics, except that a small seal came into his possession soon afterwards which he felt must have belonged to Lady Roisia (Fig. 18b). A sketch of this seal marked with a single 'fleur-de-lis' [see also Appendix X] and the description, that it was made of 'white earthlike chalk or pipe-makers clay baked', appears in his second book *Palaeographia Britannica: or Discourse of Antiquities in Britain No. II,* p. 57. [Knowledge of this book was not known to the people in Royston until I rediscovered it at the Cambridge University Library in May 1972 together with the most extraordinary defamatory book by the Rev. Charles Parkin entitled: *A Reply to the Weak, Peevish and Malevolent Objections brought by Dr. Stukeley in his Origines Roystonianae No. II against an Answer to, or Remarks upon his Origines Roystonianae No. I*]

In the *Encyclopaedia Britannica,* it states that in Medieval times seals were once again adopted and can be exampled by King Henry I (A.D. 1031-1060) who had the Royal seal of France, complete as the seal of Majesty, bearing the full effigy of the King. The original shape of a medieval seal is round; but there are exceptions, Ladies' seals and some classes of ecclesiastical and monastic seals are of pointed oval form. Pendant seals followed.

Fig. 18a.

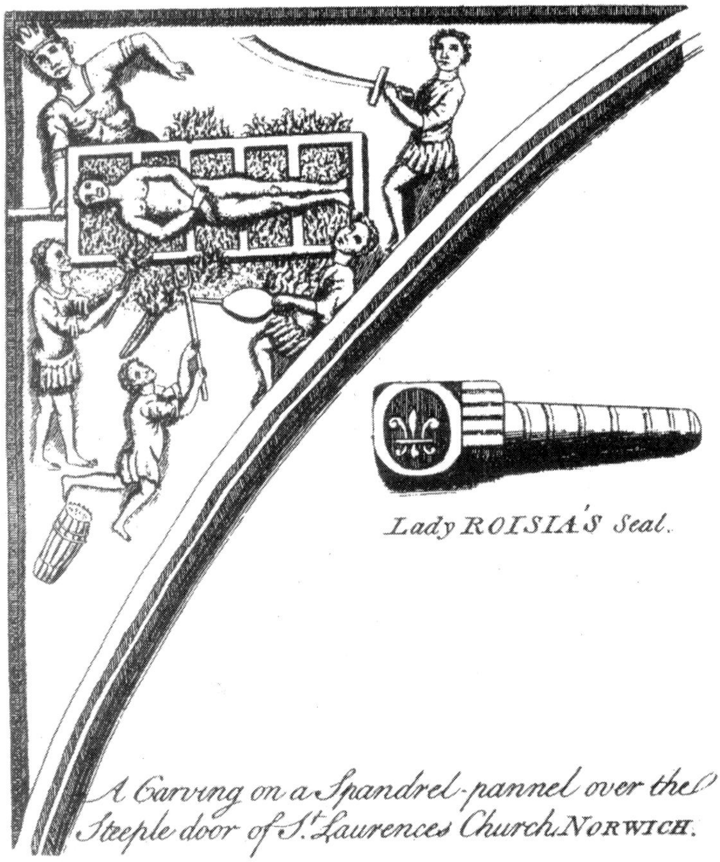

Fig. 18b.

Fig. 18a. An example of how St. Laurence was roasted on the grid-iron for his Christian values. Fig. b. The seal made of 'pipe-makers' clay', believed by Stukeley to have belonged to Lady Roisia de Vere. Both drawings come from his second book (1746).

The earliest seal of a sovereign of France to which a counterseal was added was that of Louis VII (A.D.1141) an equestrian effigy of the King as Duke of Aquitaine being impressed on the reverse. In 1154 when Aquitaine passed to the English Crown the counterseal disappeared and eventually in subsequent reigns a 'Fleur-de-lis' or the shield of France took its place.

In the middle ages the metal chiefly employed in the manufacture of matrices was bronze. Amongst the wealthy, silver was not uncommon. The ordinary seal was provided with a ridge on the back (or in some instances, with a vertical handle) by which it could be held while being used for sealing and which might be pierced for suspension.

The common material for receiving the impressions from the matrices was beeswax generally strengthened and hardened by admixture with other substances such as resin, pitch and even hemp or hair. The employment of chalk as an ingredient in many seals in the 12th century has caused them to become extremely friable. It was common practice to apply to such seals a coating of brown varnish. Besides the transparent yellowish brown of the wax when used in its natural state, as it very frequently was used in the earlier middle ages, many other colours especially red, dark green and dark brown and even black are found in Medieval seals.

Unfortunately the whereabouts of the pipe-clay seal found in Royston Cave is not known but from the sketch I think it can be assumed that it was Medieval.

In the Museum at Saffron Walden there is a badge or small plaque approximately 3 inches by 3 inches [75 mm x 75 mm] of a single 'fleur-de-lis' design stated to be probably from a 14th century tomb in the district.

HISTORY OF THE 'FLEUR-DE-LIS' SYMBOL

The history of the 'fleur-de-lis' is interesting and there are many fascinating legends relating to this symbol.

Mrs. Pritchard in her book *English Medieval Graffiti* maintains that as the 'fleur-de-lis' probably originated in the East, the Oriental conception of its significance is instructive. Yacub Artin Pacha (*Contribution à l'étude du blason en Orient*) writes: '...when the Christian cult became official in Constantinople the 'fleur-de-lis' represented the attribute of the Holy Virgin. At the feast of the Nativity, M. G. Schlumberger says, the Byzantine emperor covered his head, during the evening service, with a head-dress called 'Krinomia' and decorated with lilies, in honour of the Virgin... The Arabs themselves, from the time they appeared on the scene of history, towards the eighth century, made use of this symbol…'

> 'It is claimed that Charlemagne (782-814 A.D.), returning from fighting the Arabs in Spain had a 'fleur-de-lis' embroidered on his mantle after each campaign... If these facts could be proved, one must conclude that Charlemagne knew the significance of this symbol attributed to the Holy Virgin by' the Byzantines... As to the 'fleur-de-lis' painted on the books of Charles-le-Gros, King of France, they must have been introduced into these illuminations by an Oriental artist, who was inspired by the fashion and methods of his country.'

Mrs. Pritchard believes, beyond all doubt, that all the renowned artists of these times were Oriental monks, for the most part Byzantine.

> 'One only sees the 'fleur-de-lis' as an emblem in the arms of Europe towards the thirteenth century, when it was adopted by Louis IX following his Crusade in the East, where doubtless, he had learnt that this flower was dedicated to the Virgin Mary.' (Pritchard, 1967, 175)

The Templars adopted the 'Virgin Mary' as their patroness and the 'fleur-de-lis' was her attribute. The seal from Royston Cave had a single 'fleur-de-lis' on it. In the Tour du Coudray, Chateau de Chinon, France, there is this single emblem on a shield, another cut above the main panel attributed to artwork of the Templars (Fig. 30), also in the painted fresco at the Templar Church de Cressac (*Archeologia* No. 11 1966) there are these separated 'lilies.' (Fig. 19)

Fig. 19. A small portion of the decorated interior walls of the Templar Church at Cressac, France, showing a Templar wielding his banner. Note the emblem of the 'fleur-de-lis'.

Mrs. Pritchard also comments that in this country we have examples in graffiti of this symbol in Flamstead Church, Herts., Toddington Church Bedfordshire, Worlington Church, Suffolk. The fact that each of these 'fleurs-de-lis' is isolated and not shown as a charge on a shield makes it clear that they have no connection with heraldry. Another significance, therefore, must be found for their existence, and judging from the foregoing matter it is almost certain that these examples are symbols representing the Virgin Mary.

I would like to put forward the idea that possibly the Templars used the single 'fleur-de-lis' as a symbol for themselves, during the time they were sometimes referred to, as 'the Knights of the Virgin Mary' since the Virgin was their patron (see p. 174). Clearly, the assumption that the symbol belongs automatically and categorically to French connections, should be tempered with care and an open mind kept.

6. THE CARVINGS AND GRAFFITI

MEDIEVAL ART

Because of the composition of the carvings in the Cave, I feel it is necessary to give some account of medieval art first.

The Middle Ages had a passion for order. Theology of art was transmitted by the Church to the lay sculptors and painters of the 13th century, from one end of Europe to the other, who religiously guarded the sacred traditions so that, even in the centuries in which it was most vigorous, medieval art retained certain styles bound by religious convention, and the grandeur of primitive art. (Male, 1961, 1)

There is a category of pictures called 'devotional pictures', exhibiting the events of scripture stories. All those which express the actions, miracles and martyrdom of saints come under this class, for example, the 'Crucifixion' and the 'Last Supper' which may be so represented as to either exhibit an event, or to express a symbol of 'our Redemption'.

Our ancestors of the middle ages were not particularly concerned in drawing a strong demarcation line between the Classical, Jewish and Christian periods of history. They saw Christendom everywhere; they regarded the past only in relation to Christianity. Hence, in the early ecclesiastical monuments and edifices there is a strange assemblage of pagan, scriptural and Christian worthies, such as Hector of Troy, Alexander the Great, King David, Judas Maccabeus, King Arthur, St. George, Godfrey of Boulogne etc.

Historical subjects from the lives of saints consist principally of Miracles and Martyrdoms.

It must be remembered that the ordinary or 'common' people of the middle ages did not, and could not distinguish between miracles accredited by the testimony of scripture, and those which were fabrications, or at least exaggerations. All miracles, related as divine interventions, were to them equally possible, equally credible. If a more extended knowledge of the laws causes present day society to be less credulous, it also shows that many things were possible, under particular conditions, which were long deemed supernatural. The object was to represent the favourite patron as a copy of the great universal type of beneficence 'Christ our Redeemer'. And they were not satisfied that the resemblance should lie in character only; but should emulate the power of Christ in his visible actions.

The martyrdoms generally met with are those of: St. Peter, St. Paul, St. Stephen (protomartyr), St. Lawrence, St. Katherine and St. Sebastian. Where the patron of the church or chapel is a martyr, his martyrdom holds a conspicuous place, often over the high altar, and accompanied by all the moving circumstances, which excite the pity, horror or enthusiasm of the pious worshippers. In the best examples, the saint is seen preparing for his death, but not suffering the torments actually inflicted. The reasoning behind this is, so that the mind is elevated by the sentiment of courage, not disturbed and disgusted by the spectacle of his agonies. (Jameson, v.1, 1857 14, 16 and 17 et seq.)

SYMBOLS AND ATTRIBUTES

Fish: The fish was the earliest and most universal of the Christian emblems, partly as a symbol for water and the rite of baptism. Other symbols used are:

Crosses:

Crowns: In general, only female martyrs wear the symbolic crown of glory. It is presumed that the crown, which among Jews was the special ornament of a bride, signified the bride or spouse of Christ - one dedicated to virginity for his sake. The crown is still placed on the heads of nuns when they take their vows. For example, where St. Barbara wears the crown, it is a symbol of her martyrdom. When St. Katherine does [as in the Cave], it is not only as the symbol of martyrdom but the attribute to her rank as princess. The crown is also the symbol of sovereignty. When it is placed on the head of the Virgin, it is as the Queen of Heaven.

Sword: The sword is also a symbol or an attribute. As a symbol, it signifies generally a martyrdom by any violent death and in this sense is given to many saints who did NOT die by the sword. As an attribute it signified the particular death suffered, and that the martyr, in whose hand or at whose feet it is placed, was beheaded. In this manner it is given to St. Paul, St. Katherine and many others. It is also given to the warrior martyrs, as the attribute of their military profession. Other symbols of martyrdom are the Axe, Lance and the Club.

Wheel: St. Katherine.

Dove: Emblem of the Holy Ghost also as the Annunciation, the Baptism, the Pentecost. It is placed near certain saints who are supposed to have been particularly inspired as St. Gregory, St. Thomas Aquinas, St. Hilarius. The Dove is also the symbol of simplicity and purity of heart and as such is introduced into pictures of female saints, and especially of Madonna and Child. It is an emblem of the soul too, when it is seen rising from the lips of dying martyrs.

Palm: Ancient classical symbol of victory and triumph, assumed by Christians as the universal symbol of martyrdom.

Lily: Symbol of purity, of very general application.

Standard Banner:
Symbol of victory.

Fire and flames:
Sometimes the emblem of martyrdom and punishment, also sometimes for religious fervour.

Olive branch: Peace.

Flaming Heart: Expression of fervent piety and love.

The poniard, cauldron, pincers, shears, bell and the anvil are all attributes to other saints. And other symbols used are the anchor, lamp, ship (see p. 115), chalice, scourge, flowers, fruits, book, unicorn, church, shell and the skull which means penance. None of these latter ones are evident in the Cave.

COLOURS IN MEDIEVAL TIMES

Colours are also significant in art and I deliberately mention them for several of the figures in the Cave were painted.

Red: The ruby, signified fire, divine love, the Holy Spirit, heat or creative power and royalty. In a bad sense, red signified blood, war, hatred and punishment. Red and black combined were the colours of purgatory and the Devil.

Blue: Or the sapphire, expressed heaven, firmament, truth, constancy, fidelity.
Christ and the Virgin wear a red tunic and blue mantle signifying heavenly love and truth. St. John the Evangelist wears a blue tunic, red mantle, in later pictures the colours are sometimes red and green.

Yellow: Gold, symbol of the sun, goodness of God, initiation, or marriage, faith or fruitfulness. St. Joseph wears yellow also St. Peter with a yellow mantle over a blue tunic. In a bad sense yellow signifies inconstancy, jealousy and deceit. Judas was generally clothed in dirty yellow.

Green: Emerald, colour of spring and hope, particularly of hope in immortality and of victory.

Violet: The amethyst, signified love and truth, or passion and suffering. It is often worn by mourners. The Virgin also wears violet after the crucifixion.

Grey: Colour of ashes, signified mourning and humiliation

Black: Expressed the earth, darkness, mourning, wickedness.

THE ARTISTS

Before proceeding to describe the artwork of the Cave in detail, I would mention that, since I wrote the first account of my conclusions as to the function of the Cave, which was serialised in the *Royston Crow* (local newspaper) in October 1970, I have revised my thoughts to some extent. There is recorded evidence that the Baldock Knights Templar had a weekly market stall at Royston, commencing as early as 1199 and continuing until at least 1254. With transport difficulties of the middle ages, I questioned whether they would trundle all their wares back and forth to Baldock every market day. If not, did they have a warehouse? It is not unreasonable to assume their warehouse would have been, in all likelihood, close to the market cross, purely for convenience? I had also thought, if you have a warehouse you require a keeper and the keeper, probably a Templar himself, would have had plenty of time on his hands: he could possibly have found solace in carving the walls below the top storey? After its decoration perhaps this lower level became a chapel created for their own use, for whilst not on active duty Templars were required to make regular prayers during the day.

However, after Dr. R. C. Smail's second visit to the Cave in 1973, he felt the hypothesis of the Templars decorating the walls was unsound. In his opinion, the Templars would have employed someone else to do the work for them, not do it themselves. I had not considered this aspect and followed up his suggestion, and certainly feel he is quite right, but only for some of the more obviously important figures such as, the saints and the main crucifixion scene. It is evidenced that the pattern and way these particular engravings have been executed follow mainly the schools of art of the time, and it would seem to be unlikely that a casual person would have been fully aware of all the attitudes and attributes necessary for this art work [see also comments on p. 181 and 245]. Therefore someone, or some group of persons, must have been responsible for engaging the artist or artists. Why are there apparently no records? Was it because it was to be used for secret initiations and so deliberately omitted?

In 1986, Harold Perrett, a local artist, was commissioned to make a large reproduction of St. Katherine in fibre glass to be fixed to the barn at rear of the Cave property. When he examined the figure in situ, he realised that whoever, had carved this one and the other three figures to the left of her [Mary, Joseph and the Christ Child], had known about anatomy for the muscle formation of the arms had been carved correctly. Not only that, but the poor repair by the Ministry of Works (1950s?) had distorted the shape of her right arm and it should have been the same as the other three figures. The correct angle is discernible at the (original) shoulder.

Nevertheless, I am still of the opinion that some of the carvings were executed by more lowly people - the brown-garbed Templars maybe - and the theory is explained more fully in the conclusions.

THE CAVE ART·WORK

Note: *The Plate numbers in square brackets refer to the photographs taken by the Courtauld Institute of Art for posterity in 1972. The two modern day pull-outs are panoramas made up from a series of photographs held in Royston Museum prior to 1960 (Figs. 22 & 27). It is suggested that the reader relates to the latter two Figures together with earlier photographs referred to in the text.*

On entering the Cave (Fig. 22 - [Plate 34]) by the new entrance which lies at east, and starting on the left travelling south, there is the first niche 22 1/2 inches [0.55 m] from the ground which has been called the 'sedilia' [although it is impossible to sit in it]. The graffiti around here is very indistinct and seems to be made up mainly of scratched initials of past visitors. Then comes the next niche a few inches higher to the right.

The graffiti, just beyond, [Plate No. 25] is again faint and we have to rely on the writings and drawings of the previous authors for information (Figs. 20 & 31 Stukeley; 21a, b & 32 Beldam).

Unfortunately, as they did not have the advantage of photography, their representations are not always accurate. Beldam also states that:

> 'the figures here for some distance are nearly effaced and the first figure that can be traced, is that of a person holding a ball, or globe, in his right hand.' (Beldam, 1884, 33) (Fig. 21a)

I will make one comment here. The globe was important to the Templars, for this Globe of the world symbol was attributed to Divine Power. (See p. 102)

THE CROWNED LADY: QUEEN ELEANOR? ST. KATHERINE? VIRGIN MARY?

Beldam continues:

> 'The next is the half-length figure of a royal lady in a cloister or cell, which forms part of an ecclesiastical edifice, of Anglo-Norman or Early English architecture. The lady wears a crown, but has the air of being a prisoner; and probably represents Queen Eleanor, the wife of Henry II, who in consequence of her intrigues and violence, was imprisoned by her husband for many years, and only liberated on the accession of her son Richard I Coeur de Lion.'

Parkin supposes this figure to represent St. Katherine in prison. I am personally, not convinced this figure is of Queen Eleanor, or even St. Katherine in prison.

I suggest the image is the Virgin Mary, for there is another account similar in its essentials, and shown in what has been said to be, perhaps, the finest medieval personification of the Virgin Mary in a sculpture on Strassburg Cathedral depicted as a royal lady - the crown upon her head together with the banner of victory [royal standard - see below] and the chalice in her hand. (Hastings, 1808, vol. 12, 135)

ST. JOHN THE BAPTIST AND THOMAS À BECKET? [Plate 23]

Again indistinct: Beldam states:

> 'next to the royal prisoner and only separated from her by a royal standard, and a figure, which probably represents the standard bearer, is the shrine of the two patron saints of the Priory Church, St. John Baptist and St. Thomas à Becket.'

Stukeley recorded:

> 'William Lilly, who lives in the house just over the oratory and was very assistant in drawing out the earth, says these two figures first appeared painted over of a red colour, and I myself saw the remains of it.'

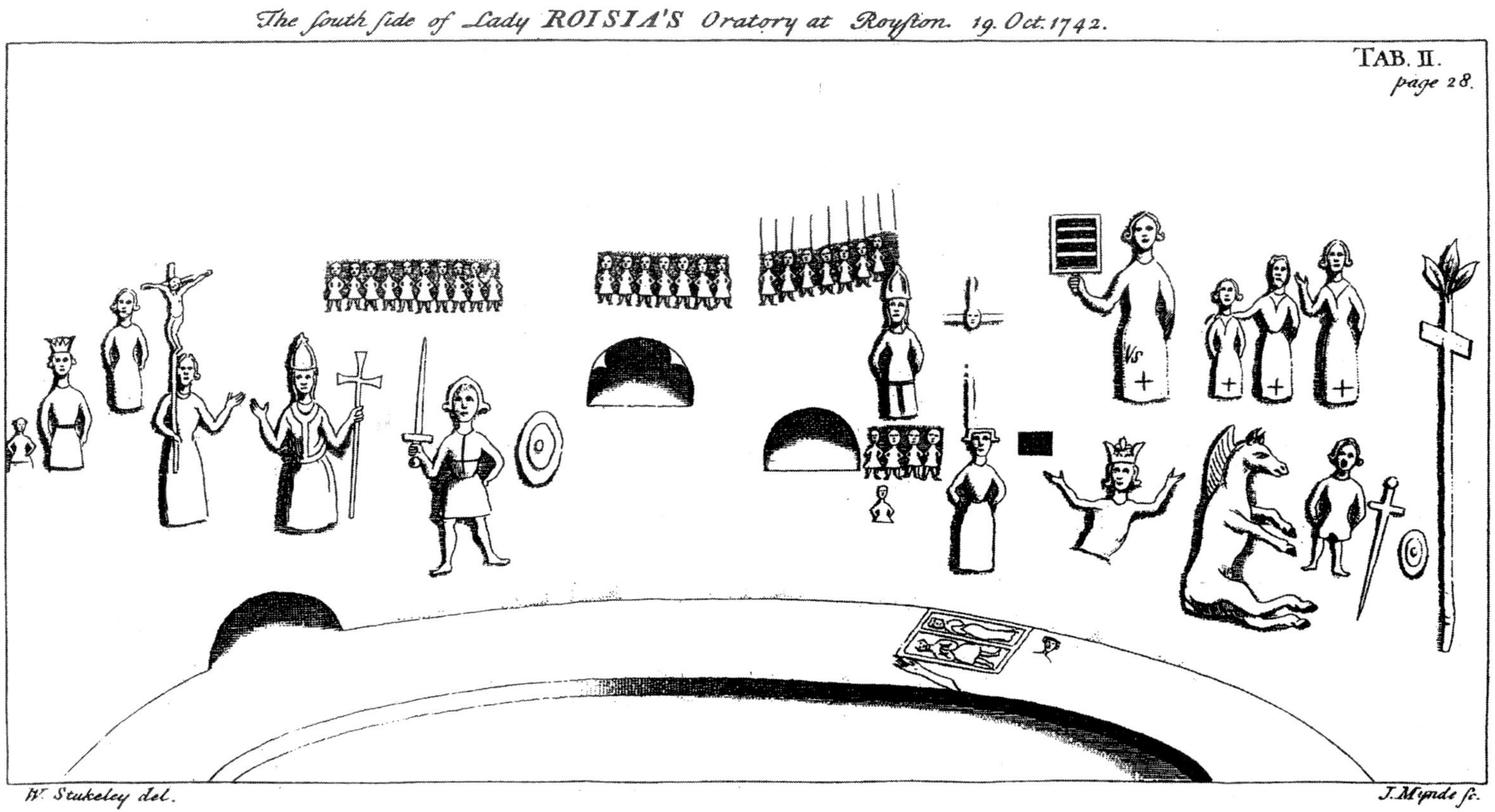

Fig. 20. *The floriat cross, to the far right of the plate, is shown as terminating in a ferule in the original plate in Stukeley's first book (1743). This copy here is from his second book (1746) where he has lengthened the cross to finish in a point. There are other small additions in this later edition, see also original sketches in Appendix X. King David (?) – the figure with his arms raised, does not have the 'WR' letters on the chest as mentioned by Beldam.*

Drawn by Mr J. Beldam

Fig. 21a Joseph Beldam's section looking south-west from the 1884 third edition of his book, 'The Royston Cave'. There are variations in the 1904 fifth edition, whether they were Beldam's own alterations or the printer's is not known.

5	The Cross of St. Helena	10	Queen Eleanor
6	The Holy Family	11	The Shrine of St. John Baptist and St. Thomas à Becket
7	St. Laurence	12	King Henry II
8	The Conversion of St. Paul	13	The Pedigree
9	William the Lion, King of Scots		

Fig. 21b.

1 Section of Cave, looking W; with the two shafts
2 Appearance of the Cave when half opened
3 Ground plan of Cave and Grave
4 Anglo-Norman Architecture
5 Norman Arch
6 The Disputed Shield
7 Kite-shaped Shield
8 Crown of Richard Coeur de Lion
9 Crown of Queen Berengaria
10 Crown of St. Katharine
11 Circular Shield
12 Another Shield
13 Crown of William King of Scots
14 The Date in the Dome
15 Lady's Head-dress
16 The Seal found in the Cave
17 The Sword of St. Paul
18 Low-crowned helmet of Henry II
19 Another Shield
20 Crusader's Helmet
21 Head-dress of the Virgin at the Cross
22 Second Date in the Cave
23 Crown of Queen Eleanor
24 Hearts in Double and Triple Lines
25 Initials of William King of Scots

Above the shrine, which is a tablet sunk in the wall, and over the head of the Baptist is a crucifixion, **'the cross being pattée'** and Parkin remarks, **'...such as was used by the Knights Templar.'** Beldam describes St. John as a venerable personage, who is bare-headed, and wearing a forked beard, furthermore:

> 'The figure is of three-quarters' length, and the legs being merely scratched into the chalk, and was possibly intended to appear as standing in the water. He wears a short tunic, and holds in his left hand, towards the figure of St. Thomas, a crown, surmounted by three drooping tendrils, probably indicating the palm and crown of martyrdom. St. Thomas is represented as a prelate of high degree, clothed in full canonicals, and wearing a lofty conical cap or mitre. He holds in his right hand, a globe, surmounted by a cross, and in his left a staff crosier. An altar marked with a cross, is cut into the space between these two saintly personages.'

Due to the condition of this graffiti little can be contradicted or confirmed.

CARDINAL OCTAVIAN AND HUGH DE NUNANT?
HERACLIUS AND THE GRAND MASTER OF THE HOSPITALLERS?
HERACLIUS WITH THE GRAND MASTER OF THE TEMPLARS?

Stukeley supposes them to represent the Cardinal Octavian, as legate from Pope Urban, and Hugh de Nunant [carrying the crucifix] King Henry II's chaplain, on a mission for the purpose of crowning his son John, King of Ireland. Another suggestion is, that the bearded man represents the Grand Master of the Hospitallers, bearing the royal standard and regalia of Jerusalem, attended by Heraclius the Patriarch; both these dignitaries having been deputed in the year 1185, to make a tender of the sovereignty of the Holy Land to Henry II, on condition of his hastening to its rescue from the Saracens. (Fig. 23)

There is yet a similar analogy I will put forward - that in 1185, Heraclius, patriarch of Jerusalem came to England accompanied by the Grand Master of the Templars to obtain aid relief from Henry II against the power of the famous Saladin, and at the same time to dedicate the Temple Church in London.

PRIORY SEAL

Beldam agreed with Parkin that the small tableau represents the shrine of the two patron saints of the Priory. Parkin supports his supposition by the Priory Seal, of which a wax impression, broken as appears in the engraving, is attached to the Deed of Supremacy preserved in the Public Record Office and described by Parkin thus:

> 'The Cross de Cruce Roheys, by which the Priory was styled, was placed in the centre of the seal between two figures, the one on the right being that of St. John the Baptist, and the other on the left St. Thomas of Canterbury.'

Fig. 22. Panorama of the Cave from the 'new' passage of 1790 in the east travelling to the south-west. Date of the series of photographs, held in Royston and District Museum, unknown, but were presumably taken before the 1960's.

He believed the legend round the seal was:

> 'St. Pr and Convent. Scor. Johis. Bapt. and Tho. Martiris de Cruce Roheys.' (Fig. 24a)

On close examination of the photograph, the crucifix, of course, does not resemble the one shown on the seal, the former having the outline of a figure on it; neither is it in between the two figures but immediately above the first one. Another small point, in the seal, St. Thomas does not hold the globe surmounted by a cross. From the state of the tableau little more can be added except to relate the following comments of Mrs. Jameson from *Legends of the Monastic Orders,* as being of interest in general.

Fig. 23. An embellished drawing, which is one drawing out of a series of water-colours by the local artist William Butler, c.1860.

ST. THOMAS À BECKET

St. Thomas à Becket was martyred in 1170, canonised by Pope Alexander III in the year of 1172. In devotional figures, St. Thomas is represented wearing the chasuble [a sleeveless garment] over the black Benedictine habit and carrying the crosier and Gospels in his hand. When represented as a martyr, he is without mitre, and the blood trickles from a wound in his head or he has a battle-axe or sword struck in his head. He is generally beardless. (See also Appendix E)

Considering the extraordinary veneration once paid to St. Thomas à Becket throughout all Christendom, but more especially in England, it seems strange that there is not now in evidence a single memorial left to him. The church which he defended, canonized him and held his name up to worship; within two years after his death his relics were laid in a rich shrine, the scene of his martyrdom became a place of pilgrimage to all nations. But kingly power uncanonised him, desecrated his shrine, buried his relics and flung his ashes into the Thames. By an act in Council of Henry VIII, it was solemnly decreed:

> 'That Thomas à Becket was no longer a saint but a rebel and a traitor; that he should no longer be called or esteemed a saint; that all images and pictures of him be destroyed, all festivals held in his honour should be abolished and the name and remembrance erased from all documents under ban of regal indignation and imprisonment during his Grace's pleasure...'

This decree was so effective in England that the effigies of this once beloved and popular saint vanished at once from every house and oratory. 'I have never met nor could ever hear', states Mrs. Jameson, 'Of any representation of St. Thomas à Becket remaining in our ecclesiastical edifices; and I have seen missals and breviaries in which his portrait had been more or less carefully smeared over and obliterated.'

But with regard to the representation of St. Thomas of Canterbury in Roman Catholic countries where they alone are to be found, in 1172, William the Good, King of Sicily began to build the magnificent church of Monreale, the interior of which is encrusted with rich mosaic; and amongst the figures of saints and worthies we find St. Thomas of Canterbury standing in his episcopal robes with no attribute but his name inscribed. It is the work of Byzantine artists and perhaps the earliest existing effigy of Thomas à Becket. His martyrdom is also represented on a cope richly embroidered presented to a little church in Agnani. On the mitre he is again represented. These two examples show how early and effectively the Church had exalted the saintly fame of Thomas à Becket. Mrs. Jameson suggests that the first example can be explained by the fact William the Good married Princess Joanna of England, daughter of Henry II who had ordered the assassination of Thomas and probably thought to honour his bride!! [SPB's exclamation marks]. As shown eastern artists were familiar with this saint.

Two stone sculptured figures were found buried in the 'middle of the wall' of the south aisle in the Royston Parish Church in 1823, both were headless. These images were lost sight of until 1859, when they were recovered from the staircase in the wall of the south aisle. Excluded from the church as being 'popish', they were preserved in the museum of the Royston Institute until the dispersal of the contents of that museum in the early 20th century. One of the images is certainly a Bishop, most probably St. Thomas of Canterbury, and it currently rests in the Chancel's south-eastern window recess. The other statue is of the Virgin and Child. The head of the infant, with a nimbus around it, was uninjured; however, the Virgin has been given a resin cast conjectural head recently, following which the repaired statue has been replaced within the Church. It is assumed that these statues were deliberately smashed at the Reformation, and that at the same time the dedication of the Priory Church to St. Thomas the Martyr of Canterbury was dropped. (Figs. 24b & c). In 1916 the Roman Catholic Church revived this saint's name in Royston by dedicating to him their Italian-styled building in Melbourn Road, copied from a church building in Rome dedicated to St. Bridget of Sweden. The architect was Father Benedict Williamson, priest to the parish, and the builders were the local firm, Jacklins, now no longer trading.

I mention here an interesting remnant of information. The Crusaders captured Jerusalem in 1099 including the Mosque of El Aksa, which building after serving briefly as the palace of the Kings of Jerusalem, was converted into the headquarters of the Knights Templar, who then officiated on the Temple compound. Apparently after Thomas à Becket's death, his four assassins travelled to Jerusalem where they took up service with the Templars and their tombs are situated near the main entrance to the Mosque. (Bishko, 1973, 20)

JOHN THE BAPTIST

The usual characteristic representation of John the Baptist is that of a tall, meagre figure, sunburnt and haggard, as one wasted with vigils and fasting, also from desert life his hair and beard are dishevelled. He is covered with a garment of camel's hair with a leather girdle: limbs and chest are exposed, the hand uplifted to warn or testify, but as messenger and precursor he generally stands with the Baptismal cup or reed cross. In the character of patron Saint and Baptist, St. John is often seen in baptisteries, with usual attributes sometimes in pictures as meditating in the desert, with the cup in his hand and a stream gushing from a rock, or the River Jordan flowing near him. (See also Appendix E)

I certainly have my doubts that the tableau is a representation of St. Thomas and St. John, although it could have remained intact since the Cave is presumed to have been filled in at the Reformation.

KING HEROD? KING HENRY II? ST. GEORGE? [Plate No. 35]

The engravings are much clearer here, although some of the wall has crumbled on the left of the picture. The figure under discussion is of a male holding a drawn sword in his right hand. He wears a low-crowned helmet. A tabard [sleeveless or shortsleeved coat] is girt about the waist, which Beldam mentions was marked with a large cross on the breast, and a smaller one on either side [The smaller ones cannot be seen now]. Above him appears an array of 'troops' (Fig. 22 or Fig. 8a showing the complete array). Parkin maintains this individual is King Herod, but Stukeley tells us it is of King Henry II and was cut in the year 1187. This figure was also painted red. Beldam thinks that this formidable personage is evidently the hero of the Cave and also presumed it to be Henry II, the reigning monarch of the time.

*Fig. 24a. The Priory Seal.
This broken wax impression is attached to the Deed of Supremacy preserved in the Public Record Office.*

Fig. 24b. The Priory coat of arms.

Fig. 24c. As a small monastery, the Priory was surrendered at the latest by the beginning of 1536. A parish was formed in 1540, and the Priory Church taken over as a parish church. The first vicar, Alexander Stookes, took office in the November. The building has subsequently been enlarged and altered over the centuries. Line drawing Alfred George, c.1980

Because there are four main figures carved on the wall which stand out, three being the saints St. Katherine, St. Christopher, St. Lawrence, I originally believed the fourth figure (Fig. 8a) was probably St. George - from the shape of the helmet, similar to Uccello's painting depicting St. George with the dragon; also of a similar one worn by King Baldwin I as illustrated in a painting: 'King Baldwin I of Jerusalem' from *Les Croniques de Jherusalem Abregies,* Osterreichische National-Bibliothek. All the aforementioned saints were revered by the crusaders.

St. George, England's patron saint, died in Diocletian's last and most savage persecution of the Christians in AD 303. He appears to have been an officer in the Roman Army and stationed in Palestine. He publicly tore down the edicts publishing the persecutions from the market place at Lydda and was at once arrested, tortured and beheaded. Such an act of courage earned the admiration of his fellow Christians who retold the story in symbols. St. George [the soldier of Christ] protects the king's daughter [the church] from the dragon [the devil or perhaps the Emperor] and triumphs. This myth was for a long time popular in Palestine, Egypt and Ethiopia, and the crusaders took to him as a paragon of knightly chivalry.

CHRIST AND THE DISCIPLES?

It will be noted that the sword extends to the centre of the figures overhead (Fig. 8a). The 'troops' are thirteen in number and are accepted generally now as being the disciples, 'twelve and one'. The small figure squeezed into the row to the right is assumed to be Judas. In Eastern art a small figure can be a demoted person. This likelihood was confirmed by Mrs. V. Pritchard, authoress of *English Medieval Graffiti* whom I visited earlier in the year (1972) and also by the late Dr. T.S.R. Boase, of Magdalene College, Oxford and former Director of the Courtauld Institute of Art in London, when he came to examine the Cave at the request of historians Drs. R.C. Smail and Jonathan Riley-Smith, both from Cambridge University, in the September of 1972. Dr. Boase felt the figure below was more likely to represent Christ the Soldier. As yet the writer has been unable to find another representation for comparison, and would still like to hold judgement as to who he represents. Another suggestion has been that he is St. Michael (see Appendix E).

CIRCULAR DESIGN

To the right of this large figure, is the first circular design (Fig. 22) (the second lies to the left of the floriat cross), believed by some to be a shield, but it is to be observed there are four circles decreasing in size which is a significant symbol and explained by Mrs. Jameson and Lady Eastlake in their book *History of Our Lord as Exemplified in Works of Art,* vol. I, where on p. 74 we read that:

> 'By the 14th century, however, the literal translation into Art of the words of scripture gave way, as regards this subject, to these theological speculations being the offspring of the schools, which mixed up astronomy and astrology in their conjectures on things beyond the reach of human reason. According to the Schoolsmen, the whole frame of Nature consisted of two parts, in the one celestial, the other elementary.'

'The celestial was divided into three principal heavens, the empyreal heaven, the crystalline heaven, and the firmament. In the firmament, again were contained the seven orbits of the seven then known planets, Saturn, Jupiter, Mars, Sol, Venus, Mercury and Luna. Next to these planets came the spheres, or the four elements Fire, Air, Water and Earth. Thus there were nine celestial circles and four elementary spheres. In these consisted the whole machine of the world, reaching as St. Bonaventura terms it, "from the hinge of the highest heaven to the centre of the earth." Art has produced this with perfect fidelity, in what the Italians call "Il mappamondo" being a nest of concentric circles, the intention of each indicated by signs and or words.'

There are some examples in art where Christ sits above the sign in the action of creator but in this case I believe it has been placed nearby. This symbol can be seen in the Templar attributed graffiti (Figs. 26 & 30) in the Tour du Coudray, Châteaux de Chinon, in the Loire Valley, France (Fig. 25 - see also Appendix VI). It was here that a number of Templars, including the Grand Master Jacques de Molay, were imprisoned awaiting trial after their arrest organised by Philippe le Bel in 1307.

Fig. 25. Châteaux de Chinon, Indre / Loire, France (three castles amalgamated into one).

In addition, there is a picture of a Reliquary in Shipley Church, shown on p. 304 of vol. II *A History of the Western Division of the County of Sussex* (*Rape of Bramber,* E. Cartwright) where several of these circles surround the Crucifixion, but the one on the right of Christ is larger than the rest - it could of course, be merely the artist filling a larger gap! This Reliquary in wood measures 7 inches long, 3 inches wide by 6 inches high [0.17 m x 0.07 m x 0.15 m] and is enamelled and gilt on the sides and ends. It is of a workmanship coeval with, or perhaps before, the donation of the church to the Knights Templar. However, W. H. Blaauw writing on the Saddlescombe and Shipley Preceptories in the *Sussex Archaeological Collections* vol. IX (1857) says that the reliquary appears to be of the 13th century. Illustrated on two of the other panels are circles containing a floriat design, very common to the Templars too.

At Strood Manor, Kent, owned by the Templars and associated with Denny Abbey in Cambridgeshire, is a zodiac painted on one of the walls. Only a portion survives today.

Fig. 26a. The three enceinte in the Tour du Coudray, Châteaux de Chinon. The circular design is similar to that found in the Cave.

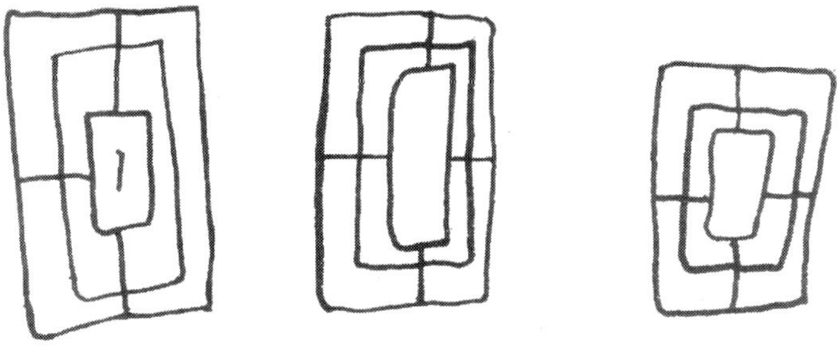

Fig. 26b. The three enceinte in the Château de Gisors, France, where Templars were also imprisoned.
It is suggested that the symbols illustrate 'enceinte' - fortified enclosure plans. French writers remark that often Templar symbols occur in threes, which had some significance now lost. Alternatively they resemble the game layout for 'Nine-men Morris' (Merelles), an ancient and popular game. Even in Britain walls marked out for the game have been found in churches, monasteries and cathedrals. (Illustrations from 'Atlantis' no. 268, 1972, 305 after Albert Héron de la Chesnaye)

NICHES AT FLOOR LEVEL

Below, is the second floor niche approximately 13 1/2 inches [0.35 m] high in the centre, 18 inches [0.5 m] wide and goes back 6 inches [0.15 m] into the wall. The first and other floor niche, which is very small indeed, lies 6 foot [1.8 m] from the end of the bottom step and measures approximately 2 1/2 inches [6 cm] high in the centre, 6 inches [0.15 m] wide and 5 1/2 inches [0.13 m] inwards. The reason for these is unknown.

THE FORTY MARTYRS? [Plates Nos. 28 and 20]

Following on to the right, two more niches had been cut into the chalk. It has been suggested that perhaps the row of figures above represent the 40 martyrs (Fig. 22). They do not add up to 40! However, in Medieval art, or perhaps better described as their 'artistic licence' of the time, a group of figures of indiscriminate number can constitute 'the 40 martyrs'. (See Appendix E)

WARLIKE GROUP?

Another construction by Beldam is that they are troops headed by a prelate in a martial vest, and wearing a peculiar kind of mitre; who seems to be offering an address from behind a battlement or a pulpit. From the shape of the headdress, I would like to suggest this is possibly a Grand Master of the Templars at the head of his armies, and indicative of their military way of life as well as religious. A small kite-shaped shield, upside down, which generally means the bearer is dead, (Pritchard, 1967, 97) is beneath the row of figures but above the largest niche, perhaps this is where they said their obligatory regular prayers for their dead brethren.

JOSHUA AND HIS FIERCE KNIGHTS?

What does seem to be agreed, is that the rows of figures represent a warlike group. The first Master of the Temple in England was one Hugh d'Argentein (another member of the family Reginald d'Argentein, a Templar, is buried in Baldock Church, pp. 174). He was succeeded by a young Norman knight Osto de St. Omer, who presided until 1153-4, then by Richard de Hastings. Under these two masters, the Templars of England embarked on one of their most innovative ventures, a translation of part of the Old Testament into the vernacular. This version of the *Book of Judges* took the form of a chivalric romance - Joshua and his Fierce Knights. The Templars constantly invoked Joshua and Maccabees, promoting themselves as latterday incarnations of the army that toppled the walls of Jericho, the army that nearly defeated Rome in the years just prior to the Christian era. The brethren encouraged the popular image of themselves as being in some way associated with the Grail Romances, as 'guardians' of that mysterious object known as the Holy Grail (Baigent & Leigh, 1989, 44 & 91) (see also p. 130). I only mention this here, as Dr. Smail said I should record all my thoughts so that in the future, others will be able to substantiate or discredit them.

Between the 'disciples' and the 'army' is 'a fish symbol of singular form scratched into the wall.' (Beldam, 1884, 38). Whether this could be construed as a the Christian symbol is doubtful. A recent child visitor said, 'It looks like a chicken with the legs scratched on, and it is running!'

I would like to suggest that as the Templars were a dichotomy - monks and warriors - perhaps the area with the 'disciples' illustrates their religious life and the 'army' their temporal and fighting life.

ST. LAWRENCE [Plate Nos. 20 and 40] (See also Appendix E)

The martyred saint (Fig. 22), engraved above and farther to the right, is obviously St. Lawrence with the gridiron, or griddle, for he was roasted alive (see also Fig. 18). Quite a large proportion of him has disintegrated, including the cross symbol noted on the early plates. The figure was badly repaired at the same time as St. Katherine. It is appreciated, however, that it is difficult to get materials to adhere to the chalk.

KING WILLIAM OF SCOTLAND AND EARL OF HUNTINGDON?

To the right and below is cut a large figure which finishes at the waist (Fig. 22). Both arms are raised and the index finger of the right hand points upwards. The person appears to be unclothed with the exception of wearing a crown. Two prominent letters 'W.R.' are engraved on the upper chest but there is no guarantee these were there originally (see comments below). Beldam assumes this figure to be King William of Scotland and considers that from the imprisoned Queen Eleanor, to the effigy of this king appears to form a consecutive story. He thinks it commemorates a remarkable event in the reign of King Henry II, interesting alike to the clergy and the people of England, and peculiarly flattering to one of the patron saints of the Priory.

The circumstances, according to Beldam, were as follows:

> 'In the year A.D.1175, great dissensions arose between King Henry and his sons who were encouraged in their rebellion by their mother Queen Eleanor. The queen, in consequence, was placed in confinement, and continued a prisoner...'
>
> 'for most of the remainder of her husband's life. Henry's sons being supported by the kings of France and of Scotland, and by other powerful chieftains, King Henry prepared for war, and resolved to combat his enemies, both at home and abroad. While still lingering in Normandy, William the Lion of Scotland made an incursion into the northern counties, where he committed great ravages; when Geoffrey, bishop elect of Lincoln, and afterwards archbishop of York, a natural son of King Henry by the fair Rosamond, putting himself at the head of a body of troops, arrested the progress of the invaders. Henry now found it high time to return to England; and immediately after his arrival hastened to the shrine of St. Thomas à Becket, who had already become the favourite saint of England. Here he performed a most severe penance, and having received absolution for the supposed murder of Becket, he proceeded to London. On the very day on which his peace had been thus made with the martyred saint, namely the twelfth of July, the Scottish king, resting in security at Alnwick and amusing himself with his companions at a tilting match, was suddenly surprised by a body of English Knights, and after a vigorous resistance, was thrown from his horse and made prisoner. The news of this capture filled Henry, and all the loyal part of the nation with joy, as it entirely broke up the hostile confederacy.'

Fig. 27. Panorama of the Cave travelling south-west to east (held in Royston & District Museum). Date of the photographs unknown, but presumably before the 1960's as the niche below the 'Arm of God' is not damaged.

> 'On the tenth of August of the following year, being St. Lawrence's day - which is indicated by the figure of the saint just above him King William did homage for his crown to the English monarch, and the Scottish prelates at the same time acknowledged the supremacy of the English church. The latter event must have been very acceptable to the whole of the English clergy, but especially to the monks of Royston, who were under the patronage of the saint to whose miraculous assistance this extraordinary success was ascribed.'

LOUIS VII OR EMPEROR DECIUS?

Beldam continues, that we may remark these groups have been differently construed by Stukeley and Parkin. Stukeley, concludes that Louis VII of France is the monarch intended; and supposes that this figure commemorates his precipitate retreat on St. Lawrence's day, from the siege of Verneuil. Parkin maintains that the frightened monarch represents the Emperor Decius, in whose reign he places the martyrdom of St. Lawrence; concluding as strangely, that the military bishop represents Pope Sixtus, a contemporary saint.

Beldam makes a parting shot by stating:

> 'The recent discovery of the initials on the breast of the figure, seems, however to settle this question.'

These letters are still very evident and were cut deep, so I am surprised they were not mentioned by the first two authors, at least by Stukeley, and included in his illustrative plates. What is more, I do not like the words 'The **recent** discovery...'

KING DAVID

When Dr. Boase saw this aforementioned figure, without hesitation, he was certain it portrayed King David, half out of the water and quoted the appropriate Latin verse from the *69th Psalm* (Fig. 28b)*. Apparently this was a normal popular symbol of the thirteenth and fourteenth centuries. David is, in a closer sense, a type of Christ, more so than any other person that the scriptures endow. His name and the idea of Christ have a mysterious and an actual identity throughout the sacred text. Through David's mouth, and in David's person, Christ soliloquises of Himself. In an earthly sense David is the only progenitor of the Lord. Christ is appealed to by the blind man as the 'son of David' and also mentioned as the 'seed of David', 'root of David' and 'offspring of David.'

Mrs. Jameson suggests representations of David may be divided into three classes: the first personal and abstract, the second typical and historical, and the third suggested by the language of the Psalms. Those which particularly illustrate the Psalms are peculiar and various. There is an illustration in the Flemish Bible of the fifteenth century held in the Burgundian Library at Brussels, where the opening passage of the *69th Psalm:* 'Save me, O God; for the waters are come in unto my soul,' is very literally translated. David is seen floating on the water with nothing on him except his crown... This is an instance rather of poverty than simplicity of conception, since the execution far outstrips the power of invention. (Jameson and Eastlake, 1864, v.1, 215). Fig. 28a shows another example.

Fig. 28a. King David standing in water with his arms raised. Illustration from a late 13th century manuscript held in Trinity College Library, Cambridge.

It is also true, from existing evidence, that King David was used in Templar Art. Ornamentation on the Templar *Inquest* (their collection of Deeds of land etc.) included, wiverns, gryphons or dragons, lions passant, floriated ornaments, palmated leaves, daisy like rosettes. King David, is seen crowned, seated crossed legs, and playing the harp: a heron, killing or feeding on a fish, is within a triangle. Two serpentine creatures, possibly wiverns, placed within a lobe from whose united foliated tails springs a vertical stem, terminating in a fleur-de-lis on which perches a bird... (Lees, 1935, xxiv). In the Tour du Coudray, in the attributed Templar panel (Fig. 30), there are two examples of 'the star of David'. Whereas David apparently appears as himself in the Cave, there is no reason why symbols were not used by the prisoners at Chinon.

** It could be said, perhaps, that the sentiments in the Psalm expressed the distress the Templars felt once they began to be discredited. (Fig. 28b)*

BRANCHED CROSS - HIGH ALTAR [Plate No. 40]

The high altar is exhibited as a branched or floriat cross, with a small niche [alveolus] below for a light to illuminate the area (Fig. 8b). Dr. Boase said that crosses were quite often branched up to the fourteenth century, and is a useful dating point. A similar example can be seen on p. 29 of *Archeologia* No. 32 beside the crucifixion scene engraved in bas-relief by the Templars at Domme, France (Fig. 29). Beldam thought the cross probably represented the Cross of St. Helena, the mother of Constantine the Great. Stukeley imagined it to be the staff of St. Christopher, commonly called the Palmers's Staff.

David complaineth of his affliction PSALMS, 69

PSALM 69

To the chief Musician upon Shoshannim, *A Psalm of David.*

SAVE me, O God; for the waters are come in unto *my* soul.
2 I sink in deep mire, where *there is* no standing: I am come into deep waters, where the floods overflow me.
3 I am weary of my crying: my throat is dried: mine eyes fail while I wait for my God.
4 They that hate me without a cause are more than the hairs of mine head: they that would destroy me, *being* mine enemies wrongfully, are mighty: then I restored *that* which I took not away.
5 O God, thou knowest my foolishness; and my sins are not hid from thee.
6 Let not them that wait on thee, O Lord GOD of hosts, be ashamed for my sake: let not those that seek thee be confounded for my sake, O God of Israel.
7 Because for thy sake I have borne reproach; shame hath covered my face.
8 I am become a stranger unto my brethren, and an alien unto my mother's children.
9 For the zeal of thine house hath eaten me up; and the reproaches of them that reproached thee are fallen upon me.
10 When I wept, *and chastened* my soul with fasting, that was to my reproach.
11 I made sackcloth also my garment; and I became a proverb to them.
12 They that sit in the gate speak against me; and I *was* the song of the drunkards.
13 But as for me, my prayer *is* unto thee, O LORD, *in* an acceptable time: O God, in the multitude of thy mercy hear me, in the truth of thy salvation.
14 Deliver me out of the mire, and let me not sink: let me be delivered from them that hate me, and out of the deep waters.
15 Let not the waterflood overflow me, neither let the deep swallow me up, and let not the pit shut her mouth upon me.
16 Hear me, O LORD; for thy lovingkindness *is* good: turn unto me according to the multitude of thy tender mercies.
17 And hide not thy face from thy servant; for I am in trouble: hear me speedily.
18 Draw nigh unto my soul, *and* redeem it: deliver me because of mine enemies.
19 Thou hast known my reproach, and my shame, and my dishonour: mine adversaries *are* all before thee.
20 Reproach hath broken my heart; and I am full of heaviness: and I looked *for some* to take pity, but *there was* none; and for comforters, but I found none.
21 They gave me also gall for my meat; and in my thirst they gave me vinegar to drink.
22 Let their table become a snare before them: and *that which should have been* for *their* welfare, *let it become* a trap.
23 Let their eyes be darkened, that they see not; and make their loins continually to shake.
24 Pour out thine indignation upon them, and let thy wrathful anger take hold of them.
25 Let their habitation be desolate; *and* let none dwell in their tents.
26 For they persecute *him* whom thou hast smitten; and they talk to the grief of those whom thou hast wounded.
27 Add iniquity unto their iniquity: and let them not come into thy righteousness.
28 Let them be blotted out of the book of the living, and not be written with the righteous.
29 But I *am* poor and sorrowful: let thy salvation, O God, set me up on high.
30 I will praise the name of God with a song, and will magnify him with thanksgiving.
31 *This* also shall please the LORD better than an ox *or* bullock that hath horns and hoofs.
32 The humble shall see *this, and* be glad: and your heart shall live that seek God.
33 For the LORD heareth the poor, and despiseth not his prisoners.
34 Let the heaven and earth praise him, the seas, and every thing that moveth therein.
35 For God will save Zion, and will build the cities of Judah: that they may dwell there, and have it in possession.
36 The seed also of his servants shall inherit it: and they that love his name shall dwell therein.

Fig. 28b. Psalm 69 in the Authorised Version of the Bible.

What is most unusual in this country is for the main altar to be on the western side of a chapel instead of facing east, towards Jerusalem. This has given rise to speculation by all. Stukeley supposed it to have been placed here, in order to correspond as nearly as possible, with the cross that was then erected above, therefore enabling any worshippers to do homage to both at the same time.

Beldam says another reason might be suggested by the necessity of leaving undisturbed the original entrance into the Cave, which was most probably by a ladder or steps descending from the eastern shaft; and that portion of the Cave may, also have been thought to be desecrated by its original pagan use. The latter problem could have been overcome easily by reconsecration and normally did not worry early Christians. I feel consideration should be given to the idea that it was deliberately placed in this area in emulation of the Church of the Holy Sepulchre in Jerusalem where the main altar was in a polygonal apse, projecting on the western face from a straight wall. (See p. 142 for further details)

Fig. 29. Crucifixion attributed to Templar artwork at the Castle of Domme, France. The Virgin Mary and the Apostle John are seen standing upright. A floriat cross is observed here and a similar one occurs in the Cave.

Comparison can also be made with the following extract recorded in *The Survey of Western Palestine* by Capt. Conder and Capt. Kitchener on p. 93 of vol III:

> 'El Habs (Lt), **A Cave with a window cut in the north face of the rock. It measures seven yards [6.4 m] by three yards [2.7 m] and contains a Latin altar of stone. The place is traditionally the retreat of St. John the Baptist in the desert. It has its altar at the West end and a rock cut door with steps on the East.'**

THE HOLY FAMILY

Higher than the altar, and to the left, are three figures (Fig. 8b) marked by crosses, thought by most to be the Holy Family including Beldam: but Dr. Boase thought this would be most surprising as Joseph is indeed rarely found in representations at that era [13th century], they were more likely to be icons of local patrons. However, since Dr. Boase's visit I have come across an obscure reference to the Holy Grail where ceremonies practised alluded to Joseph, Mary and Jesus. I have dealt more fully with this matter under the chapter relating to Templar cult.

HEART SYMBOL

Below in the centre is a heart shape with a cross within (Fig. 8b). Heart shape signs are not uncommon to the Templars and in the graffiti of No. 36 Rue J. J. Rousseau, formerly Rue Haute-Saint-Etienne, Chinon (Fig. 35), which was originally a house of the Templars. Here there are two examples to the left and right on the engraved stone. In the Tour du Coudray at Chinon there are also hearts (Fig. 30). (c/r p.110)

MARTYRDOM OF ST. HIPPOLITE? CONVERSION OF PAUL?

Lower still is a horse, overthrown and resting on its haunches, a squat figure holding the bridle and a long sword nearby (Fig. 8b). It has been suggested by a number of archaeologists, Tom Lethbridge to name but one, that this group has pagan or Celtic fertility overtones. It will be noted that the horse is phallic (it could be an addition - it is not shown on Stukeley's plates), but perhaps the phallus was deliberately omitted. The small figure shows androgynous features with female genitalia which Beldam, living in the Victorian age, presumably considered 'was not quite nice' and added a skirt in his drawings (Fig. 21a).

Lethbridge (1975, 138) thinks that the sword, indicating a cross, can be a Christian symbol, but points out it is also carried by Astarte. The horse, shiela-na-gig figure and sun disc are evidently pagan. The whole group appears to be contemporary. Astarte carries the Greek and Roman name of a Semitic fertility goddess (appearing in the Bible as Ashtoreth and corresponding to the Ishtar of the Assyro-Babylonian religion). From the meeting of Semitic and Greek culture in Cyprus, her cult spread to Greece where her identity became merged with that of various local deities as the love goddess Aphrodite (whom Homer refers to as 'the Cyprian'). She became the object of a sensual nature worship with orgiastic rites; her chief temples were at Tyre, Sidon and Ascalon [the area well-known to crusaders]. She also accumulated associations with the chase (evidenced by her late identification with Artemis at Ephesus), with the moon (often depicted as horned like the crescent moon), and with war. *(Newnes Popular*

Encyclopaedia (1963) George Newnes Ltd., Slough, Bucks, 179) Astarte in later times seems to have become St. Margaret.

In the district, another shiela-na-gig figure, or Earth Goddess, can be seen engraved in relief on the tower of the 11th century Norman church at Whittlesford, Cambridgeshire*. She displays a grotesquely enlarged vulva. The figure is unique because its sexual and fertile aspects are emphasised by its naked half-animal, half-man phallic attendant which Brian Branston suggests is a throw-back to the Cretan Goddess of Animals. The Earth Mother, with an exaggerated sexual organ, was revered by English country people from earliest times. Even though the figure is pagan it would seem to have been set firmly in the centre of medieval Christian worship, but frowned upon by the Clergy. (Branston, 1974, 152-5)

Weir and Jerman (1986, 11) suggest that the function of sexual exhibitionists is not erotic, in fact, more likely the reverse; and that such frank carvings mainly seen in tympana, capitals, corbels and friezes were more probably an element in the medieval church campaign against immorality, therefore, they were not intended to inflame the passions but rather to allay them. Another point to be borne in mind is that medieval masons did not consider such images as 'obscene'. But crude, vulgar, and not without satirical or sardonic humour - yes - for they were carried out in the full knowledge that they might shock or give offence to the onlooker.

Branston, as does Lethbridge, believes the dwarfish figure in the Cave to be a sheila-na-gig but Weir and Jerman omit any reference to it.

Parkin discovers in this group the martyrdom of St. Hippolite [Hippolytus], who was torn asunder by wild horses. (See also Appendix E)

Stukeley concludes this scene is intended to mean the conversion of St. Paul, kept on the 25th January; and the length of the sword may have been intended simply to remind the observer of the manner of his death.

Beldam scarcely doubts that the primary illusion here was to St. Paul but says it may have been subsequently degraded into a satire on the family of William 'Long Epée,' or 'Long Sword':

> 'This personage was allied by marriage to Lady Rosia, but opposed in politics to her family, and detested, both by priests and laity, for his inhumanity and sacrilege, in asserting the rights of King John. The clerical historians of the time, inform us, that the first Long Epée died an unnatural death; the second perished in Palestine; and the last of his race, being unhorsed and indelibly disgraced at a great tournament, held in the year 1250, died despised and young. It seems not impossible, that the monks of the Priory, with a mixture, by no means uncommon, with superstition and buffoonery, may have contrived, by lengthening the sword, and somewhat distorting the original figure, to make their devotion subserve their revenge, in perpetuating the disgrace of a fallen enemy.'

I fear Beldam's explanation is very far-fetched.

Dr. Boase felt that if the carvings were Templar this was more likely to represent the attributes of knighthood, the horse, squire and sword. He did not think the circular design adjacent to the sword was a shield either, and I explained there was a similar design at Chinon (Figs. 26, 30 stone D).

***Note:** *The Templars could have been aware of this 'shiela-na-gig' as they held property in Duxford, Whittlesford Hundred - see p. 183.*

Fig. 30. Graffiti attributed to the Templars. The large panel is engraved in the 'archère' on the west side. The rows of stones are designated A - D. The stones that are not engraved, to the right and below, are unsuitable being of a shelly limestone (millarge),

Note: B1 single fleur-de-lis and D3 single fleur-de-lis on a shield: B2, B3, C4 and D2 hands: B2 heart: C1 and D1 the Star of David: C2 and D1 circular designs: D2 the 'axe-head' (ancient Palestinian quaph). Drawing Prof. Raymond Mauny, 1968

ANCIENT PALESTINIAN (HEBRAIC) SYMBOL 

To the left of the small niche there is the second and more prominent ancient Palestinian symbol or axe-head in the Cave. [The first one lies to the left and down of 'Christ the Soldier' (?) and is more difficult to see there, as it is within the band of damp]. I would like to give here the translation of a section explaining why the Templars engraved their prison wall while awaiting trial at Chinon, France and, which specifically mentions this sign and its meaning. This extract also describes some of their other graffiti:

Les graffiti de la tour du Coudray, Chinon by Albert HÉRON DE LA CHESNAYE from *Chinon et l'énigme Templière, Atlantis Archeologie Scientifique et Traditionelle* No. 268 Mai/Juin, 1972. Translation, p. 296 from… Avant d'être…

> '...Before being informative signs, these engravings had been decoration on the bare walls to enable the Templars to recreate the atmosphere of their Command Residence, so finding again their purpose in life and allowing them to pray to Christ, in the same way that in our day, in settling into accommodation, one hangs up a familiar picture, before setting more useful objects in place.
>
> The main panel, or large area of engraving on the left wall of the doorway leading in, (archère – in the narrow arched opening) is the best known because it is the most clear.
>
> It portrays perhaps, the role, the mission of the Knights Templar. (The aim of drawing the figures had been marked out in an abbreviated form, before careful and fairly deep engraving of the group). The 'paleohebraique du quaph' (ancient Palestinian sign) is engraved three times on stone No. 7 or recut/repeated by the nine-segmented sextuple. It resembles a Cretan double axe: it is the symbol of double power: temporal and spiritual, it puts to death and it brings back to life. It is exactly like the two-headed Celtic hammer which has become associated with trades or the Masonic movement. In the same way, it is also the symbol of Christ, forming in those two opposite triangles, two natures, divine and human: but the vertical axe reunites the person: its top is the Deity and Deliverance for he who attains it.
>
> The Templars scarcely took liberty and physical deliverance into account: they were able to aim first for moral deliverance, to identify themselves with Christ.
>
> The Order took on itself this double function: religious and human.
>
> Religious – the Templars were monks according to the spiritual teaching of St. Bernard.
> Human – they were soldiers for defence.
> Urbanists – to construct.
> Organisers – preparing land for cultivation.
>
> But religious and human, their life was consecrated to God (Latin) – 'Not to us O God, but to Thy name be the Glory.'
>
> That is why, to the top right is a haloed figure kneeling wearing a cloak with a Templar 'mail hood' in front of him, an angel from which he is separated by an

'S' sign (like a swan's neck) in which is placed a hand [C4]. This composition suggests an annunciation scene in general the angel Gabriel is at the left and Mary at the right: the angel often has a hand raised with the index finger pointing, to make an announcement, transmitting divine power in this hand, distributing also to the Order his religious role established far away near Golgotha, to recall Christ's passion, deliverance from the guard of his Tomb, which are engraved to the left three times, calvary and the instruments of his Passion [C3].

The other Templar to the left, is military: he is defending the Holy Places symbolised by two calvary scenes which are in between.

He is carrying on top of his mantle the Templar shield, marked by the nine-segment design as on seals (Fig. 43). This last, further, possesses initiation, universal knowledge, symbolised by the Chinese Yin Yang and the sign of earth (globe surmounted by the cross) in front of him...'

To return to the 'axe-head', an example can also be observed on the left-hand side of a coffin lid, thought to be that of a Templar mason, which was uncovered at Atlit Castle in Israel (Fig. 33). Presumably the grave must pre-date the abandonment of the castle by the Templars in 1291. The photograph is held in the Museum in Jerusalem.

ST. KATHERINE

High over the altar is St. Katherine with her wheel (Fig. 8b. See also Appendix E). By her position by the main altar she is evidently the person to whom this chapel is dedicated. The Templar Church at Bodmin, Cornwall and that at Bristol were both dedicated to St. Katherine. She is shown here crowned, and the fleur-de-lis is seen clearly in the design [13th century design]. There are a series of stone figures, defaced by time, but marked with crosses, as are the saints and important figures in the Cave * (see p. 106), and together with a carved single fleur-de-lis were removed from the defunct Templar Church at Bodmin. This stonework remains today set into a small outbuilding on the same site. The fleur-de-lis appears to occur frequently in artwork of the Templars, see also examples in the Tour du Coudray, Chinon panel (Fig. 30). As mentioned before, in my opinion this symbol does not necessarily mean a definite association with France.

Stukeley ascribes the preference shown to St. Katherine in this oratory, to a great victory obtained by the Crusaders over Saladin and his hosts, on the plains of Ramleh, on St. Katherine's day, 25th November, 1177; and as the celebrated William de Mandeville, Lady Roysia's son, and lord in 'capité' of this manor [Newsells], was present on that memorable occasion. Beldam says, 'that the conjecture seems by no means improbable.'

It is worthy of note that the Templars were involved in the battle of Ramleh, and I will relate here more particulars of this historic occasion.

Fig. 31. Stukeley's drawing of 'the west side of Lady Rosia's Oratory at Royston, 19 Oct. 1742', taken from his second book (1746). It shows several small additions to the drawings, besides the lengthened floriat cross. The king and queen standing beneath St. Katherine is probably Richard the Lionheart and his wife, Berengaria. The crown over the queen is shown by Stukeley as lying on her head; in fact, the crown is suspended above the head. Queen Berengaria was never actually crowned. (See also original sketches in Appendix X.)

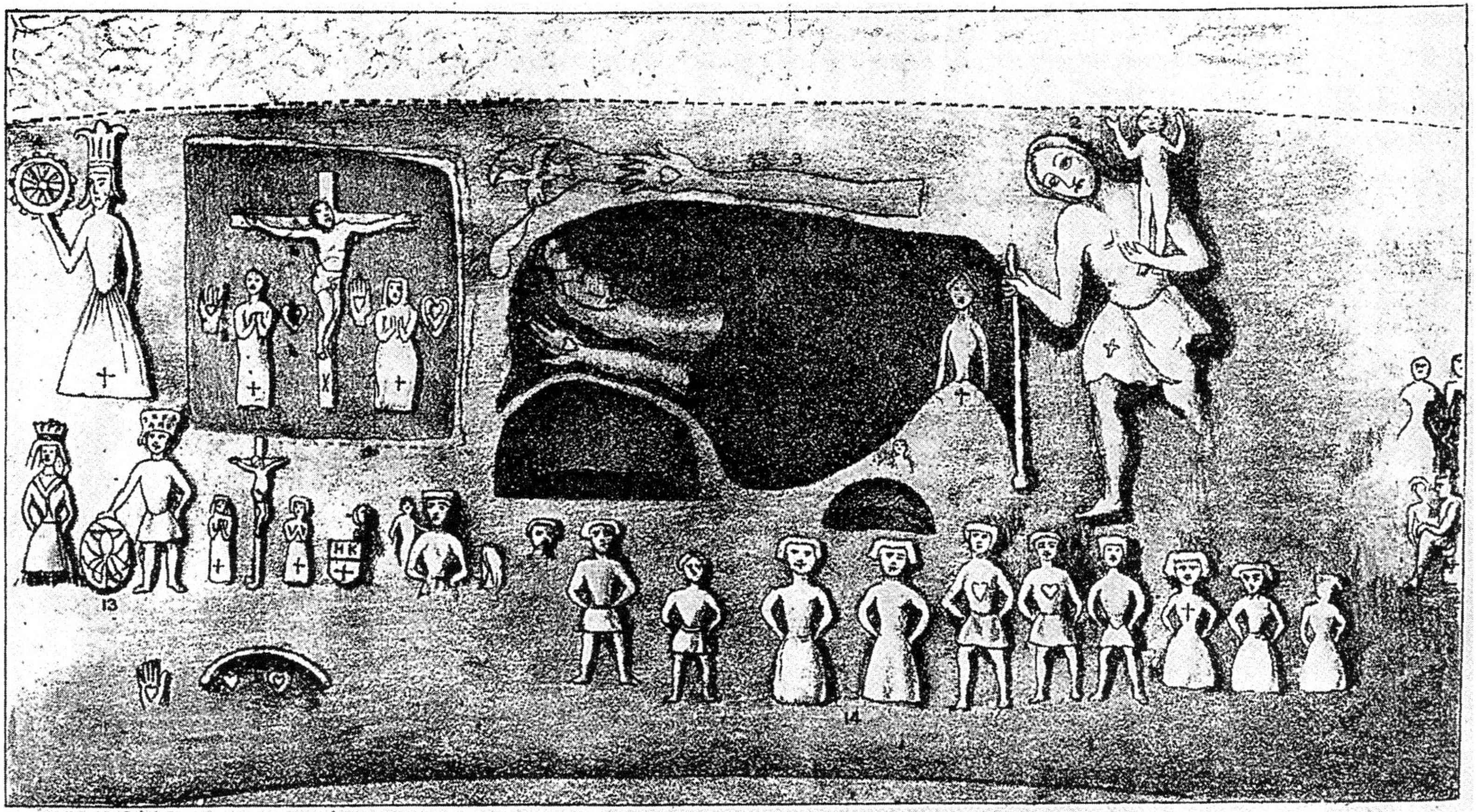

Drawn by Mr J.Beldam.

Fig. 32. Beldam's drawing of a 'section of Cave looking northwards' from the 1884 third edition.

1 *The High Altar*
2 *St. Christopher*
3 *Legend of St. Katherine*
4 *Effigy of St. Katherine*
13 *Richard Coeur de Lion and Queen Berengaria*
14 *Genealogical Figures*

Fig. 33. Stone coffin [sarcophagus] lid from the Templar castle at Atlit, Israel. Note the 'axe-head' on the left of the cross and the level on the right. The specific shape of the 'axe-head' is very similar to the large one cut in the north side of the dome of the Cave. Photo by courtesy of the Israel Dept. of Antiquities & Museums.

In the third week of November 1177, news came that Saladin had crossed the Egyptian frontier and entered Palestine by way of the coastal route. The Constable of the Kingdom was seriously ill, and Baldwin IV's leprosy now practically incapacitated him. Once more the young man's will won over his pitiable infirmity, and he acted with a speed and decision which would have done credit to a man much older and having his health. Baldwin had sent a contingent of his knights to Antioch with Philip of Flanders, but despite his reduced resources, he immediately challenged the invader. He sent out an immediate call for every man who could bear arms to join him, and hurried to Ascalon. The knightservice at his disposal numbered 500 - no inconsiderable force if one reflects that mailed knights were the armoured vehicles of the day; but Saladin's reserves were unlimited and impressed by the numerical superiority of the Muslim forces, he decided against battle, and took shelter with his forces in Ascalon. Saladin then decided to ignore the Franks and marched north to lay waste the countryside and to cut communication between Jerusalem and the coast. Baldwin's subsequent action revealed his own conception of his military duty. He had shown at Ascalon that he was not prepared to undertake battle against heavy odds: now he showed that he would rather fight than tolerate the unchecked devastation of his subjects' property.

The Temple summoned all its available knights to the defence of Gaza, to no purpose, as the Saracens marched straight on Ascalon. They intercepted the reinforcements from Jerusalem and, leaving some troops to pen Baldwin in Ascalon, continued towards the Holy City. Baldwin managed to get a message through to Gaza, asking the Templars to abandon the fortress and come to his relief - a contingency which over-confidence had led Saladin to discount. Indeed, so certain was he of victory that he relaxed discipline and allowed his troops to straggle and pillage, while the Templars by forced marches achieved the seemingly impossible.

Directly they approached, Baldwin broke out of Ascalon and conjointly with the Templars surprised the Egyptian Army at a ravine a few miles south-east of Ramleh. Many of Saladin's troops were still out on forage, and he had no time to regroup the rest. Many fled at the first impact, those who held their ground were cut to pieces, and Saladin himself only just escaped from the battlefield. Foremost among the Christian warriors was the young king with his stiff limbs and bandaged hands, more than half-blind, and 'St. George was seen to ride beside him.' (Simon, 1959, 116; Smail, 1956, 187)

** Another suggestion put forward by a visiting vicar is the possibility that the Cave figures did not have crosses on them originally, but were cut at a later date to reconsecrate the chapel if it had been thought to have been used for heretical purposes. Kuhn (1956) says that on the shores of Lake Onega in Russia there are rock-engravings which have crosses superimposed on them, crosses carved by Christian monks who thus sought to exorcize the spirits and to abolish their demoniac power.*

MAIN CRUCIFIXION SCENE - WITH HANDS AND HEARTS

To the right of St. Katherine is the main crucifixion scene with the Virgin Mary and Apostle John (Figs 8b & 27, & Appendix E). Beneath the arms of the cross two large upright hands are cut, which the writer considers to be left hands, with a heart engraved on each. There are also other independent heart designs, the one on the left is made up of two concentric hearts, and the one on the right three. The author would like to comment again that, in this instance, the crucifixion scene follows the art schools of the time, probably between the 12th and 14th centuries, with the exception of the hands and hearts: Christ's head is turned to the right, his body curved, and the feet appear to be crossed. Below his feet is a St. Andrew's cross.

THE CRUCIFIXION IN ART

There are various different categories into which the crucifixion is classed. When the Virgin and St. John stand on each side as solemn witnesses to the act, this is simply known as 'doctrinal'. Whereas, 'historically devotional' art, is portrayed when the real figures of the scene are preserved, and saints and devotees are introduced. In early crucifixes Christ is represented young, beardless, always without a crown of thorns, not always with a nimbus, yet alive and erect. His feet are always separate and with two nails upon the foot board, or to which they were attached. The arms are at right angles to the body, the hands straight, the eyes open. An example of this composition occurs in the Templar attributed graffiti in the castle at Domme,

France (Fig. 29), and on the Templar Cross at Le Temple, Ille-et-Vilaine, also in France (Figs. 34a, b, c).

The figure of Christ is sometimes draped to the feet and to the wrists, or the cloth around the loins extends to the knees in front, and lower still behind with no signs of bodily suffering. Often the sun is seen on the right of a crucifix and the moon on the left.

Later on, the Saviour's person changes slowly in character - the head falls more on one side, always on the right, the body becomes less straight, while the four nails remain. These signs of natural suffering appeal to the onlooker's sense of tenderness and compassion, no longer permitting faith to be the paramount feeling.

The crucifixion which figures the Virgin and St. John standing alone on each side of the cross is most frequent. It embodies and isolates the passage from the Bible:

> 'Now there stood by the Cross of Jesus his Mother, and his Mother's sister Mary the wife of Cleophas, and Mary Magdalene.' 'When Jesus therefore saw his mother, and the disciple standing by, whom he loved, he saith unto his mother, "Woman behold thy son." Then he saith to the disciple, "Behold thy mother." And from that hour that disciple took her unto his own home.' *(John* XIX 25 - 27)

During the 13th and 14th centuries, the Virgin was still semi-upright. The Virgin depicted as fainting at the cross occurs later on, of which instances can be seen in the 14th century. The 15th century saw her seated on the ground, but by the close of that century and the beginning of the 16th century she was laid lower still, in fact nearly flat. (Jameson and Eastlake, 1864, v. II, 183)

ST. ANDREW'S CROSS SYMBOL

Christ, the second person of the Trinity, is represented by the St. Andrew's Cross (Twining, 1885, 8) and beneath the feet of Christ in the main crucifixion scene in the Cave, this sign is observed as already remarked. It was also recorded by Stukeley in his drawing, and presumably was not a random scratch.

HAND SYMBOL

The symbol of the hand is used throughout the whole range of early Christian art to express the first person of the Trinity, God. It has its origin in the innumerable texts of the *Old Testament,* especially in the *Psalms,* which speak of the Hand of God, not to be confused with the Arm of God.

Therefore, in any scene where the power of God is specially manifested, or where the Almighty is described in the Bible as holding direct communication with man, the hand symbol is used. Such scenes are far more common in the *Old Testament* than in the *New,* for in the earlier stages of the world's history God saw fit to control human affairs by communicating openly with his chosen agents, but afterwards he made his unseen influence felt by inspired prophets, through his Son, and intervening only at rare intervals. Although there are so many passages in the *Old Testament* describing God dealing with man, only a limited number were selected for illustration. Amongst the principal scenes in which the hand symbol occurs in the *New Testament* are the Transfiguration, Crucifixion, Ascension, Christ in Glory.

The hand symbol at the crucifixion refers to our Lord's works *(Luke* xxii 46) 'Father, into thy hands I commend my spirit.' The position of the hand is generally facing upwards or downwards in the centre of the picture, or inclined diagonally from one of the upper corners. The attitude of the fingers is either that of giving benediction, or outstretched with the fingers sometimes close together, or the *Alpha* and *Omega* signs are added (early Christian art), or rays of power are seen issuing from the tips of the fingers.

The early Christians, during the first four centuries adhered to the scriptural view of the case, and the first person of the Trinity was almost always, symbolised by the hand. But, from the 9th century onwards the difficulty of representing God as man without diminishing those feelings of reverence and awe, which would naturally deter the artist from approaching so sacred a subject, was avoided by assuming the identity between God the Father, and God the Son. The Almighty is therefore shown as a bearded man, with cruciferous nimbus round the head; and except for the surroundings, there is no means of distinguishing between the figure of the Creator and that of Christ. (Allen, 1887, 161)

To summarise briefly: in this case it is evidenced that the hand symbol was rarely used in later centuries and by the attitude of Christ on the main crucifixion in the Cave with head slightly turned to the right, the body not rigid, also the appearance of the feet crossed, points to the fact it was cut after 1200 when hand symbols would be unusual. Included in the graffiti from the Templar house in Rue J. J. Rousseau, Chinon (Fig. 35), is a hand comparatively close to the pattée crucifix (Héron de la Chesnaye, 1872, 309). Although the hand symbol is not associated with a crucifixion in the Tour du Coudray, at Chinon, there are three of them exhibited in the panel (Fig. 30), An explanation on these hands has been translated from the French, viz:

> 'What do these three open hands mean. Let us take another look at what P. Bosiaux-Defrance said:
>
> The palm of the open hand diffuses vibrations which can either be invigorating or calming. It was part of the druid magic inherited by St. Bernard.
>
> The hand of beautiful Fatima eldest daughter of the prophet has remained famous in a similar way in the Islamic world and is still quite commonly found as a symbol of protection and healing.
>
> The magic power of the hand in certain conditions holds the opponent in respect - hands more than lips participate in prayer. The troubadours and their jugglers always accompanied their mystical songs with symbolic gestures. (See XII century Romanesque paintings in Tarant church and the painting in Sainte-Radegonde chapel in Chinon, with such characteristic hands)...'

Le Temple, Ille-et-Vilaine (7.5 km east of Questembert, on D136), Department Morbihan, France

Fig. 34a. (Above left) The rectangular Templar church with a cross pattée over the doorway. Photo Sylvia Beamon, 1989

Fig. 34b. (Above right) The cross opposite the Templar church. Photo Alan Beamon, 1989

Fig. 34c. (Right) Enlargement of the crucifixion scene on the cross. Claimed to be of Templar origin, dated to early 14th cent. Photo Sylvia Beamon 1989

Also under esoteric lore the right hand is supposed to be the practical hand, the hand devoted to the things of the world. The left hand is the spiritual hand, that which is devoted to metaphysics. Even though there is lack of good evidence, the writer thinks consideration should be given to the suggestion that in the case of the Cave, the hands are likely to be associated with the ideas from the East, where many Templars spent much of their life, and that they represent protection and healing.

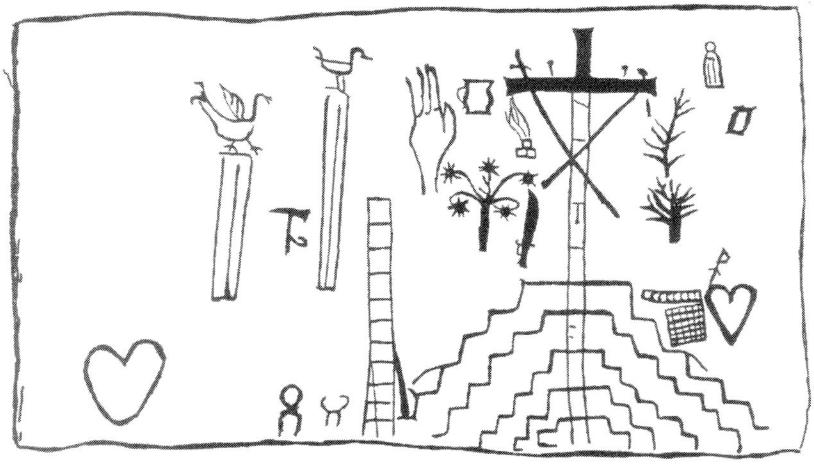

(Dessin de Bernard NISSE.)

Fig. 35. A former Templar house, no. 36 *Rue J. J. Rousseau, Chinon, France. Note: hand, hearts and the cross pattée. ('Atlantis' 1972, 309)*

THE HEART

Below the figure of St. Katherine towards the right is a small crucifixion tableau, again with the Virgin Mary and the Apostle John (Fig. 27 & 8b). Christ's arms in this instance are raised almost above his head. Immediately beneath is yet another hand with a heart, also the Cretan/ancient Palestinian symbol with a single heart to the left and a double heart to the right (c/r p. 98 and 100-2)

The heart is found frequently in the catacombs. It may either have signified truth and sincerity of those who were buried there, or the love of mourning friends, and besides these, it may have had an illusion to that purity of heart by which alone we can see God. (Twining, 1185, 119). Another complexion, according to the Aryan faith as interpreted by the Hindus, is that a heart within a heart, or a Lotus within a Lotus indicates the cycle of creation. (Chaplin, 1935)

KING AND QUEEN - KING RICHARD AND QUEEN BERENGARIA?

Next to the crucifixion are two figures, one with a crown suspended above but not resting on the head, and the larger of the two crowned and holding a shield in the right hand (Fig. 27 & 8a), This figure has been repaired badly. Beldam says:

> 'The king stands clad in complete armour, wearing his crown, and resting his right hand on a large kite-shaped shield, marked with a fanciful device. The queen, who is only of three-quarters length, appears on the other side of the

shield. A crown is placed above her head, but scarcely appears to touch it, and a veil descends from her head-dress on either side, down to her shoulders. She wears an elegant stomacher, adorned with a collar and a brooch, and her whole costume resembles the style and fashion of royal ladies of the twelfth century.'

The detail is not evident today.

Beldam continues:

'They may either represent King Henry II, who took the vow, although he never went to the crusade; in which case the lady will be Queen Eleanor, however her disgrace and imprisonment makes this supposition less likely. Or, far more probably, King Richard I, Coeur de Lion [1157-1199], the most distinguished crusader of his age, and Queen Berengaria, whom he married, and caused to be crowned on his way to the Holy Land. But this lady was never crowned in England, and after her husband's death, her rights as queen dowager were for some time denied her by her brother-in-law, King John; a circumstance which may possibly account for the peculiar position of the crown.' [Bob Edwards, a friend, pointed out another example of a floating crown hovering over the head of Edward V, one of the princes in the Tower (c.1483), who was not crowned but deposed, and is seen in a stained glass window in St. George's Chapel, Windsor.]

Beldam also thinks that this group having been placed immediately below the effigy of St. Katharine and the high altar, may be intended to commemorate the date of the agreement made between King Richard and Philippe of France, which was in November, 1189, and contained a condition to unite their forces for the crusade on the following Easter-day.

The author agrees with Beldam's deductions that these two figures are most likely to be Richard I and his queen.

The device on the shield is unusual and various suggestions have been put forward that it looks like a scorpion, scarabaeus or a bird. The writer tentatively suggests it is an eagle, a late symbol of the Templars.

King Richard had many contacts with the military brethren. Whilst on a crusade in 1189 he diverted to the island of Cyprus where the Templars joined him in the sack of the ports, and castles of Famagusta and Nicosia. Finally, Richard conquered the island. Two years later, in July, 1191 when Acre in the Holy Land surrendered, Richard and Philippe divided the city, and King Richard made his quarters in the Templar house. He was very close to Robert de Sablé, the Templar's new Grand Master at that time, and negotiated the sale of Cyprus to the Order a few months later.

When John, was usurping his brother Richard's position in England, the true king appealed for assistance to the Master of the Temple, to 'get him home', and it was agreed that Richard could travel to Europe disguised as a Templar knight. Unfortunately, he was captured in Vienna and imprisoned for a while, even the Templars could not guarantee him a safe journey back. (Burman, 1984, 114-6)

Another symbol lies below, near the branched cross, resembling either an oval shape or a badly shaped square marked with a cross (Fig. 27). It is difficult to see clearly.

Next to the lesser crucifix is a shield which Stukeley states:

> 'The fess upon it is very plain, high raised, and the other marks or sketches so like to cross crosslets .. .'

But Beldam, over a 100 years later, remarks:

> 'The six crosslets appear to be two letters 'H.K.' above the fess, with a calvary cross beneath it.'

Due to deterioration it cannot be agreed upon nor denied.

HOLY SEPULCHRE? [Plate No. 31]

Above the large niche there had been an incumbent figure (Fig. 27 & 8b) but little is left since a large portion has broken away, only a head and the feet marked with a cross remain, but Stukeley and Beldam fortunately, both recorded it (Figs. 31 & 32). Over the head is a cupped hand and higher still is the dove representing the Holy Spirit. Adjacent to the dove is a large arm and hand assumed to be the Arm of God. The Dove, third person of the Trinity, is often represented above the head of Christ (Twining, 1885, 55). It has been suggested by several people that what is symbolised here, is the Holy Sepulchre and the Resurrection. The writer agrees, and would point out that the 'feet' appear shrouded and at the end of the inset tableau is another figure which she thinks could be Mary Magdalene holding the stone that has been rolled away from the Sepulchre. (See also p. 249 and Appendix E)

ROW OF FIGURES

Below the niche begins a row of figures, some with hearts or crosses on (Fig. 27 & 8c), From their dress, the carvings are assumed to be of late 13th century date. Beldam (p. 44) considered that they are icons of local patrons, and amongst others, lists the following names taken from the earliest charters of the Priory as possible benefactors: Eustace de Merk; Ralph de Rochester, Hawysia his wife, William de Rochester his heir; Alicia de Scales, Richard de Clare, Warin de Bassingbourne, Reginald de Argentine. And then last but not least as being members of the first noble family, lords 'in capité' of the manor of Newsells - Geoffrey de Mandeville, Lady Roysia herself and finally the distinguished crusader William de Mandeville which Beldam considers was possibly the founder of the oratory.

Perhaps another look should be taken at the 'dress' and in particular the supposed feminine headdresses. The writer located an illustration from the *Codex Maness* in the Heidelberg University Library of a Templar wearing a very similar headdress and attired in long robes. (Fig. 36)

Fig. 36. If this illustration of a Templar is viewed minus his beard he could easily be assumed to be a lady! (Codex Manesse, "Grosse Heidelberger Liederhandschrift", Zurich, beginning 14th century)

ST. CHRISTOPHER [Plate No. 36]

On the right is a large image of St. Christopher the patron saint of travellers, carrying the Christ Child on his left shoulder (Fig. 27 & 8c & Appendix E). He is sited in the position he is usually found in churches, on a north wall near an entrance. From his stance, he is also assumed to characterise 13th century art. Some people consider that the person to the left [Mary Magdalene? q.v.] is holding a lantern to guide him across the River Styx. Cottered Church, Hertfordshire has a dilapidated distemper painting of St. Christopher, also on the north wall of the nave.

Stukeley mentions in his first book (pp. 32-34) that St. Christopher was used as a form of protection against tempest and earthquakes, and knowledge of this saint was brought from the Holy Land and often painted in churches. He mentions that in Westminster Abbey - between the monuments of Shakespear and Gay - he saw a similar picture of St. Christopher in a huge proportion. Stukeley also refers to an old record in the *Court of Liveries,* 32 Henry III, m.7. that an image of this saint was to be painted in the queen's chapel at Winchester [not located].

[Plate No. 32] (Fig. 27 & 8c) There is an unusual symbol a couple of feet or so on from St. Christopher, and because there seems to be no similar symbol in any other location known to the writer, no comment can be made.

TWO UNKNOWN FIGURES

Next, are two figures that seem to be unconnected with the rest of the carvings [the left-hand head is a replacement] (Fig. 27, see also 8c). Consideration should be given to the idea that this pictorial impression represents the Templar sign - two knights sitting on a horse - the symbol of poverty (see Figs. 37a & b). The shape of the hips should be particularly noted, perhaps this representation was never completed. About 1975, a Barrister visited the Cave and suggested the following connection. He said that a lantern had been found at the Inns of Court with the Pegasus Horse painted on it. It was realised that something else was painted underneath. The painted wings of the horse were removed and there emerged two figures seated on the horse. The Inns of Court had been Templar property. From another source we do have mention of a representation of two serving brethren with one arm round each other; whilst the right hand of one figure holds the chalice, the other has a book under his arm which alludes to the vessel, and therefore they are as one with the Chalice of the Grail. (Yarker, 1909, 197)

Fig. 37a. A Templar seal – The Symbol of Poverty – illustrating two men sitting on and sharing a horse. Sceau d'un Precepteur des Chevaliers: "Sigillum Militum Christi", 1298. (Charpentier, Louis (1967) 'Les Mystères Templièrs', Robert Laffont, Paris). (See also p. 137-8)

Below to the right is the sign of the moon. The Crescent Moon in Muslim symbolism was in all antiquity and the middle ages the symbol of Byzantium, and which is now the symbol of the Turkish Empire, is a direct inheritance from Byzantium's mythical foundress Keroessa, the daughter of the moon goddess Lottera. (Hastings, 1908 vol. 12)

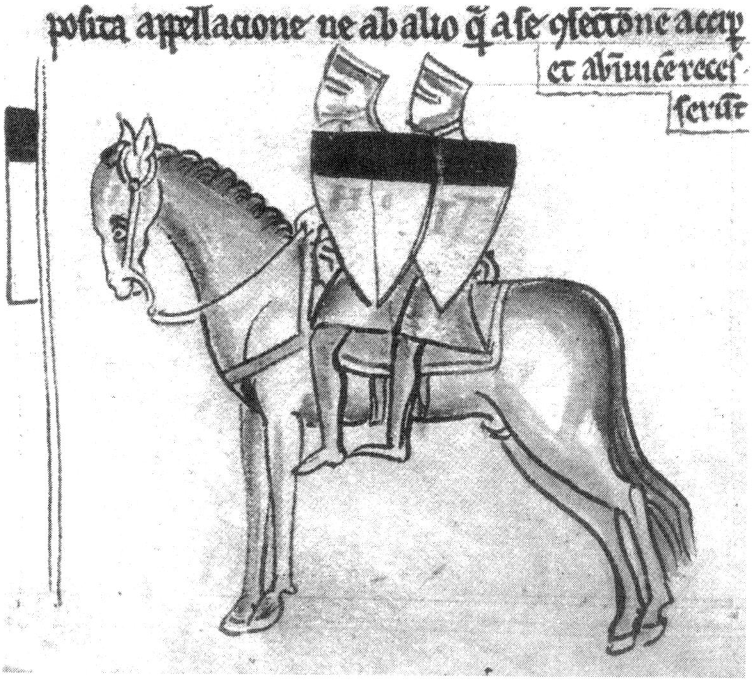

Fig. 37b. Two Templars astride a horse, carrying the Templar design kite-shaped shield apiece. The standard 'Beausant' stands nearby. ('Historia Major' by Matthew Paris, 13th cent.) By permission of the Master and Fellows of Corpus Christi College, Cambridge and the Conway Library, Courtauld Institute of Art.

In 1977, Mark Stevenson, noticed some 6 feet [1.8 m] above the left hand side of the 'grave', what appears to be outlines of rigging for a ship; alternatively, he thought the striations could be the cords or the means by which a pottery lamp would have been suspended. (Stevenson, M. (1978) *Royston Cave* in *Hertfordshire Past* No. 5, pub. jointly by Herts. Arch. Council & Herts. Local Hist. Council, ed. A. Jones, pp. 29-31)

[Plates No. 12 and 16] These last two plates show the area above the designated 'grave' and brings us back to the new entrance, having completely circumnavigated the bottom section of the Cave.

UPPER STOREY OR VERANDAH [Plate No. 37]

Above the 'frieze' and the line of a natural fault in the chalk bedrock, and commencing again from the east travelling south, very indistinct graffiti is evidenced here. There are three small niches. Moving along, another niche, wide as well as long, has several potent crosses around it [Plate nos. 17 & 19]. The writer believes the larger niches were used as cupboards for storing cheese and butter (Fig. 38a).

Continuing on: One crudely scratched face, is seen clearly from the floor, and two more are faintly drawn above. Beneath them is a zig-zag which runs into the small kite-shaped shield. Whether these are true symbols is somewhat doubtful but the face may be a symbol for air and the zig-zag for water, as illustrated on p. 16 of *Signs and Symbols* by G. Oliver (1826).

The most prominent symbol [Plate no. 38] appears to be the sign of the sun (fire). In the spurious Freemasonry of the Egyptians the blazing star was the symbol of Horus, son of Isis - the sun - the primordial principle of existence. (Mackey, 1860, 325) Next to it is probably a mason mark, the reversed level or tau and illustrated amongst other symbols by Yarker (1909, 147) where he says: ' ...there are certain ancient symbols, some of which have the appearance of Roman letters but are not really so, which are found sculptured on stones in Egypt and elsewhere, and found in later times in this country as Masons' Marks.'

[Plate Nos. 14 & 30] The largest Cretan/ancient Palestinian sign in the Cave can be easily picked out from ground level. Above are other letters or signs including a large 'B' (this letter was important to the Templars and evidenced in the graffiti at Chinon Fig. 30). Two interlaced triangles are close by. The possibility that these are just haphazard graffiti cannot be discounted (Fig. 38b).

ENTRANCE SHAFTS [Plate No. 21]

The original entrance shaft, sealed by the road above, is sited on the north wall through which the boy first entered in 1742 after the Cave's discovery. Two foot-holds are viewed below.

[Plate Nos. 41 and 29] This second entrance shaft, also sealed above, was found supposedly 'bricked-up' in 1742 but it has since been opened, except for the remaining three courses of clunch blocks painted red (see Fig 6a). The top left-hand block has the date '1347' engraved on it (not readily visible today), discovered by Beldam. Baring-Gould, (1911, 224) mentions that high up are two dates cut in the chalk, in Arabic numerals, that have been erroneously read as '1347' and 'Martin 1350 February 18,' but these should read respectively '1547' and '1550', as Arabic numerals were not in use in England in the 14th century, and the name of 'Martin' and the 'February' are distinctly 16th century in character. Beldam also concludes that a fraud could have been practised and the '5' altered to a '3'.

This entrance was more than likely used as an air vent, but notice should be taken of the smoothness of the wall in this area. The author suggests that the raising and lowering of sacks of goods for marketing, onto the verandah or flooring, could have caused this wear. Immediately beneath at ground level lies the 'grave' or sump. It is possible that the latter was a continuation of the shaft and was dug right down to the floor in prehistoric times in search of flint, or for another function (Romano/British - Beldam, see p. 17), and at a later date the rest of the chalk material was extracted to form the chamber.

[Plate No. 27] Higher still in the dome (south), the damage to the chalk wall was caused by the National Westminster Bank's former vault [old post office?] breaking into the dome when it was built during the 1960s. The author believes that this breakthrough has caused more problems with water gaining a collection point and trickling down to the floor. Finally, in the top of the dome is a grille set in the pavings in the street above. The dome was sealed when the Cave was opened in 1742 but it is suggested by the 'denehole' expert Rod Le Gear of *Subterranea Britannica* and *Kent Underground Research Group,* that the Cave could have been initially created as a 'denehole' to dig chalk out to marl the fields. Not that it is necessary in Royston, but the chalk could have been transported to other areas which needed the earth to be broken up or to counteract an acid soil. The practice of marling has been well known since Roman times. (See also further comments in the Conclusions)

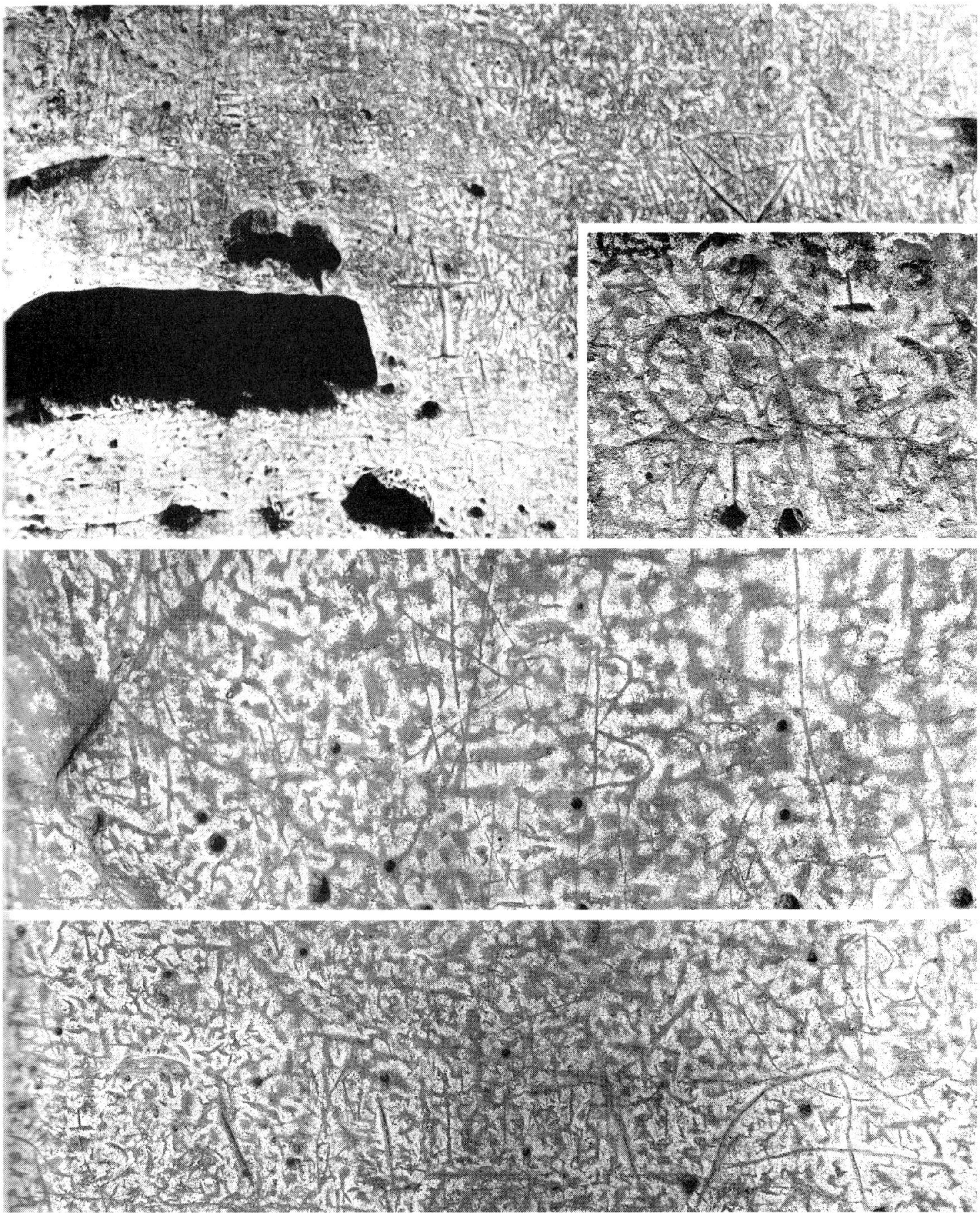

Fig. 38. Upper storey of the Cave

MEDIEVAL GRAFFITI

Although this chapter has run to great length, something must be said of other graffiti attributed to the crusading period in England, particularly local to the Eastern counties. Was it a frequent activity, for example? It did occur comparatively often, but whether it was Templar or not is another matter, and would appear to be almost unprovable unless written records survive. Several instances have been chosen below:

BEDFORDSHIRE, EDWORTH - The Knights Templar owned property in this small hamlet of Edworth, just inside the Bedfordshire county. Inside the church of St. George on the wall near the south doorway is a 'swastika pelta' 4 x 4 ins [10 x 10 cm] with four lines. Only a part of the graffito has survived. The 'swastika pelta'* is sometimes called 'Solomon's knot' which should not be confused with the 'Solomon's seal' [or the 'star of David'], a six pointed star. The 'swastika peltae' disappeared in England after late 13th century.

CAMBRIDGESHIRE, DUXFORD - In the church of St. John, belonging to the Templars before 1275 until 1308-12, is a careful drawing of the 'swastika pelta'. (Pritchard, 1967,33-4, 178) (Fig. 39)

Fig. 39. Example of a 'swastika pelta' from the Church of St. John, Duxford, Cambs. Rubbing by Violet Pritchard, 1967, 33

CAMBRIDGESHIRE, GREAT WILBRAHAM - The church of St. Nicholas at Gt. Wilbraham was owned by the Templars from 1226-1308 and on the south east respond of the transept arch there are two 'swastika peltae', one the same dimensions as for the Edworth example but with six lines, and the other slightly larger, also with six lines. (Pritchard, 1967, 178)

ESSEX, STEEPLE BUMPSTEAD - amongst the many graffiti in the Church of St. Mary the Virgin at Steeple Bumpstead, is yet another example of the swastika pelta. However, it is a hat with a tall feather, together with a Christian prayer, 'God help me' that is important here because they are dated in Latin to A.D.1301 which is rare. The prayer is repeated several times on church pillars. There is a parallel to the drawing of the hat in a Western graffito on a pillar in the Church of the Nativity at Bethlehem. The shape of the hat with a feather is so like the one at Steeple Bumpstead that it is impossible to ignore the resemblance. Mrs. Pritchard claims that the historical evidence makes it possible that the graffiti at Bethlehem could be connected with the crusades and, although it may seem a far journey from Steeple Bumpstead to Bethlehem it is permissible to suggest that the Steeple Bumpstead hat represents the crest of some crusader. (Pritchard, 34, 79-83)

HERTFORDSHIRE, ANSTEY - At the time of the 'Domesday Book' (1087) Count Eustace of Boulogne held Anstey, and according to tradition he built the castle there. It was in existence in 1141, when the manor was acquired by Geoffrey de Mandeville. He controlled all the castles in Hertfordshire, except Waytemore (Bishops Stortford) (H. Douglas-Irvine in *V.C.H. East Herts.* (1914) vol. IV. 12). There appears to be a link between Anstey Castle and the graffiti in the church of St. George. The castle which was 'under demolition order' in 1218, probably acted as a quarry when the church was being built. Therefore, some of the graffiti, belonging originally to the castle is likely to have become incorporated in the church, for example, one drawing of a cart is seen upended - not impossible for an artist, but unlikely.

Most of the graffiti in this cruciform shaped church are drawn on the walls which join the west arch of the tower on the north and south sides facing the nave. There are many drawn crests and kite-shaped shields which give the impression of great activity either in war or the tourney; especially fine is a crested helm on a horse's head. The shields are considered, in the main, to be of the 13th century, and one may have belonged to the Balliol family. (Pritchard, 1967, 91-99)

SUFFOLK, WORLINGTON - The graffiti in All Saints Church at Worlington are exceptionally important as they certainly appear to be connected with the crusades, but apart from the graffiti there are other points to consider if this connection is to be proved. For instance, it is not known if Worlington had been a starting point for a crusade and, or, a landing place for ships from the continent. London perhaps was not a safe meeting place in those times and to have used a port on the south coast may have presented too difficult a journey across country. The Icknield Way on the other hand passed near Worlington and could have brought men from many parts of England.

There are a number of shields drawn in Worlington Church but there are no crests, a fact which may indicate that the graffiti belonged to a time before they began.

The arms consisting of a cross (in its older form pommée and later potent) between four plain crosslets are well known to have been the arms of the Crusaders' Kingdom of Jerusalem. Probably in their earliest form there were more than four crosslets which Matthew Paris writing about 1250 describes the arms as 'scutum aureum crux alba cum multis parvis crucibus albis' [gold shield, white cross with many small crosses]. Another shield in All Saints Church shows the arms with these extra crosses exactly as Matthew Paris describes.

The cross fitchée (cut to a point) is believed to have been introduced into armorial bearings by the crusaders who, like the early Christians, are said to have made wooden crosses which they sharpened at the lower end in order to fix them into the ground. These crosses were used during the crusaders' devotions and could be used wherever they went. The fact that the graffiti shows this cross alone unconnected with a shield suggests that it represents one of the early wooden crosses. (Pritchard, 1967, 159. 162)

There are other instances, similar to the above, and I would refer the reader to Mrs. Pritchard's book. But, none of the aforegoing graffiti can be comparable to the design and magnificence of those in the Royston Cave, which although today may appear crude to our sophisticated eyes, must have been quite striking when painted and freshly cut. (See also comments on the 'fleur-de-lis', p. 73)

* *Note that the swastika symbol itself is seen at Denny Abbey in a glass fragment (Fig. 57f). To draw a 'swastika pelta', it is necessary to first draw a swastika, then carry lines from it.*

MASON CONNECTION WITH THE TEMPLARS

The topic of masonry has been touched upon before in this text but the relationship between the Masons and the Knights Templar is discussed more fully here and in Chapters 7 and 8.

Clavel, quoted by Oliver (1826), says in the 17th century a grave was discovered in Germany of a Templar who died before the dissolution of the Order. On it was 'a stone cube inscribed with the square and compasses, the pentalpha, the celestial sphere, a star of five points, and several other stars.' The square, level, compasses, compassed with quadrant, interlaced triangles, the flaming star, tau cross of Egypt are found in Templar churches at Erfurt, Shoengraben and Prague. Such decoration may be due to the Masons who erected these churches; and the symbolism, equally with the Reception of a Templar, have points of affinity. As remarked, the Templars were extensive builders, and Jacques de Molay, the last Grand Master, praised the zeal of his Order in decorating churches when answering charges brought against them in 1310; hence, the alleged connection of Templar and Freemasonry is bound to have a vein of truth.

Nicolai, quoted in *Acta Latamorum,* asserts that in Italy there are several churches, formerly belonging to the Templars, which perpetuated the name 'l'église de la Mason'. Besides the symbols already noted above an old writer Assemau, mentions a shield on which is a lamb, a cup, and two crossed torches. The last was a Mythraic symbol, the chalice or cup was a common symbol of the Order. They used the cross pattée, equi-limbed cross, the Latin cross, the patriarchal cross, and in later times they adopted the eagle as a symbol. Von Hammer, confirmed by Hallum and other writers, states that in various preceptories, their most secret place (crypt) contained indecent emblems sculptured, but not described in any way. (Yarker, 1909, 195/6)

It is beyond doubt that after the Norman conquest in 1066, the predominant genius of masonry was French; the design, planning and oversight were French and the labour Anglo-Saxon, although the latter were soon strong enough to transmit their own style in combination with the French. The fall of Jerusalem in 1187 brought back from the East many artisans to the West, whose influence is traceable in the early pointed style, or as it is termed the 'Lancet' or 'Early English.'

TRAVELLING MASONS AND CRUSADING INFLUENCE IN ARCHITECTURE

In 1190 Bishop Jocelyne obtained a Charter from William the Lion of Scotland to establish a 'Fraternity' to assist in raising funds in order to build the Cathedral of Glasgow, Strathclyde; it supposedly implies the existence of a band of travelling Masons. The same bishop undertook the erection of the Abbey of Kilwinning, Strathclyde, and the Templar Preceptory at Redd Abbey Stead was built at the same time.

During the reign of Henry II, the Grand Master of the Knights Templar superintended the Masons, and employed them in building their Temple in Fleet Street, AD 1155. Masonry continued under the patronage of this Order till the year 1199, when John succeeded his brother Richard on the throne of England. (Preston, 1861)

In the reign of Henry III thirty-two religious houses were constructed and the Templars built their *Domus Dei* at Dover. The beginning of this King's reign is the period when Laymen, freeing themselves from the Monasteries, came to the front as builders, and leaders of working Masons. It is also the beginning of a more highly finished style of pointed Gothic introduced by the Masons who had returned from Palestine. (Yarker, 1909, 304, 315-17). Templar architecture was usually Byzantine in its characteristics, reflecting influences beyond Rome's sphere of control. Two graves of Templar Master Masons were found at Atlit, Israel. (Baigent & Leigh, 1989, 136)

Templars sponsored their own guilds, and also acted as patrons and protectors for other guilds of craftsmen including stone-masons. They seem on occasion to have become members of such guilds themselves. Occasionally, skilled artisans would be taken in as 'associates' of the Temple and live in self-contained villages attached to preceptories. They then enjoyed many of the Order's privileges, including exemption from tolls and taxes! (Baigent & Leigh, 1989, 136)

MASON MARKS

Referring to Palestine, Conder (1881) comments that a far safer indication of Crusading work lies in the mason marks. No buildings except those of the 12th and 13th centuries in Palestine have mason marks. These marks are finely cut on the best dressed stones of interiors and vary in size from one inch, or two, to three in length. They include every letter of the alphabet except

'D G Q and X' with various geometrical signs. The same marks are found in buildings separated by the entire length of the country, and have no reference to the position of the stone in the building but seem rather to be those distinctive of the workmen employed. Some structures have a great variety, others the same repeated. As a rule, the larger buildings appear to have a larger number of different marks, the smaller fewer, therefore intimating that a large number of Masons were employed on the more important buildings etc. There is no question over the date as each mark is distinctive of one man, for the 13th century marks, and although similar, are not identical with those of the 12th century buildings. These remarks only apply to the masonry of the interior.

The Jews were not a great building people. The influence of the Western nations is to be noticed in later Jewish buildings. The great buildings of the country of Palestine are to be ascribed to the Byzantine and Crusading Christian epochs.

The writer has a theory that a clue to the marks may lay in squares, some divided into four and others five, cut on walls of a few Churches, together with the use of the compass and level the necessary tools for geometry from which, of course, are created squares and circles: but this is probably only part of the answer. From Roman times the word 'PATERNOSTER', sometimes associated with *alpha* and *omega* symbols, is translated as 'Our Father' the first words of *The Lord's Prayer* and linked to Christianity. It can also be a muttered prayer or spell. These letters occur quite often in mason marks - perhaps just coincidence. Three scholars working independently in the 1920s found that the 25 letters (five by five) could be rearranged to form 'Pater Noster' twice in the shape of a cross centred on the single letter 'N' with two 'As' and two 'Os' left over.

'Magic Square':	(Form 1) ROTAS	(Form 2) SATOR
The same letters in	OPERA	AREPO
'paternoster' turn up in	TENET	TENET
this perfect palindrome	AREPO	OPERA
widely known in Europe	SATOR	ROTAS

Top to bottom, bottom to top, side to side, the same words are created in the square. Both forms carry several interpretations. Form 1 is assumed to have a pre-Christian origin and only later adopted by Christians who discovered its linguistic capabilities for their own purposes. Christian examples are noted from the 4th century AD in Form 2; even as late as the 1870s, it was regarded as an instrument of great power and used as a charm for seamen, tin miners and streamers in Cornwall. Gérard de Sède thinks Templars used the 'magic square' as a code between themselves, since other words can be found within, TAROT, ARTOS, PORTA and the signature of the order O.T., all of which were believed to be of significance to some members of the order imprisoned at Gisors in France.

Practically any mark could fall within the category of being able to be fitted into a square or a circle and a lot more research is needed. Most artisans were illiterate, it would have been far easier for masons to have been taught, at Guild meetings for example, to remember the word 'paternoster', learn by rote the palindrome and furthermore, recognise the letters in the 'magic square'. (Beamon, Sylvia P., *Mason Marks*: Paper read at SFES Symposium 1991, Kefermarkt, Austria)

7. TEMPLAR CULT

RELIGION AND MAGIC

Religion can be vague, intangible, and 'beyond' human existence; it means different things to different people through the eons of time. Even in Neolithic times it is assumed from the arrangement of burials that there was ritual and possibly a form of belief. Man's interminable questioning. Does each society determine what life is to be from the cradle to the grave, or is it destiny? If it is destiny, can it be altered by making sacrifices and atonement to a God or several Gods? For example, will the rains come at the right time of year to ensure a harvest?

Religion and magic have one main similarity, that of being concerned with the supernatural. Magic differs from religion in that it is manipulative in essence, and yet this magical manipulation is conducted in an atmosphere of fear and respect, marvel and wonder too, similar to that which characterises the religious relationship. (O'Dea, 1966, 7)

Malinowski maintains that magic has an end, in pursuit of which, the magical ritual is performed by the religious rite - yet has no purpose - for it is not a means to an end, but an end in itself. The religious rite 'expresses' the feelings of all concerned: 'While in the magical act the underlying idea and aim is always clear, straight forward and definite, in the religious ceremony there is no purpose directed towards a subsequent event.'

Malinowski also thinks magic and religion are similar, in that they both 'arise and function in situations of emotional stress' and both open up avenues of escape from certain situations and impasses. Both exist in an atmosphere of the miraculous and surrounded by taboos and observances which mark off their acts from those of the profane world. Magical beliefs are simple with a circumscribed technique, spell and rite, whereas religion has more complex aspects and purposes. (O'Dea, op. cit., 9)

Freud's 'Frustration Hypothesis', although formulated this last century can equally be applied to earlier times. Primarily, he maintains that religion is a pleasant illusion in response to the frustrations of 'nature' with its uncontrollable catastrophes, its destructive forces from the outer world, and the decay of the body.

Secondly, there is the suppression of instinctive desires - sexual, aggressive and egoistic - by the forces of civilisation, that are assisted by the internalisation of these restraints in the superego of the individual.

Thirdly, the relative deprivation of the working classes, or lower order, by other sections of society in which they find themselves.

He finally suggests suffering is easier than pleasure and can only be obtained from the momentary satisfaction of pent-up needs. (Argyle, 1958, 161)

TEMPLAR HERESY

What was the Templar heresy? There are various opinions. According to Wilche, Ranke, and Weber it was 'the unitarian deism of Islam' (Bussell, 1918, 803). Lecouteulx de Canteleu thinks, however, it was derived from heretical Islamic sources, and relates that whilst in Palestine, one of the Knights, Guillaume de Montbard, was initiated by the Old Man of the Mountain in a cave of Mount Lebanon (*Les Sectes et Sociétés Secrètes,* p. 85). That a certain resemblance existed between the Templars and the Assassins has been indicated by von Hammer-Purgstall, J, (*History of the Assassins,* (1835 English translation) p. 80). The Templars, as far as can be discovered, were, or became, anti-Christian deists. Loiseleur considers that their ideas were derived from Gnostic or Manichean dualism - Cathari, Paulicians, or more particularly Bogomils [their name signified in Slavonic as 'friends of God'], whose doctrine is summarised as follows:

God the Supreme Father, has two sons, the elder Satanael, the younger Jesus. To Satanael, who sat on the right hand of God, belonged the right of governing the celestial world, but, filled with pride, he rebelled against his Father and fell from Heaven. Then, aided by the companions of his fall, he created the visible world, image of the celestial, having like the other its sun, moon, and stars, and last he created man and the serpent which became his minister. Later Christ came to earth in order to show men the way to Heaven, but his death was ineffectual, for even by descending into Hell he could not wrest the power from Satanael, i.e. Satan. (Webster, 1955, 63 et seq.)

This belief in the impotence of Christ and the necessity therefore for placating Satan, not only 'the Prince of this world,' but its creator, led to the further doctrine that Satan, being all-powerful, should be adored. Nicetas Choniates, a Byzantine historian of the twelfth century, described the followers of this cult as 'Satanists,' reasoning that: 'considering Satan powerful they worshipped him lest he might do them harm.' Subsequently, they were known as Luciferians, their doctrine, as stated by Neuss and Vitoduranus, holding to the conviction that Lucifer was unjustly driven out of Heaven, but one day he will ascend there again and be restored to his former glory and power in the celestial world.

The Bogomils and Luciferians were thus closely akin, whilst the former divided their worship between God and His two sons, the latter worshipped Lucifer only, regarding the material world as his work and by indulging the flesh they were propitiating their Demon-Creator. It was said that a black cat, the symbol of Satan, figured in their ceremonies as an object of worship (Fig. 40), also that at their horrible nocturnal orgies sacrifices of children were made and their blood used for making the eucharistic bread of the sect.

To return once more to the Templars, they recognized at the same time a good God, incommunicable to man and consequently without symbolic representation, and a bad god, to whom they give the features of an idol of fearful aspect. Their most fervent worship was addressed to this god of evil, who alone could enrich them. 'They said with the Luciferians:

'The elder son of God, Satanael or Lucifer alone has a right to the homage of mortals: Jesus his younger brother does not deserve this honour.'

Fig. 40. The engraved head of a cat can be found on the right of the Grand Master's Chapel, Temple Bruer, Lincolnshire, as about knee level. Photo M. Clancy, 1988.

The cat: why would there be a portrayal of this animal in a Templar Chapel? The cat symbolises the varying power of the sun and the waxing and waning of the moon, in fact, the splendour of the night; also can denote stealth, desire and liberty. If black, it is lunar (as belonging to the moon), evil and death. As regards Celtic symbolism it is associated with Chthonic powers or funerary. By Christians the cat was seen to relate to Satan, darkness, lust and laziness. But perhaps the answer lies in the Templar connections with the East where in Egyptian symbolism it is sacred to Set as darkness, and as lunar it can be an attribute of Isis and of Bass, the moon. (Cooper, J. C. (1978) 'An Illustrated Encyclopaedia of Traditional Symbols', Thames & Hudson, London, p. 31)

The Templars were not specifically 'accused' of idolatry at their trials although they allegedly worshipped a cat in contempt of Christ. There was supposedly a woman in England who said something about a cat that talked which she had seen through a crack in a Templar building. Where is not known.

Although it is not possible to find these ideas so clearly defined in the confessions of the Knights, some credence is lent to this theory by those who related that the reason given to them for not believing in Christ was: 'that He was nothing, He was a false prophet and of no value, and that they should believe in the Higher God of Heaven who could save them' (Michelet J. (1841-51), *Le Procès des Templièrs,* II, Paris, 404. Cf. Ibid. p. 384). According to Loiseleur, the idol they were taught to worship, was the bearded head known to history as *Baphomet,* representing, 'the inferior god, organiser and dominator of the material world, author of good and evil here below, him by whom evil was introduced into creation.'

The large floriat pointed cross, likely to represent the main altar, is cut on the western wall of the Cave (Figs. 8b & 27), although by some, it is more acceptable as a sword. A sword was used in Templar rites and as a cross in the field of battle. One of the charges brought against them, when the sect was dissolved, was that they spat upon the cross and denied Christ. Inquisitors were told that it was a test of fidelity and the denial was an imitation of St. Peter's denial of Christ - three times. Other excuses were given for spitting or trampling on the cross.

The rites of the Templars were a closely guarded secret, but some of them can still be found today in the Freemason chapters. When a mason initiate is 'raised' to the position of Master Mason there is an involved ordeal based on the legend of Hiram Abiff, architect of King Solomon's temple, who died rather than reveal the secrets of masonry (some say he was killed). It involves the initiate being 'murdered' and then 'raised from the dead'. Several Masonic temples have an actual hollow which is used as a 'grave'. (See also p. 139)

SKULL AND CROSSBONES

Similar to the Celts and other sects, it is also claimed that the Templars worshipped a skull and crossbones which may possibly have been images representing 'Death and what lies beyond.' (Gardner, 1968, 79) Or, perhaps it was a tangible relic to represent *Baphomet.* According to the Inquisition records, from the interrogations following the Templar arrests in 1307 in France, among the confiscated goods of the Paris preceptory was a reliquary in the shape of a woman's head. It was hinged on top, and contained what appeared to have been relics of an odd kind, and was described as follows:

> "...a great head of gilded silver, most beautiful, and constituting the image of a woman. Inside were two head-bones, wrapped in a cloth of white linen, with another red cloth around it. A label was attached, on which was written the legend CAPUT LVIIIm. The bones inside were those of a rather small woman."

However, a Templar knight whilst under interrogation, when confronted with this feminine head, declared it had no relation to the bearded male head used in the Order's rituals. Baigent (1982) points out that the 'm' in 'Caput LVIIIm - Head 58m' may not be an 'm' at all but ♍ the astrological symbol for Virgo.

There is another 'head legend' traced back to at least a late 12th century writer, Walter Map, and to another writer nearly a century onwards who recounted a similar tale, but neither specified a recalcitrant Templar! Yet by 1307 this enigmatic story had become traditionally linked with the Templars and mentioned repeatedly in the Inquisition records. A variant of the story follows:

> 'A great lady of Maraclea was loved by a Templar, a Lord of Sidon; but she died in her youth, and on the night of her burial, this wicked lover crept to the grave, dug up her body and violated it. Then a voice from the void bade him return in nine months time for he would find a son. He obeyed the injunction and at the appointed time he opened the grave again and found a head on the leg bones of the skeleton (skull and crossbones). The same voice bade him 'guard it well, for it would be the giver of all good things', and so he carried it away with him. It became his protecting genius, and he was able to defeat his

> enemies by merely showing them the magic head. In due course, it passed into the possession of the Order.'

At least two knights said they were familiar with the story, but it must be remembered that they were under interrogation.

It is possible that this narrative is symbolic of some initiation rite, involving a figurative death and resurrection. A woman Yse, probably Isis, is mentioned in one tale which takes the legend back into time almost immemorial to those of Tammuz or Adonis, whose head was flung into the sea, and of Orpheus, whose head was flung into the river of the Milky Way. The magical properties of the head also evoke the head of Bran the Blessed in Celtic mythology and in the *Mabinogion.*

Nevertheless, the inquisitors certainly believed in the importance of the 'cult of the head', and they itemised that in each province they [the Templars] had idols, namely heads: they adored these idols... : they said that the head could save them: that it could make riches... : it made the trees flower: made the land germinate: that they [the Templars] surrounded or touched each head of the aforesaid idols with small cords, which they wore around themselves next to the shirt or the flesh. (Baigent, Leigh, Lincoln, 1982, 54-5). The references to the trees flowering and the land germinating could easily be construed as 'fertility' rituals.

A human skull, claimed by Stukeley to have been female, and bones were found in the Royston Cave but, as far as can be ascertained, not a complete skeleton.

CULT OF THE HEAD

A 'cult of the head' survived until recent times in the Fontanelle underground catacombs of Naples, Italy. Five caverns were used for the rituals. They were closed by the Church authorities in the 1980s and three were destroyed by the earthquake in 1988. The ritual specified that a young girl should ask for special favours of the family (who wanted a skull) to place a skull in a box. Beforehand, the girl had to undertake certain rites underground, for example, traversing a maze as from prehistoric times. Once the connection between the family, the girl and the skull had been completed, the skull became a protector of the family. The Catholic church frowns greatly upon these rituals and has tried to stamp them out. Around the caves are several paintings. Where the painted head should be is an actual inset skull, and in a couple of cases only a portion of the bone survives. Professor Alfonso Piciocchi has made a special study of this 'cult of the head'. One point worth mentioning is that in one or two of the other paintings, not containing a skull, the eyes in the head are shown as complete circles, exactly the same as the small head, thought to be Templar work, at Denny Abbey (Fig. 41). The Templars were well established in Italy and could have been aware of these ancient rites. [Isolated heads can be seen in the Cave and in the graffiti in the Tour du Coudray, Chinon.]

THE TURIN SHROUD

Before leaving the matter of the head completely the Turin Shroud should be touched upon. The Shroud has been housed in Turin, Italy for many centuries and on rare occasions displayed to the public. It is claimed to have been in the possession of the Templars between 1204 and 1307, and if folded, would have just exposed the head. At Templecombe in Somerset, a reproduction of a head painted on a wooden panel was found, which bears a striking resemblance to that on the Turin Shroud [Fig. 42]. The author was in contact with the Rector, Rev. A. Marshall in 1978 and his comments are worth recording:

> 'This panel painting of our Lord's Head was discovered in an outhouse of a cottage belonging to Mrs. A. Topp in Templecombe High Street in 1951. During a gale the plaster of the outhouse ceiling collapsed revealing the panel in the roof, covered with coal dust. The key-hole and hinge marks indicate that at some time it had been used as a door in the cottage coal house.
>
> This life-size painting, Medieval in style, is one of the most remarkable portraits of its kind in the country. Although previously dated about 1314, present day research suggests that it is of earlier origin and probably connected with the Knights Templar...
>
> In the year 1185 the Knights Templar acquired the property of the Manor on the south side of the village (hence the name Temple Combe) and established a Preceptory, or station, for members of the Order. In its day it was a place of some importance. The preceptor, who resided here, was responsible for managing the Templar's estates in the West Country, admitting new members to the Order, and training men and horses for service in the East. The remains of the old Templar buildings are still to be seen at the Manor House in Templecombe. It is believed that this painting was originally one of many similar portraits in the possession of the Templars and used in their religious rites. When the Order fell into disrepute in the 14th Century, its members were accused, amongst other things, of 'idolatry' - of worshipping a strange image. Could this be one such 'idolatrous image' which escaped the inquisitor's attention? Although the top portion of the panel is missing, it does not appear to have included a 'halo' which is usually featured in all Medieval paintings of Christ. During the suppression of the Order, the absence of the 'halo' in their portraits - which Templars maintained were paintings of Christ appears to have been used as evidence of idolatry. The omission of the 'halo', together with the striking similarity between this panel painting and the figure imprinted on the Holy Shroud at Turin Cathedral (the linen cloth believed to have been used to cover the body of our Lord in the Sepulchre*), has led to a new theory. It has been suggested that, during the Crusades in the East, the Templars obtained the prized possession of the Holy Shroud, brought it to Europe and, from it, copied their paintings...'

It should be noted that none of the religious engravings in the Cave have 'haloes' either. An exception, is a scratching of a cat with a halo; some say it is not a cat but a serpent. Whatever it is, it lies close to the floor (to the right and down from the hand, heart, double heart and 'axe-head' grouping (c/r p. 110, see Fig. 27).

I did not mention the impression in the previous chapter since it does not appear in the antiquarians' text or drawings. It is possibly a later addition, if not, then perhaps it did have some significance. (See also Fig. 40)

***Note:** *After extensive examination, and many tests including C14 (carbon fourteen tests), the Turin Shroud was pronounced in 1988 as being a forgery and could not date from the first century AD. In February 1992 an expert Dr. Ian Wilson claims it may be genuine after all, as carbon dating is increasingly in question!* [2009 – its authenticity is being debated again]

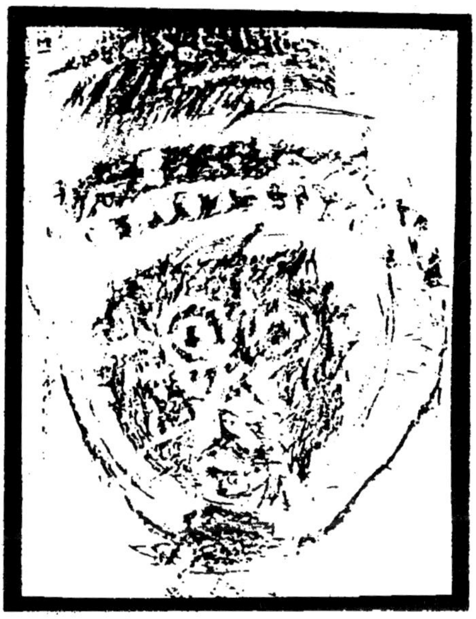

Fig. 41. Rubbing of a head with circular eyes from a pillar in the Templar portion of Denny Abbey, Cambridge. Not to scale. From author's own collection.

Fig. 42. Painted wooden panel from Templecombe, Somerset.

THE HOLY GRAIL

At the time when the Order of the Templars was at its height, there was a peculiar Culdee legend travelling around. [The Culdees were one of a fraternity of monks, living in Scotland from the 8th century, in groups of cells]. This legend termed the *Quest of the Sangraal,* supposed there was a lost cup, which had contained the blood of Christ, and could only be found by a chaste knight who journeyed in search of it. If found, it had various magical properties and ambiguous answers to enquiries could be read upon it. There were certain ceremonies practised alluding to Joseph, Jesus and Mary, said to have been of Culdee origin that have a sober resemblance to the Quest. The Mystic tradition may have had the old blood baptism of the Mysteries. (Yarker, 1909, 191 et seq.) [The Holy family is represented on the Cave wall and it is unusual for Joseph to be included in the Medieval period under discussion]

There are various legends regarding the Holy Grail. In the oldest account of the legend of Titurel, he builds the Grail Temple, but in a version completed by Alfred von Scharfenberg, it was Parsifal, Titurel's grandson, who was selected to build a Temple in the middle of a square of wood. The Temple itself to be round [as are some Templar churches] etc., to hold the Grail and to be guarded by chaste Temple or Templar Knights. Lecterns to have carved Apostles, Martyrs, Prophets and their 'wise Saws.' The groining of the roof to show a lamb holding a red cross banner it its claws [a Templar Standard]. In one of these manuscripts, England is named in connection with four crowns, four virgin martyrs, and their legends. (Yarker)

Bruges, in Belgium, has been named by one writer, Paul de Saint-Hilaire, 'the City of the Grail'. Partly, this title is generated by the presence of a relic of the Holy Blood kept in the church of the same name in the centre of the city. It is still possible to visit this sacred object for it is displayed daily at certain times. Inside its glass container is what looks like dry red dust - and is supposed to radiate energy. It was the Templars who are reputed to have brought the Holy Blood to Bruges. Suggestion has been made that St. Bernard of Clairvaux, related to one of the founding knights and mainly responsible for writing the *Rule* of the Order, may have communicated some knowledge to the brethren that is found in coded form in the pages of the *Queste del Saint Graal.* This document was written by Cistercian monks of whose Order St. Bernard was both founder and head. Firm evidence for the support of this theory is lacking. (Matthews, Green, 1986, 58-9, 92)

There is a surviving legend associating the revered vessel with Glastonbury and giving an account of the romances of King Arthur. Another claim is made for a Sapphire Cup in the Monastery of Richeneau, Lake Constance, Switzerland, founded by Charles Martel in AD 725; there is yet a third claim for a cup said to have been brought from the East by the crusaders, and lodged at Genoa, Italy, which is now believed to be made of green glass. (Yarker, op. cit.)

And what exactly was this Holy Grail, Sangraal, Chalice, Cup and why was it searched for with such fervour? This illusory tenuous object was not real but symbolised the search for the 'meaning of life' or *raison d'être,* and because this cup was supposed to have held the blood of Christ who knew the meaning of existence, the Knights of the Round Table, Knights of the Temple and other legends connected with the Holy Grail probably took it as an attribute. They did not really search literally for a cup but for the reason of being, that which all nations, all creeds, for all time have searched. More than likely several cups were actually made, many people require an actual object to venerate in order to accept an idea, just as the Cross was adopted to symbolise Christianity. The Chalice of course, is still used in Communion services today.

JOHANNISM

It is here that we reach a further theory with regard to the secret doctrine of the Templars - the most important of all. Since it emanates from Masonic and neo-Templar sources it effectually disposes of the contention that the charge brought against the Order, of apostasy from the Catholic faith, is solely the invention of Catholic writers.

In 1842 the Freemason Ragon related that the Templars learnt from the initiates of the East, 'a certain Judaic doctrine which was attributed to St. John the Apostle: therefore they renounced the religion of St. Peter' and became Johannites (J.M. Ragon, *Cours Philosophique et Interprétatif des Initiations anciennes et Modernes*). Eliphas Levi (1861) expresses the same opinion.

Apparently these statements are founded on a legend which was first published early in the 19th century. Besides publishing the list of all Grand Masters, known as the *Charter of Larmenius,* said to have been preserved in the secret archives of the Temple, these works also reproduced another document drawn from the same repository describing the origins of the Order. This manuscript written in Greek on parchment, dated 1154, purporting to be partly taken from a 5th century manuscript, relates that Hugh de Payens, first Grand Master of the Templars, was initiated in 1118 - in fact the year the Order was founded - into the religious doctrine of 'the Primitive Christian Church' by its Sovereign Pontiff and Patriarch, Theoclet, sixtieth in direct succession from St. John the Apostle. According to the Abbé Gregoire and Abbé Munter, the authenticity and antiquity of these documents were beyond dispute. Gregoire, referring to the parchment manuscript of the Levitikon and Gospel of St. John, said: 'Hellenists versed in paleography believe this manuscript to be of the 13th century, others declare it to be earlier and to go back to the 11th century. However, Professor Thilo of Halle and Matter believe that they date from the beginning of the 18th century.' The antiquity of the manuscript containing the history of the Templars therefore remains an open question.

However, the history of the Primitive Church is given below:-

> 'Moses was initiated in Egypt. Profoundly versed in the physical, theological, and metaphysical mysteries of the priests, he knew how to profit by these so as to surmount the power of the Mages and deliver his companion. Aaron, his brother, and the chiefs of the Hebrews became the depositaries of his doctrine...
>
> The Son of God afterwards appeared on the scene of the world ... He was brought up at the school of Alexandria... Imbued with a spirit wholly divine, endowed with the most astounding qualities (dispositions), he was able to reach all the degrees of Egyptian initiation. On his return to Jerusalem, he presented himself before the chiefs of the Synagogue... Jesus Christ, directing the fruit of his lofty meditations towards universal civilization and the happiness of the

> world, rent the veil which concealed the truth from the peoples. He preached the love of God, the love of one's neighbour, the equality before the common Father of all men...
>
> Jesus conferred evangelical initiation on his apostles and disciples. He transmitted his spirit to them, divided them into several orders after the practice of John, the beloved disciple, the apostle of fraternal love, whom he had instituted Sovereign Pontiff and Patriarch...'

Here we have the whole Cabalistic legend of a secret doctrine descending from Moses, of Christ as an Egyptian initiate and founder of a secret order. A theory, of course, absolutely destructive of belief in His divinity. The legend of the *Order of the Temple* goes on to say:

> 'Up to about the year 1118 the mysteries and the hierarchic Order of the initiation of Egypt, transmitted to the Jews by Moses, then to the Christians by Jesus Christ were religiously preserved by the successors of St. John the Apostle. These mysteries and initiations, regenerated by the evangelical initiation (or baptism) were a sacred trust which the simplicity of the primitive and unchanging morality of the Brothers of the East had preserved from all adulteration ...
>
> The Christians, persecuted by the infidels, appreciating the courage and piety of these brave crusaders, who, with the sword in one hand and the cross in the other, flew to the defence of the holy places, and, above all, doing striking justice to the virtues and the ardent charity of Hugh de Payen, held it their duty to confide to hands so pure the treasures of knowledge acquired throughout so many centuries, sanctified by the cross, the dogma and the morality of the Man-God. Hugh was invested with the Apostolic Patriarchal power and placed in the legitimate order of the successors of St. John the apostle or the evangelist'.

Such is the origin of the foundation of the Order of the Temple, if it can be so, and of the fusion in this Order of the different kinds of initiation of the Christians of the East designated under the title of 'Primitive Christians' or 'Johannites'. As Nesta Webster endorses, it will be seen at once that all of this story is subtly subversive of true Christianity, and that the appellation of 'Christians' applied to the Johannites is really not accurate. What may be regarded as certain, is that a sect existed long before the time of the Crusades corresponding to the description of the Johannites given by Eliphas Levi, in that "it was Cabalistic, anti-Christian, yet professedly founded on the doctrines of one of the St. Johns". Whether it was by this sect that the Templars were indoctrinated must again remain open. M. Matter objected that the evidence for such a conclusion is lacking, and lies in the fact that the Templars expressed no particular reverence for St. John. But, Loiseleur asserts that the Templars did prefer the Gospel of St. John to that of the other evangelists, also that modern Masonic lodges claiming descent from the Templars, possess a special version of this Gospel said to have been copied from the original of Mount Athos. (Loiseleur, op. cit., 52) It is also said that *Baphomets* were preserved in the Masonic lodges of Hungary, where a debased form of Masonry, known as Johannite Masonry, survives to this day.

If the Templar heresy was that of the Johannites, the head in question might possibly represent that of John the Baptist, which would accord with the theory that the word *Baphomet* was derived from Greek words signifying 'baptism of wisdom'. Moreover, this would not be incompatible with Loiseleur's theory of an affinity between the Templars and the Bogomils. The Bogomils also possessed their own version of the Gospel of St. John, which they placed on the heads of their neophytes during the ceremony of initiation, (Ibid, p. 51: Matter, op. cit. III, 305) giving as the reason for the peculiar veneration they professed for its author that they regarded St. John as the servant of the Jewish God Satanael. (Hastings (1908) *Encyclopaedia,* article on Bogomils). Eliphas Levi, even goes so far as to accuse the Templars of following the occult practices of the Luciferians, who carried the doctrines of the Bogomils to the point of paying homage to the powers of darkness.

Dr. Ranking, who devoted many years of study to the question, arrived at the conclusion that Johannism is the real clue to the Templar heresy. He stated in a paper published in the Masonic journal *Ars Quatuor Coronatorum,* that 'the record of the Templars in Palestine is one long tale of intrigue and treachery on the part of the Order,' and finally:

> 'That from the very commencement of Christianity there has been transmitted through the centuries a body of doctrine incompatible with Christianity in the various official Churches...
>
> That the bodies teaching these doctrines professed to do so on the authority of St. John, to whom, as they claimed, the true secrets had been committed by the Founder of Christianity.
>
> That during the Middle Ages the main support of the Gnostic bodies and the main repository of this knowledge was the Society of the Templars.'

Webster questions: What is the explanation of this choice of St. John for the propagation of anti-Christian doctrines? What else than the method of perversion which in its extreme form becomes Satanism, and consists in always selecting the most sacred things for the purpose of desecration. Precisely then, because the Gospel of St. John is the one, of all the four, which most insists on the divinity of Christ, and the occult anti-Christian sects have habitually made it the basis for their rites.

THE ROSICRUCIANS

Before I explain about this sect I wish to make it quite clear that I do not think it has anything at all to do with the fact that Royston was at one time known as Rose Crux.

The Rosicrucians appear to have been the outcome of both the Cabalistic movement and the 16th century teachings of Paracelsus. The earliest intimation of their existence was given in a series of pamphlets which appeared at the beginning of the 17th century. The first of these entitled the *Fama Fraternitatis; or the Discovery of the Fraternity of the most Laudable Order of the Rosy Cross* was published at Cassel in 1614 and the *Confessio Fraternitatis* early in the following year. These contain what may be described as the 'Grand Legend' of Rosicrucianism, which has been repeated with slight variations up to the present day. Briefly, this story is as follows:

> 'The most godly and highly illuminated Father, our brother C.R. that is to say, Christian Rosenkreutz, a German, the chief and original of our Fraternity, was born in 1378, and some sixteen years later travelled to the East with a Brother P.A.L., who had determined to go to the Holy Land. On reaching Cyprus, Brother P.A.L. died and 'so never came to Jerusalem' Brother C.R. however, having become acquainted with certain Wise Men of 'Damasco in Arabia' and beheld what great wonders they wrought, went on alone to Damasco. Here the Wise Men received him and he then set himself to study Physick and Mathematics and to translate the Book M into Latin. After three years he went to Egypt, whence he journeyed on to Fez, where 'he did get acquaintance with those who are called the Elementary inhabitants, who revealed to him many of their secrets... Of those of Fez he often did confess that their Magia[n] was not altogether pure and also that their Cabala was defiled with their religion, but notwithstanding he knew how to make good use of the same.
>
> After two years Brother C.R. departed the city of Fez and sailed away with many costly things into Spain, where he conferred with the learned men and being 'ready bountifully to impart all his arts and secrets' showed them amongst other things how 'there might be a society in Europe which might have gold, silver, and precious stones sufficient for them to bestow on kings for their necessary uses and lawful purposes...'

Christian Rosenkreutz then returned to Germany, where 'there is nowadays no want of learned men, Magicians, Cabalists, Physicians, and Philosophers.' Here he 'builded himself a fitting and neat habitation in which he ruminated his voyage and philosophy and reduced them together in a true memorial.' At the end of five year's meditation there came again apparently into his mind the wished-for Reformation: accordingly, he chose to form a circle of initiates, 'some few adjoyned with him,' the Brethren G.V., I.A., and I.O. - the last of whom 'was very expert and well learned in Cabala as his book H witnesseth'. So began the Fraternity of the Rosy Cross. Five other Brethren were afterwards included, all Germans except I.A. and these eight constituted his new building called Sancti Spiritus.

Finally Brother C.R. died and the date generally given is 1484.

While declaring their belief in the Christian faith, the *Fama* goes on to explain that:

> 'Our Philosophy is not a new invention, but as Adam after his fall hath received it and as Moses and Solomon used it... wherein Plato, Aristotle,

> Pythagoras, and others did hit the mark and wherein Enoch, Abraham, Moses, Solomon, did excel, but especially wherewith that wonderful Book the Bible agreeth.'

It can be seen that, according to this manifesto, Rosicrucianism was a combination of the ancient secret tradition handed down from the patriarchs through the Greek philosophers and of the first Cabala of the Jews. (Webster, 1955, 86 et seq.)

The *Grand Legend* of Rosicrucianism rests, however, on no historical evidence; there is, in fact, not the least reason to suppose that any such person as Christian Rosenkreutz ever existed. The Illuminatus von Knigge in the 18th century asserted that:

> 'It is now recognised amongst enlightened men that no real Rosicrucians have existed, but that the whole of what is contained in the *Fama* and the *Universal Reformation of the World* [another Rosicrucian pamphlet which appeared in the same year] was only a subtle allegory of Valentine Andrea, of which afterwards partly deceivers (such as the Jesuits) and partly visionaries made use of in order to realise this dream.'

What then, was the origin of the name Rose-Cross? According to one Rosicrucian tradition, the word 'Rose' does not derive from the flower depicted on the Rosicrucian cross, but from the Latin word *ros,* signifying 'dew', which was supposed to be the most powerful solvent of gold, whilst *crux,* the cross, was the chemical hieroglyphic for 'light' (Mackey, 1860, 265) It is said that the Rosicrucians interpreted the initials on the cross INRI by the sentence *Igne Nitrum Roris Invenitur* [The natron of dew is found in the fire] (Ibid., p. 150). Supposing this derivation to be correct, it would be interesting to know whether any connection could be traced between the first appearance of the word Rosie Cross in the *Fama Fraternitatis* at the date of 1614 and the cabalistic treatise of the celebrated Rabbi of Prague, Shabbethai Sheftel Horowitz, which appeared in 1612. (*Jewish Encyclopaedia*) Although this book has often been reprinted, no copy is to be found in the British Museum. A simpler explanation may be that the Rosy Cross derived from the Red Cross of the Templars. Mirabeau who, as a Freemason and an Illuminatus, was in a position to discover many facts about the secret societies of Germany during his stay in that country, definitely asserts that 'the Rose Croix Masons of the seventeenth century were only the ancient Order of the Templars secretly perpetuated.' (Mirabeau, *Histoire de la Monarchie Prussienne,* V. 76)

Lecouteulx de Canteleu is more explicit: (*Les Sectes et Sociétés Secrètes,* p. 97)

> 'In France the Knights [Templar] who left the Order, henceforth hidden, and so to speak unknown, formed the Order of the Flaming Star and of the Rose-Croix, which in the fifteenth century spread itself in Bohemia and Silesia. Every Grand officer of these Orders had all his life to wear the Red Cross and to repeat every day the prayer of St. Bernard.'
>
> Eckert states: '...the ritual, symbols and the names of Rose-Croix were borrowed from the Templars, and that the Order was divided into seven degrees, according to the seven days of creation, at the same time signifying

> that their 'principal aim was that of the mysterious, the investigation of Being and of the forces of nature.' (*La Franc-Maçonnerie dans sa véritable signification,* II, 48)

Another work, *Examination of the Unknown and Novel Cabala of the Brethren of the Rose-Cross,* agrees with the assertion that the chief of this 'execrable college is Satan, that its first rule is denial of God, blasphemy against the most simple and undivided Trinity, trampling on the mysteries of the redemption, spitting in the face of the mother of God and of all the saints.' The sect is further accused of compacts with the devil, sacrifices of children, of cherishing toads, making poisonous powders, dancing with fiends etc.

Nesta Webster maintains and the writer agrees, that although all this would appear to be quite incompatible with the character of the Rosicrucians, as far as it is known, the practices already described were by no means imaginary. When the fame of the Rosicrucians was first voiced abroad in the 17th century, black magic was still, a horrible reality, not only in France but in England, Scotland, and Germany, where sorcerers or witches of both sexes were continually put to death. As much as the methods employed against these people may be deplored, it would be idle and stupid to deny that the cult itself existed and to question the supernatural origin of their actual cult. A society known as the Rosicrucians still exists today.

SECRET STATUTES

The official statutes of the Knights Templar contained rules, not only about keeping knowledge of the statutes secret, but also the secret enterprises of the Order; and members could be punished accordingly for breaking any of these regulations. (De Sède, 1962, 144 et seq.)

Master Roncelin explained that the secret statutes of the Templars were never translated into any current language of that day; and were never handed down to mere brethren (2nd. part of article 6). This supposedly leaves room to suggest that secrets did exist for second degree members, which were contained in documents in a form of cyphers, and disappeared from the Temple, never to be traced again.

But there are some very curious articles, in the third part, for example, where they deal with monuments erected or used by the Templars, and about precautions to be taken to hide the activities going on there. According to the eminent French archaeologist, Emile Male, the 'transept' [croise - cross] form apparently was derived from both the Byzantine and Arab art of fortifying their castles, a military art which goes way back to ancient Assyrian times.

In architecture, the Templars followed the Justinian tradition, copying Syrian fortresses but in a simplified form. This building tradition was characterised by three enceintes often in octagonal form, even though the octagonal form lacked any military value as such, however, for the Templars this form had a symbolic meaning, because this geometric figure contains the cross pattée as the emblem of their Order. (De Sède, 1962, 145, 146)

Monsieur Paul Naudon, architectural historian, is of the opinion that when Templars, aided by Christian labourers, founded their commanderies throughout Europe, they brought with them the secrets and traditional rites of Byzantine and Tarouq musulman schools of art, which both have their foundations in hermetic syncretism. These principles were adopted in the way they constructed their buildings.

TEMPLAR SEALS

Waxed seal impressions were used for sealing writs and documents of importance, in particular for land purchases and exchanges. The Grand Master had his own seal and preceptories or commanderies owned one as well. For what purpose exactly the secret seals were used is not known. Several seals are shown below (Figs. 43a & b, see also pp. 70-72; Figs. 37a, 56d, 57c):

1. This seal of a Grand Master shows a cupola surmounted by the Templar cross above a gallery of four arcades - Byzantine style. The wording: S'TVBE TEMPLI XRI (abridged) represents SIGILLUM TUMBE TEMPLI CHRISTO [seal of Christ's Temple Tomb]

2. Seal no. A.D.N. 9861 represents two Templars on a horse both holding lances, and from the viewer's standpoint are seen galloping from right to left. Sometimes referred to as 'the symbol of poverty' as they have to share one horse. The horse, messenger of the divine, is their support and unites them in fraternity. The horse symbolises *rites de passage,* for their entry into the world, their span of life, then as the horse is permitted access to Paradise, it can conduct the dead through to immortality. Another suggestion is that the two riders represent Gemini the twins (Dioscuri - Castor and Polux, as sons of Zeus), who sought Sagittarius with his arrow. The twins symbolise the knowledge of incarnation. Sagittarius takes the arrow/lance from the riders and together with their horse guides them through the door to the 'other world'. It is through the intercession of the arrow that Sagittarius can convey them to heaven and also symbolises the spirit of the Templar who aspires to the divine.

3. An abraxus [secret seal]: with the words *Secretum Templi,* but with the cross shown on the reverse side. (*Archives Nationales,* D.9860 bis), This abraxus shows a Gnostic symbol. It is composed of a personage with some of the body covered with armour but the chest area garbed in a court robe. In place of the two legs, there are two serpents, each terminating in two heads. The head is that of a cockerel.

   This seal, with the secret figure, belonged to the Grand Master too, and was actually used on a French charter dated October 1214. It has been suggested that the figure illustrates the famous idol *Baphomet,* which the Templars supposedly adored and were accused of worshipping at their trials. Hammer-Purgstal claims the Templars were gnostics and *Baphomet* is *Baphometides* - the baptism of wisdom - and the baphomet figure itself is the Gnostic symbol. However, it is suggested that *baphomet:* 'Bios - Phos - Metis' signifies Life, Light and Wisdom, or alternatively is representative of the hermaphrodite, Hermes-Aphrodite, of Knowledge and Love.

There are other secret seals.

4. The seal (*Archives Nationales* D.9863) is on a charter between the Templars and the Abbey of Saint-Victor in Paris, March 1259. Again two soldiers on the same horse with mail even covering most of their heads. They both have lances and shields. The symbol on the shields is formed by the St. Andrew's cross and the Greek cross, and when joined together resembles the British flag. This symbol is noted in several other places in France and can be seen in the Tour du Coudray dungeon, Chinon (see Fig. 30). The inscription reads: SIGILLUM MILITUM XPISTI [Seal of the soldiers of Christ], and the Templar cross is present.

5. *Agnus Dei* [Lamb of God] seal occurs in the arms of Templar houses, commanderies and fortresses. In particular it is noted in the arms of the commandery of the Temple of London where it carries the cross pattée. (The Pegasus horse [winged] is seen in the Inner Temple), Other examples exist in France, Germany and Britain. (Carny, 1972, 336-48) (See also Figs. 56d & 57c)

Fig. 43a. French Templar Seals (not to scale)
Note: the design of the shield on seal no. 4 is similar to that seen on stone C3 Fig. 30 in the Tour du Coudray, Chinon.

Fig. 43b. English seal of the Temple Church, London.

FREEMASONRY

What, if anything, can be gained from examining certain rituals and symbols of Freemasonry which revealed itself to the world in 1717, the given foundation date? Robinson (1989) maintains that there are much more direct Templar connections than would be expected, and they survived from the middle ages through a clandestine form of masonry. Certain aspects of Freemasonry rituals, rather than with the 'furniture' of the modern lodge room, are interesting, after all secret meetings 'on high hills and in deep valleys,' or in 'barns and cellars', certainly did not include an altar, candlesticks, columns, or chairs. Nor would they have included the *Holy Bible* (which still brings criticism to Freemasonry today for referring to the Holy Book as an item of the 'furniture' of a lodge room). In the period under examination individuals did not have Bibles, at least not legally. The elements they could have had were the circle, the mosaic pavement, and the compass and square. The circle that is at the centre of the Masonic lodge is in four parts: first, the circle itself; next the point in the centre of the circle; and then two parallel lines, one on each side of the circle. In Masonic lore the circle is the boundless universe, the point in the centre is the individual Mason, and the lines on two sides of the circle are the staffs of St. John the Baptist and St. John the Evangelist.

Robinson suggests a medieval Mason would have prepared the meeting place by initially clearing an area of his choice: then after cutting two sticks, say four feet long, he would hold or tie them at one end, spreading them out at the other end to make a crude compass. Whilst holding one end of one stick firmly to the ground, he would rotate the other to scratch a circle in the dirt. The end that was held in place naturally left a point in the centre of the circle. The two sticks placed on either side of the circle, finally created the total symbol. At one point in the ritual, the Masons in attendance would walk around the circle, a reverential act now known as the 'circumambulation of the lodge.' Initiation ceremonies of the Knights of the Temple took place in their own churches, which were usually circular in shape to emulate the Church of the Holy Sepulchre in Jerusalem. When Templars processed around their circular churches they had only one way to go - in a circle, just as today's Masons travel in their 'circumambulation' of the lodge.

As regards the Masonic mosaic pavements, Robinson thinks it could have been indicated on the ground by scratching a checkerboard, or by using any black and white material. There is no regulation as to the size or number of the squares. He draws on the connection that the symbolism possibly began as one white square and one black because the battle banner of the Knights Templar, the *Beausant* was a vertical design consisting of a black block above and a white block below (see illustration on Fig. 37b). The black block signified the black world of sin the Templar had left behind, and the white block symbolised the pure life he had adopted as a soldier for Christ. Masonic historians say the origin of their mosaic pavement came from the East.

It is tempting to wonder why a checkerboard is shown in the Priory coat of arms and the colours for Royston are black and white. A checkerboard is also shown in the Coat of Arms for the town, which was granted in 1952:

> 'The centre feature of the shield is the black and white Stewart (for Stuart) cheque which refers to the association that James VI of Scotland and I of England had with the town. The Royal Stuarts of Stewarts (Stewards) derived their name from the hereditary Office of the Lord High Steward of Scotland, and their Coat of Arms bore this chequy fesse.' (*Royston - Official Guide and Town Map,* 1973, 17)

Early in the 17th century, this king took a liking to the good hunting facilities, especially for hare, around Royston causing many grievances among his not so loyal local subjects by his excessive hunting activities. His palace still survives in Kneesworth Street.

Baigent and Leigh (1989) also trace the rise of Freemasonry from the absorption of Judaic and Islamic beliefs by the Templars, and from the architectural practice of the Middle East which their artisans adopted. They believe the Templar refugees in Scotland, particularly the stone-masons, passed on these traditions and secret rituals to operative stone-masons there, and that these were accepted into an elite body of the nobility. Furthermore, the two authors suggest that Freemasonry was taken over by the Jacobites and used as a secret society dedicated to preserving the dynasty of the Stuarts. The earliest surviving minutes of Dunblane No. 9 Lodge, dated 1696, are signed by some of the principal Jacobite conspirators. The higher degrees of Freemasonry were in existence in Scotland long before the formation in 1717 of the Grand Lodge in London which has been seen as an Hanoverian attempt to counter the Jacobite monopoly.

McKerracher (1991, 168) expresses his conviction that the connection between the Templars and Freemasonry in Scotland can be seen on a 14th century gravestone at Kilmory Chapel which quite clearly portrays a Masonic set square together with a Templar Cross. (See also Fig. 33 where a set square is engraved on a coffin lid from Atlit, Israel.)

The notion of Templar heresy is very complicated and this chapter has attempted to give some meaning to their underlying esoteric thought.

8. TEMPLAR CONNECTIONS WITH ROUND CHURCHES, AND SOME EARLY MODELS OF THE HOLY SEPULCHRE

The study of 'round churches' has led to the general opinion that most of the circular churches of England, as well as those of a similar character and date in other countries, may be justly attributed to Knights Templar influence. The brethren proudly esteemed, as a shrine, the church of the Holy Sepulchre in Jerusalem, above all other earthly objects; and this sanctified circular building was to affect the design of some crusader churches away from the more usual cruciform plan. It can be looked upon as a natural consequence of such enthusiasm, that when the Templars became a rich and powerful body, acquiring establishments in many of the countries of Europe, they should want to imitate the revered structure. This appears to have been actually the case with those who settled in Britain, as they built circular churches in several places. Round churches are not exclusive to the Knights Templar themselves, the Hospitallers built a few too. One or two others were built by private individuals, as exampled by the chapel of St. Mary Magdalene in the courtyard at Ludlow Castle and another at Northampton. Some of the round churches, both abroad and here, were dedicated to the Holy Sepulchre.

ISRAEL:

Church of the Holy Sepulchre, Jerusalem

To pilgrims and crusaders alike the Church of the Holy Sepulchre was the final object of their devotions; they did not have any doubts at all, either from the historical or archaeological angle as to the survival of the rock-cut tomb, or to its specific location. Calvary and Christ's tomb had been revealed by the Christian community in Jerusalem to St. Helena, Christian mother of Constantine, the first Christian Roman Emperor. St. Helena had the site uncovered. Nearby, in' an underground chamber originally cut in the rock for water storage, she found parts of a cross which she and posterity have accepted and venerated as being that on which Christ had died. (Smail, 1973, 127). [q.v. Beldam suggested that the floriat cross in the Cave represented the Cross of St. Helena and it was aptly symbolized by the production of buds and flowers perpetually renewing itself.]

Constantine undertook the re-sanctification of the spot in 325 AD. 'The pious Emperor,' wrote Eusebius of Caesarea, a Palestinian contemporary of the event, judged it incumbent on him: 'to render the blessed locality of our Saviour's Resurrection an object of attraction and veneration to all.' He issued injunctions therefore, for the building of a house of prayer. Eusebius goes on to say:

> 'that the tomb had been completely buried by the ungodly men who set themselves to assign to darkness and oblivion that divine monument of immortality.'

The area was levelled and the rock around the cave sepulchre cut away leaving it as a detached feature. It became the central point of a round church building under a conical roof; the grotto in which the Cross had been found became the crypt of a second, lying to the east, a large basilican church, known as the Martyrium, with a single apse at its western end, opening into an atrium, approached through an impressive triple entrance - parts of which still survive in the Russian hospice. During excavation work in 1990 a single fleur-de-lis, scratched on a door jamb, was uncovered. It is suggested that it was incised by a crusader. Between the rotunda and basilica stood Calvary, reduced to a formal cube of rock, in a paved and colonnaded courtyard. (Smail, 1973, 126)

Constantine's church survived 300 years and it was not until 1048 that the Patriarch Nicephorus, largely financed by the Emperor Constantine Monomachus, undertook a new restoration. The ruins of the domed rotunda were reconstructed, supported on a circle of eighteen pillars, with the tomb as its central feature. The main altar was in a polygonal apse on the western face from a straight wall with four doorways, stretches of wall still survive with upper windows visible above later rebuilding. There was no attempt to rebuild the Martyrium (Fig 44a). [NOTE: The main altar in the Royston Cave is on the western side too and not on the east as is usually found in oratories, chapels and churches in this country and Europe, q.v.]

Mosaic and painting also played a great part in the decorative scheme. One must imagine the Church of the Holy Sepulchre glowing with subdued richness. Abbot Daniel describing the rotunda in 1106 lists figures of apostles in the arches above the tribune, and a considerable iconographic scheme, centring on the Anastasis, Christ releasing the souls of the just from limbo, above the altar. This was on the wall removed to make the opening through to the Crusaders' church but similar designs seem to have been used, possibly reused, by the crusaders in their apse. References to the mosaics continued to be made until the 17th century, by which time they were much obliterated.

Some of the crusaders seem to have been fascinated by this Byzantine inheritance, for William of Tyre tells how Godfrey of Bouillon's companions used to complain of the time he spent in churches, asking about the meaning of each image and picture. Paintings [*iconae*] presumably on panels, were also hung from the arches. Of all this lavish decoration, there survives today, in the chapel of Calvary, only a fragment in mosaic showing Christ in Glory. It could be either Byzantine work of the mid-11th century, or crusader-Byzantine work of the mid-12th, probably the latter, for the inscription is in Latin. [It should be remembered that the figures carved in relief in the Royston Cave were in the main painted.]

The main facade opened on the parvis or court of access on the south side (Fig. 44b). George Sandys describes it as follows:

> 'The Frontispiece opposing the South, of an excellent structure; having two joyning doors, the one now walled up supported with Columns of Marble, over which a Transom engraven with historical figures; the walls and arches crested and garnished with flority...'

'Garnished with flority' is a picturesque term for the elaborate friezes, much influenced by classical prototypes such as can still be seen at Baalbek, Tyre, and elsewhere, that divide the facade into its two stages and provides a cornice below the dome. Deeply undercut, large in scale, inventive in design, the friezes of the south facade are outstanding examples of a Franco-Byzantine style, and appear to be the product of a mason's yard where local carvers were employed under Western supervision. (Boase, 1967, 2-3). [Royston Cave has a deep frieze above a natural bedrock fault which practically encircles the Cave below which, are the carvings.]

The Church of the Holy Sepulchre, Jerusalem

Fig. 44a. Court of access on the south side.

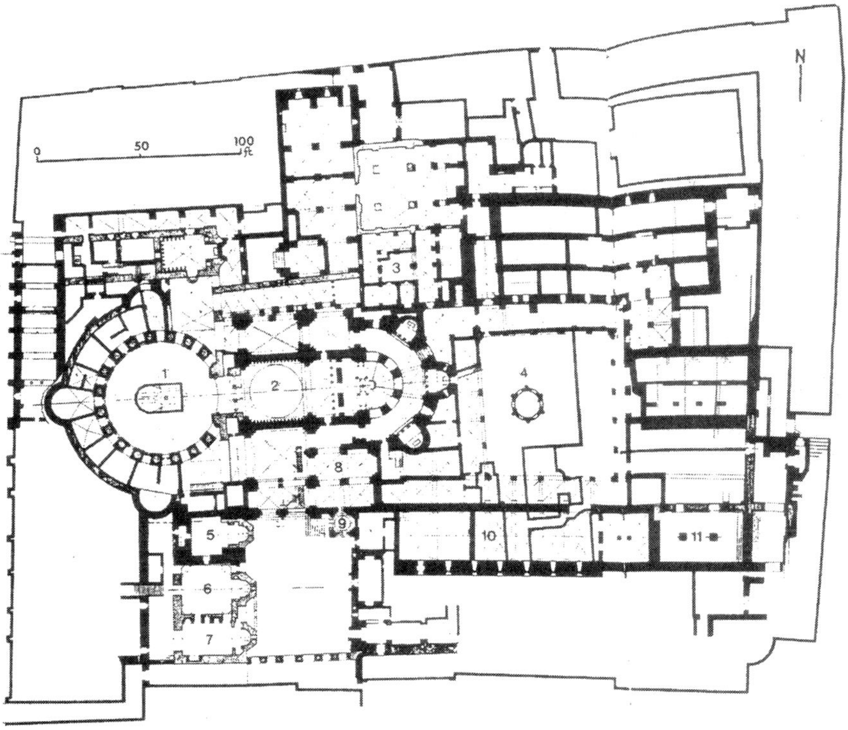

Fig. 44b. Plan of the church in the 12th century (after R.C. Smail, 1973, 129)

1 Christ's Sepulchre
2 Crusader Choir
3 Cloisters of the Cannons
4 Cloisters of the Cannons
5 Holy Trinity Chapel with belfry above
6 St. John's Baptistry
7 St. James' Chapel
8 Calvary Chapel
9 Calvary Porch
10 Refectory
11 Kitchen

Dome of the Rock, Jerusalem

The Temple area, called the 'Hram al-Sharif', is the platform where the original Temple stood, and on which stands the Dome of the Rock (Figs. 45a, b & c). This latter structure, rivalling in attraction with the Holy Sepulchre Church, was readily accepted and incorporated into Christian mysteries by crusaders, unlike the early Christians to whom the Temple compound had been a 'polluted' place from the other religious factions.

The Dome itself, visible from so many points of the city, one of the world's great masterpieces, was built by the Caliph Abd-al-Malik ibn-Marwan, between 685 and 691 AD. In conception it was a Byzantine building, a great dome set on an octagon, dazzlingly decorated with mosaics and Cufic inscriptions. Its floor plan consists of two sets of interlocking squares: the inner pair determines the circumference of the dome itself; the outer pair delimits the octagonal exterior of the building. (See Resistivity Report p. 27 Royston Cave floor was cut with two squares forming an octagon.) In the transformation from an Islamic shrine to a Christian church, masons carved steps into the rock itself, and had an altar raised atop its pitted surface. (Landay, 1972, 70, 95) The outer covering of Persian tiles replacing mosaic patterning was added to it by Sulaiman the Magnificent in 1561.

To the crusaders, whatever its architectural style, it was *Templum Domini,* and during their occupation span of eighty-eight years, it was served by a community of Augustinian canons. The Templars adopted it as their mother church. The sacred rock that it covered was associated with Abraham's sacrifice, Jacob's dream, and David's threshing floor, and in all probability was the actual site of the Temple altar.

About 1142 the structure had been re-dedicated as a Christian church. The naked rock, sacred to Jew, Christian and Moslem, was covered over with marble pavement, and surrounded with a great iron grille. The mosaics, some of them dating back to the original construction were fortunately preserved, as were many of the Arab inscriptions. To these splendid works, the crusaders added mosaic or painted representations of the events of scripture specially connected with the site, and placed Latin texts in great characters round the inside of the Dome.

In the Dome of the Rock there is a doorway, leading down to the cave beneath the rock, which exhibits or did, until comparatively recently, a tympanum with two curling acanthus sprays and a central branch ending in a cone. In the cave itself is a carved niche with acanthus whorls and linked columns which is similar to the design on the tomb of Baldwin V in the Holy Sepulchre, as evidenced by Elzear Horn's drawing of the 18th century. The tomb was destroyed, or at least dismembered, by the Greeks in 1809. On the child king's death, Guy de Lusignan seized the throne with aid from the master of the Temple, and it would have been fitting enough that the tomb should have been ordered from the Templar's own yard. (Boase, 1967, 19). Acanthus whorls can also be seen in Templar art work on the walls of Cressac Church, France. It also occurs in the decoration of the Metz church, France, that is if during restoration work it was religiously copied from the original design.

Fig. 45a.

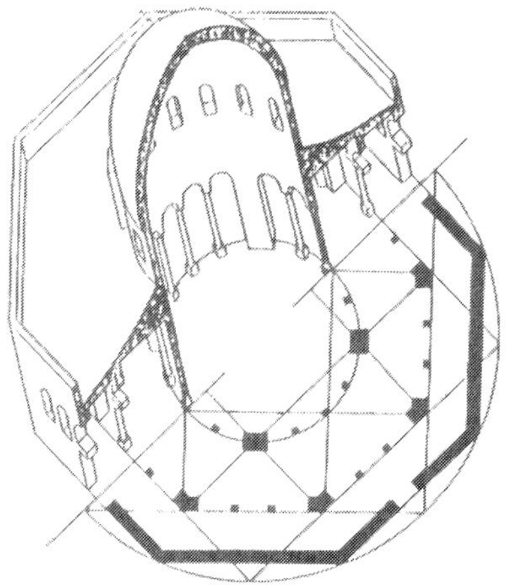

Figs. 45b & c.

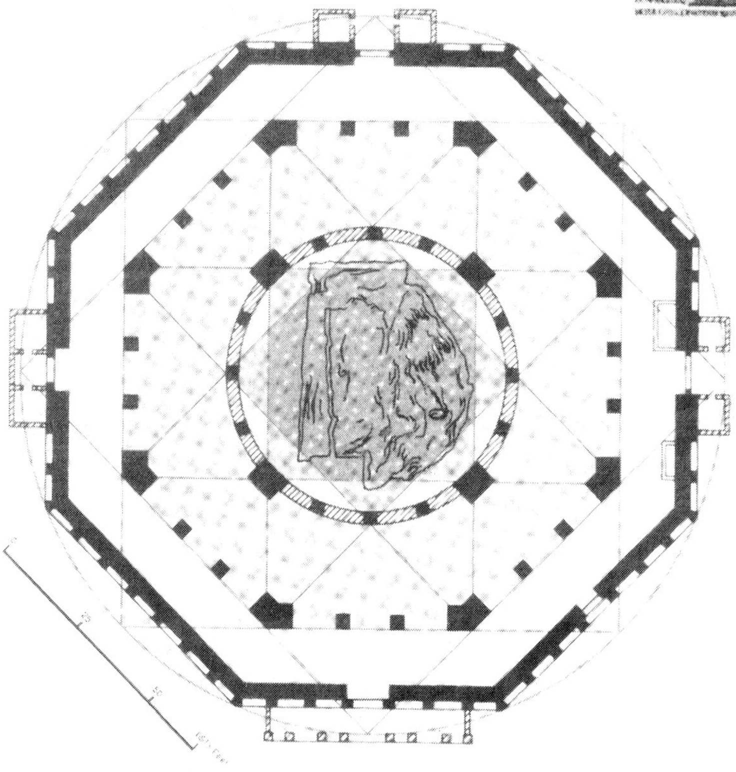

The intricate mathematical relationships on which the design of the Dome of the Rock is based, are both aesthetically intriguing and architecturally sound. The floor plan (left) consists of two sets of interlocking squares: the inner pair determines the circumference of the dome itself; the outer pair delimits the octagonal exterior of the building. The result is a soaring central cupola building (left top) encircled by two concentric ambulatories. (After Francis and Shaw, 1972, 70)

Dome of the Chain, Jerusalem

Throughout the platform in Jerusalem, small shrines were built with open arches and cupolas, modelled on the 8th century Dome of the Chain that the crusaders found there.

Al-Aksa Mosque, Jerusalem

At the south end of the enclosure stood the al-Aksa [al-Aqsa] Mosque, known as *Templum Solomonis.* There had been a mosque here since the early days of the Conquest: it was the place of general worship, whereas the Dome, despite its size and magnificence, was essentially a shrine. Constant rebuilding had taken place, however, and the crusaders found the mosque as a triple-aisled basilica with a dome over the crossing. They thought it to be originally the Palace of Solomon and therefore a fitting residence for their kings. It was shared initially; part served the kings of Jerusalem as a royal residence while the rest was converted into the headquarters and barracks for the Order of the Temple. Eventually, when the royal court moved to the Tower of David, it was handed over in its entirety to the brethren. It is interesting to note that they showed a certain tolerance in religious matters outside their own, and set aside an area for Muslim worship. The colonnaded area that adjoined al-Aksa on the west gave way to the Templar armoury and provision stores, and the vast substructure beneath the mosque dating back to Herodian times, which still survives today, became a vaulted stable that could easily accommodate four hundred horses. (Landay, 1972, 95; Riley-Smith, 1987, 55)

The Templars' design for the mosque's conversion into a church never seems to have been completed. Probably it was an adaptation of the existing building.

Atlit Castle Church, Atlit (South of Haifa, Israel)

Within the inner ward of the Templars' own Atlit Castle [Athlith] was a dodecagonal church [twelve angles and sides] with three radiating chapels and vaults supported on a central pillar, but only foundations now remain. The shape recalls the Temple at Jerusalem, the Dome of the Rock, and is a native example of the round church associated with Templar holdings in Europe.

JORDAN:

Church of Hebron (23 miles [36.8 km] SSW of Jerusalem)

The crusaders were, as befitted the impulse that had sent them forth, active church builders. Some of these churches were adaptations of earlier buildings. At the town of Hebron, formerly in Palestine, the massive enceinte with its huge masonry is a Herodian construction; the church was based on Byzantine foundations but altered to carry 12th century groined vaults. Hebron was in 1119 the scene of a striking incident. The Patriarchs, Abraham, Isaac, and Jacob, were known to have been buried in vaults under the mosque that had now been occupied and was being rebuilt by Augustinian canons. Beneath two small, probably Umaiyad cupolas, two eyeholes (one of which is still open) looked down into indeterminate caverns. To the Latins the relics of the patriarchs were inviting 'finds' or trove. Researches were undertaken and eventually, after various disappointments, a well-built tomb chamber was opened containing bones which were acclaimed as those sought for.

Some seventeen years later an account was drawn up based on the narrative of participants. It is one of the earliest reports of an excavation. The caves had long been closed: the mosque itself still somewhat difficult of access and no unbeliever was allowed explore its lower regions.

In 1917, when the English occupied the town, an officer, investigating the enclosure, penetrated into a subterranean chamber which held what seems to have been some form of tomb slab, but he had no knowledge of the archaeological interest of the place where he found himself, nor did the circumstances of the moment permit closer examination, which is a pity. (Boase, 1967, 63, 86, 88)

ITALY

The stimulus given by pilgrims' accounts of the Holy Places led to the construction of models of them in the West. As pointed out above the chief shrine of all was the tomb of Christ in the Rotunda of the Church of the Holy Sepulchre. The oldest copy of this, though frequently restored, is probably that in the Church of San Stefano at Bologna. By tradition this group of buildings, which formed a 'New Jerusalem' including the main sites of the Passion, was founded by S. Petronio in the 5th century. Destroyed by the Huns in 903 it was rebuilt by Abbot Landulf in 1180. A contemporary chronicle states that the abbot devoted special care to the reproduction of the Lord's Sepulchre, setting out the work himself with a measuring reed, for he had passed many days in Judaea collecting all the vestiges of Christian antiquity. The church itself is dodecagon; the tomb chamber has an altar on the top approached by two staircases. It has been largely restored but may represent an early pre-crusading work.

FRANCE

In France the church of Neuvy-Saint-Sepulchre was founded in 1045 (although the existing work is probably 12th century) *ad formam Sancti Sepulcri Ierosolimitani;* it is a rotunda with side tribunes but the central shrine has gone. By 1079 it was paying tithe to the Church of the Sepulchre in Jerusalem.

The round church of St. Benigne at Dijon, built by William of Volpiano in 1001, may have been another imitation, as also the rotunda at Charroux in Poitou, consecrated in 1095, of which only the central piers and the lantern, standing unbuttressed and magnificent, still remain.

GERMANY

Eugene Voltz, a French architect and conservator, wrote a most illuminating article in *Archeologia* (1972), entitled *La Chapelle des Templiers de Metz.* He outlined the history by explaining that 16th century chronicles record that the Knights Templar were first established at Metz, Lorraine, France [formerly Germany] in 1123 by Philippe de Vigneulles under the Episcopate (1120-1162) of Etienne de Bar in the reigns of King Louis le Gros (+1137) and the Emperor Henry V (+1125). According to one critic, he thinks the foundation date of 1123 could be somewhat premature and cites an abbey charter of Sainte-Glossinde, noted by the learned

Benedictine historians of Metz, together with later historians that this did not come about until 1133 under a title of 'Poor Knights of Christ'.

The oldest recorded date with certainty is 1147 when two brothers, Gerard and Guerin de Bosanville, departed for the second crusade and were taken on from Metz by St. Bernard himself. From the number of its establishments, it is evident the Order was already well settled in Lorraine. Within the diocese of Metz alone, Cattenom, Gelucourt, Pierrevillers and Richemont are mentioned as holdings of the Order. For reasons of Templar territorial organisation, the commandery [usually called preceptory in Britain] at Metz held jurisdiction over the establishments of Trois-Eveches, of Lorraine, and the Duchy of Bar.

It is curious to find at Metz they attracted certain masons who joined the Templars towards the end of the 13th century to help with building work. There was a certain Jennas Clowanges, a mason, known to have joined in 1285. There is an inscription on a tombstone, considered to be genuine, discovered in 1861 in the chapel which commemorated a certain brother chaplain who was Master of the Masons of the Temple and died 1287:

...FREIRES CHAPELENS KI FUT MAISTRES DES MAZONS DOU TANPLE...

In 1312, the Vienne Council for Churches decided to suppress the Order. Although some Templars were being burnt at the stake in France at that time, unique action was taken by the Inquisitor of Trois-Evenches who upheld, at the provincial Council of Mayence, that the knights were beyond suspicion. The Order disappeared from Germany, and doubtless from Metz too, towards 1319. Part of their establishment went to the Teutonic Knights, another part went to St. John of Jerusalem or Rhodes.

After Metz was joined to France, in 1556 further construction work took place in the citadel, and the Hospitallers who had lost their quarters, moved into the Templar accommodation. Later, the former commandery of the Templars plus a nearby hostel and chapel became a storage for gunpowder. In 1859 after the construction of a new artillery magazine, the chapel became classed as an historic monument and escaped demolition with the adjacent buildings (Figs 46a & b).

The chapel oratory is orientated towards the East, although there is quite a deviation of the axis. The plan is that of a massive octagon, almost perfect in dimensions, measuring internally 8.40 m N-S, and 8 m E-W direction. Within the very thickness of the wall the interior arched faces have been cut except, near the entrance to the chancel, to form a rotunda. At the end of the chancel is the sacristy. It must not be forgotten the usage made by the Templars of the central area for 'circumambulation', a feature of medieval church activity, and other rituals. The oratory the Templars built at Laon in 1140 is without doubt the prototype plan of Metz.

Heavy restoration work of the interior took place in 1863 and it is not possible to know whether the original decoration was meticulously followed. Nevertheless, since little known Templar artwork survives it could be useful to record what does remain.

The Chapel at Metz, France (formerly Germany)

Fig. 46a. Portion of a line drawing of Metz Chapel, 1849, after de Migette (Archeologia, 56, 1973); Sixteenth century chronicles record that the Knights Templar were first established at Metz, Lorraine, France in 1123. The plan of the Round Church is based on a massive octagon.

Fig. 46b. Plan after Charles Czarnowski.

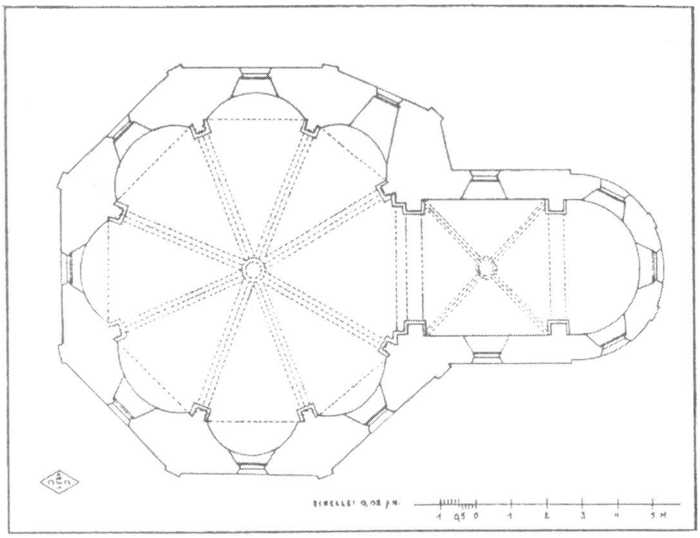

Quite a lot of the original wall paintings are deteriorating. Above the right hand side lintel of the main entrance, close to the arcading, are the remaining fragments of the original cross of the Templars.

Under the restoration, leaded windows were reconstructed to enhance the chancel which had a lot of mosaic on the walls together with medallions, in the 13th century tradition, that represent episodes from the life of Christ and seem to show activities of the knights. But most attention should be given to the mural pictures of the 14th century, of which interesting fragments, partly faded [changed] and partly effaced have been conserved inside a little niche in the meridional side of the rotunda. The Virgin is sitting within a trilobed arch surmounted by pierced fretwork of quatrefoils wearing a crown with a veil, encircling a young face, falling in elegant folds over her shoulder. Her left hand is holding an upright crucifix quite close to her face while the index finger of her right hand, held at breast height, is pointing at the Saviour on the cross. A smaller figure, kneeling in devotion, can be seen in the left hand corner of this panel, wearing a white robe with a cross on the left shoulder, and clasping his hands together in an imploring attitude.

Noted not far away is another crowned person seated, accompanied by a standing female figure, and to the right of the group, there are three forms apparently like wheels which give an impression of the martyrdom of St. Katherine. On the tympan, at the back of the niche, again to the left, is a 'saint' [unknown] wearing a mitre holding a cross in front of him with a trilobitic arch around him. Amongst other decoration is a roundel portraying the lamb carrying the cross, a Templar symbol - see also the seal found at Denny Abbey, Cambridgeshire Fig. 57c.

SPAIN

At Segovia, the church of La Vera Cruz is a dodecagon building with a single aisle; within the central row of pillars is a model of the Sepulchre, a two storied building with steps going up to it as at Bologna. This was a Templars' chapel, built in 1208, and certainly intended as a model of the Jerusalem church. It is interesting as an example of a polygonal not circular copy, which from the tomb chamber in its midst must represent the Rotunda, not the Templars' mother church, the octagonal *Templum Domini* or Dome of the Rock.

ENGLAND

As far as it is known in all the English examples, the 'round' formed the nave of the church to which a small chancel was attached at the East end. Four of these churches survive in London, Cambridge, Northampton and Little Maplestead.

Temple Church, London

The most interesting portion of the Temple Church, called by earlier writers simply 'the Round,' was consecrated in AD 1185, by Heraclius, patriarch of Jerusalem who was accompanied by the Grand Master of the Temple on his arrival in England to obtain aid from Henry II against the power of the famous Saladin. It was dedicated to the Virgin Mary. The oblong portion was consecrated on Ascension Day, 1240, in the presence of the king and much of the nobility of the kingdom. As there was a considerable lapse in time between the erection of the two portions, there was consequently a great variation in style (Figs. 47a, b & c). This church was burnt out by German incendiary bombs on the night of 10th May, 1941 but was restored and rededicated on 7th November, 1958.

At a period, earlier than that to which the building of this church can be assigned, the Templars had a place of religious worship in Holborn, near Southampton Buildings, the remains of which were uncovered in 1875 (Fig. 47d). The historian John Stow, 1598, tells us:

> "...This temple was left and fel to ruine since the year 1184 when the Templars had builded them a new Temple in Fleet street, neere to the river of Thames..."

Part of the first Temple Church [their first church in Britain] was discovered on pulling down some old houses in 1595, when it was found to have been built of Caen stone, and in a circular form. From the same chronicler we learn that the 'new Temple', was often made a 'storehouse for men's treasure.' (*Saturday Magazine,* 1842, No. 654, St. John Hope, 1908, 178)

With reference to the interments in the Temple Church two ancient manuscripts, written by the Monks of Walden Abbey, maintain that Geoffrey de Mandeville, Earl of Essex being slain by an arrow in 1144 was taken by the Knights Templar to the Old Temple and was afterwards removed to the New Temple and buried *in porticu* before the western door of the church.

Fig. 47a. The 'New Temple', London. Line drawing from 'Saturday Magazine', August 27th 1842.

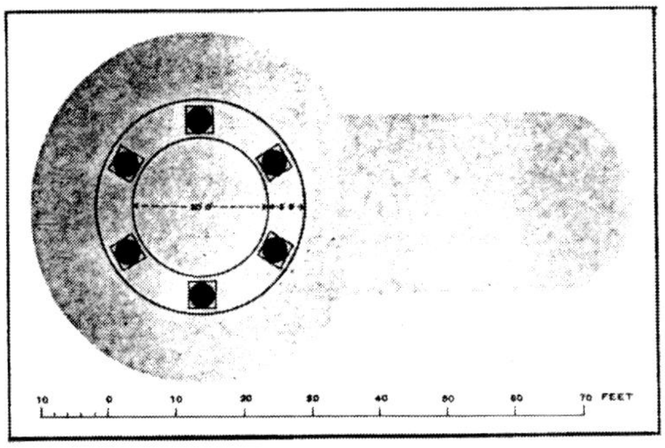

Fig. 47b. Plan: Remains of the church of the Old Temple in London, uncovered in 1875. (After St. John Hope, 1918)

Matthew Paris records that William Marescal [Marshall], the elder, Earl of Pembroke and Royal Protector, dying in 1219 was entombed in the middle of the Church of the New Temple and near to him William and Gilbert Mareschal two of his sons, successive Earls of Pembroke. Burton, the antiquarian and member of the Inner Temple 1622 in his *History of Leicestershire* (p. 222) tells us that in his time:

> 'There was in the round walk at the west end of the church, where many of the said Order lay buried, their portraits being cut in stone, some of them cross-legged, and who were of the chief est houses of the nobility as Vere, Earl of Oxford; Mandeville, Earl of Essex; Marshall, Earl of Pembroke; Bohun, Earl of Hereford and Lord Ross'.

Richardson comments that this passage including Vere, Earl of Oxford and Bohun, Earl of Hereford is repeated word for word in Nichols, *Leicestershire* vol. III p. 945, except he adds William son of King Henry III to the number. However, there is some doubt whether all are accurately named or that they were indeed Templars with the exception of the Marshall family. (Richardson, 1843, 10)

Interestingly enough, these cross-legged effigies do appear to have been placed in the Temple Church, to the memory of a class of men termed 'Associates of the Temple' or 'Confrères'. As explained in Chapter 4, though not actually admitted to the Holy vows and habit of the Order, they were received into a section who had spiritual connection with the Templars which can illustrate the superstition and credulity of the times.

Many piously-inclined persons of rank and fortune, brought up amid the congenial pleasures and the luxuries of the world, were anxious to participate in the spiritual advantages and blessings believed to be enjoyed by the holy warriors of the Temple in respect of 'good works' done by the fraternity: but they could not bring themselves to submit to the severe discipline and gloomy life of the regularly professed brethren (Addison, 1852, 310). For the purpose of turning these expectations and sensitivity of such persons to a good account, which no doubt society today would call exploitation, the Master and Chapter of the Temple assumed the power of admitting them into spiritual association and connection with the Order so that, without renouncing their pleasures or having to give up their everyday way of life, they might share in the merit of the 'good works' performed by the Templars!

The Temple Church, London

Fig. 47c. Line drawing of the interior of the circular portion of the church, prior to it being bombed in WWII, and subsequent restoration. (Illustration taken from 'Saturday Magazine', No. 654, September 10th 1842)

Fig. 47d. (below) Plan after Walter H. Godfrey. (Undated - pre 1972)

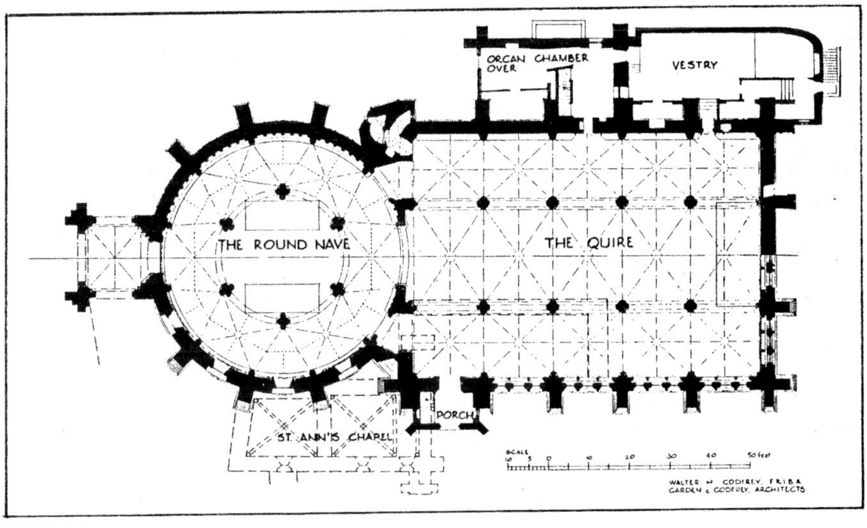

It is presumed that the Monumental Effigies, by attitudes in many instances, were used to some extent in lieu of inscriptions. Thus the crossing of the legs, implied a vow taken by a crusader, yet it does not necessarily mean an actual pilgrimage had been made - some straight-limbed effigies were of *bona fide* crusaders. To continue, the hands in prayer, indicate that he died a natural death, and an earnest Christian too. The drawing of the sword that he died in action; sheathing it, that he died after vanquishing his enemies. The lion at the feet indicated valour: the dragon, sin.

The cross-legged effigy of Geoffrey de Mandeville is of Sussex marble and represents him in ring mail. The hauberk and surcoat descend below the knee. This is believed to be the only example of a monumental effigy with a tall cylindrical flat-topped helmet over a hood of mail. The shield is curious and Gough describes it as the earliest example known of sculptured armorial bearings on a monumental effigy in England. The *Chronicle of Walden* states that on his promotion he augmented his family distinction by adding to his shield an escarbuncle which is a charge consisting of eight rays, four of them making a common cross and the other four a saltire. This charge is on the shield and is represented raised on a diapered field, with three plain spaces left, somewhat resembling a fess dancette. (Richardson, op. cit.)

[Both authors, Addison and Richardson, mention Lady Roisia, wife of Geoffrey de Mandeville who constructed for herself a cell, and refer to Stukeley.]

After the demise of the Templar Order, the last Master of the Temple of London was imprisoned and later died in the Tower of London.

Holy Sepulchre Church, Cambridge

Referring to the round church in Cambridge (Figs. 48a & b), there have always been links between this Templar church and the St. John hospital (Hospitallers) which stood where St. John's College now stands. Both these sects were usually close together. It is thought that initially the Holy Sepulchre Church was probably a wayside oratory for the offering of prayer for those connected with the crusades.

Fig. 48a. Some controversy does surround this church inasmuch that some individuals believe it never had any connection with the Order of the Templars.
But it must be remembered that Templar records for this county are sporadic.
Line drawing by Alfred George, c.1985.

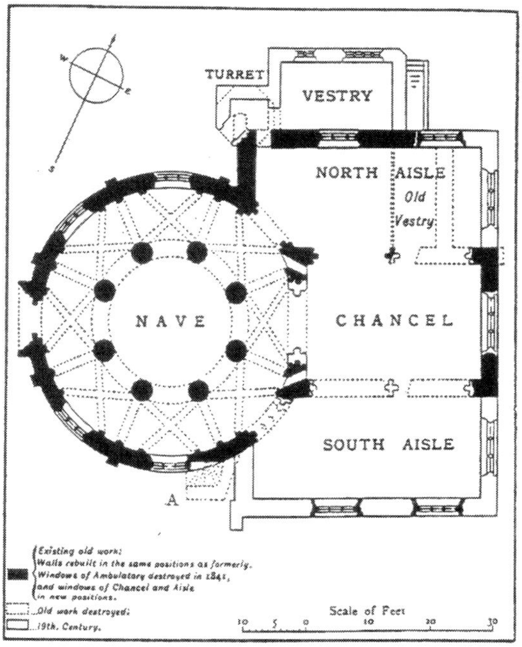

Fig. 48b. Plan of the Holy Sepulchre Church (Round Church), Cambridge.

'A' – Position of the stairway to the gallery in the Round Church which was destroyed in the restoration of 1841.

The exterior was also much altered..

Although the records relating to the time of the erection of this building have all been lost, the peculiarities of style are sufficient to establish satisfactory evidence as to its date. It is asserted that the present round church was built in the reign of Henry I, or between the first and second crusades, and may therefore be considered the oldest church of this form in England. There exists in the chronicles of Ramsey Abbey (20 miles [32 km] north west of Cambridge) a charter in which Reinald, the abbot (1114-1130) grants to Randolf with the Beard of Cambridge, to Robert, to Auger and others of the 'Fraternity of the Holy Sepulchre', the churchyard of St. George and the neighbouring land for the construction of a church there in honour of God and of the Holy Sepulchre, which was to be subject to Ramsey abbey.

Church of the Holy Sepulchre, Northampton

Like the other 'round churches' of the 12th century, this church owed its origin to the crusades too. Simon de Senlis, the first of the Norman Earls of Northampton, was a member of the powerful Bouteiller family of Senlis, Grand Butlers of France. Earl Simon took part in the first Crusade but returned to Europe before the capture of the Holy City. The church in Northampton, founded c. 1100, is a reproduction, on a somewhat smaller scale, of the Church of the Holy Sepulchre, Jerusalem and was evidently intended by its builder as a thanks-offering for his safe return (Figs. 49a, b & c). It must have been well advanced, if not completed, when Earl Simon granted it to the Monastery of St. Andrew, a house of Cluniac Monks then recently founded by him in Northampton. Early in the next century he made a second journey to Jerusalem, but died on his way back c. 1115 and was buried in the Priory of La-Charité in France.

It is suggested that crusaders used this church, before and after their travels, particularly as two of the Crusades started from Northampton. The same may be said of Richard Coeur de Lion. He kept his Easter in Northampton immediately after his return from captivity; scarcely would he omit to visit the 'Round Church' which would so well recall to him the shrine for whose recovery he had suffered. It is further suggested that the new aisle, with an altar dedicated to St. John the Baptist and Thomas à Becket which was added about the time of his visit, may have been built as the result of a royal donation. (Sergeantson, Revd. R. M., revised by Tibbs, Revd. H. A., (undated, before 1971) *A Short History of the Church of the Holy Sepulchre, Northampton,* The Church Publishers, Ramsgate)

Fig. 49a. (right) Church of the Holy Sepulchre, Northampton, from an early 19C. engraving.

Fig. 49b. (below) Probable form of the original church (not to scale). (After Sergeantson)

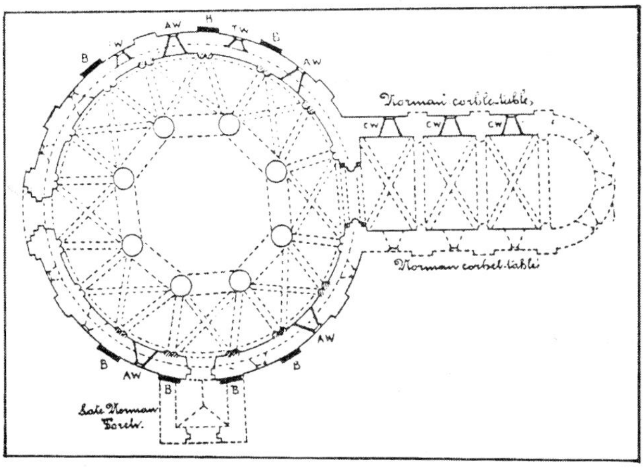

Fig. 49c. Line drawing of the interior of the Holy Sepulchtre Church, Northampton from 'Saturday Magazine' No. 656 September 24th 1842.

St. John the Baptist Church, Clerkenwell, London (Hospitaller)

Although the Hospitallers were founded in 1099, their first English house was not founded until c. 1140 in Clerkenwell when the apsidal quire of its church, with an underlying crypt, was begun. Gradually a large circular nave was built, presumed to have been supported by a ring of pillars, and remains of this nave were discovered in 1900 by H. W. Fincham. Later the eastern limb was greatly enlarged on a different plan. In 1185 the completed church was hallowed by Heraclius, the Patriarch. (St. John Hope, 1918, 65) (See also p. 82)

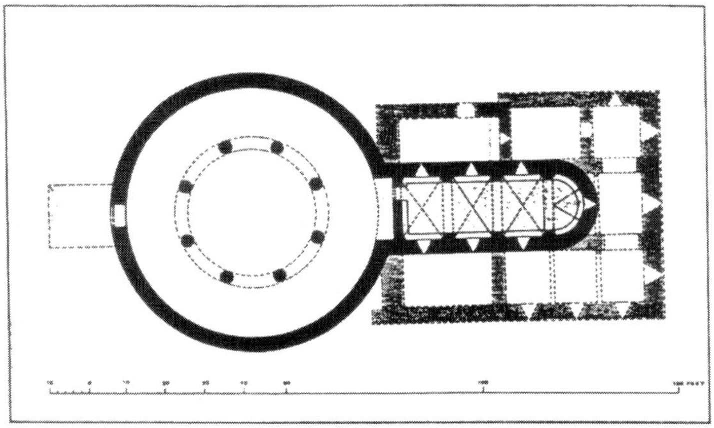

Fig. 50. Priory church of St. John, Clerkenwell. Crypt plan showing apsidal quire and round nave. The later extension of the presbytery and quire are shown in dotted lines. (After St. John Hope, 1918)

St. John The Baptist Church, Little Maplestead, Essex (Hospitaller)

Little is known about the first Church, at Little Maplestead, Essex believed to have been built by the Hospitallers c. 1186. The church, dedicated to St. John the Baptist, was probably of circular plan copied from that of the mother house in Clerkenwell. At the same time suitable domestic buildings would have been erected, adjoining the church to include a chapter house, refectory, dormitory and various subsidiary structures grouped around a courtyard. Not a trace of the Knights' first church nor the domestic buildings remain, and even their site is uncertain.

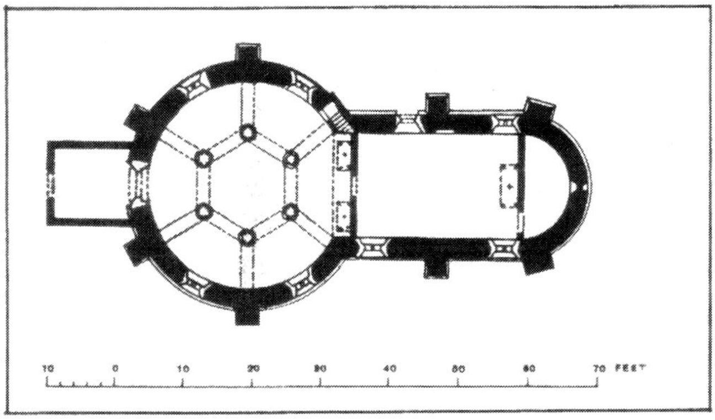

Fig. 51a. Plan before the drastic restoration in 1852 of the Hospitallers' church at Little Maplestead, Essex. (After St. John Hope, 1918)

From the point of view of church history and architecture the extant Little Maplestead Church is of great importance because it is the latest in date of the four remaining round churches still standing in England (Figs. 51a, b & c). It was built c. 1335 taking the place of an earlier structure. It consists of a spacious aisleless chancel terminating in a semicircular eastern apse - the only 14th century example of this type now existing in England - a six-sided 'nave' [not eight] surmounted by a low belfry and surrounded by a circular aisle, a modern west porch and a south vestry.

Why the circular plan as late as the 14th century was adopted is still a matter of speculation but it is suggested that the plan may have been influenced by the earlier round church. (Dickinson, P. G. M. (1967) *The Church of St. Giles, Great Maplestead and The Round Church, Little Maplestead,* Anglia Echo Newspapers Ltd., Haverhill, Suffolk)

Fig. 51b. (left) Earlier line drawing of Little Maplestead Church, Essex before restoration. From 'Saturday Magazine' No. 659 October 8th, 1842.

Fig. 51c. (right) This illustration from a postcard on sale in the church in the 1980s depicting it as it is in the 20th century.

The Templar Church at Temple Bruer, Lincolnshire

The remains of the Templar church and the conventual buildings have been effectively hidden by farm buildings. The foundations of the circular church, just over 50 feet [15 m] in diameter, were uncovered in 1908 between the tower and the line of three low buildings which stand along the farm road at the far side of the field in the foreground Figs. 52a, b & c). The purpose of the tower is not known for certain except the 'ground floor' may have been a private chapel and chapter house as evidenced by rows of sedilia [stone seats] and the piscina [stone basin with an outlet used in the Mass]. (See also pp. 125 & 169-71)

A controversial excavation plan, from an earlier excavation by the Rev. G. Oliver during 1833-4 (Fig. 52d), still exists in the Ross Manuscripts held at the Lincolnshire County Council Central Reference Library. He published it in a paper entitled *Temple Bruer and its Knights* in *Lincolnshire Topographical Society Transactions* 1843, but W. H. St. John Hope, in his article on *The Round Church of the Knights Templars at Temple Bruer, Lincolnshire,* debunked quite a proportion of both the former's writings as well as the excavation plan itself. In particular, he related to the non existence of a "narrow subterranean passage" coated with "plaister" beneath the tower, a walled-up skeleton in a small chamber, and other vaults and arched passages beneath the church. The latter had supposedly contained burnt skeletons and other weird finds which Oliver conjectured was connected, in some measure, with Templar initiation. St. John Hope comments:

> "As Dr. Oliver does not describe his dreadful chamber [the one with the immured skeleton] but merely says one was found, he was probably putting on record something that had been told him, which his horror of the Templars and all their works caused him to imagine a reality." (St. John Hope, W. H., *Archeologia,* vol. LXI, Society of Antiquaries of London, 1908, 177-198)

Fig. 52a. North view of Temple Bruer drawn by Samuel Buck, 1726.
This is the only illustration of the round nave to survive.

Fig. 52b. Temple Bruer, Lincolnshire. Drawing of the surviving one of two towers from the north by Thomas Hearne (1744-1817). The original is held in the Usher Gallery, Lincoln.

William de la More, Preceptor of Temple Bruer and the Prior of all England, together with his knights were arrested in 1308 and imprisoned initially in Claxlede Gate and elsewhere in Lincoln. In November 1309 they were tried in the Chapter house of the Cathedral for blasphemy, infanticide, cruelty and debauchery. Although they escaped with their lives, as elsewhere in this country, they were stripped of their estates by the Crown. (*The Heath Trail, North Kesteven,* c. 1990). It was probably such information that fuelled Oliver's conjectures.

St. Katherine's Church (formerly Church of the Holy Cross), Bristol

In 1145 the Templars were given some land, then in the manor of Bedminster by Robert, Earl of Gloucester, for the building of a small church and dwellings. An archaeological survey carried out in 1966 resulted in the discovery of these foundations within the ruins of the present church. Their market, the 'Stallenge' was held in Temple Street, marked on old maps by the Stallenge Cross. The construction of this Templar round church showed interesting similarities with the Temple Church in London. The dimensions are also the same, (within a few inches) as the North porch of St. Mary Redcliffe, which is the oldest part of that church and of eastern design, not in keeping with the rest of the church. The significance of this, if any, has yet to be determined. (Extracted information by P. Marshall pers. comm. from *Bristol Past Revisited with Sperry Local History Group* published 1981)

Fig. 52c. Temple Bruer, Lincolnshire. The published plans from Sir William H. St. John Hope's excavation of 1907. (Society of Antiquaries of London, vol. LXI, pl. XX, 1908)

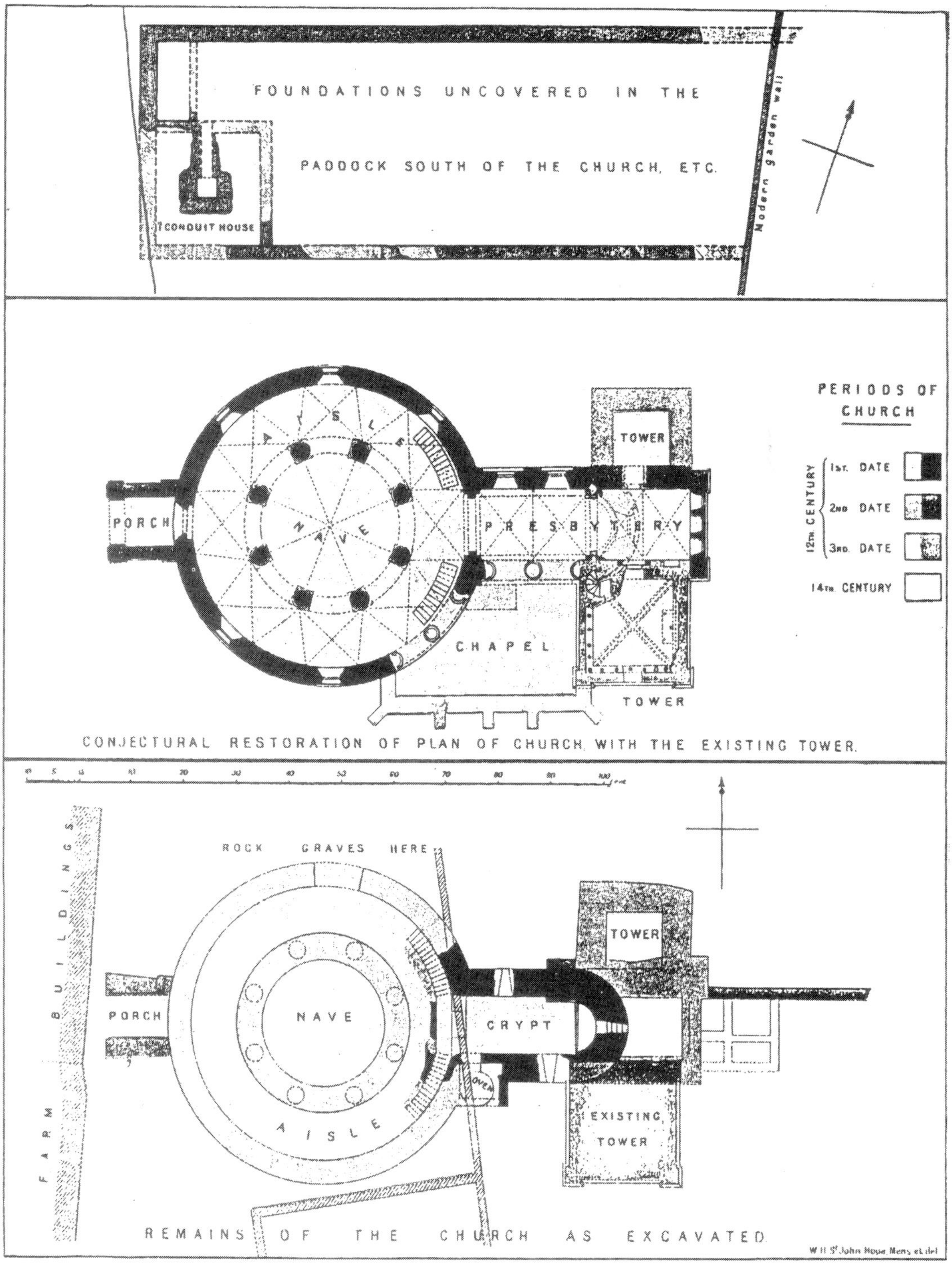

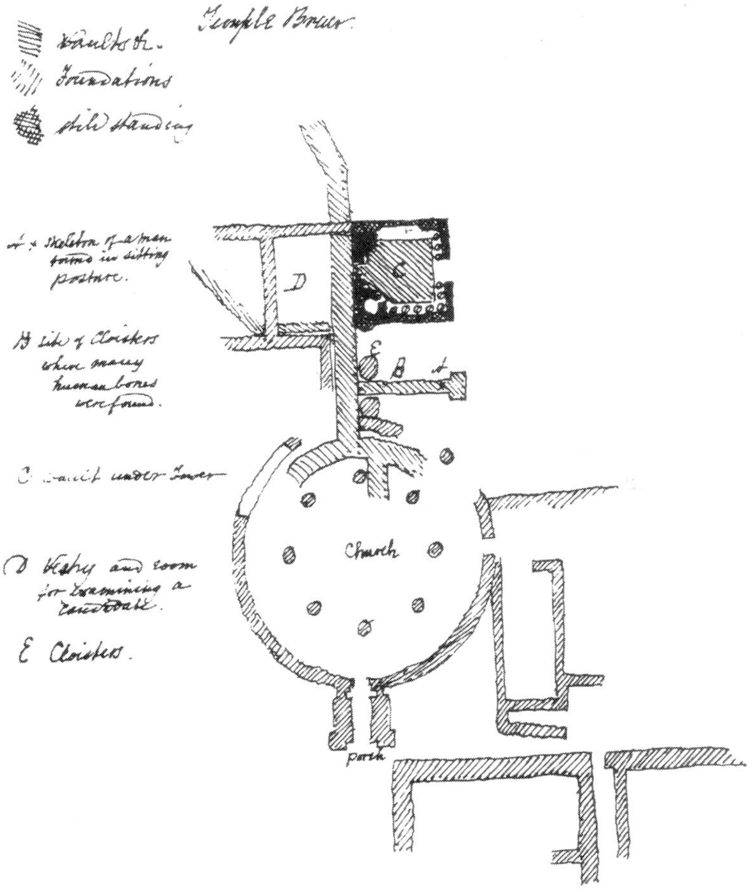

Fig. 52d.
Temple Bruer
Rev. G. Oliver's original excavation plan c. 1833 which has since been under dispute.

St. Michael's Church, Garway, Hereford & Worcester

Lands including the site of an earlier church were given to the Templars during the reign of Henry II, possibly about 1165-80, the gift being confirmed in 1199. Jacques de Molay, when Grand Master of England, visited their commandery in 1294. At the dissolution of the Order the preceptory and Templar church, with a round nave and square chancel, passed to the Hospitallers. An excavation in 1927 resulted in finding the foundations of the round portion of the Church. Some decoration attributed to the Templars c. 1210 remains in the chapel, south of the chancel, incorporated in the present church. The corbels outside the East window are carved on the right with the head of a Grand Master of the Order wearing the mitre, and on the left with a dead man's face (sic). The 14th century piscina is ornamented with fish and a curious winged cup, believed to be probably in reference to the Holy Grail (Fig. 53), while the inside of the doorway is grotesquely adorned with the carving of a foot and leg on one side and on the other two fish tied together by the tails. (Church leaflets by Kathleen A. Whittaker, BA; Joan Fleming-Yates, both undated c. 1989)

Fig. 53. St. Michael's Church, Garway. Ornamentation with the fish and a winged cup, probably relating to the Holy Grail. Photo Olive Davis, 1989

DISCUSSION

In South Italy at Brindisi the Romanesque church of S. Giovanni al Sepolcro, also known as 'dei Templari and dei Cavalieri Gerosolimitani', is a circular church with a projecting apse. If 1045 can be taken as the foundation date for the Neuvy-Saint-Sepulchre, French example, it appears that a custom, which preceded the crusades, gained momentum with their preaching and expeditions. Under the patronage of the military orders several such chapels were built in the 12th century, the period in which they were most numerous. Later examples are on a simpler scale. A surviving reference to the chapel 'made to the lykness of the sepulkyr of owre Lorde at Jerusalem' which William Wey set up at the Priory Church of Edington in Wiltshire has disappeared, and it is unlikely that it was a main architectural feature of the church Certainly the Chapel of Calvary, the Church of Bethlehem, and the Mount of Olives, to which his Will refers, were models constructed in wood. (Boase, 1967, 110)

In France the Templar chapel at Laon is octagonal whilst the Paris Temple church is circular. In England there were Templar round churches, at Cambridge, Dover, Bristol, Garway, Temple Bruer, the Old and New Temple churches in London, and elsewhere. There were also those built by the Hospitallers and private individuals. The circular shape rather than the polygon seems to have been favoured by the English. In no English instance does a copy of the tomb chamber still exist. (Unless it can be proved that the Royston Cave was indeed 'a copy'.)

What has been shown in this chapter is that the military Order of the Temple were church builders, adapters of church buildings and not averse to making copies of the Holy Sepulchre Church. They were used to, and surrounded by, decorative paintings in these edifices, and indeed were certainly very familiar with underground sites.

9. LOCAL TEMPLAR / HOSPITALLER HISTORY

Although Hospitaller history is mentioned, the main emphasis has been placed on that of the Templars and their property. With the exception of Baldock, which has even named one of its schools after the Knights Templar, very few people today are aware of the extent this Order played in the general society of the Middle ages, and the amount of land they accrued locally. It will be becoming obvious to the reader that the same names keep recurring in the text, from those buried or recorded in the Temple Church in London and those who owned land in Hertfordshire and the surrounding counties:

HERTFORDSHIRE

Weston - Broadwater Hundred

Weston, a Hertfordshire village, in close proximity to Baldock, about four miles [6.4 km] east of Hitchin, was one of a group of manors, of which Hitchin was the *caput* [head or top one], held by Earl Harold before the Conquest, and by the king in 1086 (Fig. 54a). The *baillia* [outer enclosures] seems to have included the Templars' lands in the two counties of Hertfordshire and Bedfordshire, on the great fees [property] of the earl of Pembroke, of Bernard de Balliol, and of Simon de Wahull, the chief donors in this district, with smaller donations on the fees of less prominent landholders. The arrangement of these entries in the Templars' *Inquest,* at first sight seems confused and disorderly, but becomes intelligible once it is realised that the actual units of the fiscal organisation were the large manorial properties, from which the grants were made: donations by Gilbert, earl of Pembroke, in Weston and Baldock, with a *Summa* [abstract] for Weston, Buckland and Reed; the Balliol donation in Preston, with a *Summa;* and the Wahull donations in Langford and Sharnbrook, in Bedfordshire, with a *Summa* for Langford. A collection of small gifts in both counties from various benefactors, has a *Summa* of six marks: the Bedfordshire vill of Millbrook, with its mill, has a separate *Summa,* and a *Summe* of churches and mills end the section. The rents for Baldock and Sharnbrook are not summarised, and there is no *Summa summarum* for the two counties at the close of the fifteen pages, or seven and a half folios, of the manuscript which are devoted to the record of the rents and services due to the Templars from their tenants in Hertfordshire and Bedfordshire.

The Weston donation of Gilbert de Clare, earl of Pembroke, must have been made between 1138, when the earldom was created by King Stephen, and 1148, the year of Gilbert's death. It was sufficiently important for the earl to style himself, 'Comes Gilbertus de Westone', in his charter confirming the liberties of Weston church. The whole gift comprised of four carucates [a carucate - as much land as an ox could plough in a season] at Weston with the advowson [the right of presentation to church benefice (living)] of the churches of Weston and Baldock, and about 150 acres in the vill of Baldock, some two miles north of Weston. It also included the mill of Radwell in Bedfordshire (*sic*)*, a mile [1.6 km] to the north again. Altogether, property which in 1185, yielded a yearly income of over £20.0.0.

*Note: *In 1937, H. C. Andrews, the Hitchin historian wrote to Miss B. A. Lees explaining that, throughout her work, she had wrongly identified this Radwell (Hertfordshire) with Radwell near Felmersham over 5 miles north-west of Bedford in Bedfordshire. She gratefully acknowledged his correction and all later copies of the book were to be corrected.*

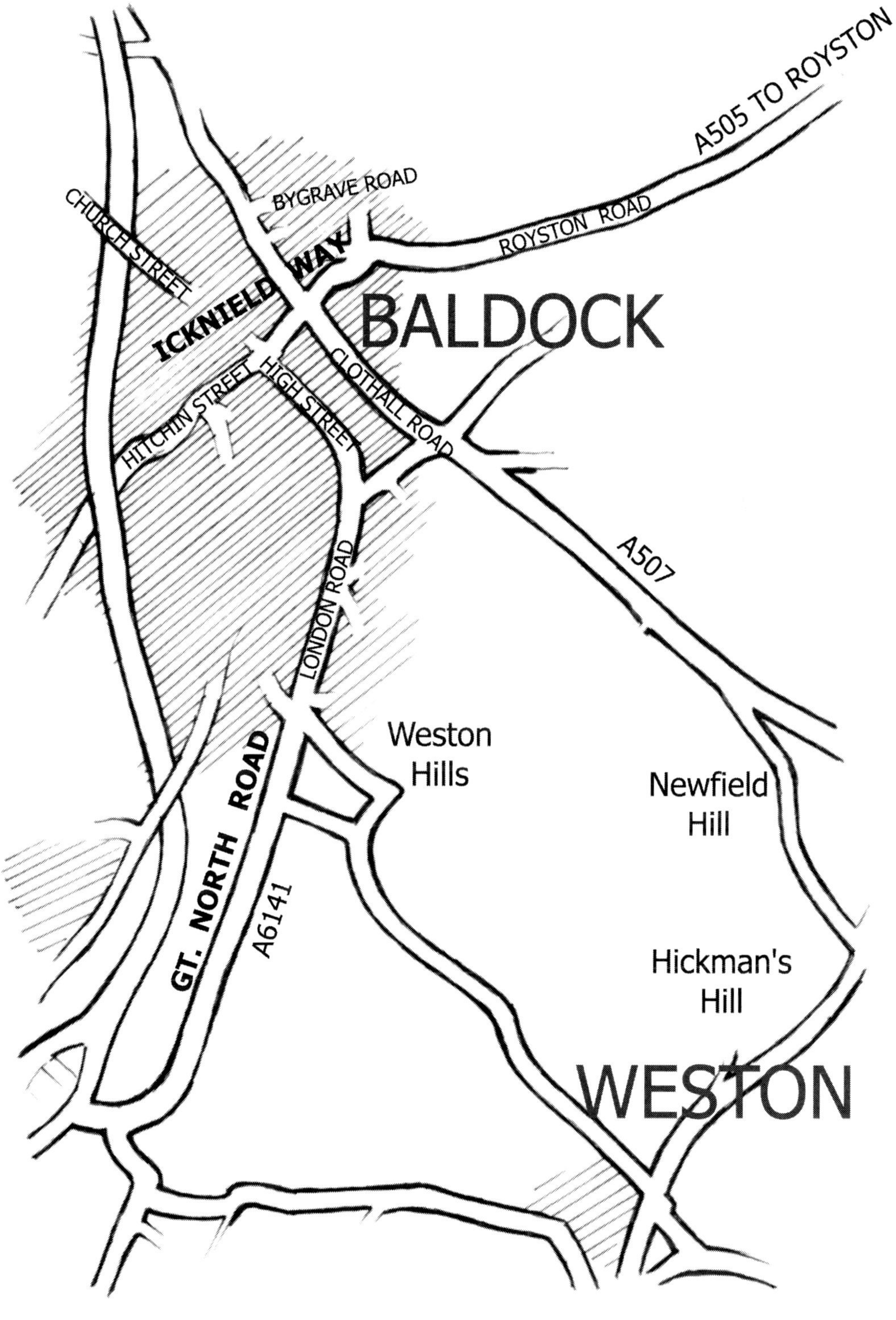

Fig. 54a. Area of Baldock, Herts. sketch by Yuri Leitch

In the early 13th century, when William Marshal, earl of Pembroke (Fig. 54b) (who had married Isabel de Clare, daughter of Richard Strongbow, earl of Pembroke, and the granddaughter and heiress of the original donor), confirmed the first earl's gift, he included in it: The church of Weston, with its pertinencie in wood and plain [area of woodland and meadow belonging to it], and (as confirmed by Earl Gilbert's charter), ten librates of land [librate is an amount of land worth £1 - the area of which depended on the value of the pound and on the soil quality of land] in Weston manor. It was on this land which the Templars had built the 'borough' (burgum) called 'Baudac' [Baldock] the site of the Templars' special buildings; the wood called Langenache, and the mill and miller of Radewelleshevedt [Radwell]. These details were summarised later by the 15th century Hospitaller John Stillingeflete, who had probably seen the Marshal's charter, which was transcribed in the Hospitallers' *Register* of 1442. By that time the outstanding features of the donation were the church of Weston and the 'borough' of Baldock, though the land in Weston manor and the wood of' Langnoke' were not forgotten. The earlier, 14th century, Hospitallers' *Report* to the Grand Master also records former Templars' property in 'Langenok' and 'Wylie' with the villa of Baldock and the church of Weston, *in proprios usus* [appropriated to pious uses], the whole estate valued at 38.5 marks (£25.13s.4d.) and farmed out for a term of 10 years.

The Weston grant, in all probability, acquired additional importance when a Hertfordshire man, Hugh of Argentein, was head of all the brethren of the Temple in England, not merely as a local preceptor, but as a *procurator,* or business agent. The Argenteins were lords of the manor of Great Wymondley, close to Weston, and apparently as early as 1142, King Stephen gave 40 shillings' worth of land in the Hertfordshire vill of Dinsley to God and the brethren of the Knighthood of the Temple of Jerusalem and to Hugh of Argentein. A Robert de Argent' held in Baldock in 1185, and one of the lesser Weston donors, Walter Fitz Hubert, gave the Templars a few acres in the field of Graveley, between Great and Little Wymondley. All these indications, slight though they may be, point to the intimate feudal and local connection of the Templars with this district in the reigns of Stephen and Henry II.

At Weston proper, the settlement was more purely agricultural, and much of the former manorial organisation seems to have been retained. Here the Templars held in round numbers about 250 acres.

The altar dues from the two Hertfordshire churches of Weston and Baldock, part of the benefaction of earl Gilbert of Pembroke, amounted to 13 marks (£8.13s.4d.) a year. In the 13th century the church of Weston was appropriated by the Templars and a vicarage was instituted there. In 1338 the Hospitallers held the church of Weston *in proprios usus.* (Lees, 1935, cxxix, cxxxvi, cxl, cxliv)

Still remaining in Weston Park are a string of four fish-ponds, including one from its shape, called the 'Horse-shoe Pond'. They originally belonged to the Templars. There used to be a mass of sweet rushes growing in the ponds, which when trodden on gave off a lovely scent. These were used for strewing on floors in houses in the medieval period, but most of these rushes today have been smothered by the common flag. At least one large field on the site was a Templar vineyard. The owner, Mr. J. M. Pryor, maintains that scattered masonry elsewhere on the estate indicates the whereabouts of some Templar buildings destroyed in the past.

Fig. 54b. Effigy of William Marshal, earl of Pembroke (d.1219) armed as a Crusader.

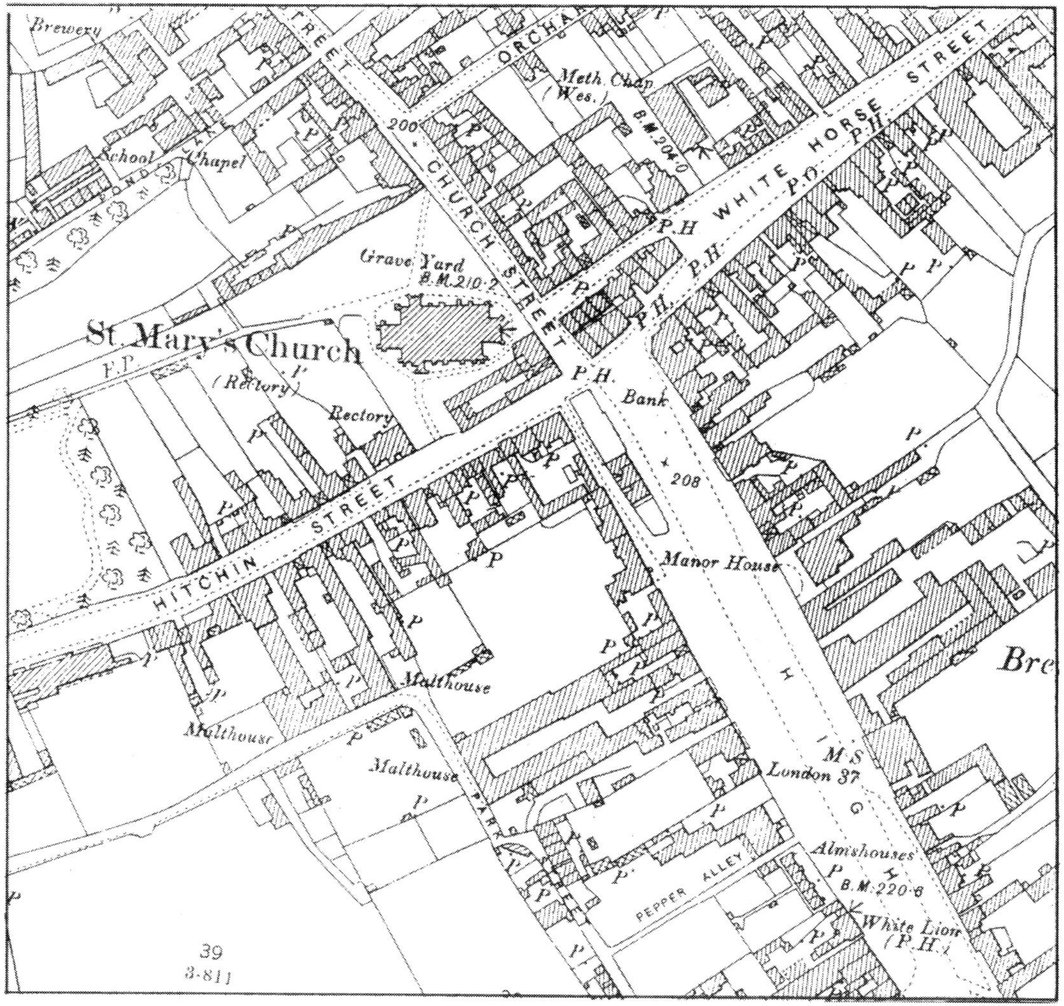

Fig. 54c. Centre of Baldock. OS map dated 1898 (with permission of the Controller of HMSO © Crown copyright), showing an arrangement of buildings erected between two roads in White Horse Street pointing to a medieval post-Domesday development similar to that at Royston when market stalls became permanent shops between the High Street and Upper King Street.

Baldock - Broadwater Hundred

There are interesting parallels between the foundation of a new town at Royston ** (see p. 169), and the almost contemporary foundation of Baldock only nine miles [14.4 km] to the south-west. In each case a religious house was responsible for the new community and for the privileges of market and fair which were given to the townsmen. Each site stood in open country where the Icknield way, following the foot of the chalk hills, intersected a north-bound road from London. The present main road (A1M) comes to Baldock through Hatfield, but the alignment of Parish boundaries and a partly disused succession of lanes and footpaths suggest that an older route approached Baldock up the river Beane from Hertford.

The intersection of the two important roads at Baldock made, as at Royston, a right angle (Fig. 54c). At Royston, the north-bound main road was widened to give room for the market-place. At Baldock, the transverse road was widened and at the head of the triangle of open ground a new church was built. The diversion of the North road and the abandonment of the route from Walkern to Baldock may date from the setting out of the market-place along the south-western arm of Baldock's cross-roads, for it is into this arm that the present route leads.

Just as at Royston, Baldock lay on the edge of several Parishes, three in this case, and not far from the meeting place of five. As hinted to before, the king gave charters for a market and fair in 1199, but even in the great survey of Templar possessions in 1185, an active town was in being. The description of Baldock is very different from that of the men and their holdings in Weston two miles [3.2 km] away, where the Templars maintained a demesne [an estate] on which villeins [peasant workers] worked, rendering both rent and labour services. In the town, no services were rendered, the Templars being receivers only. The area of field-land, about 100 acres, was too small to maintain the 122 tenants whose names appear in the survey. A typical entry is:

> 'Ricardus de Herford tenet iii acras de burgagio in villa de Baldach.'

The surnames of some of the tenants indicate what alternative occupations they held, rather than working in the fields, and how the Templars found it profitable to relieve such men of their obligation to do agricultural work, by taking instead only a money rent.

Historians are certain that the town was a new and deliberate settlement because of the absence of early references, and from the words used by the earl of Pembroke in the early 13th century, ratifying the grant of his ancestors:

> 'confirmavimus...Illas decem libratas terrae...In eodem manerio in qua terra ipsi (i.e. The Templars) construxerunt quendam burgum qui dicitur Baudoc.'

The name of the new town itself, 'Baudoc' is believed to be corruption of 'Baghdad', a name brought from the east by the Templars, but the reason for this curious choice of name remains unexplained (see also Appendix VIII). The commercial optimism of the Templars must have been exceedingly high if they hoped to create a new Baghdad in Hertfordshire (Beresford & St. Joseph, 1958, 230-1).

****Note.** *There is a curious remark in a booklet entitled 'The Origin and Antiquity of Royston, and its Oratory' published in* 1825, *Royston (author not named) as follows:*

> *'Royston has been accounted a place of great antiquity by most authors who have mentioned it. It has been affirmed that a Roman Town once stood here, which was entirely destroyed at the invasion of the Picts, about the year 450. '* [2009 – p. 9]

There are no references, so from wherever this information was picked-up, it is certainly a mystery or *the figment of someone's imagination. Recent excavation work at Baldock, however, has shown that a large settlement did exist there in Roman times.*

Fig. 54d. An early 20th century line print of Baldock with a view of St. Mary's Church.

A COMPARISON BETWEEN BALDOCK AND TEMPLE BRUER, LINCOLNSHIRE

A comparison can be made with the Knights Templar's village of Bruer [heath], later called Temple Bruer, in Lincolnshire, which was planted, like their new 'Baghdad' or Baldock, in open country and in heathland, as indicated by the actual name. The foundation charter of the preceptory (c. 1150) delineated an area *de terra astata et brueria* on the plateau south of Lincoln, between the Lincoln-Sleaford and Lincoln-Stamford roads (Fig. 55a). It was to become one of nine preceptories for Lincolnshire.

Although there is no entry in Domesday Book, the survey of the Templars' estates in 1185, gave a separate section to Bruer and a separate *summa* of its income, treating it as a full manor. By 1185, the village was already a generation old. Around the preceptory had settled 37 tenants inhabiting 34 tofts. Ten of the villagers each held field-land, amounting to a single toft [a homestead, or the land where one has stood] and a single bovate [a variable measure related to the amount of land an ox could plough in a year and the soil quality – generally recorded as 1/8 of a hide, 7/32 acres], probably of 24 acres. The villagers paid the Templars a rent in money, in hens and in services, or boon-works – in other words – gifts and favours to be given in return. The surnames of the tenants, in 1185, indicate peasant migrants from local villages. Except for a weaver and a shepherd, occupational names are absent, in contrast to the list of tenants that same year in the equally new foundation of Baldock.

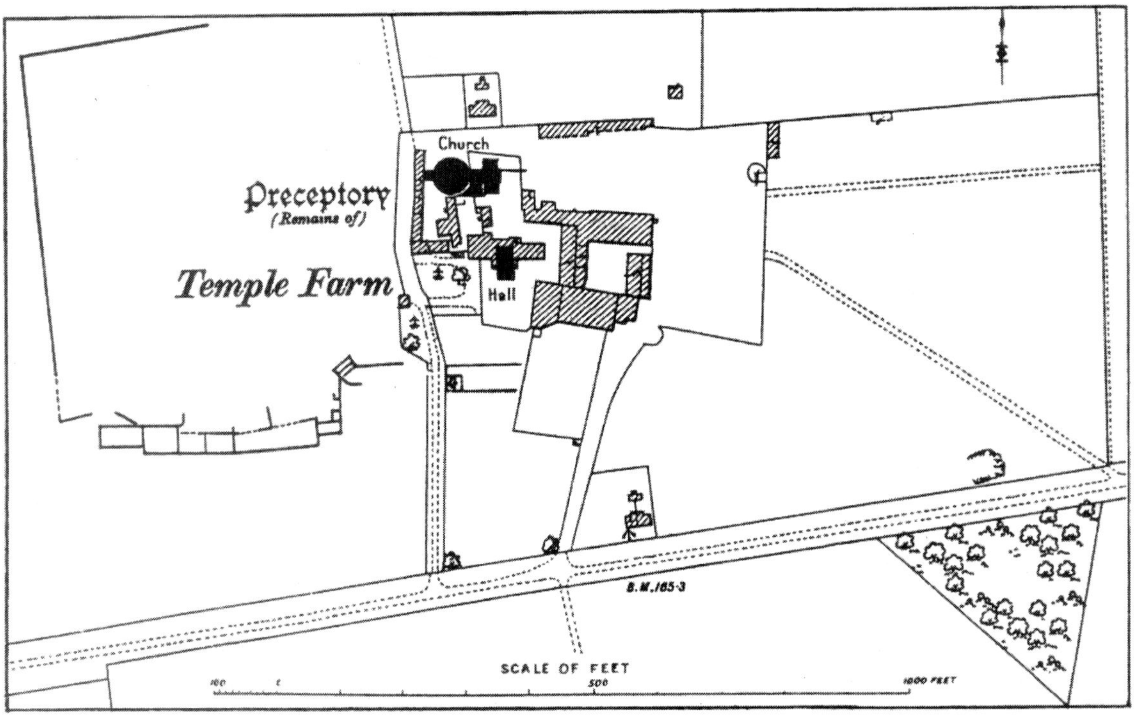

Fig. 55a. Plan of Temple Bruer site showing discoveries in 1907 based on 1:2500 O.S. map).
(After St. John Hope, 1908)

There is little doubt that the new village of Temple Bruer was created here, settlers being encouraged by the brethren who needed a labour force for cultivation of their lands. Although the 1185 survey suggests a simple, rough-and-ready allocation of land for the maintenance of the incoming peasantry, the Templars had no intention of Bruer remaining solely an agricultural village. A weekly market began to be held on the third quarter of the 12th century, where at least grain and wool was sold.

The subsequent fate of the village is not known. When the historian Leland visited Bruer in 1538-9 he said:

> 'greate and vaste Buildings, but rude at this Place, and the Este end of the Temple is made opere circulari de more…'

An engraving of the ruins published by Samuel Buck in 1726 includes part of the circular church adjacent to the tower (Fig. 52a). All that remains today is a single large farm besides a fragment of Templar building (Fig. 55b). This village was never well placed in relation to long-distance traffic, being midway between the Lincoln-Stamford and Lincoln-Sleaford road which formed the boundary of the heath (bruer) in the foundation charter. As mentioned before the Templars were equally unfortunate in an attempt to establish a roadside market at Walshford Bridge in their Yorkshire manor of Robston, and the Knights Hospitallers failed at the Fosse Way site of Eagle, Lincolnshire, in 1348. (Lees, 1935, clxxxi; Beresford & St. Joseph, 1958, 162-3). When under the latter Order, Temple Bruer was for sometime run jointly with the commandery at Eagle. About 1308 Bruer had been the second richest preceptory in England with an income of over £177. Even though its income was slightly higher under the Hospitallers, due to inflation, its real value slumped considerably.

Fig. 55b. The renovated tower of Temple Bruer. Photo Sylvia Beamon, 1991.

LOCAL MARKETS AND FAIRS AT BALDOCK AND ELSEWHERE

In days gone by, fairs were usually held on feast days. First the people gathered to perform their religious duties and afterwards came business and pleasure. Our present word 'holiday' meaning a day of enjoyment is derived from 'holy day', a feast. Fairs were at first normally held in the churchyard, but during the reign of King Edward I, a law was passed forbidding this usage. The 'George and Dragon' at Baldock almost certainly originated as a booth in the churchyard in which 'church ales' were drunk and mystery plays performed, such as the story of 'St. George and the Dragon' which was brought back from the Holy Land. (Gray, undated c. 1960, 8)

The need for salt for preserving meat had much to do with the creation of markets. This valuable commodity could not be universally obtained; hence it had to be conveyed to centres where it was exchanged for goods common to that district, and the plaee where these exchanges or barters were effected came to be called markets. They were originally on the boundary between the two 'marks' and the spot was often indicated by a stone, the precursor of the 'market-cross' of medieval times. It is possible that the base of Royston Cross had been as such a 'marker' stone (q.v. Chapter I). An example of a market stone is the 'four shires' stone at Moreton-in-Marsh, which is situated at the junction of the four counties of Gloucester, Hereford, Worcester, and Warwick (Willis, W. R. (1898) *Markets and Market Laws* in *Bygone Hertfordshire,* ed. & pub. by W. Andrews, 233-243)

The 13th century saw an unprecedented phase of urban expansion and a proliferation of market places. Towns already established in 1200 grew quickly and many newcomers were added to the urban pattern. Some villages acquired town status and at least 65 new towns were planted where no previous settlement had existed. In addition, about 2500 market charters were granted, most of them to rural communities. Consequently, considerable movement of agricultural produce must have existed between these market places and the farms of peasants and lords alike. The produce would have been transported to market in sacks carried by pack-horses or in carts. And besides that required to feed the local inhabitants, a proportion was destined for export after having been collected into large consignments by travelling merchants.

An eminent 13th century lawyer, Henry de Bracton, considered that the length of a 'reasonable day' spent in marketing could be transformed into the linear equivalent of 32 km. Buying and selling would occupy at least a third of the day, leaving a third for the journey to market and a third for the return home. The maximum range of a market journey was therefore, in Bracton's own precise phrase, 'six miles and a half and the third part of a half or just over 10 km. Most medieval English markets were not places of permanent trading, but like the periodic markets of primitive economies today, were used only on one specified day of the week when temporary booths and stalls were set up and rented by traders for the duration of marketing. (Fox, 1970, 658, 660-1)

As referred to under Royston, there is evidence of a dispute between the Knights Templar of Baldock with the bailiff of the Wednesday market in Royston as to whether they were entitled to free stallage to sell their wares. The prior of the house of St. Thomas and St. John backed his bailiff to exact the tolls. An appeal was made to King John, who at that time was believed to be at Ashwell, and may have settled the dispute personally. The outcome was that the Templars' privilege could not be resisted, and the prior and convent had to refund the whole of the money taken from the Templars' stall, an amount of thirty-seven shillings. (Salmon's *History of Hertfordshire*). The amount involved indicates that the stallage was considerable, or that the dispute was of long standing, probably the latter.

Baldock is 9 miles away from Royston, approximately 14.5 km, as already remarked, and is separated by an undulating road that in places is certainly steep. It would seem that the Templars did indeed have an excessive day if they travelled to and from Baldock in one day to attend Royston market. Or did they stop overnight? Presumably not at the Priory for obvious reasons.

In 1199 King John granted the Templars at Baldock the right to hold a yearly fair on St. Matthew's day and four days following, i.e. September 21st to 25th. In the first year of Henry III's reign, the king confirmed to the Knights Templar and their successors that they should hold one Fair yearly in the Town of Baldock on the feast of St. Matthew the Apostle, and also one market day on Wednesday. This grant has the words 'fratibus leprosis apud Baudac', from which it is gathered that the Templars had some place of 'retirement' or haven, at Baldock for those of their brethren affiicted with leprosy, a disease very common in England then. The site of this Lazar House is assumed to be now covered by some cottages close to the railway, but the memory of the house was kept alive by the narrow thoroughfare called 'Clothall Road, formerly Pest House Lane.' [site of Lazar House uncovered by excavation, 2003-5: Mark Phillips, 'Four millennia of human actions along the A505 Baldock bypass.' in *E. Anglia Arch. Rep*. 128 pub. 2009.]

Richard, earl of Strigul, who married Isabel, the sole daughter and heir of Richard Strongbow, gave further liberties and privileges to the Manor. He also gave to the Templars the Mill of Radwell-e-the-bed with two husbandmen in that town, and the Templars, (or rather the Knights Hospitaller, their successors in title), held it till the reign of Henry IV when John de Wheathampstead, a famous Abbot of the Monastery of St. Albans, amongst other property purchased the Mill and also the advowson of the Rectory. Previously, under the charter granted by Henry III, the Master of the Templars had claimed in the reign of Edward I [son of Henry III], very large liberties with exemption from all secular service, soc., sac., toll, etc., and a discharge in all things in all places, from all toll and all secular services and customs. Also claimed was the collection of the assize of bread, wine and ale, Tumbrel and Pillory view of frankpledge [a mutual suretyship by which the members of a tithing were made responsible for one another]. All these privileges were upheld by Edward I and allowed to the Master.

On the dissolution of the Knights Templar and the subsequent union of most of their land with that of the Knights Hospitaller of St. John of Jerusalem, this Manor became vested in the latter. Apparently, the people of Baldock did not take kindly to the new custodians of the Manor. In 1312 a commission was appointed to enquire into a disturbance at Baldock. When Geoffrey de la Lee *** (see p. 182), the King's Custodian of the Templars' lands in Hertfordshire, came to collect the rents, tolls and profits of the fair, he and his men and their servants were assaulted, robbed and three men were killed. Among the list of people charged was John Werri, Chaplain, probably the Templars chaplain at Baldock Church. On February 12th 1312, this John Werri was pardoned of the sentence of outlawry passed on him for his part in the death of the three men. (Gray, op. cit. p. 9)

In the seventh year of the reign of Henry VII that sovereign *Letters Patent* granted to John Kendal, Lord Prior of St. John of Jerusalem, gave him, his fraternity, and successors, liberty to hold a market on the Wednesday in every week of the year free from all tolls, taxes, tallages etc. and two fairs annually. From the last lease, which the Knights Hospitaller granted of the Manor of Baldock, it appears that the annual value was then £12 per annum. By this, Thomas Docwra, the Prior, with the consent of the Chapters assembled at their house of St. John of Clerkenwell, granted a lease in 1422, for a term of 21 years, to one John Bowles, gentleman, of the Manor and Lordship of Baldock. It included all the rents, perquisitions of court view of frankpledge; profit of fairs and markets in consideration of an annual rent of £13., and for entertaining the Prior's servants and three or four horses once in every year. At the

Dissolution, in Henry VIII's reign, the Manor fell into the hands of the Monarch, by whom it was granted to Thomas Rivett. (Brown, Charles, *Baldock and the Knight Templars* held with H. J. Gray's notes on Baldock)

The fair on St. Matthew's day is today kept on October 2nd and 3rd, the difference in date being caused by the omission of eleven days from the calendar in 1752. Royston's fair follows on from the Baldock fair. Could it possibly have had a connection with the Baldock Templars, or even with Royston Templars? Perhaps just coincidence.

THE CHURCH OF ST. MARY THE VIRGIN (BALDOCK)

Chauncey, in his *History of Hertfordshire,* states that the Knights Templar built a Church at Baldock. A date of 1150 is suggested but no confirmation can be found. The present Church, although mainly erected during the 14th and 15th centuries was, as pointed out by Mr. Millard in a paper read before the East Herts. Archaeological Society in 1908, a reconstruction in a new form and doubtless an enlargement of a previously existing Church (Fig. 54d). The chancel end was retained, and to this day remains in use as the sanctuary.

The oldest and most interesting memorial in the Church is a grey marble slab to the memory of Reginald de Argentine. Round the margin is the remains of an inscription in Lombardic or Gothic letters, much worn, of an early French inscription in rhyme which fortunately was carefully noted by earlier church recorders:

"Reynaud de Argenthem ci gist
Que ceste chapele fere fist
Fu chyvaler Saynt Marie
Checun prodom pur s'alme prie."

A translation reads:

Reginald de Argentein lies here [Reginald Argentein III]
Who caused this chapel to be made,
He was a Knight of St. Mary,
Let every good man pray for his soul.

The expression 'Knight of St. Mary' is taken to mean he was a Knight Templar whose patron was the Blessed Virgin Mary. [The symbol of the Virgin Mary being the single fleur-de-lis, q.v.]

The Rev. Thomas Cole visited the Church in 1757 and recognised two neat plain small shields, 'Gules, three covered cups, argent,' on the stone as being the Argentine arms, and was able to ascribe it to Reginald de Argentine. The family was connected with Baldock in 1214 and earlier: their Manor being in the parish of Melbourn, Cambridgeshire. The slab today has only the indentations for a brass floriated cross (q.v., see also Chapter 6) and the shields. Although the church was the parish church of Baldock, it was in actual fact a chapel for the Knights Templar whose chaplains served the church and acted as the parish priests. It is concluded that the tomb is that of the renovator or later builder of the church who died in 1307. An inscription of about the same date, previously existed on a stone near the north door. This has been almost entirely worn out - the letters *"le xl Jours"* are all that can be made out, and it has been suggested that this stone recorded another member of the same family. (Gray, c. 1960 op. cit., 37-39)

Baldock had an interesting local sidelight, in the first known entry of a presentation to the Church of Baldock. 'On June 14th, 1308, Henry de Craystok was presented to the Vicarage of the Church of Baldock (in the diocese of Lincoln) which was in the King's gift, by reason of the lands of the Knights Templar being in his hands.' (Cal. Pat. Rolls, 1307-1313 p. 79)

Hitchin: Temple Dinsley - Preston parish, Hitchin Half-hundred

Although the Templars had demesne at Weston, they do not appear to have had a house or preceptory on the manor in 1185. By that date the preceptory at Dinsley was probably the centre of all the Hertfordshire and Bedfordshire estates. A few entries relating to property at Buckland and Reed, to the east of Baldock, separate the Weston and Baldock returns. After Baldock, the *Inquest* enters the rents from several small grants in Bedfordshire and in the Hertfordshire vills of Rushden, Buntingford, Corneybury, and Cottered, all within easy reach of the second great Hertfordshire donation, with which it proceeds to deal. This was the Balliol estate in the neighbourhood of Hitchin, which was known to later history as Temple Dinsley. (Lees, 1935, cxxix, cxl, et seq.)

The name of Dinsley does not occur in the *Inquest,* and were it not for the survival of a few charters in the Hospitallers' *Register,* there would be little to connect the preceptory with Bernard de Balliol's gift of eight carucates, in 'villa de Prestune', which the 12th century rental records. The somewhat spectacular circumstances in which Bernard de Balliol gave the Templars 15 librates of land in Wedelee ' ...que est membrum de Hichen' have caused this grant to be generally accepted as marking the foundation of the important Hertfordshire preceptory of Temple Dinsley.

> 1147 (Eastertide) At the Chapter of the Templars, in the Round Church of the Templars in Paris, Bernard de Balliol, Lord of Hitchin, granted to the Knights of the Temple of Solomon fifteen librates (about 780 acres) 'of my land which I possess in England in perpetuity, freely and without any custom, Wedelee by woodland. And I make this gift in the chapter which was held at Paris in the octaves of Easter, the apostolic legate Eugenius being present and the king of France, and the Archbishops of Sens, Bordeaux, Rouen and Trascunnie and one hundred and thirty brethren, Knights of the Temple, arrayed in white cloaks.' Wedelee was the early name for Preston (11) (115.73)

The above being a translation of the charter by B. A. Lees, on p. 214 of *The Inquest.*

The charter seems to have been drawn up shortly before the French Crusaders started on the ill-fated Second Crusade. In reality, Dinsley is not mentioned either in this charter or in its confirmation by King Stephen, given in London, which describes the gift as in the manor of

Hitchin [Heicchen]. However, another royal charter, of approximately the same date (dated by D'Albon in a manuscript transcript of this charter: 1147, 28 avril - 1154) confirms a grant of waste land [*vastum terre*] in Dinsley, *sicut Bernardus de Baillolio ...illud dedit.* Even the 15th century Stillingeflete, who knew the Balliol charter of 1147, referred to it as giving land 'in Hychin et Prestone.'

The true founder of the Templars' Dinsley estate seems actually to have been King Stephen himself. Five years before the Balliol grant, in 1142, the king on his northern progress gave full liberties and free customs [*liberales consuetudines*] to the brethren of the Temple at Jerusalem, *in terra sua de Dynnesleya,* by a charter issued at Ipswich. He also confirmed, at York, John the chamberlain's gift of an acre of land in the same place. Later in the year, at Oxford, Stephen appears to have added two mills, worth two pounds, to the previous donations. It was witnessed by Earl Geoffrey de Mandeville of Essex and by the constable Robert de Vere; they also witnessed several other charters besides this one. Deneslai, a seven hide-manor, was a member of the Hitchin manorial group in 1086 - a group which included that Welei which may perhaps be identified with the Wedelee of the Balliol charter of 1147, while Preston was a hamlet of Hitchin.

All these places were close together, and the permanent association of the name 'Temple' with Dinsley (similar examples being, Cressing Temple, Temple Cowley, Temple Guiting, Temple Bruer etc.) suggests that the preceptory proper, the house and chapel, where many future provincial Chapters were to be held, may have been built on this manor, perhaps on the *vastum terre de Dynnesleya* which Stephen confirmed to the Templars in the latter part of his reign.

The two Dinsley mills (likely to be at Wellhead and Charlton) which Stephen gave to the Templars probably in 1142, are not entered in the *Inquest,* perhaps because they were on demesne land: however, they are referred to in Charters held in the British Museum [Add. Ch. nos. 35543 late 12th century, and 35436 early 13th century].

Clutterbuck, (1815-7, vol. III, 26-7) gives information on additional land belonging to the Order. Matilda, daughter of Matilda and William de Luvetot a Yorkshire family, who when she was seven years old and in the custody of Ralph Murdac, was certified 32 H. II [1185] (or thereabouts), to have the Town of Dineley (in Hertfordshire) in Dower, which was valued at £12 per annum.

> "Matilda, the daughter and heir of William de Lovetot, was by King Richard I, married to Gerard de Furnivall, who came out of Normandy".

This lady was a great benefactor to the Knights Templar in lands, tenements, meadows, and pastures in this place. King Henry III granted the Templars free warren in all their demesne lands of Dynnesley, Stanho, Preston, Charleton, Walden, Hiche, Chelles, Sevecamp and Benigho in Hertfordshire. The same king, by his charter dated 9th February in the 11th year of his reign [1227], confirmed to them all the donations of his predecessors and of their other benefactors, with soc. and sac., etc. (see details in Appendix VIII)

King Edward I, by his Charter dated the 22nd November, anno 9 Edward I [1280] (reciting a Charter of King Henry III, his father dated 12 of June, anno 37 H.III) confirmed to the Master and Brethren Knights of the Temple and Solomon in England, all their honours, lands, royalties, etc.

Previously, in the 6th year of Edward I [1277-8] there was a *quo warranto* against the Templars in common with other privileged persons, requiring them to show by what authority these privileges were claimed, and they answered by the grant of King Henry III.

The Templars exercised almost regal sway over their lands which grew in area and value until at one time, besides Hitchin and Wymondley, they extended into the parishes of Kings Walden, Abbots Walden (now St. Paul's Walden), St. Ippollyts, Offley, Pirton, Ickleford and Astwick. The house was held in great esteem by the Order, and General Chapters were held there on several occasions. It is assumed that Temple Dinsley must have witnessed many wondrous and spectacular displays of chivalry, an echo of which still lingers in the name of 'Pageant Field'. The sporting rights attached to the estate were of great value and no doubt must have given the Knights good hunting and entertainment. A 13th century charter - most likely translated wrong - gave rise to the tradition that the owner of Temple Dinsley has the right to stand on the doorstep of Stagenhoe [present day premises of the Princess Helena College] on Christmas Day and fire off a gun (sic). Reason unknown. [2001 – excavation failed to locate evidence of the preceptory]

In 1218 an agreement was reached with the nuns of Elstow near Bedford for the provision of a chaplain resident at Dinsley to celebrate mass on Sundays, Wednesdays and Fridays in the morning, and vespers in the afternoon, unless the festival fell in the week when that was counted as one of the three days. The priest received one silver mark annually plus four pounds of wax for the chapel lights. The Templars undertook to pay the nuns the tithes previously paid to the Church at Hitchin on all lands ploughed, and on any part of the ground newly broken up and sown. That part of Dinsley where the priest lived became known as Preston.

Dinsley Castle, which probably had been previously a prehistoric stronghold and stood on the site of what is now Castle Farm, was held by the Balliols and the Templars, and from it dominated the countryside. The powers of the Knights included the much prized right of 'gallows'. In 1286 Gerle de Clyfton and Johannes Tykkul were hanged for stealing a silver chalice and four silver spoons from the priest at Temple Dinsley, and the same fate overtook Peter son of Adam for torturing a woman.

In 1308 the six brethren in residence were arrested, two being taken to the Tower of London and four to Hertford Castle. On 2 August 1309 a Papal Bull was issued dissolving the Order. The manor was assigned to the unpopular Geoffrey de la Lee, but the local inhabitants seem to have much preferred their old masters and the change was accompanied by serious riots similar to those at Baldock.

One of the objects of suppressing the Order was to gain possession of their vast riches, but when the Commission of Enquiry visited Temple Dinsley no trace could be found of the treasures of gold, silver and jewels. The Templars are thought to have buried them or thrown them into one of the many ponds in the grounds, but their actual hiding place still remains a mystery.

Dinsley Castle was dismantled and let to the Prior of Wymondley for a rent of 10 shillings a year. The preceptory at Temple Dinsley was handed over in 1348 to the Knights Hospitallers who continued in possession until the dissolution of the religious houses in the reign of Henry VIII. The preceptory was pulled down c. 1542 by Sir Ralph Sadleir [a Puckeridge school has been named after this man]. Only a few traces remain today. Two houses of different periods with extensions and alterations have been subsequently built on the site. In 1935 the Princess Helena College moved from its former premises at Ealing to this Temple Dinsley property. (Historical notes from the Princess Helena College, c. 1980)

RELICS

Relics of Templars' occupation are scarce in the country at large. In the 1880s' excavations, and tillage brought to light tangible evidence of the brotherhood at Temple Dinsley's former preceptory. Human remains were found in the kitchen yard. Among them lay a pewter chalice with baluster moulding on its stem, classified as being of early 14th century date (Fig. 56a) of a type such as it was customary to include in ecclesiastical interments. Two similar examples, to that already found here, may be seen in the British Museum. At the same spot a grave stone cover of the 13th century, carved with a cross bottony [also referred sometimes as floriated], was unearthed and is today preserved in St. Martin's Church, Preston (Fig. 56b). It is presumed to have marked the grave of some Master or Preceptor of the Order. From one of the estate ponds a 14th century bronze jug was recovered, its whereabouts today is unknown.

Fig. 56a. Pewter chalice found at Temple Dinsley when the grave of a Templar preceptor was dug up in 1880s by Mr. W. Ransome of Hitchin. Reproduction by permission of the British Museum

Fig.56b. Stone grave cover carved with a cross bottony which marked a Templar preceptor's grave. Photo Sylvia Beamon, 1991.

Found on the site of Preston Castle, was a medieval brown earthenware chafing dish (a vessel for heating with hot coals; a dish for cooking on the table) in the shape of a bowl standing on a short foot (Fig. 56c). It measured 6.5 ins [0.16 m] high and 9.5 ins [0.25 m] across the brim. The holes which pierced the foot and sides were to admit air, and for the convenience of carrying it, a looped handle was attached to one side. At the proceedings of the Society of Antiquaries in London in 1869, Mrs. E. Mayle exhibited and presented a water-colour drawing of the vessel. Mrs. Nina Freebody, a local historian, discovered in 1984 that although the watercolour remains in the Society's care, the dish itself has not been seen, nor recorded elsewhere.

In 1909, when the comparatively modern house was undergoing further refurbishment, and foundations for a new west wing were being dug out, several tiles of the 13th century were uncovered. Originally, they probably formed part of the chapel floor. One tile exhibits the familiar *Agnus Dei* with a halo, and bearing a pennon, the staff of which is surmounted by a Maltese cross. This, the badge of the Knights Templar is found on the seals attached to the Order's charters and other documents, and is referred to several times elsewhere in the text both abroad and in this country.

Another tile, of similar dimensions, roughly 5.5 ins square [0.13 m], has the same coarse red body glazed on the exposed surface and bears a crude impression in yellow of a coat of arms. The details of the arms have run considerably in the firing, but were sufficiently clear to be recognised as 'Ermine, on a chief Azure three lions rampant and belonging to the Le Sauvage family'. An important link. was found between a member of this family and Temple Dinsley. It concerned a lease of property in Brampton (Derbyshire?), which had been given to the Templars by Hugh Fitz Ingeram, to Hugh Fitz Peter of Brampton at an annual rent of 13d. and half a silver mark death dues. The business was transacted c. 1241 at a chapter at Temple Dinsley headed by Brother Robert de Samford Master of the Templars of England who humbly subscribes himself as *"Milicie Templi in Anglia minister humilis"*. [see Appendix VIII for the full text of the deed]. Fr. Tho. Le Sauvage was one of the witnesses to the document, held in the British Musuem, which is some 5 ins by 2 ins [0.12 x 0.5 m], written in a fine contracted script. Attached is a green wax seal in perfect condition showing the Lamb of God, within a circle inscribed *SIGILLUM TEMPLI* (Fig. 56d)

Fig. 56c. Chafing Dish found at Preston Castle (formerly Dinsley Castle) near Hitchin.

TESTIS SVM AGNI.

Fig. 56d. Knights Templar seal with the 'Agrus Dei'.

It has been surmised that he must have been an important person amongst the Templars, for it was not only at Dinsley that his memory should be so perpetuated, but also in a wider sphere of the Order's activities. Only the more prominent members of those who met together in chapter placed their hands to the serious financial business of disposing or letting of its lands.

Several errors in the indexing of manuscripts have occurred in the past. The deed above was ascribed to the chapter at Dingley, Northamptonshire, but the Templars never had a Preceptory there. It is also possible that the 'Brampton' was not in Derbyshire but indeed in Cumberland, and the writer, H. C. Andrews, FSA, of the typewritten notes entitled *Some Relics of the Knights Templars at Temple Dinsley* (undated, presumably pre-1918, held in the NHDC Hitchin Museum & Art Gallery) sought the Le Sauvage family in the north as he realised a close tie connected them in their common ownership by the Balliol family. His search rewarded and

Brother Thomas Le Sauvage of the Dinsley Templars was found in the Balliol lands as Lord of Stratteford, now known as Startforth, in the liberty of Richmond, Yorkshire.

THE CHURCH OF ST. MARY THE VIRGIN, HITCHIN (Fig. 56e)

A monk, Hildebrand of Hitchin, writing about the Church (between 1297-1305) remarked:

> "the rood loft was brightly painted at the expense of the Knights Templar who live nearby. It is indeed right that they should endeavour by charity and good work to make their peace with Heaven, which cannot love their arrogance or their licentiousness; in their evening feast they often take too much wine, and it is credibly reported that their cries and their unpleasing songs can be heard in the town."

Fig. 56e. St. Mary's Church, Hitchin showing the south porch. c.1990. Two stone effigies of knights transferred from Temple Dinsley Church in St. Mary's in the 1540s still remain.

The rood loft was a screen, which would have joined those portions surviving in the north and south aisles, with, above it a large crucifix. The latter, it was said, survived until the 18th century. Alan Fleck reasons that the Templars' carousing could be heard at the distance of three miles is unlikely, nevertheless, is an interesting social comment. (Fleck. A. (1984) *Concerning the Names of the Saints in Old Hitchin Life*, vol. I, No. 4, *Hitchin Historical Society*, 5-10) [The monk's first sentence illustrates that the Templars knew of suitable painters or had painters within their own brethren.]

Three effigies lie in the north aisle window sills of the church. Sculptured in Purbeck marble of the 13th century, the westernmost effigy represents a knight in mail beneath a kite-shaped shield, suspended from a wide guige which passes over the right shoulder. A belt, girded a little above the hips, once supported a sword, worn on the right side, but of this only a fragment remains. There was a tradition of longstanding in the Parish, that this forlorn, dismembered figure was brought from Temple Dinsley when the preceptory of the Templars was demolished and that it represented their founder, Bernard de Balliol, sometime lord of Hitchin manor. This tradition was confirmed by the discovery at Temple Dinsley of the foot of a mailed figure in Purbeck marble too, which not only matches with but fits onto the mutilated figure in the north aisle. (Note on an ancient effigy existing in the parochial church of St. Mary, Hitchin by F. S. Clarkson, in *St. Albans and Herts Architec. & Arch. Soc. Trans.,* 28-29)

The area of Hitchin, doubtless, meant something to Balliol, for he chose out of all the churches in his gift to be buried in the preceptory of his Knight Templars at Dinsley 1167. (Hine, 1929, 411)

Cottered - Odsey Hundred
Aspenden, Throcking, Wyddial, Graveley - Edwinstree Hundred

In the reign of Edward the Confessor, Cottered formed part of the demesne lands of St. Peter of Winchester. The Norman Conquest did not disturb this tenure, and in 1086 the manor of Cottered was held by Bishop Walkelin of Winchester. On his death in 1098 it appears to have been detached from the bishopric and to have become part of the honour of Boulogne. Queen Maud, daughter of Count Eustace of Boulogne and wife of King Stephen, is said to have granted half a virgate of land in Cottered to Reimer of Wivellelme, to hold of the Knights Templars. Her son William de Blois granted the honour of Ongar to Richard de Lucie, and apparently part of his lands in Cottered were granted at the same time, and became the manor of Cottered. Maud, the daughter and heiress of Richard de Lucie, married Richard de Rivers in the reign of John, when the overlordship of Cottered then descended with this family, and was held in 1303 by John Lord Rivers. (*V.C.H. Herts., 228*)

During the 13th century the Templars held land at Aspenden, near Hitchin and in the neighbouring villages of Throcking and Wyddial. (Lees op. cit., 71) Willelmus de Therefeld (Therfield) gave some land in Graveley to the Templars.

Rushden - Odsey Hundred

The Knights Templar seem to have had a small holding in Rushden, Bedfordshire (sic), attached to their manor of Temple Dinsley, in 1309, the year of the suppression of their order [sic], when a report was ordered to be made on all their lands in Hertfordshire. After the grant of the Templars' lands to the Knights Hospitaller, this estate probably became amalgamated with the Hospitallers other holding in Rushden. (*V.C.H. Herts,* vol. III, 268-9) (see also p. 197)

*** **Note:** *A William Lee of Radwell owned property in Royston known as 'Cave property' at the time of the Reformation - see chapter 2. It is interesting to conjecture that he is a relative of Geoffrey de la Lee. Could there be some connection perhaps of a small piece of property being purchased by the family of the Custodian of the Templar lands in Hertfordshire and passed down 200 years? The Templars also of course, had previously owned land in Radwell. More research into these questions is necessary and continuing.*

CAMBRIDGESHIRE

As B. A. Lees explains, although no Cambridgeshire land is entered in the *Inquest,* the Templars were holding of the Prior and Convent of Ely at Denny and elsewhere in the County in 1176. This is shown by the *compositio* [arrangement] made in the same year with Richard of Hastings, 'Minister of the Temple', and his Chapter, which settled certain questions at issue concerning estates at Deneia, Elmencia, and Beche. That the Templars were recognised as being a social and economic power in Cambridgeshire in the 12th century may be gathered from contemporary references to their local possessions and activities: their land at Waterbeach, near Denny or at Wendy, not far from the Bedfordshire border, and their attestations in charters and agreements. In particular, an original cyrograph, probably dating between 1176 and 1185, should be noted. It is witnessed by three officials of the London Temple - the Master, Richard; William the chaplain; and Roger, the 'commander' or preceptor - while William le Brun, one of the parties to the agreement [*conventio*] which gave him the enjoyment of property in Fordham and Isleham, in Cambridgeshire, may be the Templars' London tenant, Willelmus Brunus, who held a messuage of them at a yearly rent of 17 shillings in 1185.

Duxford - Whittlesford Hundred

Other spellings of Duxford are, Dodeswurd, Dokesworth, Dokesworthe, Dokisworthe, Ducheswrd, Dukesworth, Dukeworth, Dukewrth, Doksforth.

It is interesting to find that at Duxford, which is only 8 miles [13 km] from Royston on the Icknield Way, Templars were residing there. About 1235 Sir William de Colville, a Templar himself, founded a priory or preceptory at Whittlesford bridge where travellers could find shelter and the sick could be attended to. This foundation is to be distinguished from the manor which another member of the Coleville family gave to the Knights Templar at Duxford in 1273 which was situated nearer the village and included 30 acres of arable land with some meadows, a water mill, a free chapel and a fair (Lysons, 1808). The chapel, which can be seen from the main road (A505) today, is administered by English Heritage and annually attracts a small number of tourists.

At the Chapter of the Templars held in London at Easter 1273, Guy de Foresta, the master, granted a lease of certain lands at Pampisford, the rent to be paid to the 'Temple at Duxworth'. The seal bears the device of the Pascal Lamb with the words *'TEMPL. DOKSFORTH,'* and the first witnesses were Brother Walter de Wilbraham and Brother Baldwin de Akeny. This is the earliest direct reference to the preceptory.

John Mohun, Preceptor of Duxworth, was arrested with the rest of the Templars in the county on 10th January, 1308. At the time there seems to have been no brother with him, and he was probably the sole professed member of the house, for John Creke, the local Sheriff, found only one bed with its furnishings in the chamber, and this he valued at the preceptor's rate of 20s. Neither is there any mention in the sheriff's account of the secular chaplain with whose stipend of 5 marks the house, according to Philip de Thame, had been charged by the founders. The office may have been empty at the time, since the books and ornaments of the chapel were sent to Cambridge Castle. Mohun was charged at his trial with having spoken contemptuously of the immortality of the soul - perhaps in excuse for the neglect of that Chantry. There were fifteen dependants, of whom the majority were outdoor servants: the others, being the preceptor's secular squire or groom, a reeve, a porter and cook. The buildings consisted of a hall and chamber, with a buttery and a bake house.

Mohun had been 38 years in the Order and had nothing to say about the details of admission and funeral rites at his trial. He was however, the object of the only damaging piece of outside evidence recorded against a Cambridgeshire Templar. An Austin Friar, William de Bernay, said that:

> 'he had heard some brother of the Temple of Duxford beside Cambridge in Ely diocese whose name he knew not (but he believed it was the preceptor of the place), say that "no man had a soul after death any more than a dog."'

On 3rd June 1309, Duxford together with Denny, was committed to Master Roger of Wingfield who, in 1310, was appointed keeper of all the Templar lands in England, and it apparently remained in Wingfield's hands until November 1313. (Saltzman, 1948 *V.C.H. Cambridgeshire and Isle of Ely,* vol. II, 262)

Two more earlier historical references to the Templars are worth recording here:

1276 – The fee of William le Goys of Dokesworth owes suit; the fee of Colvill, which the Templars now hold there, used to owe suit; the tenements of Henry de Lacy and Ralph de Dukesworth now do suit to the court of the honor of Brittany at Badburham; (R. Hund.I, 55) (Farrer, 1920, 269)

1279 – The Templars have a demesne manor there and 4h. 20 a. [4 hides 20 acres] which they hold of Roger de Colevill in alms and he of the earl of Aubermarle for 1 fee and the earl in chief; the abbot of Tyleteye holds of the master of the Templars by the old gift of William de Colevill 70 a. for half mark rent; the prior of Wytlisford Bridge holds one and a half virgates etc. in alms by the gift of the bishop of Ely, in whose gift it was by the grant of William de Colevill, he holds of Roger de Colevill and he of the Earl of Aubemarle; R. Hund.II 580-84 (Farrer op. cit.)

Eventually the properties, including the priory at Whittlesford and the priory and Templar lands at Duxford, were granted to the Knights Hospitaller, and the first Hospitaller to be appointed prior by the Bishop of Ely was William de Sauston in 1313, the Lord of Dale Manor, Sawston.

In 1538 and the years following, the monasteries, including all the Hospitaller houses throughout the country were dissolved and their properties confiscated and later sold to the highest bidder, in most instances by Crown Commissioners. In 1547 the Priory at Whittlesford bridge and other Hospitaller (formerly Templar) lands and properties in Duxford, Sawston and elsewhere, were granted to Sir Richard Long, whose grand-daughter married William Lord Russell, father of the 4th Earl of Bedford. Afterwards it was in the possession of the Webbe family.

These Duxford lands now comprise the lands of Temple Manor, and include Temple Mill and Temple Farm. The name perpetuates the former association with the Templars. (Teversham, undated, 2-3)

Wilbraham or Great Wilbraham - Staine Hundred (Wilburgham, Wilburham)

The records show that in 1226 seisin [possession, now as freehold] to be made to the Templars of the land of Peter de Malo Alneto, son of Hugh, in (Great) Wilburgham, which the same Peter gave to them; (ib.109b; Pat. Roll, 1226, 30)

1236 – Robert de Insula holds in Wilburham 'Regis' 2 h. in socage [tenure of lands by service fixed and determinate in quality] of the honor of Brittany; Ralph son of Fulk [this family had connections with Royston] holds 40 a. there is socage of the same honor; the same Ralph and John son of Henry hold 1 geldable [taxable] hide; the Templars and William Pikot hold 3 non-geldable [non-taxable] hides; (Lib. de Bernewell, 262)

1279 – The King (more probably count Alan Rufus) retained the other moiety [half: one of two parts or divisions] of the vill and gave a fourth part thereof to Picot his serjeant to keep a sparrow-hawk; Roger Loveday now holds it by the feoffment [gift of a fief: a fief being land held in fee or on condition of military service] of William Pikot; Henry III gave three-fourths of that moiety to Hubert de Burgh, who exchanged those three parts with the Templars for a manor called Weston prope Mare; (ib. 491) [Exchanges of land appear to have been quite common.]

1279 – The earl of Oxford holds Little Wilburham. [Relative of Lady Roisia]

And as late as 1284 there was a grant to the Templars of £20 of land in Little Wilburgham; (Quo War.107 b) (Farrer, op. cit., 123)

Great Wilbraham Church remained appropriated to the maintenance of the sick at Denny, even after the Templar foundation of a preceptory in 1226 in its own parish. The Preceptor of Wilbraham was responsible for the annual payment of 40s. in augmentation of the stipend assigned to the vicar, c. 1240.

In 1308, Richard Petevyn, Preceptor of Wilbraham, was arrested at Dinsley, where he had originally been received into the Order by Humbert Peraut, the master in England, at the Chapter of 1266, together with William de la Forde and Thomas of Toulouse. Petevyn had been a Templar for 42 years and was presumably on a visit to Hertfordshire at the time of his arrest. Two other brethren, who were arrested at Wilbraham, had both spent comparatively short service in the Order: William de Thorp, described as *'custos'* not preceptor, had been received by the Grand Preceptor of Yorkshire, six or seven years before in the Chapel at Foulbridge. William Raven had been received by William de la More, the arrested Master at Templecombe, Somerset [who in 1300 had been the preceptor at Temple Bruer], together with a knight of the Order, since dead: although about 100 seculars had been present at the time of his reception, only two brethren were there, one of whom, John de Walpole, *serviens literatus* afterwards instructed him [William Raven] for a month in the *Rule*. He said that he had made no other formal profession after this reception, and had spent the whole of the five years, which had elapsed since it took place, at Wilbraham. [See also Appendix C]

The house of the preceptory seems to have been a small manor house and very simply furnished. The only ornaments in the chapel were a vestment, with towels, worth a mark, and one silver chalice, together with the necessary books. In the chest, for transmission to the Master, was £4. The most elaborate fittings in the house seem to have been those for dairying, with presses for cheese, a churn, a large fixed cauldron for heating milk and other utensils.

Following the arrests of the brethren, John Creke, Sheriff, with the preceptory of Wilbraham, formally took over the manor of Carlton and the churches of Great Wilbraham and Wendy.

On the 21st December, 1313 the manors of Wilbraham and Duxford with the churches of Great Wilbraham and Wendy were handed over to Brother William de Sauston of the Hospital of St. John of Jerusalem. (*V.C.H.* vol. II, op. cit., 263)

Waterbeach - North Stow Hundred

(Beche, Waterbeche, Waterbeyche)

The following historical references prove the Templars were not only very active in the district, but it was over a long period of time:

1158 – The knights of the Temple are pardoned 31s. of the old donum of co. Camb; P. 166.

1166 – Robert the chamberlain [see Wendy also]

ante 1185 – The monks of Ely, or their tenant, gave to the Templars. [The editors of the *Monasticon Anglican* suggest that the Templars were placed in the cell of Denny in lieu of the monks who had been placed there by those of Ely; op. cit.VI, 1549] two thirds of the vill of Waterbeach (4h.) (Lib. de Bernewell, 242)

1207 – Michael son of ...tenant, acknowledges that a messuage in Beche is the right of Hermericus, master of the Temple, who grants the same to Michael; (Camb. Fines (Rec. Com.) 317)

1236 – The Templars hold two-thirds of the vill of Waterbeche in free alms of the fee [feudal tenure] of Ely; (Lib. de Bernewell, 242)

1279 – The master of the Templars claims the advowson of the church of Waterbeyche with Elmeneye of the fee of the bishop of Ely and renders to the prior of Ely 4 m. a year.

The master of the Templars claims the advowson of the church of Waterbeche against the prior of Bernewelle and states that Richard de Hastinges, prior of the Templars, was seised thereof in the time of Henry II and presented his clerk. The suit fails; (Lib. de Bernewelle, 135.) (Farrer op. cit., 190)

Fig. 57a. Section of southern Fenland. (After Christie & Coad, 1980)

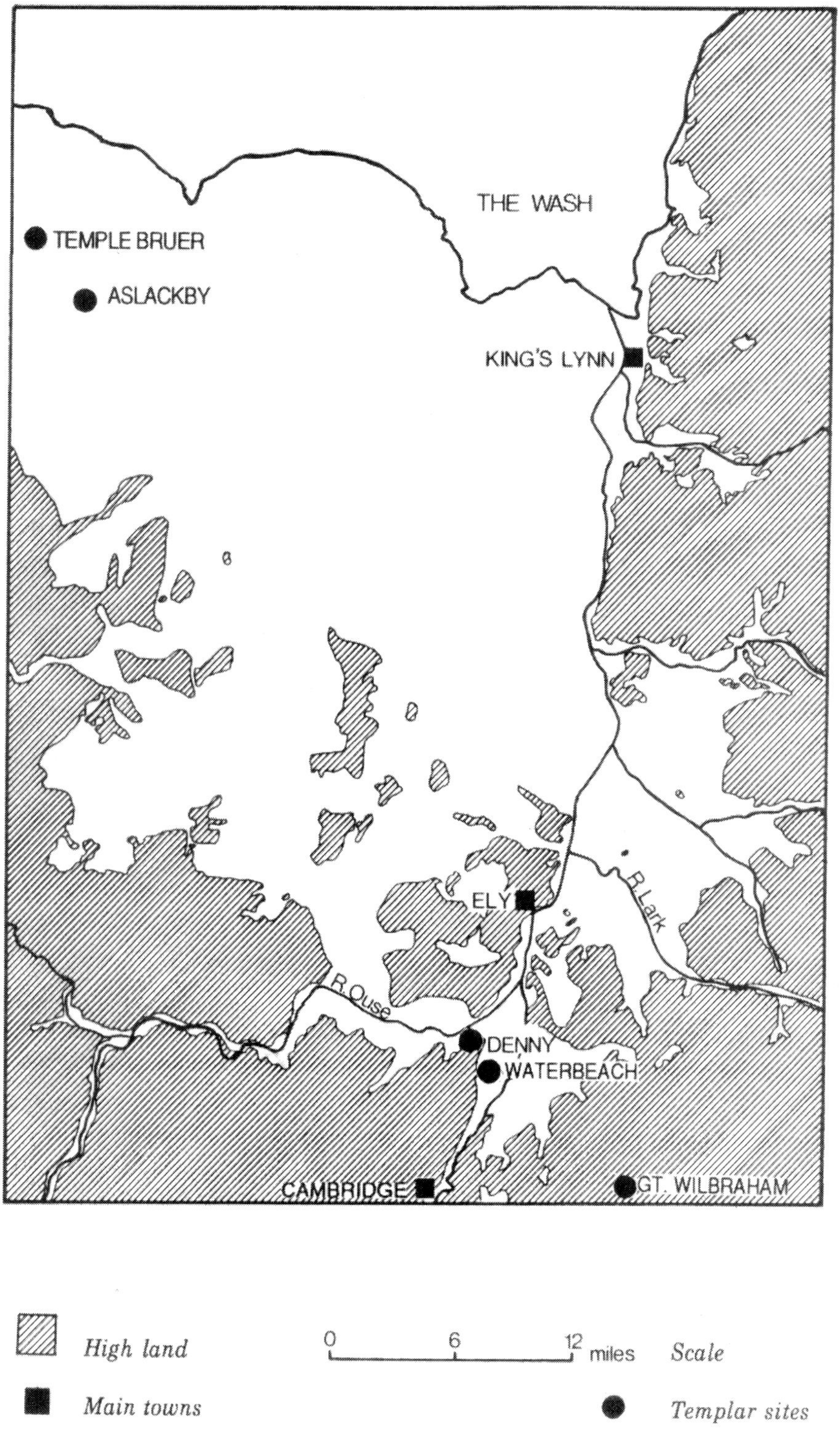

Denny Abbey (formerly Denney) - Northstow Hundred

Denny Abbey, in the parish of Waterbeach, is sited on a small island consisting of mainly gravelly loam soils, between the river Cam and the river Ouse in the Fens (Figs. 57a & b). It lies close to the A10 road, 7.5 miles [10.4 km] NE of Cambridge towards Ely. About the middle of the 12th century Robert, chamberlain of the Duke of Conan IV of Brittany held of the duke, as Earl of Richmond a manor in Waterbeach of which Godric, son of Radfrid Brito, was tenant in fee with the 'islands of Denney and Elmeney'. Robert also held Wilbraham and Wendy of the Earl and his first intention may have been to found a cell of Ely and Elmeney, but before 1159 he had built a church in honour of St. James and St. Leonard on the larger island of Denny. He endowed this with all the land that Godric had held of him, two parts of the isle of Elmeney and nine acres in the open fields at Waterbeach, then handed it over to the Benedictine Order of Ely under a monk, named Reynold as prior, in the presence of Bishop Niel, who dedicated the church.

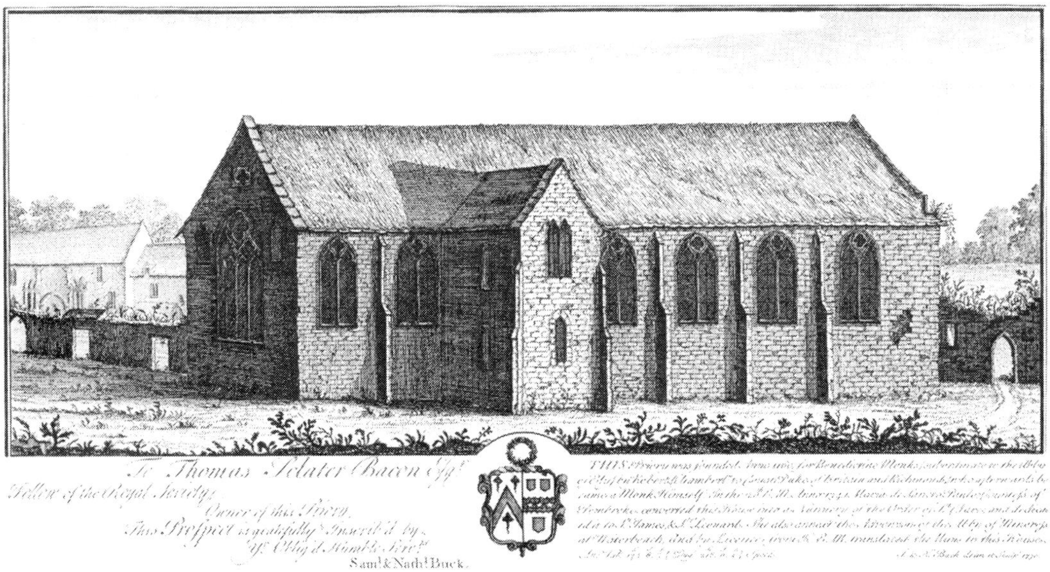

Fig. 57b. North-east view of Denny Priory, Cambridgeshire, 1730

A little later Conan confirmed to the monks serving God at Denny his Chamberlain's gifts of the tithe of his demesne at Wendy and Wilbraham, Wendy church, and with the Bishop's consent the advowson of all churches on his land in Wendy, Wilbraham and Kirkby (not located, possibly Lincolnshire). Robert himself became a monk at Ely, probably about 1159, and died shortly afterwards. His priory had a very short existence.

The first of the Cambridgeshire estates on which members of the Templars lived together under their *Rule* was at Denny, which was transferred to them by the community at Ely in 1170.

A Bull of Alexander III of 17th October c. 1173 confirms to the Master and brethren of the Temple the gift of Wilbraham church made to them by 'Nicholas' Bishop of Ely, with the consent of' 'R.' and Gilbert his son, founders and patrons of the said church. The copy is exceedingly inaccurate, but it would seem that Bishop Niel who died, 30th May 1169 had already transferred part of the gift of Robert (who died c. 1160), and his son George, to the Templars. Another Bull, probably at the end of 1174, confirmed to the Templars land given them in Waterbeach by George the chamberlain (who died before Michaelmas 1175) and Geoffrey, Earl of Richmond, who succeeded to the honour in 1171, with the consent of Geoffrey's father, King Henry II. A third Bull of 6th May, c. 1177 confirmed an agreement between the Templars and the monks of Ely about the churches of Kirkby, Wilbraham and Wendy, and the places of Denny, and Elmeney etc.

It is not possible to say how soon Denny became a hospital for sick and superannuated members of the Order. However, when Hugh, Bishop of Ely - either Hugh Balsham after 1257 or more likely Hugh Northwold between 1229 and 1254 instituted Robert de Swaffham as vicar of Great Wilbraham in the presence of the Master of the Temple, a composition was made by which the great tithes of the church were allotted to the support of the infirm brethren of the Order of Denny [c/ref Great Wilbraham]. The only other infirmary [excluding lazar houses, e.g. Baldock] for Templars known to have existed in England was that attached to Eagle, one of the early houses in Lincolnshire, and seems, like Denny, to have occupied a special position in their economy. It is quite possible that Denny with its ready built church and monastic buildings was acquired by the Templars with the object of using it for their sick from the very first.

A seal was found at Denny, when exactly is unknown, but it was before 1870, when an illustration of it was included in the *Ross Manuscripts for Temple Bruer* held by Lord Monson, Lincoln (Fig. 57c). The seal was attached to an agreement between the master and brethren of Temple Bruer and the Lord Henry de Colville respecting some exchange of lands etc. dated c. 1258. Robert Sutton was then preceptor. The name of Colville has cropped up again, probably a relative of those who held land in Duxford.

Although Denny held an important position in the Order, and the Templars of Cambridgeshire were comparatively numerous, it is improbable that a 'knight' was often, or perhaps ever, a preceptor of that establishment. Neither the management of an estate, which was the purpose of all preceptories, nor the care of the sick being the special business of Denny, were primarily the affair of combatants. Consequently, in England preceptors were more often 'servitors' rather than knights. Sometimes they were chaplains. Of the 135 Templars brought to trial in the British Isles, six only are described as *miles* [soldiers] and eleven were priests, none of whom came from Cambridgeshire.

John de Creke, Sheriff of Cambridgeshire and Huntingdonshire, kept account of the manors of Denny, Wilbraham (c/r), Carlton and Duxford (c/r) in Cambridgeshire with two in Huntingdonshire. The list of portable property found by him at Denny in 1308 gives a clear idea of the furnishings of a Templar house. Except in the chapel, there was no ostentation of wealth. Each brother, of whom there were eleven counting the preceptor and invalids, had a bed which, with their tunics and a clothes bag was valued, in the case of the preceptor, at 20s., and for the rest at a mark. There were also four mazers and six silver spoons. In the chamber together with the beds was a chest; the hall was furnished with two long trestle tables, two tables dormant; two wash-basins, and a form; the kitchen and bakehouse were well equipped with pots and pans etc.

The church was rather better furnished than the parish churches belonging to the Temple in Cambridgeshire. The main items confiscated were its three silver chalices, a silk altar cloth and its sets of vestments. No secular chaplains are known to have served this church, but priests must have been provided from outside the organisation of the Temple, for none were found among either the brethren or the *corrodarians,* being pensioners, here at Denny.

William de la Forde, had been *custos infirmorum* [infirmary warden] at Eagle and may have been appointed to Denny for that reason. As mentioned before he had been received into the Order about 42 years previously at Dinsley, together with Richard Petevyn and Thomas of Toulouse, and must therefore have been of advanced age when he was arrested in 1308. Of the brethren arrested with him, William de Chesterton and William de Wells were old and infirm; John de Hauville insane; William de Scotho, who had been preceptor in 1286, probably elderly; Roger de Dalton had been received at Balsall; Hugh de Tadcaster was presumably a Yorkshireman; John de Newent (he and Dalton were the only young men at Denny) and Roger de Ludlow probably came from the Marches; Alexander de Bulbecke and Robert Scot would appear to complete the number. (See Appendix C)

Fifteen Templars in all were arrested in Cambridgeshire, of these ten or eleven were sent from Denny, three or possibly four from two other houses. In 1309 they were handed over to the Constable of the Tower of London and the trials dragged on until 1311. None of the Cambridgeshire brethren admitted anything material, and against those from Denny there was little of the outside hearsay evidence which was freely accepted in this country. The preceptor had apparently attended most of the chapters, since his admission to the Order, for he said he had seen as many as a hundred brethren admitted, of whom only John de Newent and William de Chesterton were, at the time of their arrest, members of his own house at Denny. As *infirmarian* at Eagle he had seen the funerals of sixteen brethren, whereas none of the others gave evidence of having seen more than one or two.

Hugh de Tadcaster was porter [*claviger*] in the Temple as a secular, and asked the Master to admit him to the Order; this was done at Flaxflete, Yorkshire. Later he had seen the admission of Michael Baskeville, the London preceptor, who was a servitor, and that of a Knight of Dinsley, where he stated the reception of the knight was exactly the same form as his own. He had seen two other admissions, the latest being three and a half years before at Sutton in Essex.

Robert the Scot had been twice admitted to the Order. He had first joined it 26 years before in Syria, but afterwards apostasised [*ex levitate*] and remained outside it for two years. He then repented and went to Rome to confession at the Pope's penitentiary, on whose advice he sought readmission. This brother resumed the habit with 'alacrity and much penitence' at Nicosia in Cyprus, which after 1291 became the Templars headquarters. He had probably only retired from active service and come to England - where he had been placed with other superannuated brethren at Denny - shortly before the fall of the Order, for he had seen no admission in England. Like Tadcaster and others he testified that all the funerals of which he had knowledge were held in public.

On one of the chief points brought against the Templars, that of allowing lay absolution, William de la Forde, as preceptor of a house where the confession of the sick and aged made it of particular importance, gave very clear evidence. He said lay preceptors absolved their brethren, not from mortal sin, but from acts of canonical disobedience openly confessed in chapter, simply as an act of forgiveness, and that he believed the same was done in all other religious Orders. His evidence was borne out by the Preceptor of Duxford, William Raven of Wilbraham, Scotho, and also Dalton who had been professed only four years and had never seen another admission or funeral.

On 12th July, 1311, William de la Forde, Robert Scot, Raven, Scotho, and Tadcaster abjured and were absolved. The next day Newent abjured, so did Welles, and Chesterton who had been a Templar for 30 years and the former for 26 years, with three other crippled brethren. All were allowed to abjure privately in All Hallows Church, close by their place of imprisonment in the Tower of London.

Robert Scot and Roger Dalton, were handed over to John Ketene, Bishop of Ely 'to place in certain monasteries to do penance', with an allowance of 4 pence a day for each of them. Other Denny Templars were delivered to the Bishops of Lincoln, Norwich, Salisbury and Worcester. Later, it is found that Roger de Dalton was keeper of the Hospitallers' *camera* [legislative chamber/treasury?] of Ashley [? possibly near Newmarket, Cambs/Suffolk] in 1338. (*V.C.H.* vol. II, op. cit, 259-260)

The house of Denny was dissolved between 1308-12, after the suppression of the Templars, when it was granted by the Crown to the Hospitallers as happened to most of their property. It is unclear why in 1324 it seems to have reverted back to the Crown, one suggestion being that the Hospitallers had no use for it. In actual fact, it probably never had been handed over officially, for the Grand Prior of the Hospitallers was known to have complained several years later that the king was still occupying, or had re-occupied, certain Templar estates including Denny and Strood in Kent. (Rigold, 1962, 6-7) Three years later Denny was granted to Mary de Valence (formerly of St. Pol), widow of Aymer de Valence, Earl of Pembroke. It was Mary who was responsible for establishing the third monastic community to occupy Denny when in 1339 she received licence to transfer from Waterbeach the house of the Franciscan Order of Minoresses, which process was not completed until 1351. (Christie & Coad, 1980, 140-1). The Countess, a kinswoman of the king, was also given the Templar property at Strood and she brought the holding revenue to Denny. Apart from Strood's value as an estate, it had been conveniently placed, near the main road to the continent, for Templars to lodge in when travelling on business.

EXCAVATION OF DENNY ABBEY BETWEEN 1968 AND 1975

The excavations carried out by Patricia Christie and J. G. Coad concentrated on the 12th century church and the area to the north. They revealed a remarkable building sequence on this site which was occupied successively by Benedictine monks, Knights Templar, and Franciscan nuns verifying on the ground the historical documentation. After the Dissolution, the 12th century church was incorporated in a farmhouse. An examination of the foundations enabled a building sequence to be suggested for the upstanding remains. Standing remains of Templar preceptories are rare in this country, and Denny is the only example of an existing monastic site being adapted for Franciscan use. Drastic alterations in the 14th century were effected by building a new church to the east and converting the existing Templar church to residential use for the nuns. [see Fig. 57b. far left, note the incorporated arch – 1730]

The Templars occupied Denny for over 100 years and during that time considerable structural additions and modifications were made to the original Benedictine plan, and included buildings to the north of the church. The fact that Denny was an infirmary would have influenced the layout of the buildings.

Three intact burials and part of a fourth are ascribed to the Templars' era (except nos. 2 & 3 could be earlier). Burial no. 1 (dated to the 13th century), found west of the church, is orientated E-W with feet to the east, and was lined with clunch blocks set in mortar. Remains of a pewter chalice were found by the head and a decorated lead plate was found on the abdomen of the body. The plate or disc (146 mm dia. 2 mm thick max.) is unusual, for which no known parallel is known. On one face only is a roughly executed compass-drawn design of three concentric rings, which encloses intersecting arcs in the form of an attenuated cross with equal arms, except it cannot be seen as a *pectoral cross* in the normal sense due to its being inscribed on a flat circular sheet of lead (Fig. 57d). It lacks the depressed centre normal in a priest's patten but from its design (known from churches in East Anglia), and the fact a chalice was in the grave also, supports its possible use. Alternatively, it could have been let into a wooden coffin lid or formed the top of a wooden box for holding the wafer.* (See comments on p. 194)

In 1972 I visited the site several times and was permitted to take rubbings of the mason marks and other graffiti on the standing fabric. One in particular, on the south outside wall of the refectory (15th century), was a swastika (Fig. 57e). This motif appears in a small piece of glass found from a square border in a diamond-shaped frame (from the west range) dated to the 14th century (Fig. 57f). (Christie & Coad, 1980, Fig. 20, p. 205). There is no reason why the later swastika could not have been copied from that originally seen in the glass window, or the stone was a reused one. An exciting find for me was a metal object with opposing 'fleur-de-lis'. Alas post archaeologically it has been recognised as a 16th century book binder's punch.

On one occasion I enquired what the Templars did for water and whether any medieval wells had been found? Dr. Christie took me across the yard where there was a cistern which the archaeologists had uncovered, still containing water. This was a clunch-built structure with brick on edge roofing, set into the natural gravel, plastered internally on the north and east wall, with an internal diameter of 5 ft 2 ins [1.57 m]. Shallow gullies, at the natural gravel level, led to four round headed culverts feeding the cistern from the four cardinal points with surface run-off rain water. An inner tank, 2 ft by 2 ft 6 ins [610 x 762 mm], of three courses of clunch, was set within the main structure. Maximum height from the top of the brick opening to the base of the clunch coursing in this tank was 5 ft 5 ins [1.65m]. The surviving roof over the culverts and part of the tank had a square brick-built opening that once supported a timber hatch cover. Surrounding earth contained a quantity of shellfish remains. The excavation report maintains that it is not possible to date this cistern with certainty, although a Templar date seems likely. (Christie & Coad, 1980, op. cit., 138, 167-8, 189, 260-1)

Finds from Denny Abbey (57c-f) and elsewhere

Fig. 57c. Seal with the Pascal Lamb, found prior to excavation, and recorded in the Ross Manuscripts in Lincoln (not to scale)

Fig. 57e. The swastika motif (not shown to scale – 80 mm by 80 mm) on the south outside wall of the refectory. Thought to be of 15th century date. Rubbing from Sylvia Beamon's collection, 1972.

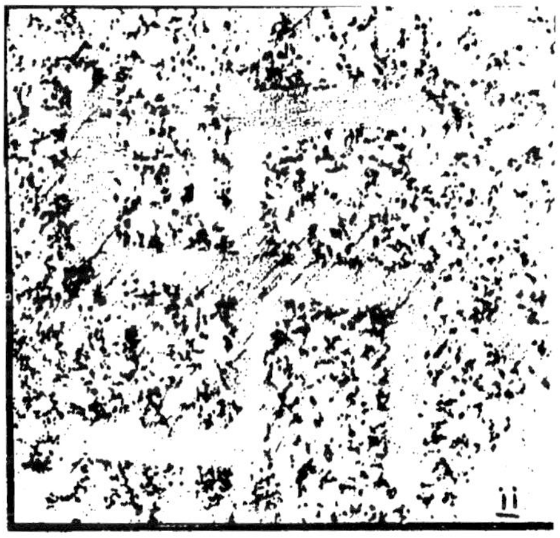

Fig. 57g. The swastika symbol 100 x 107 mm engraved on the south wall of St. Michael's Church Tower, Garway, built by the Templars.

Fig. 57d. Decorated lead disc (not to scale). 146 mm diameter, 2 mm thick, decorated one face only. Three outer concentric rings, 7-8 mm apart. The area forming the attenuated cross were drawn from four (still visible) points on the second outer circle. (Christie & Coad, 1980)

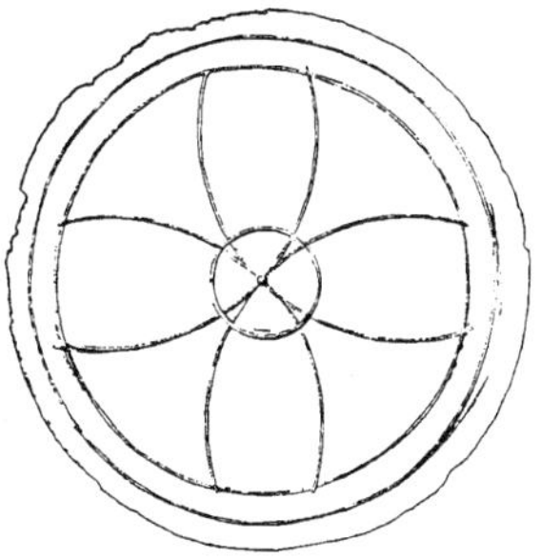

Fig. 57f. A small piece of glass of 14th century date, exhibiting the swastika, which can represent many things – e.g. 'the sun' or 'symbol of light'. Scale 2 : 3 (Christie & Coad, 1980)

Fig. 57h. Engraving of Templar coffin lid in the Holy Trinity Church, Bosbury, Hereford.

After this last visit, I have often wondered whether the depression or 'grave' area in Royston Cave, was in fact a sump for water and perhaps fed by a culvert which could be behind the 'bricking' (clunch blocks) which has never been broken into approximately 15 ft [4.5 m] above it. A run-off surface water well was located a few yards from the Cave. Depth to the water level was only 11 ft [3.35 m]. It still had a rusted pump attached in the early 1970s when examined, which has since been removed and the area covered over.

* **Note:** *The author questions whether the 'disc' was part of a ceremonial staff, an insignia of office, similar to that shown being clasped by the Templar in the illustration from Dugdale's 'Monastieon' shown in Fig. 13, or on a Templar coffin lid in Holy Trinity Church, Bosbury, Hereford.(Fig. 57h).*

Wendy - Armingford Hundred
(Wandei, Wandrie, Wendei, Wendena, Wendey, Wendeye, Wendie)

From some of the examples already quoted it will be realised that the Templars were well established locally from the middle of the 12th century. Several points of interest remain to be noticed as follows:

1155-75 – Hugh prior of Bernewelle recovers the church of Wendei (Wendena), which had been lost through the negligence of his predecessors: (Lib. de Bernewell, 65) (Farrer, 1920, 17 et seq.)

ante 1159. Robert, chamberlain of Conan Earl of Richmond, gave to the monks of Denneye in Waterbeach the church of Wendei and the ninth garb of his demesne there; (M.A. VI. 1552b). Earl Conan confirmed this gift. (ib.)

1159 – The Templars were pardoned ... (see under Royston Property)

1169 – Nigel bishop of Ely confirmed the gift which Robert the chamberlain made to the monks of Denneye; (M.A. VI. 1549)

1199 – William de Scalers demanded against Hugh de Scalers land in Wendei held by knight's service; (Abbrev. Placit. 99)

t. John. Robert Engaine, knt. gave to the Templars the manor (sic) of Wendy; (M.A. VI. 834b)

After 1205 Ralph Belet ... (see under Royston Property)

Two further entries concern Ralph son of Fulk and his progeny. This family founded and held the patronage of the Hospital of St. Nicholas at Royston. (q.v.)

1236 – Ralph son of Fulk, Hugh Giffard, William Engayne, John, son of Henry and Alice Sauns Manche pay half mark for frankpledge of Wendeye; (ib. 273)

1266 – Grant for life to Matilda, wife of Ralph son of Ralph son of Fulk, taken at Kenilwrd, that of the manors of the said Ralph in Wendeye and three other places she shall have £5. a year for her and her children's support; (Cal. Pat. R1266, 526)

And a final extract for this section states:

1276 – The township of Wendeye is held by socage of the honor of Richmond and owes suit which has been withdrawn; the brethren of the hospital of Senegey [Hospitallers] have appropriated a tenement in Wendeye of the fee of Richmond and for ten years past they have withdrawn suit to the sheriffs turn; (R. Hund I, 51)

There seems to be no doubt that the Templars were in Wendy a very long time before the Knights Hospitaller arrived. Wendy adjacent to Shingay is known today as Shingay cum Wendy.

MINOR CAMBRIDGESHIRE PROPERTY

The Knights Templar besides having preceptories at Denny, Duxford and Great Wilbraham were given a lot of land in Cambridgeshire. They had land at Pampisford (Chilford Hundred), Carlton (Radfield Hundred) and some small tenements at Knapwelle [Cnapwell] (Papworth Hundred). The Templars claimed liberties in Boxworth. An entry for Papworth Everard and Papworth Agnes states:

> Papewurd hundred was amurced 2 m. for default of warranty; of this the Bishop of Ely was pardoned 16d. and the Templars 2d. (P. 57).
>
> In the villages of Ashley (Asle) and Wilnesle, Cheveley Hundred, the Master of the Knight Templars held 300 acres of land (1276). (Farrer, op.cit. 46, 62, 90, 92, 97)

On the All road from Royston at Abington there is a cafe named the 'Temple Cafe', and this is situated on Templar land at the crossroads (now known as the 'Four Went Ways Roundabout'). This crossing was quite an important one since the roads led to Colchester, Newmarket, Cambridge and Royston (one road being the Icknield Way).

BEDFORDSHIRE

Edworth - Biggleswade Hundred

Land in Edworth was given to the Templars and the records are contained in the Sussex charters (Lees, 1935, 222). (See also p. 118)

Apart from the rents from Cockayne Hatley, Edworth, and Sandy, which are entered in the *Inquest* between two sets of Hertfordshire entries, the returns for the Bedfordshire estates of the Templars are arranged in three main groups, for Millbrook, Sharnbrook and Langford.

Sharnbrook - Willey Hundred
(Sarnebroche)

Where services in kind were rendered, William Trichet had granted 20 acres of demesne land, but there appeared to be no signs of a preceptory, except the Fine of 1254 could indicate otherwise.

Amongst other donors of land at Sharnbrook was Alice or Adeliza, daughter of Hugh, Count of Clermont who married Gilbert fitz Richard de Clare and was the mother of Gilbert, Earl of Pembroke (1138-48) the benefactor of the Templars in Hertfordshire (Lees, 1935, 75). Furthermore, a Fine recorded at Bedford 12th November 1254, translated from Latin, states:

> "Brother Rocelinus, Master of the Knighthood of the Temple in England, by John de Taney, his attorney, against William de Stanbrigge and Elicia his wife: Land at Sharnbrook. Plea of covenant. Right of the Master and Brethren, as of their gift, to hold of them and the heirs of Elicia free of all secular service. Clause of warranty. William and Elicia further granted that henceforth they would not claim common pasture for their beasts in that baulk called ROWEBALK, between the land of the Master in Sharnbrook and that formerly belonging to Roger de Loring, extending in length to the baulk called CHILDESBALK, and in width from the way leading from the Master's house towards Sharnbrook as far as LE TEMPLE SLADE, where a water leat runs. For this the Master gives them land in the same vill, in the field called Poverescroft; to be held from the Master and his successors free of all secular service. The Master and Brethren grant that William and Elicia may build and enclose a courtyard outside their door without hindrance."

The assumption is that the Master wanted the baulk [a division between pieces of arable land] to be enclosed and added to other of his land. This sort of 'waste' was normally available for communal grazing. The Master was evidently resident at Sharnbrook, unless 'Master's house' simply means one owned by him.

The 1279 *Hundred Rolls* mentions that 'The Master of the Temple of Jerusalem' held part of Sharnbrook, with view of frankpledge, etc., and the other part was held by the Prior of Newnham, who had demesne land, manor house, fishing rights etc. There is no suggestion by that date that the Master was resident in the parish, although the Templars still held houses and land as follows:

> A 'messuage' [house and grounds] and 9 acres of land, of the Prior of Newnham, rent 2s, 10 acres of land 'in free alms, given in the time of King Henry, son of King John' 22 acres of land; 3 roods of meadow, 'in free alms ...' (as above), held of Elena de Pentyn (part of the Barony of Beauchamp)
>
> And:
>
> 'The Templars of Jerusalem hold in this vill, without tax or fee, whatsoever of the Honour of Gloucester was given by Alice de Clermund in the time of King Henry son of King John in free, pure and perpetual alms, not performing service to the lord king or any other, and they have free view of frankpledge of their tenants ...' [A list of tenants and sub-tenants follows.]
>
> Item: The Templars hold in this vill 26 acres of land and 6 acres of wood, of the gift of a certain Richard Taysi, in the time of King John, of the aforesaid Fee of Gloucester.

Item: The Templars hold in this vill, in a place call Alfey, 27 acres of land and meadow...'

By 1331, the Templar holdings at Sharnbrook had been passed to the Knights Hospitallers, who in the 12th and 13th centuries held a quantity of property at neighbouring Riseley and Melchbourne. They would seem to have been very influential in the area, holding courts at their 'seat' at Melchbourne. Reminders still remained of the Templars in the 16th century with fields in Sharnbrook continuing to have names such as 'Temple Leys', 'Temple Hills' and 'Temple Corner'. Recorded as late as 1882 are 'Temple Woods' and 'Temple Spinney'.

KNIGHTS HOSPITALLER

Rushden - Odsey Hundred

The Knights Hospitaller held lands in Rushden which were attached to their Shingay preceptory in Cambridgeshire. Probably the land attached to it in Rushden represents the half hide which Earl Roger held in Broadfield, in 1086, for there is no further trace of this holding in Broadfield; also the boundaries of the manorial holdings do not seem to correspond with the present boundaries of the parishes.

In 1198 the Knights Hospitaller, who held land in Rushden, were fined for receiving a fugitive, Ralph Rusticus. They continued to hold these lands until the close of their Order, after which the preceptory of Shingay and its appurtenances in Rushden and elsewhere was granted by Henry VIII to Sir Richard Long in tail-male in 1540. There is no record of the Rushden estate after this date. 'Shingay' survived as a wood's name on the 1845 tithe map. (*V.C.H. Herts.*, 268-9)

Chippenham - Staploe Hundred

(Chipeham, Chippeham)

Like Denny for the Templars, the preceptory at Chippenham was a hospital for sick Hospitallers, perhaps even from its foundation. It was founded by William de Mandeville [Lady Roisia and Geoffrey de Mandeville's younger son] in 1184 and received from him manorial rights and a comparatively small endowment of land. The other Hospitaller preceptory at Shingay, is fully described under Royston.

Two later references verify that in:

1279 – The abbot of Waleden has the church of St. Margaret the virgin in Chippeham in *proprios usus* with 45 a. of land by the gift of William de Mandeville; the prior of the Hospitallers holds the manor of Chippenham by the gift of William de Mandeville, earl of Hereford, temp. Henry II; (ib. 505). [Hereford is correct. It is easy to see how confusion arises between the county names, changes of status of individuals and is the reason why many documents get misfiled, lost, and spread around the country.]

1302-3 – The prior of the Hospitallers holds the manor of Chipeham of the earl of Hereford; F.A. I, 143 [Note again: Hereford] (Farrer, op. cit., 149)

The interesting examples quoted before and those below illustrate how the various families, Mandevilles, de Scales*, Ralph fitz Fulk belonged to a close-knit community as their names occur time and again through the centuries.

Shepreth - Wetherley Hundred
(Seperee, Seperei, Shepere, Shepereth, Chepereye, Sceperet, Schepere)

1167-69 – Earl William de Mandeville gave to the Hospitallers 100s. of rent in Seperei, which King John confirmed in 1199; (R.Chart.16)

1231-32 – Fine between Robert son of William le Keu and Ralph fitz Fulk, who had been called to warranty touching land in Shepereth. (Cal. of Camb. Fines 15)

1243 – Ralph fitz Fulk holds in Seperee quarter fee of the barony of Geoffrey de Scalers: (T. 354 b)

1251 – Grant to Geoffrey de Scalers, keeper of the land and heir of Ralph fitz Fulk of certain dates for repayment of £45 and 3 palfreys owing to the king by the said Ralph; (Excerpt e R Fin., II. 115)

1265 and 1266 – Grant to Matilda, wife of Ralph son of Ralph fitz Fulk, taken at Kenilworth, for her life by way of humanity, that of the manors late of the said Ralph in Chepereye (Shepreth), Wendeye, Aspenden and Bradefeld, which the king gave to William Giffard, late extended at £16.12s.10d. a year, she shall have the manor of Bradfeld etc. for maintenance of herself and children; (Cal.Pat. 1265 R.469)

1278 – 54 a. of land used to be geldable in the vill of Sceperet and have been alienated to the liberty of Brittany; the abbess of Chateriz holds 50 a. of the fee geldable of Simon Martyn and they have been alienated by the liberty of Ely; also of the same fee half acre has been alienated to the hospital of Schenegeye (Shingay) (R.Hund.I,50)

1279 – Walter Martyn holds half fee in Shepere of Richard de Frivill; 40 a. of the kings's fee were given to the nuns of Chateriz by Simon Martyn, father of the said Walter, 30 years since; in the time of Robert Martyn 20 a. of that fee were alienated to the abbot of Wardon etc.; Ralph fitz Fulk, knt., holds quarter fee in Schepere of the fee of Scalers; William de la Haye hold 1 h. in Schepere of the prior of the Hospital of St. John of the fee of Mandevile and renders 100 s. to the prior; the abbess of Chateriz holds there one and a half hides (8 score acres) of the fee of Boulogne with the advowson of the church, but the tenement has been drawn into the liberty of Ely, how it is not known; (ib.II, 561-62). (Farrer, op. cit., 231)

****Note:** Robert de Scales, whose family held Chelmsford Hundred in Essex, also held Sandon (see chapter 11). This family is sometimes muddled up with the d'Eschalers (de Scalers) family, members exampled above, whose name lingered in the manor of Challers, in Reed (Herts.) and is still preserved as 'Scales Park'. Hardouin d'Eschalers had an extensive fief, including Babraham, Little Carlton, Histon and Great Chesterford, in Cambridgeshire. His descendants were benefactors of the Cluniac Priory of Lewes, Sussex on which early in the 12th century Hugh de Scalariis bestowed the Hertfordshire churches of Widdial, Reed and Little Berkhamsted.*

10. TEMPLAR PROPERTY IN ROYSTON

Having looked at the Templar and Hospitaller holdings in the two counties of Hertfordshire and Cambridgeshire in some depth, Royston, with 'a foot in each' county (Odsey Hundred and Ermingford Hundred), is now to come under scrutiny.

The following paragraph recorded in *A History of Hertfordshire, 'Odsey Hundred',* is of special interest for it claims the Templars did have property in Royston itself, as early as the 12th century:

> 'From the first the situation of the town on the crossroads in the midst of the barley-growing country must have caused the markets and fairs to prosper. In 1291 they were valued at £9.13s.4d. In 1223 and 1226 the maximum price of wine was fixed at a higher rate in Royston than elsewhere, owing to the distance of the town from the coast. The prior made good his right to the market and to the fairs at Whitsuntide and the feast of St. Thomas in 1278. The prior had been involved in disputes with the Abbot of Westminster and the Master of the Knights Templar, who claimed exemption from toll in all English markets. In 1247-8 the Abbot pleaded the charters of Edward the Confessor and William I against the claims of the prior (Assize R.318. m. 5 d.) The dispute with the Templars, **who owned property in Royston,** [Attached to Shingay preceptory *L. and P. Henry VIII* xv, 613 (I)] began in 1199 and was still continuing in 1200. (*Rot, Cur. Reg.* (Rec. Com.), i, 229; ii, 82, 143, 217, 218). This plea concerned 'liberties', probably the exemption from toll claimed by both parties. Salmon (*History of Hertfordshire,* 356) states that the prior was obliged to restore 37s. taken from the Templars as stallage).'

It was really quite a large amount of money which the Prior had to give back to the Templars, see previous comments under Baldock (p. 172).

IMPRISONMENT OF TEMPLARS IN ROYSTON

Evidently, in the middle of the 13th century brethren members were still travelling to Royston for marketing, and the assumption is that they came from Baldock. In 1254 the Master of the Templars impleaded the prior for imprisoning and beating certain of his men who had come to the market on the Templars' business. (*Abbrev. Plac.* (Rec.Com.) 137). The markets and fairs were frequently disturbed during the 13th and 14th centuries.

More detailed references are as follows:

> 'Hereford: Prior de Cruce Roys summoned to answer the Master of the Templars why he instructed Richard Bucke (Buche) and Simon Heggeswell (Heggeswet), concerning the plea that they took and held prisoner the men of the said Master coming to the market of Cruce Roys for the business of the Templars and beat them. The prior defends himself and seeks judgement:

'quare si debet eidem precepto respondere quousque convincet (convincatur), Ideo consideratus (consideratum), est quod prior inde sine die quo usque factum fuerit convictum.' M. 21.

[[to be postponed] ...if he must answer the summons until it was proved ... therefore it was decided that the prior would be [relieved] thereof indefinitely until the deed should have been proved.]

The Master impleads the same men concerning the same (said trespass) and they do not come. The Sheriff answers that they were not found and it is testified that they dwell in Crucem (Crux) Roys; the Sheriff is to take them and have their bodies etc. M. 21. (Roll 21)

[The names and other words in round brackets indicate variations in different references.]

It will be noticed that Hereford instead of Hertford is the heading. Frequently Royston occurs under Herefordshire, also Huntingdonshire in the Rolls Series etc. besides of course, being included in the Hertfordshire and Cambridgeshire records.

In August 1971, I wrote to the Hertford County Record Office asking them if they knew where in Royston the Templar property was sited? They answered that the writer of the Royston section of the *V.C.H.* seems to have known that the Templars owned property in Royston only from a grant made in 1540 which is calendared in *Letters and Papers Foreign and Domestic of the Reign of Henry VIII,* vol. XV. Sir Richard Longe was granted properties in Royston, and many other places, 'of the preceptory or lordship of Shingay'. None of the properties are described in any way: The writer of the section is now dead.

They went on to say that unfortunately, there are no documents listed in the indexes and calendars in their office relating to Templar lands in Royston, or to the estates of Sir Richard. There is no mention of the property in Dugdale's *Monasticon.*

TEMPLAR PROPERTY IN SHINGAY?

I think I should mention at this point that there is some controversy over Shingay and whether, in fact, the Templars ever did have a preceptory there.

In an article by W. M. Palmer, (1904) *Notes on the Early History of Shingay,* he records that:

'About the year 1140, or within 50 years of the existence of the Order, the Earl's only daughter Sybil, gave the manor with all its appurtenances to the Knights Hospitallers of St. John of Jerusalem.'

'In a paper on Shingay, read before the Cambridge Antiquarian Society on March 3rd 1890, it is stated, apparently on the authority of Camden, that the Manor was given by Sybil to the Knights Templar, and was held by them until the Order was suppressed. But this is directly contradicted by the official record, viz: the *Charter Roll of* 1199, which recites and confirms various gifts to the Hospitallers amongst which is Sybil's gift of 'Senegia'. This gift refers to the manor only, the rights of the church of Shingay had already been given away. Dugdale in his *Monasticon* vol. II p. 966, quoting the ecclesiastical historian Orderic Vitalis, states that Earl Roger himself gave the tithes of Shingay to the monastery of St. Evroul in Normandy. The confidence usually placed on the accuracy of this writer has caused this statement to pass unquestioned hitherto. But it must always have seemed curious to anyone who has studied the matter, that no further reference to a connection of St. Evroul with Shingay should have been found. Whereas, on the other hand, the Abbey of St. Martin at Seez in Normandy, constantly appears in records such as ecclesiastical taxation rolls, as having an interest in Shingay. The earliest mention of any connection between Seez and Shingay in any English record is in the taxation roll known as Pope Nicholas's *Valor* 1291, where the following occurs:

> Portio Abbatis de Sees in ecclesia de Shenegeie indecimabilis... - 1 10 0'
>
> [The portion of the Abbot of Sees in the church of Shingay, not titheable - 1 10 0]

In Pope Innocent's *Valor of 1254*, there is no mention of Sees under Shingay, although in connection with Orwell, there is (see Earl Roger's Charter below). Again in the account of the English possessions of the Order which was sent to the Grand Master in 1338, is this entry.

> "Item Abbati de Sees quondam patrono ecclesie de Shenegeye, per compositionem ratione prioratus per annum – 20s."
>
> [Item: To the Abbot of Sees, formerly the patron of the church of Shingay, by agreement because of the Priory each year – 20s.]

The connection is also mentioned in the *Nonae Roll* (1342) under 'Wendey cum Shenegeie' .

This connection of Seez with Shingay had led Mr. Palmer for some time to believe that the historian Orderic had made a slip, and had written St. Evroul instead of Seez. Then the discovery of the following charter settled the matter as far as Palmer was concerned - but does it? It is taken from Lechaude d'Anesy's *Cartulaire de La Basse-Normandie,* a three volume collection of charters and other records relating to the possessions of the religious houses of Normandy in England. This charter is also included in J. H. Round's *Calendar of Documents preserved in France, Illustrative of the History of Great Britain and Ireland* vol. I 1899.

Carta Com Rogeri (See Appendix D for the Latin)

A translation of the charter appears in the *Newsells Park Estate Ownership Calendar,* 1929 as follows:

> Calendar of documents preserved in France. A.D. 918-1206 p. 233. Abbey of St. Martin, Sees (Benedictine). (? 1087(9)-1093) 656.

Charter of Roger (earl) of Shrewsbury giving for the souls of his most sweet William Duke of the Normans and King of the English and of Queen Mathildis for his own and for those of his wife Mabel and all his predecessors and successors, with the consent and approval of his sons and daughters to God and St. Martin of Sees and the monks there serving God, in alms for ever, Fissaburna (Fishbourne, Sussex) and Wath (Sussex) and Hanton (Southampton, Hampshire) with all its appurts, and Arintonam [Harrington, Co. Northampton] and the tithe of Senegaia (Shingay) and Orunvelle (Orwell), and Herlingtone (Arrington), and the church of Hertinges (Harting, Sussex) for a brother of the countess Mabel, who was made a monk in that monastery. Robert the sheriff son of Tetbald gave Totintona (Tottington, Sussex, Upper Beeding) to the same saint at his death, with the consent of (earl) Roger and his sons. Norman the huntsman, with the consent of them all give the tithe of all his lands. Eudo son of Hubert gave the tithe of Neiselles.

All these gifts were made in the time of the most excellent duke of the Normans and king of the English, William and of queen Mathildis. Earl Roger, Hugh his son granting it, gave St. Martin of Seez the church of Dodelabria with all its appurts, and Belingeham wholly free of all forfeitures.

Testantibus:- (names of the witnesses given in Appendix D)

N.B. Neiselles is indexed as Newsellbury in Barkway, Co. Herts.

ARRINGTON

I will digress here and explain why in the *Carta Com Rogeri* recorded in W. M. Palmer's Notes he has asterisked 'Arintonam' as 'Arrington' and yet I have given this place as (Harrington, Co. Northampton).

When checking this charter and the present day naming of the places mentioned I found that 'Herlingtone' was indeed Arrington which puzzled me as to why it should then read, 'Arrington, Shingay, Orwell and Arrington' again. I telephoned the Record Office at Cambridge, to ask whether they could throw any light on this minor point and they suggested I contacted Northampton Record Office to see whether the Earl of Shrewsbury had ever had land at Harrington, although they themselves thought it still meant 'Arrington, Co. Cambridge'.

The Northampton Record Office sent me the following extract from *The Place-Names of Northamptonshire* by Gover, Mawer and Stenton. C.U.P. 1933.

'HARRINGTON 73 F 12.
Arintone 1086 DB, -na C. 1090 France, Harinton' 1166 P(p) Hederingeton' 1184 P (p), Hetheringtone 12th Survey et passim to 1379 Cl. with various spellings – inton(e), or -yngton. Haderington c. 1210 Wells R, -inton 1234 Cl, Hatherinton 1237 Cl. Eringtona 1225 Bracton, Etherinton 1275 RH.'

They also enclosed an article on Harrington from *The History and Antiquities of Northamptonshire* from the collections of John Bridges, compiled about 1720, but not actually published until 1791 vol. II (Rothwell Hundred).

> 'This lordship soon after the conquest appears to have been in the possession of Roger de Montgomery earl of Shrewsbury. He was the father of Maud wife to Robert earl of Morton half-brother to the conqueror, and gave eight hides of land in Harington to Grestein Abbey in Normandy founded by Herlewine de Coutevill the said earl of Morton's father. At the time of the general survey Grestein Abbey had five hides and a third part of one hide in Arintone. The arable land was ten carucates, in demesne were three carucates, and seventeen villanes with thirteen cottages had five carucates, and four socmen had two carucates... '

The above article answered one question and created another. Who was Maud if Sybil was the only daughter of earl Roger de Montgomery?

I wrote to the Cambridge Record Office enclosing photostats of the information from Northampton, and received a reply on the 10th August explaining that:

> '*The Dictionary of National Biography* provides details of Roger de Montgomery's children. It seems he married twice, and had five sons, Robert, Roger, Philip and Arnulf,* and four daughters, Emma, Matilda (Maud) Mabel and Sybil. It was Matilda who married Robert, Count (Earl) of Mortain, who was half-brother of William the Conqueror. John Bridges is referring to the same people when he says Roger's daughter Maud was wife to Robert Earl of Morton, W. M. Palmer is presumably mistaken when he states that Sybil was the only daughter of Roger, but he must have been repeating a statement made in one of his sources, Dugdale's *Monasticon Anglicanum* or the Charter Roll. The *D.N.B.* [*Dictionary of National Biography*] provides the further information that Sybil was, by Robert Fitz Hamo, mother of Matilda, the wife of Robert Earl of Gloucester, but does not mention a granddaughter named Sybil, so I think she must be Roger's daughter.' [* no mention of the fifth son.]

I am trying to show, by the digression, that however careful you are as a serious historian, and Palmer certainly was, minor errors are inevitable, either from misinformation from your sources, or the accidental misfiling of documentation beyond your control etc.

KNIGHTS HOSPITALLERS AT SHINGAY

Referring back once more to Shingay, it seems that the Master of the Shingay 'Hospital' was a very powerful man in the county. His preceptory was the fourth wealthiest in England as early as 1338, and when the Knights Hospitaller Order was suppressed in 1540, there were rents payable to him from many villages in Cambridgeshire, as well as other places in Bedfordshire, Buckinghamshire, Essex, Hertfordshire and Huntingdonshire.

The confiscation of the property of the Knights Templar at the beginning of the 14th century added much to the power of the Order in general, as well as to most individual preceptories, and Shingay was no exception to the rule and we find in *Originalia 32 Henry VIII* m. 29 that the preceptory had property in the following places: Sawston, Wendy, Clopton, Croydon, Guilden Morden, Steeple Morden, Abington, Litlington, Bassingbourn, Kneesworth, Whaddon, Meldreth, Melbourn, Shepreth, ROYSTON, Tadlow, East Hatley, Wimpole, Orwell, Bourn, Longstowe, Cambridge, Dry Drayton, Haslingfield, Horseheath, Barton, Babraham, Borough, Comberton, Chesterton, Caldecote, Dullingham, Eversden, Grantchester, Harston, Shudy Camps, Histon, Impington, Trumpington, Whittlesford, Westley Waterless, Madingly.

In February 1972, I wrote to the Curator of the Library and Museum of The Grand Priory in the British Realm of the Most Venerable Order of the Hospital of St. John of Jerusalem in London, asking several questions relating to property ownership by both the Orders. She replied that they have no records of any Hospitaller property in Royston, and as far as she could find out the Hospitallers and the Templars did not both have property at Shingay. The Curator also thought that W. M. Palmer's information is correct about Shingay, as she had found confirmation from Tanner de Thomas, *Notitia Monastica,* 1787, Cambridge:

> 'A preceptory of Knights Hospitallers of St. John of Jerusalem, given to that Order by Sibyll a de Raynes daughter of Roger, Earl of Montgomery AD 1140. It was worth at the suppression £171.4s.6d. per annum Dugdale: £175.4s.6d. Speed: and was granted, 32 H. VIII, to Richard Longe.' [As mentioned before in the *Odsey Hundred.*]

ROYSTON TEMPLARS AND WENDY TEMPLAR PROPERTY

In view of the evidence, I think it can be assumed that the Templars owned property in Royston, which was taken over by the Hospitallers after the downfall of the Templars, and then added to Shingay preceptory. The confusion with regard to the connection of the Hospitallers and Templars with Shingay, arises perhaps from the fact that both Orders had possessions in Wendy. Robert Dengayne, Chamberlain of Conan, Earl of Britainy and Richmond, in the early part of the 12th century, gave a manor in Wendy to the Hospitallers, and the tithes and advowson of Wendy to the Priory of Ely (*Mon. Ang.* vol. I p. 4.) The monastery afterwards exchanged their rights in Wendy with the Templars, for some land in Waterbeach. In 1308 just after the lands and possessions of the Templars had been seized by the king, the corn tithe, etc.

> '...blada perveniente tam de decimis quam de exitu dominicarum ecclesie sic venditis in grosso' [The grain which comes both from the issue of demesne of the Church so sold together] - of Wendy was worth £15. 13s. 4d. (*Land Revenue, Miscellaneous Rolls No. 20 Templars' Lands*).

In the 1338 report, under a list headed:

> 'Extenta bonorum quondam templi' [Extent of the goods formerly of the Templar church] is stated:

'Ecclesia de Wendye in proprios usus valet per annum 20 marks.' (£13.6s.8d.)

[...The church of Wendy for its own use is worth 20 marks per year.]

Yet at the same time the Manor of Wendy, an ancient possession of the Hospitallers, was worth £11.6s.0d. (*Camden Society,* Publ. O.S. 65).

Perhaps another reason for the confusion arose because of a namesake connected with the Templars in close proximity. The following entry is found in *Feudal Cambridgeshire* by William Farrer and on page 17 he states:

> 'After 1205 Ralph Belet for himself and Sibyl his wife acknowledged that the 4th part of the advowson of the church of Wendie was the right of the master of the Templars and remised the same from the heirs of Sibyl.' (*Abbrev. Placit.* 78b)

I first discovered this reference in the Bibliothèque Nationale in Paris in October, 1972 where I went to study the unpublished works of the Marquis d'Albon in their manuscripts room. * (See p. 207)

There is no doubt at all that the Templars were established at Wendy in the middle of the 12th century for there is a reference in 1159 that 'the Templars were pardoned 9s.11d. out of 10 m. [marks] imposed upon Erningeford [Ermingford] hundred for a murder: P. 54.'

The weekly market at Royston was the subject of an Inquisition held here in the reign of Henry VI, in the year 1425, which is recorded in a Latin document now in the Public Record Office, of which the following is an extract. The reference is apparently to the small portion of the market which extended into Cambridgeshire at the Cross:

> 'Inquisition taken at Royston in the County of Cambridge, Wednesday after S. Michael's Day, 3 Henry VI, in the presence of Nicholas Parys, Escheator of the Lord King in the said county by the oath of Thomas Taylour, John Andrews, Henry Tebowde, John Politede, John Strete, Roger Plasle, William Brammistone, Thomas Arnbrok, Richard Fuller de Bassyngburne, Roger Fyn, John Cosy, and John Balle, Jun., Jurors. Who say that Richard Hugh, prior of Royston, holds a market in Royston every Wednesday throughout the year, whereof neither he nor his ancestors hold a charter of the king. The market is worth 6d. the year. From the first year of Henry V until now the said prior and his predecessors have received the issues and profits of the same, for which they are responsible to the king. In the witness whereof, etc.' (*Escheators Inquisition* 2-3 *Hen. VI,* Series 1, file 556, Public Record Office.)'

The Royston jurors of Henry VI's reign evidently forgot the history of their own town. It certainly seems extraordinary that the prior was not able to satisfy them that a charter had been held by his 'ancestors', or predecessors, as far back as the reign of Richard I. The contention may have been that the charter did not apply to Cambridgeshire. The value stated as the worth of the market is only intelligible on the assumption that, as it was the Escheator for Cambridgeshire who was taking action, it may have been in respect of 'part of ye markit for fowles, butter, cheese, and such like commodities,' which Layer says extended into Cambridgeshire. (Kingston, 1906, 37-8).

I would like to suggest that the 'Cave', which was under the butter market, was itself situated in Cambridgeshire and therefore on the land appertaining to Wendy. However, I realise there are certain questions that still remain to be fully answered. Geoffrey de la Lee was given the custodianship of Templar lands for Hertfordshire in the 14th century. William Lee of Radwell, owned property in Royston. Could he be related in some way to Geoffrey de la Lee? (c/r p. 21 & 164) William Lee's will (1527) attests:

> '...as to the disposition of all my lands and tenements which I have within the counties of Hertford and Cambridge...'

And why, in another portion of the Will, not quoted before in Chapter 2, did he make a bequest to Wendy church?

> '...I bequeath to the High Altar in Radwell Church xij d. Item to the High Altar in Wendy Church 3s.4d...'

Surely there must be some connection. Did the family enjoy rents or property originally owned by the Templars for services rendered to the Crown? The Will of course, was honoured before the Reformation.

Finally, in this section, there is evidence in Royston of a Templar specifically named. It was not market day so presumably he had not come into the Town on business. Did he, therefore, reside here?

> "(Sept.) 1234 Cal. Pat. Hen. III 1232-47 p. 70.
> Prohibition of a tournament to be held at Royston on Thursday before Michaelmas next, in the form whereby the tournaments of Northampton and Cambridge were prohibited before.
>
> **Mandate to the Prior of R. to go with John the Templar to the said place and prohibit the tournament and show these letters."**

A CURIOUS CONVERSATION WITH A FRENCHMAN

In 1971 I went to the Châteaux de Chinon to visit both the engraved panel in the Tour du Coudray and to meet Yvon Roy, later to be the author of the controversial book *Le Testament des Templiers à Chinon,* published in 1974. Professor Raymond Mauny translated for me. Monsieur Roy gave me some intriguing news:

He had found in the French archives some information that the Templars owned in Royston an orchard, barn and a cave and that these should be connected by a passage. Great care must be taken in attempting to open the tunnel as it will be 'snared as for rabbits'. He qualified the statement by saying it was man-trapped.

[An example of a man-trap can be seen in a 'souterrain' at Motte de Monsavignac, (Commune de Tourliac 47) France, where a small bottle-shaped cavity had been constructed in the approach tunnel as a protection from intruders.] It was Monsieur Roy's remarks which were, in part, the reason for the excavation of the floor of the Cave in 1976 (q.v.).

He further said the Cave had been two storied and I should look high up on the walls for more information. Not only that, but the Templars had been associated with Shingay. He specifically mentioned the name of 'de Rochester' (see p. 219) before I showed him *Newsells' Deeds*. Monsieur Roy told me to look in Sussex as de Rochester had gone to Sussex to found a preceptory. [I have been unable to uncover any information to this effect.]

On being shown a photograph of the king-post in the adjoining property to the Cave he said he felt it was the right architecture for the Templars. I mentioned the Cave flooded from time to time; he laughed and said there was a small natural spring in it. This was disproved by Dr. Colin Forbes, Department of Earth Sciences formerly Geology Department, Cambridge University, but the sump probably contained water and could have been known in France as 'point d'eau' [area of water but not necessarily a spring]. (See Appendix I)

Monsieur Roy had never visited the Cave and was very interested in seeing photographs of the carvings. In his opinion overall the pictures illustrated the fact the Templars were searching for the Holy Grail linked with the legends of King Arthur. Of St. Katherine he said she was the only other legendary female figure after the Virgin Mary, about which many tales were interwoven. He supposed the horse belonged to Sir Lancelot and had some connection with Sir Lancelot's father, Ban, and King Arthur. The representation of St. Christopher caused great hilarity to the Frenchmen present, which to this day has eluded me, and no doubt has some sexual connotation. It seems that St. Christopher has his knee bent and is holding his staff (stick) which is stuck in the ground, and by the crossing of the river Styx [represented by the staff] the new man is resurrected. Apparently, there is a play on words and it is a French/English joke!!

Regarding the row of figures on the north wall, he remarked that apparently nine girls and nine boys had to be sacrificed in theory every year, which was part of the legend of St. George and the Dragon. He maintained the Templars held blood sacrifices, probably of sheep.

I tried over several years to obtain the references for the information he gave me, but he never replied to my letters or those of my French colleagues. It is, of course, possible that other documentation survives somewhere in France.

***Note**: *The Marquis D'Albon vols:* LX, *LXI, LXII and LXIII are a collection of letters and copies of manuscripts handwritten at the turn of the century. These four volumes dealt exclusively with all matters concerning the Templars in England and are not indexed in any way. There are 71 volumes in total, and the rest deal with other countries. Regrettably, the Marquis died at the early age of 46 years, not long after his published book of 1913.*

11. LOCAL FAMILIES

This section can be considered as being rather heavy going, and the writer suggests that the not so-serious historical reader should skip various passages. However, to promote evidence for this working hypothesis it is necessary for all of it to be incorporated in the text.

EUDO DAPIFER

Eudo Dapifer was supposedly the youngest son of Hubert de Rie. There is a legend attached to this family which purports to explain why they became so highly favoured and given such large grants of land in England after the Conquest.

The legend is as follows:

> The scene is set in Normandy in the year 1047, at the Castle of the Lord of the little town of Rie in the Bessin, three leagues south of Bayeux. The Lord himself is standing in the early morning leaning over the gate between the church and the rising ground on which the castle was built. Presently his meditations are interrupted by the sound of a galloping horse. In the travel-stained horseman who is urging his weary steed past the gate, the Lord of Rie recognises his young sovereign, William the Bastard, of Normandy, fleeing for his life from his cousin Guy the Burgundian, and sundry other traitors. The name of the Lord of the Castle was Hubert de Rie, who after entertaining and remounting the Duke, directed three of his stalwart sons to conduct. their 'prince' in safety to Falaise; while he himself went back to his station at the gate, in order that he might detain and misdirect any pursuers. In such manner he took fortune by the hand, and she never left him and his house in 'his' own or the next generation. Hubert de Rie was a made man; the serious conduct by his house were never forgotten either by the Conqueror or by his sons William and Henry. Needless to say Hubert and his stalwart sons crossed over the 'silver streak' with Duke William and took part in the so called Conquest... (John Frome Wilkinson, Rector of Barley).

King William conferred upon Eudo 25 lordships in Essex, 7 in Hertfordshire (including Abbotsbury near Barley), 12 in Bedfordshire, 9 in Norfolk, 10 in Suffolk besides others, and he held land in twelve counties at the time of the *Domesday Survey.*

Of Hubert's other sons, Robert became Bishop of Sees(z); Hubert the eldest was made Castell an of Norwich Castle; Ralph was given manors in Nottingham, Derby, Leicester, Stafford and Lincoln and he was also Castellan of the Castle of Nottingham. Adam, yet another son, was seated in Kent where he held great estates under Odo, Bishop of Bayeux and was one of the Commissioners for the Great Survey of England known as the *Domesday Survey* (1086). There was one daughter Albreda, who married Peter de Valoines which connection, together with the family connection of the de Clares through Eudo's wife Lady Rose (Rohesia), eventually helped to reinstate Eudo in favour with Henry I.

Colchester

In the time of William I, Colchester was under the charge of one of the conqueror's special favourites, Eudo of Rie (also spelt Ryes), the Dapifer or Seneschal of Normandy. The king conferred upon him all the crown properties and revenues of the town of Colchester to which William Rufus added an estate in Greensted, across the river. Besides these he held over 60 manors, of which, as mentioned, 25 were in Essex. Eudo was a man greatly beloved and respected by the townspeople for his justice and generosity. Colchester castle, whose ruined keep still stands, was built by him about the year 1076; twenty years later he founded the Benedictine Monastery of St. John, outside the walls south of the town. He also built a hospital for lepers. On his death in 1120 at his Castle of Preaux in Normandy, his body was brought over to Colchester, and buried in St. John's Abbey. He bequeathed his manor at Brightlingsea together with his corpse, £100, a gold ring etc. to the Abbey Church at Colchester.

Soon after the foundation of the abbey, St. Botolph's Priory was built near it by one Ernulf, for the Order of Canons Regular of St. Augustine. [It is not known if this Ernulf was related to Eudo Dapifer. The name was to be given to Geoffrey de Mandeville and Lady Roisia de Vere's eldest son, see below.] This was not only the first monastery of the Order in England, but it received authority from the pope over all the other English Houses of the same class. The presence of the abbey and the priory, besides Eudo's great establishment at the castle, naturally gave an impetus to the prosperity of the town, which continued until the reformation. (The grants made to Eudo appear to have been only for his lifetime, for when he died his possessions in Colchester, including the castle, were appropriated by the king). Though it had lost its great benefactor, Colchester continued to thrive. St. John's Abbey became one of the most powerful in East Anglia. It was free from all outside jurisdiction, and was granted many special privileges and immunities. Its Abbot was one of the twenty-eight in England entitled to wear a mitre.

Margaret, daughter of Eudo Dapifer married William de Mandeville (the first) and in her own right became Seneschal of Normandy. She was mother of Geoffrey de Mandeville, first earl of Essex, and also of Beatrice who married William de Say. (*Cartulary of St. John's, Colchester. Monasticon* vol. IV sub title, *St. John's Colchester* vol. II, 268) (Extract from: *A Contribution called Colchester in Olden Times* by Joseph W. Spurgeon incorporated in *Bygone Essex* edited by William Andrews, F.R.H.S. 1892)

Eudo Dapifer's Honour of Walbrook

A feudal court was held by each lord of a fee for his tenants. This feudal court, the *libera curia,* so difficult to isolate from the franchisal or manorial assembly with which it was frequently merged, is, if important enough, sometimes called a *curia militum,* or *curia militaris.* (Courts so different in importance as those of Harewood, Yorks., where there were three fees, and Plympton, the *caput* of the honour [a group of manors held by one lord] of Devon, where there were 89, are both so styled. Other examples are the courts of Newport (Isle of Wight) Dudley, Warwickshire, Skipton-in-Craven (Yorks.), Alnwick and the ecclesiastical courts of the Archbishop of York at Ripon, and the Bishop of Hereford at Hereford. The courts of the

Honours of Gloucester and Lacy were both 'of knights and other fee tenants'. Later the courts of the Constable and Marshall were to be styled *curia militaris*). Of such courts the present note, although concerned primarily with that of the honour of Walbrook, is also associated with that of the honour of Mandeville.

When Eudes the Sewer (Eudo) died without heirs in 1120 his great honour escheated [property that falls to the state, or feudal lord, for want of an heir] and was disintegrated, only 53 fees of it being eventually re-granted by Henry II shortly after his accession, to his Chamberlain Warin Fitzgerold. For these fees which lay chiefly in Kent and Essex, a court was held. It comes to light only in the late 13th century, as a double court, held alternately at Arkesden, Essex, and Walbrook in London every three weeks. Suit [process or act of suing] was done to it from five counties. So far as may be known from the essoins [excuses for not appearing in court], suit in each honour was done to the *curia militum* exclusively by military tenants.

At some time during the 12th century, the fee certainly was called the fee of Colchester. In this, as in the Mandeville honour, the chief castle of the fee is apparently never the meeting place of the honour court.

The fees of the court of Walbrook and Arkesden are thus the fees of the honour of Eudo the Sewer. Arkesden he held in demesne in 1086, and if, as some have thought probable, he held lands in London, it was in the ward of Walbrook around St. Mary Woolchurch and St. Stephen's including the site of the later Stocks Market and the modern Mansion House. It was here that Eudo, according to a charter of disputed genuineness, had a stone house. (Previte-Orton, 1931, vol. XLVI, 623 notes and documents *Eudo Dapifer's honour of Walbrook*).

Newsells/Newsellsbury

In Hertfordshire, Eudes the Sewer held Newsellsbury in 1086 for five hides and half virgate, with which two hides and 20 acres of barley were worked with the ploughs of Newsellsbury; in Layston 6 acres and in Reed 1 virgate; in Suffolk in Eriswell 6 carucates, in Chelsworth (Cocleswrda) 8 carucates, in Lakenheath and Brandon two carucates, William de Aubervill (Odburguille) held in Barley four and a half hides and ten acres.

Eudes gave the Church of Newsells to St. John the Baptist's Colchester and temporarily William I gave tithes of Newsells to St. Martin's Sees, but before 1120 these lands were incorporated in the honour of Boulogne.

William Page (1912) was assured that not all of Eudo Dapifer's property locally reverted to the Crown. It is interesting to find it connected with the Mandeville family for a while. This William de Mandeville, is not to be confused (as Stukeley did) with William de Mandeville, earl of Essex, son of Geoffrey (first earl of Essex) and Lady Roisia. The William mentioned here, was of the 'de Say' family line descended through Geoffrey's sister Beatrix, whose family on inheritance took both the name of 'de Mandeville' and the title (see p. 211 & 218).

DE VALOINES (VALOYNES, VALOGNES)

VALOGNES. *Paly wavy argent and gules.*

Benington

This village was the head of a Saxon lordship of some importance, which apparently extended into Sacombe, Layston, Ashwell, Hinxworth and Radwell. Held in the time of Edward the Confessor by Ælmar, William the Conqueror granted these lands to Peter de Valognes, who was sheriff of the county in 1086. Peter, as successor to Ælmar, made Benington the head of the Valognes barony, which was sometimes styled later, the honour of Benington. He is thought to have acquired some land in Graveley, Chesfield (Chisfield) manor through Adam Fitz Hubert (see connection below). This manor was then held of Benington Manor as of the Valognes baronry. (*V. C.H., Broadwater* 1912, 87)

Radwell Manors

In the reign of Edward the Confessor and in the early days after the Conquest there were two manors in Radwell. The larger of these was assessed at 4 hides and had a mill attached worth 8s. It was held before the Conquest by Alnoda, a man of Archbishop Stigand. In 1086 it had become part of the extensive lands of the Bishop of Bayeux and was held by him by Adam son of Hubert de Rye. On Adam's death his lands passed to his brother Eudo Dapifer. When Eudo died in 1120, Radwell apparently passed to his sister Albreda the wife of Peter de Valognes, as mentioned the Sheriff of Hertfordshire, and then became amalgamated with the other manor of Radwell.

The smaller manor in Radwell was assessed in 1086 at only 2 hides and had a mill worth 6s.8d. It was formerly held by Ethelmaer (Ælmar) of Benington. Ethelmaer's brother held half a hide of it under him, however by 1086 Radwell had passed with Ethelmaer's other estates to Peter de Valognes and was held of him by Roger.

After Peter de Valognes had acquired the second manor, the two conjoined properties became known as the Manor of Radwell. On the death of Peter de Valognes his lands descended to his son Roger. It was Roger de Valognes who probably built the masonry works of Benington Castle upon the earthworks possibly thrown up by his father. Roger was a partisan of Geoffrey de Mandeville, during the period of anarchy in Stephen's reign. He was present with Mandeville at Stephen's celebrated Easter Court in 1136 and died in 1141 or 1142. He had a son Peter, who appears to have died without issue, and to have been succeeded by his brother Robert. This Robert left an only daughter Gunnora, who married Robert Fitz Walter. In the struggle between King John and the barons Robert Fitz Walter was one of the leaders of the latter party and when Louis of France arrived in England he joined with William de Mandeville earl of Essex (see comments c/r p. 210) in subjugating Essex and Suffolk. Robert Fitz Walter had by Gunnora a daughter Christine (Christina/Christiana), who married William de Mandeville, earl of Essex and as Christine Countess of Essex (de Mandeville) she held of the gift of her father the honour of Valognes four fees, including Radwell. She died without issue in 1233, and Radwell seems to have passed to her step-brother Walter Fitz Walter who died in 1257. (Page, 1912, 243; *V.C.H., Broadwater,* 73-74)

Ashwell Manor, Hertfordshire

Ashwell Manor was originally part of the demesne of the Crown, and granted by Edward the Confessor in his first charter to the Abbey of St. Peter, Westminster, dated December. The *Domesday Survey* records that of the 6 hides at which Ashwell was assessed. The Abbot himself held two and a half in demesne, the manor at this date being evidently a large one, with land for twelve plough-teams and meadow sufficient for six. Peter de Valognes held half a hide and Geoffrey de Mandeville one virgate of the Abbot (*V.C.H. Hertfordshire,* I, 313a). These tenements held by Peter de Valognes and Geoffrey de Mandeville must not be confused with their independent holdings in the same parish. (*Assize R.* 325 *Hund. R. (Rec. Com.)* i, *193;Plac. de Quo Warr. (Rec. Com.)* 275, 288)

In the reign of Henry II (1154-89) Robert de Valognes, grandson of Peter held 14 librates of land here which descended to his daughter Gunnora, the wife successively of Durant de Catelli and Robert Fitz Walter. As mentioned, Christine daughter of Robert and Gunnora married William de Mandeville, earl of Essex, and possibly Ashwell was settled on her, for she granted 'all her men in the vill of Ashwell' to the Priory of Walden in Essex.

Hinxworth Manors

Peter de Valogne's holding was a berewick [a subsidiary or outlying estate] of his holding at Ashwell, and the overlordship descended with his manor there (q.v.) until the death of his daughter Christine. (Page, 1912, 234)

DE VERE

VERE. *Quarterly gules and or with a malet argent in the quarter.*

Alberic de Vere, like Eudo Dapifer, came over with the Conqueror, and was also in high favour with the Norman king. His second son, also named Alberic or Aubrey, de Vere had a family of seven children, five sons and two daughters Roisia and Alice. Roisia de Vere married Geoffrey de Mandeville, grandson of Eudo Dapifer, and became by marriage the grand-daughter of the earlier Lady Roisia, wife of Eudo Dapifer, and thus she comes upon the scene two generations later than the first Lady Roisia, who was known to be connected with Newsells and possibly with the Roys Cross.

It was of course, to Lady Roisia de Vere that Stukeley gave credit for the engraving of the oratory, she was certainly a pious lady and donated much to religious institutions. By her first marriage to the earl of Essex she had four sons, Ernulf who was banished from the realm after the civil war, Geoffrey, second earl of Essex, on whose death without issue, his brother William took the title, and Robert who is presumed to have died young. After the death of her husband Geoffrey in 1144, Roisia married Pagne de Beauchamp, third baron of Bedford, by whom she bore one son Simon and three daughters.

Alberic de Vere III, Roisia's brother was made the first earl of Oxford, and their father was given Colchester Castle by the Empress Maud. (Round, 1892). Alberic (III) founded a monastery at Hatfield Broad Oak, attaching it to the existing Saxon structure in 1135. The monastery was of the Benedictine Order [Black Monks - monks who wore black garments as opposed to the Augustines who usually wore brown], and was a 'cell' to the larger Abbey Church of St. Melanius at Rennes in Brittany. The family continued interest in this village as evidenced by a Robert de Vere's effigy, which was completed c. 1270, clad in crusader vestments holding a shield, clasping his sword, and laid originally, with crossed legs, before the monastery's high altar. [This person, in all probability, was a nephew of Lady Roisia] (*St. Mary's Church, Hatfield Broad Oak,* leaflet, undated c. 1988)

Gilbert de Vere, brother of Lady Roisia, uncle of William de Mandeville, was made Grand Prior of the Order of the Hospital of St. John of Jerusalem in 1195 and was buried there.

DE MANDEVILLE (MAGNAVILE, MAUNDEVILLE)

MANDEVILLE. *Quarterly or and gules.*

At Saffron Walden, the Manor of Waledana (Valley of the serfs) in Essex, was granted by William the Conqueror to Geoffrey de Mandeville, shortly Mandeville, grandson of the original owner about 1120, and was to be occupied for a period of only about 100 years. This grandson, who became the first earl of Essex, owned extensive lands in Normandy, Middlesex, Essex and Hertfordshire. He married Lady Roisia de Vere

The Priory of St. James was founded by Geoffrey de Mandeville [first earl of Essex] in 1130. It was situated in the western part of the town at a spot in the angle made by two streams meeting, the Cam and the one descending from the Castle. The Priory was made an Abbey in 1190 and played an increasingly important part in the development of the Town, as the Abbey acquired more property and land in Walden.

A tradition, which has reached down through the ages, maintains that the Mandeville family held Newsells in *capité,* and I have examined the Charters granted both by Matilda and King Stephen which are shown in Appendix A.

For the Second Charter of the Empress Matilda, again recorded in the *Great Coucher of the Duchy,* J. H. Round has taken for the following text the transcript from the *Great Coucher* in Lansd. MS 229 (fo1. 10) and also collated Dugdale's transcript, among his manuscripts at Oxford (L. 19), *'ex magno registro in officio Ducatus Lancastrie.'* He also collated another transcript which is among the Dodsworth manuscripts (xxx. 113), and which was made in 1649. Unfortunately, it was not complete, however, another transcriber began to copy the charter but also stopped almost at once. The variations in the Dodsworth and Dugdale transcripts are slight. (See Appendix A)

By comparing this charter, with those preceding it, the historically dubbed 'unscrupulous earl' Geoffrey de Mandeville had yet again won more advantages by this last change of front and switching Crown allegiance. It is to be noted that a further grant namely:

'...totam terram quae fuit Eudonis Dapiferi in Normannia et Dapiferatus ipsius'

[...the whole land which belonged to Eudo the Steward in Normandy and the Stewardship of the same.]

with a conditional proposal that Geoffrey should also, in exchange for the grants he had already received, obtain that portion of the Dapifer's fief which lay in England. The large estate which this successful minister had accumulated in the service of the Conqueror and his sons had escheated to the Crown at his death, and is entered accordingly in the *Pipe-Roll of 31 Henry I.* This has an important bearing on the noteworthy admission in the charter that Geoffrey is to receive the Dapifer's fief not as a gift, but as his right (*rectum suum*). This expression is referred to by Mr. Eyton in his manuscript as placing beyond doubt the received statement that Geoffrey was maternally a grandson of the Dapifer, whose daughter and heiress Margaret had married his father William.

In view of the evidence aforementioned, I can see no reason why the Mandeville family could not have lived at Newsells even for a short spell, as believed by Stukeley, who in his second book (1746) on p. 113, gives the following Empress Charter to Geoffrey de Mandeville which he claims was in a book by Lord Burghley (unfortunately not titled) as his evidence:

> 'Matilda imperatrix Henrica Regis filia et anglorum Domina concessit Comiti Galfrido Essexiam sicut Galfridus avus aut wilhelmus pater ejus tenuit concessit etiam ei Turrim Lundoniae cum castello quod subtus est et vicecomitatum Essexiae pro trecentis libris sicut Galfridus avus tenuit. Et vicecomitatum de Hertford pro sexaginta libris vicecomitatum lundonie et Midlesexie pro trecentis libris. Et etiam hereditabiliter justiciarium Lundonie, Midlesexie, Essexie et de Hertfordshire. Testibus: Roberto Comite Glocestrie, Milone Comite Herefordie, Rogero Comite Cornubie, baldwino Comite Devoniae, Gileberto Comite Penbrokie, Comite Hugone de Norfolkia, et Comite alberico [Stukeley thinks the last name is Geoffrey de Mandeville's father-in-law, Alberic de Vere, earl of Guisnes].'
>
> [The Empress Matilda daughter of king Henry and lady of the English granted Essex to count Galfridus (Geoffrey) just as Geoffrey his grandfather or William his father had held it. She also granted to him the Tower of London with the Castle which is beneath it, and the earldom of Essex for £300 just as Geoffrey his grandfather had held it, and the earldom of Hertford for £60 and the earldom of London and Middlesex for £300 and also by way of inheritance the justiciarship of London, Middlesex, Essex and Hertfordshire...]
> (See Appendix A, the content is similar to Queen Matilda's Charter c.1142)

Stukeley goes on to state [concerning Lady Roisia]:

> '...that the estate of Newsells was her first husband's so that she had been in possession of it from about the year 1130.'

In the next paragraph, referring to the Priory he says:

> 'Besides, it well became the founders of the priory, who held their estates under her, at least by the gift of her predecessors, by that kind of tenure which our ancestors called hoke-land [a Saxon term for land held by title from the Crown. The tenants were probably exempt from a number of public services, such as defence and bridge-building. Alternatively called charter-land and deed-land]...'

Later on, when her husband Geoffrey was ravaging the Eastern Counties and had his property confiscated by King Stephen, nowhere is it mentioned as to where his wife and two younger children were living at this time, with the exception of Ernulf the eldest, who was with his father.

Following the serious disagreements between the earl and his king, which had culminated in the confiscation of property, with the exception of Ramsey Abbey, the situation also led to Geoffrey being excommunicated from the church because he had turned the monks out of his abbey to use it for himself. When he died in 1144 at Burwell Castle, Cambridge, the Knights Templar took his body to London encased in lead where it lay for some time in the garden. Years later, after a pardon and absolution was obtained through the monks of Walden Abbey, he was finally buried within the Temple Church (see Chapter 8).

It is worth noting here that both the Holy Sepulchre Church, Cambridge and the church of St. Mary the Virgin, Burwell (built adjacent to the castle) were subject to Ramsey Abbey.

Geoffrey de Mandeville, the first earl, witnessed several charters for land etc. to be given to the Templars, so also did his son Geoffrey de Mandeville, second earl who for example, confirmed a grant of Sawallus de Osevilla giving a small stream to the Templars during the time he was earl (1156-1166). (Leys, 1938 & 1941)

WILLIAM DE MANDEVILLE

William was the younger son of Geoffrey de Mandeville and Lady Roisia de Vere. It is known that William de Mandeville together with Philip, earl of Flanders, went on a pilgrimage to Jerusalem in 1176 and associated themselves with the brethren of the Temple and the Knights Hospitaller when Harangh Castle was besieged.

To illustrate the high standing of this member of the Mandeville family and his connection with Richard Coeur de Lion, I give the following information.

On Sunday, 3rd September 1189, King Richard was crowned in Westminster abbey. The writers of the time gave a minutely detailed account of the ceremony which has been closely followed in all subsequent coronations:

> The clergy, dressed in copes of purple silk, went in procession, preceded by acolytes carrying a cross, candles, and thuribles of incense, to Richard's chamber in Westminster palace and escorted him to the abbey over linen cloth laid the whole way, with 'glorious song'. The procession was led into the abbey by clerks carrying holy water, crosses, candles and thuribles. Then came

> the clergy in due order, first the Priors, next the Abbots, and then the Bishops. In the midst of them walked four barons carrying golden candelabra.
>
> Next came the king's regalia. Godfrey de Luci carried the cap of state, John Marshal the golden spurs, William Marshal, newly married to the great heiress of the earl of Pembroke, carried the golden sceptre surmounted by a golden cross, and the earl of Salisbury carried the golden verge with a golden dove at its end. Three earls, David of Huntingdon, the brother of the king of Scots, John, Richard's brother, and Robert earl of Leicester, carried swords with golden scabbards. Next came six earls and barons carrying a chest on the top of which were the royal insignia and garments, and after them William of Mandeville, earl of Essex, carried the golden crown studded with rich gems.
>
> After the crowning and the mass the king returned in procession to his chamber, where he laid aside the heavy crown and vestments and put on lighter ones for his comfort during the coronation feast.

When Rannulf Glanville, Henry's Chief Justiciar resigned or was deposed in 1189, at the Council at Pipwell, Richard appointed Bishop Hugh of Durham and William of Mandeville, earl of Essex and Count of Aumale, as joint Chief Justiciars.

William de Mandeville had married Hadwisa, the heiress of the Count of Aumale, and had assumed that title in his wife's right. He had gone on a crusade with count Philip of Flanders and had helped to win the great victory at Ramleh in 1177.

Stukeley regales the story that just over ten years later in 1188:

> "...when half the kingdom was rushing into the crusade, so zealous then was mankind in the cause of religion? But this spirit rais'd in our monarch Henry II, and his people, was quench'd by the pernicious machinations of the French king who broke the truce, seduc'd the king's sons again to rebel."
>
> "This same year, Hovedon tells us, Albemarle the possession of William de Mandevile was burnt by the French. He in return, burnt S. Clare; and a beautiful grove which the French king had planted, the then king of France cut down the fine elm near Gisors, where the conventions between the two monarchs us'd to be held: as if he meant never more to treat of peace..." (1746, 116)

The meadow in which the ancient elm stood was called 'Champ Sacre' and the site had been deemed sacred since pre-Christian times. The tree had given shade and provided the setting for numerous meetings between Henry II of England and Philippe II of France in the 12th century (Fig. 58). During the skirmish between the opposing forces the tree was felled, the French holding the field at the end of the day. Richard Coeur de Lion; Henry's eldest son and heir, apparently spilled a considerable amount of blood. (Baigent, Leigh, Lincoln, 1982, 90)

Fig. 58. Meeting place under the elm on the plain near Gisors where the kings of France and England settled their differences.

As King Henry's closest friend, William had accompanied him on his last wild flight from Le Mans in June 1189. Richard liked and trusted him too, and after appointing the earl as one of the Chief Justiciars he sent him on a mission to Normandy. (*Gesta,* vol. II, 91)

When earl William died childless at Gisors [Stukeley says it was at Roan in the November of 1189 and where he was interred (1746,116)] of an acute semi-tertian fever, the king gave his widow Countess Hadwisa, whom Richard of Devizes describes as 'a woman almost a man, lacking nothing virile except the virile organs', to his friend William of Fors. Hadwisa showed her mettle by refusing to marry him, whereupon the king ordered her estates in Yorkshire to be seized and had stock to the value of £114.1s.4d. sold from them. The countess then gave in and married the man of the king's choice. (Richard of Devizes. PIO; *Pipe Roll* 6 *RichardI,* p. 163)

Hadwisa did not inherit earl William's estates in England, which would descend to the nearest heir of the Mandeville line. The estates were claimed by two descendants of Beatrice (Beatrix), earl William's aunt; Beatrice de Say, the elder daughter of Beatrice's elder son William, who was married to Geoffrey son of Peter; and Geoffrey de Say, the younger son of the elder Beatrice. These relationships are indicated by the accompanying table:

Earldom of Essex Table

William of Mandeville, d. 1130
(m. Margaret daughter of Eudo Dapifer)

- Geoffrey of Mandeville, d. 1144 (m. Roisia de Vere) created earl of Essex by King Stephen
  - Geoffrey de Mandeville earl of Essex d. 1166
  - William de Mandeville earl of Essex d. 1189
- Beatrice, d. 1144 (m. William of Say)
  - William of Say d. 1177
    - Beatrice, (m. Geoffrey son of Peter who took the name of de Mandeville and the title)
    - Matilda, m. William of Buckland
  - Geoffrey of Say d. 1214

Geoffrey of Say offered 7000 marks 'to have the land that was earl William's'; Geoffrey son of Peter offered only 3,000 marks 'to have earl William's land as the inheritance of Beatrice of Say, his wife, provided that he will be of such service to the lord king that it shall be in the king's pleasure whether he chooses to accept it or not'. Geoffrey of Say paid nothing, whilst Geoffrey son of Peter by Michaelmas 1190 had paid 900 marks. Needless to say, Geoffrey son of Peter was given possession of the land. Richard's charter, dated 23rd January 1191, at Messina, gives Geoffrey son of Peter and his wife Beatrice, the lawful and nearer heir, all of earl William's land, thus ignoring the claims of Beatrice's younger sister Matilda, who was entitled to half the inheritance. In 1191, Geoffrey son of Peter paid 1,460 marks to discharge of his promise, in 1192, 140 marks; and in 1193, with unusual promptness, he paid the debt in full. Geoffrey received only the lands; although he had been receiving the 'third penny' normally given an earl from his county since Easter 1190, he was not formally made earl of Essex until John's coronation. (*Ancient Charter,* pp. 97, 108-10; *Pipe Rolls* 2 *Richard I,* pp. 104, 111; 3 *Richard I,* p. 29; 4 *Richard I,* p. 171; 5 *Richard I,* p. 5; *Howden,* vol. IV, p. 90)

GEOFFREY DE SAY

A Geoffrey de Say c. 1228 granted the manor of Saddlescombe, some four miles [6.4 km] north west of Brighton to the Templars with the assent of William de Warenne, earl of Surrey, who added a grant of 40s. rent from Lewes. (*V.C.H, A History of Sussex,* 92) [Geoffrey de Say, son of Beatrice was dead by this time. At the present time, it is. unclear from whom he is descended - he is possibly Geoffrey son of Peter who may have inherited the de Say lands too.]

GEOFFREY SON OF PETER (GEOFFREY de MANDEVILLE, EARL OF ESSEX)

In 1198, to take Hubert Walter's place as chief justiciar Richard appointed Geoffrey son of Peter, the next most experienced and capable man in the kingdom. A man of modest origins, he served Henry II in several capacities and had been Sheriff of Northamptonshire during the last five years of Henry's reign. Richard, when he came to the throne, released Geoffrey from his crusader's vows, and named him as one of the justiciars who were to be associated with the chief justiciar in the Government of the country. He was sheriff of Northamptonshire again from Michaelmas 1191 to Easter 1194 and of Essex and Hertfordshire from 1190 to 1193; he had served as an itinerant justiciar throughout the reign, and he had been chief custodian of the royal forests during both reigns. His prudent marriage, of course, enabled him to greatly increase his wealth and importance. Because he signed many documents as Geoffrey de Mandeville, as was his right, it has caused quite a few historians to be confused with the lineage through from the original Geoffrey de Mandeville who came over with William the Conqueror.

DE MERK (MERC, MARC)
DE ROCHESTER (ROUCESTRE, ROUCESTRIA, ROFFA, ROSSA*, ROUEE)
DE SCALES (SCALARII, SCALIER)

The Deeds of Newsells Park Estate

SCALES. *Gules six scallops or,*

The first reference to the de Merk family in the *Newsells Park Estate Calendar of* 1929, occurs after 1120 when Eudo Dapifer died. Newsells then evidently reverted to the crown and was granted by King Henry I to Eustace Count of Boulogne. The overlordship remained in the honour of Boulogne. Members of the Merk family were the immediate tenants. Eustace de Merk was witness to the charter of Eustace Count of Boulogne confirming Barkway Church to Colchester Abbey. It appears possible that he was already tenant of Newsells under the count.

1189-1199. Sir Eustace de Merk Knight was styled 'Lord of Newsells' and founded a Chapel at Royston within this Lordship. He was also styled 'de Rochester' and was succeeded as tenant (apparently within his own life-time) by his nephew Ralph de Rochester. Ralph was preceded by Baldwin de Rochester probably his father. Newsells was the *caput* or head of the Baronry which Ralph held of the honour of Boulogne. Ralph's son and heir William de Rochester died shortly before 24th October 1249.

From these deeds it would seem that there is a rather large gap from 1120 to 1189. Assuming Eustace de Merk was 20 years old, I doubt if he would have been much younger to sign the charter, he would have been between 89 years and 99 years when styled 'Lord of Newsells'. I suppose it is possible but more likely there were several persons named 'Eustace de Merk'.

Stukeley states in his second book that both Eustace de Merc's ancestor and Ralph de Rochester's father Thomas had their estates in Newsells given them by Eudo Dapifer. Another reference in the *History of Essex* by Morant, vol. II, 145 states:

> 'The Manor of Rivenhall was in the lordship of the earl of Bulloin [Boulogne] and the heiress of that family marrying King Stephen, it came by that means into the Crown.
>
> In the reigns of King Henry II, Richard I, and John, Baldwin de Osterwich held knight fees here. Under him they were holden in 1210 of King John by Ralph de Roffa or Roucester: whose ancestors enjoyed Nusels in the parish of Berkway in Hertfordshire, of the gift of Eudo Dapifer. This Ralph had issue William, Peter and Alice. William de Roffa the eldest son, held the manor of Rewenhalle and Advowson of the church of the king in *capité,* by the service of one fee and a half. And under him Hugh de Essex held in Rivenhall 180 acres of arable, meadow, pasture and a water-mill. William de Roffa was succeeded by his brother Peter then aged 40 years. But he dying without issue all his estates came to his sister Alice who brought them in marriage to Robert de Scalariis, otherwise Scales, descended from Scalier, who came over with William the Conqueror.' [for Roffa read Rossa]

This is the first mention that the property of Rivenhall, Essex and that of Newsells was linked.

I found out from Mr. Clement Dale, the Newsells Estate Manager, in the 1970s that this estate covered 2,500 acres, virtually half the size it had been in earlier times. Originally, it extended nearly to Barley incorporating Cokenach [Cochenach], Reed and Therfield. Also included were several manors which still survive to this day, 'Abbotsbury' on the Cokenach Estate, 'Mardleybury Farm' Reed End, 'Queensbury' and 'Reed Hall'.

Unfortunately, Stukeley did not always give his references, nevertheless, if he is correct and the 'de Rochesters' were given estates in Newsells, could that mean they did not have the property in its entirety? Or did they sub-let some of the manors? Both Stukeley and Beldam assure us that the Mandeville family, as well, actually did live at Newsells for some time, perhaps they too lived in one of the Manor houses on the estate.

Going back to the deeds the next entry records:

> 1249. His brother (of William de Rochester) Peter de Rochester, a parson of Rivenhall, County Essex, who took the habit of a Knights Templar shortly before his death, succeeded him.

1255. On the Saturday before Ascension Day as he lay on his death bed he granted Newsells Manor to his sister Alice, widow of Robert de Scales.

The scanty information above requires evaluation, and of course, it is often disputes which contain considerable information. To begin with, the first known tenant of the fee was Eustace de Merc, founder of the Priory of Crosroys of Royston. In 1170 a mark was levied from the land of Eustace de Merc in Cambridgeshire for a default, and in 1174 the farmer of the honor of Boulogne claimed allowance of £4 of land which Eustace de Merc had that year in Layer, Essex while the honor was in the king's hands down to 1179. He had a crown gift in 1184, and in 1186 was an overseas envoy for the crown with Godfrey de Luci and Guy de St. Valery when they were provided with two ships for their passage. He appears to have had land at this time in Yorkshire.

In 1185 Ralph de Roucestre ['Rossa', Rochester] gave 20 shillings for the right of nine marks against Robert de London in Kent. In 1198 he was essoined at Hertford by Gunter de Berqueia [Barkway]. In 1200 he had a suit with Eustace de Laghefare in Essex, whereupon an assize came to recognise if Eustace de Merc, maternal uncle of Ralph de Roucestre was seized of two carucates in Larer [Lagefare] at his death which Eustace de Lagefare held, who claimed to hold the land of the king, that both he and Ralph were of one stock [*stipes*], he being of the elder birth. Afterwards they came to an agreement whereby Eustace was to hold of Ralph certain tenements in Layer for half fee. In 1201 Ralph gave 30 marks in lieu of service overseas in respect of five and two third fees of the honor of Boulogne in Suffolk and elsewhere. It appears probable that he was son of Ralph de Roucestre who joined with Eustace de Merc in the foundation of Royston Priory. In 1208 Ralph owned 20 marks in Norfolk and Suffolk for the grand assize touching one knight's fee in Estmore and Barton.

In 1212, Ralph de Roffa or Roucestre, held one and a half fee in Newsells of Barkway of the honor of Boulogne. In 1217-8 the same Ralph held of this honor in Rivenhall, Essex, Barkway and Newsells Herts., Eriswell and Chelsworth, Suffolk., 5 fees; and in High and Little Laver, Essex, half fee which Richard de Roucestre and Eustace his brother held.

Ralph de Roucestre gave to Colchester two thirds of the tithes of Eriswell and Chelsworth, including lands of the demesne granted in fee by his father and by himself; he also confirmed the tithes granted by Eudes the Sewer and Eustace count of Boulogne. Another Ralph de Roucestre also granted the same monks three half-virgates in Barley. Some reference to the family of Roucestre will be found in Clutterbuck's *History of Hertfordshire,* vol. III p. 365.

In 1216 Ralph's lands were seized and committed to the king's Bailie, but on Henry's succession he had writs of reseisin [restoration] to the sheriffs of Hertford, Cambridge, Norfolk and Suffolk. In 1236 William de Roucestre, son and heir of Ralph de Roucestre, gave relief of £27.10.0d. for his inheritance held of the honor of Boulogne. It is uncertain if this was the same Ralph as that named above, or his son.

> In 1248 William de Roucestre died seised of lands in Eriswell held of the king as of the honor of Boulogne for two fees, the manor of Rivenhall with the advowson of the church similarly held for one and a half fee, and the manor of Newsells similarly held for one and a half fee, of which Ralph de Handleye held a fourth part; Peter his brother, aged 50 or 60 years, was his heir. Peter de Roucestre gave relief in 1249 of £25 upon succeeding to his inheritance, and shortly before his death on Ascension Day, 1255, as Peter de Roucestre, parson of Rivenhall, he granted the manor of Rivenhall to his nephew (*nepos*) Robert de Scales and the manor of Newsells to Alice wife (*recte mother*) of the said Robert, on condition that they founded a chantry for his soul's welfare; shortly before his death he assumed the habit of a Templar.

Does this last paragraph point to an important piece of the jigsaw? Did the de Scales family found a small chapel with the Templars in Royston for their forebear's soul? Regrettably, no formal document seems to have survived, should this have been the case.

With the exception of John the Templar, who went with the Prior to stop a tournament in Royston, this is the strongest evidence of Templar involvement by a local man owning local land; taking upon himself the Templar habit. As will be seen from the following documentation the transference of the two conjoined properties Newsells and Rivenhall to the de Scales family was not straight forward:

> In 1255 Robert de Scales had exemption for life from being put on assizes and the like, and the same year an enquiry was directed to be made as to what state Peter de Roucestre was in when he granted the manors to Robert and Alice as just described. In the following year Robert de Scales and Alice his mother gave 17 marks of gold for seisin of the manors of Rivenhall and Newsells, which sum they paid into the wardrobe [for livery] in three sums amounting in all to £113.6s.8d., for this they had acquittance in 1260 to the barons of the exchequer. (Farrer, 1925, III, 268: XI, *Honor of Eudes the Sewer*)

For the interest of the more discerning reader, the reference has been detailed below. (See Appendix B for the Latin version)

Translation from *Chancery Inquisitions Post Mortem Henry III:* File 19 (2) (Calendar (p. 100) No. 367) originally copied from the *Cartulaire Générale de L'Ordre du Temple 1119-1150. Recueil des Chartes et des Bulles relatives à l'ordre du Temple,* vol. LXI still in manuscript form in the Bibliothèque Nationale in Paris.

> 'The enquiry held at Wautham before Roger de Thurkelby and Henry de Mara on Wednesday after the feast of St. Andrew the Apostle concerning the Manor of Rewehal in the County of Essex and concerning the Manor of Neweseles in the County of Hertford in the eleventh year of the reign of King Henry son of King John.
>
> By order of the shrievalty of Essex and Hertford these must appear before the aforesaid Roger and Henry on the day and at the place appointed all those good and loyal men who were present at the former hearing of the case of the manors

of Rewehal and Neweseles as well as others by whom the facts of the case can be better and more fully gone into and an enquiry made into the assertions by which Lord Robert de Scales claims that the aforesaid Manor of Rewehal in the County of Essex was given to him by Peter de Rossa uncle of the same Robert and by which Alice de Scales claims that the aforesaid Manor Neweseles in the County of Hertford was given to her by the said Peter and that the findings in the previous enquiry were inconclusive. By these men can be gained a better idea of the truth of the matter; when before what witnesses. What was the condition of the said Peter when the aforesaid enfeoffments were granted and whether they were granted when the said Peter was in a fit state to know what he was doing or not. These manors were transferred into his own hands by the king as if they were to remain his property because the said Peter, at the time when the aforesaid enfeoffments ought not to have been granted, was lying at death's door and in so low a state that these said enfeoffments ought not to be valid.

Henry of Bathomia says on behalf of the king, that the aforesaid Peter was in no position to grant the enfeoffment of the said manor of Rewenhall to the said Robert because the said Peter had leased the aforesaid manor to the Master of the Knights Templar in England for a period of six years of which three were still to run when the aforesaid Peter died. He also states that the said Master of the Knights Templar was at that time not in those parts, so he could not have handed back the said manor to the said Peter. He says also that the aforesaid Alice had possession of the manor of Neweseles in Peter's lifetime and to his knowledge but that without consent or the wish of that same Peter she had taken possession of the said manor. He further states that the aforesaid Peter, when he hadn't the right to grant the aforementioned enfeoffments, was in no fit mental state to be able to grant to them the enfeoffments of the said manor and that it was when he was at death's door that they installed themselves in the said manors.

Gilbert Manduzt, John de Boksted, Radulphus Marcel, Richard son of John de Teye jurors at the first hearing and Peter of Radley, Adam de Loges, Alexander de Beynflat, Thomas Burdun, Gibertus Chippenmere, John de Broke, John Adgar, Willelm de Chemino, Robert de Hebrugge, Thomas de Thopingho, John Le Marzun de Torbinges, jurors of the County of Essex came along. Peter of Radlegh and other jurors who were not present at the first hearing say on oath that the aforesaid Peter for three years and more before his death had leased the manor of Rewehal with its appurtenances to the said Master of the Knights Templar in England. The tenancy was for a period of six years for £22 per annum of which the said Master paid to the said Peter £66 for three years in advance. At Easter day in the fourth year next before the death of the same Peter the said Master paid to the said Peter the pounds that were due. After Easter Peter realising that he was failing told the aforesaid Robert and Alice to come to him.

They will say that on the Sunday before the Ascension of the Lord in the 39th year between the first and the third hour Brother Willelm del Estre preceptor of Kersing and Wyham and Brother Radulphus of Bedford and Brother Willelm of Wyham fratres of the Knights Templar came by the wish of the Master himself and they believe that it was for this reason that Brother Radulphus came from London and gave back to the aforesaid Peter the aforesaid manor with the appurtenances and the deed of covenant of the Lord King from whom they asked it. The said Peter on the same day gave to the Brethren of the Knights Templar about 100 acres of land in the aforesaid manor for alms for ever. On the same day before the 9th hour the aforesaid Robert and Alice came to this same Peter at Rewenhal to the houses attached to the church at Rewenhal and as he was Rector of this same church on that day he granted the aforesaid Robert the manor of Rewenhale and the said Alice the Manor of Neweseles and on the following Sunday had the deeds of the manors drawn up for the enfeoffments of the aforesaid manors about the first hour and with his own hand put the seal to the deed of the aforesaid Robert and that Richard the chaplain of the said Peter in the presence and at his request sealed the deed of the aforesaid Alice because Peter was too weak to do it and the said Peter received their homage for the aforesaid manor but they say that he was unwilling to hand over those deeds to them until both of them took an oath that they should find a chaplain forever to celebrate for his soul.

He said that the aforesaid Robert should also give his own manor at Hoo in the County of Norfolk, if he should recover from the illness from which he was then suffering, to be held by him for all his life. That the aforesaid Alice should give to him the manor of Hicelingfield in the County of Cambridge to be held in the same way. Immediately they had taken the oath, he handed over the deeds to the aforementioned with his own hand and he instructed his servant Alfred to put the said Robert in possession of the said manor of Rewenhal which he did on the next Monday following before the first hour. So this same Robert on - day received the homage of the free men and the fealty of the villeins of the same manor and they cut down ash trees and distributed them and broke the earth for a vineyard and put in a fish pond and his possession was peaceful until on the eve of Whitsun the sheriffs and bailiffs of the County of Essex put him out. On that same Sunday the said Peter instructed Willelm Martel with his serving man to attend on Alice with *letters patent* which he had taken out at Neweseles to give her possession of the aforesaid Manor. On the Tuesday before the Ascension of the Lord the said Willelm along with John the serving man of the said Peter came to that same place and had a full court summoned to the same place and had the *letters patent* of the said Peter read concerning the granting of possession to the said Alice which he had recently got and about the first hour put her in possession of the said Manor. She herself received the homage of the free men and the fealty of the villeins of the aforesaid manor. On the Wednesday, the vigil of the Ascension of our Lord,

> she caught a deer in the park of this same manor and sold it and gave away the trees in the same park and had them felled. So she remained in possession until Friday in Whit week when the bailiffs of Our Lord the king threw her out and they say that the aforesaid Peter died on the day of the Ascension of Our Lord next following after the ninth hour and that a little before his death on the same day he put on the habit of the Templars. They say that he was of this mind from the day he granted them the enfeoffment and ever afterwards until his death. And the aforesaid were the jurors who were present at the first hearing from the County of Essex and likewise Robert de la Rohele Stephanus Camerarius and John son of Gilbert were the jurors of the County of Hertford who were present at the first hearing; Alan of Wadlington, Walter Hacun, Willelm Basset, John son of John, Brian of Trokkinge, Willelm son of Bernard, Robert de la Dene, Willelm de Hodenho, Theobald de Mora and Richard Dignon testified to all this on oath. John of Coggeshal and Radulphus of Wyrham named as witnesses to the deeds of both Robert and Alice testified to this too on oath. John of Coggeshal and Radulphus of Wyrham names as witnesses to the deeds of both Robert and Alice testified on oath to this same thing. Mjellus Trot, Albredus de Haselingfield, Johannes de Camera and Willelm Marcel servant of the said Peter who were present when he granted the enfeoffments of the said manors were sworn and examined individually and they tell the same story on oath. Alice proposes in her place Robert de Scales or Radulphus of Wyrham or Willebruum of Wytewell.'

There is a rather odd little reference written in English on the back of *Harl:7* b. document regarding Alice de Scales (F.8):

> 'Alice de Scales to Osbert, Prior of Cruce Roys. She has granted to Ric. de Clare earl of Glouc. and Hereford the Patronage and advowson of the Priory of Cruce Roys with all her rights in the Priory.'

It is undated (see penultimate paragraph under 'De Clare family'). Obviously she was able to act accordingly once the acquittance had taken place in 1260, therefore presumably the document is dated after this date.

A later entry maintaining that Peter de Rochester was a Templar is confirmed from Reaney, *Early Essex Clergy*, 136-7:

> 'PETER DE ROFFA. In 1264 Nicholas de Audeleg' failed to establish his claim to the advowson (Nicholas de Audeleye held the advowson of the prior of Royston in 1263 (*Essex Fines,* i, 259 v. also *Cal. Pat.,* 1266-72. p. 283 and *Essex Fines* i, 270) The jury declared that the last parson Peter, who had been admitted, instituted, and died parson, had been presented by Ralph de Roff,' grandfather of Ralph, who now claimed the advowson (*Assize Roll* 1197 m. 5d v. also *Essex Fines,* i, 259). He is almost certainly to be identified with Peter de Rossa the parson of Rewenhale who died on Ascension Day, 1255. He was a nephew of Robert de Scales and became a Templar a little before his death (*Cal. Inq. p.m.* Henry III, vol. 1. No. 367 p. 100)'

The last reference being taken from the same document as that related above.

There is further evidence that other members of the de Rochester family were either Templars or at least connected with the Order. I record below two Charters contained in B. A. Lees book, *Records of the Knights Templar in England and the Inquest of 1185:*

> *MS Cotton Nero E.* VI, fo. 130 c. 1153-85.
> Thomas de Boklandia (1) amicis et vicinis suis omnibusque fidelibus sancte matris ecclesie salutem. Sciat dilectio vestra me dedisse quatuor acras et dimidiam fratribus templi Salomonis in perpetuam elemosinam pro anima mea et animabus omnium amicorum meorum et concessisse. Et volo quod teneant eas libere et quiete ab omni seruicio seculari scilicet duas acras in crofto iuxta ecclesiam et unam acram iuxta Herynge stratam et aliam in crofto Wulfrici. Hiis testibus. Humfrido Capellano. Waltero sacerdote. Baldewino sacerdote. Baldewino de Roucestria (2) Henrico de Shallers. Euerardo Lucas. Baldewyno Nepote Baldewini de Rouee (3) Humfrido Medico. Rogero Feuerelle. Henrico de Huchyntone. Baldewino Mercatore. Alfrido. et frater Affricus istam elemosinam ad opus fratrum templi Salomonis recepit.
>
> [Thomas de Boklandia [sends] greeting to his friends and neighbours and to all the faithful of the church of St. Mary. Know that I have given for love 4.5 acres to the brothers of the temple of Solomon in perpetual alms for my soul and for the souls of all my friends, and have granted it. And I Will that they hold them [i.e. the 4.5 acres] quietly and free from every secular service: namely 2 acres in a croft next to the church and 1 acre next to Herynge Street and another in Wulfric's croft. With these witnesses: Humphrey the chaplain, Walter the priest, Baldwin the priest, Baldwin de Roucestria, Henry de Shallers, Everard Lucas, Baldewyn nephew of Baldwin de Rouee, Humphrey the doctor, Roger Feuerelle, Henry de Huchyntone, Baldewin the merchant. Alfridus. And brother Affricus received these alms for the use of the brothers of the temple of Solomon.]

Notes:

1. Buckland, about eight miles east of Baldock, Herts.

2. This may be taken without hesitation as referring to Baldwin of Rochester, a name which occurs below as Baldewinus de Rouee. Ralph of Rochester, well known in the twelfth century, may have been the son of Baldwin.

3. Rouee is one form of the name Rochester. Baldwin of Rochester is mentioned in an Essex charter of c. 1153-4. The family, whose name was Merk, though several members of it were called de Rouecestria held in Essex and Suffolk as well as at Barkway and Newsells, near Reed, Herts.

> *MS. Cotton Nero,* E. VI, fo. 290 (15th century transcript) De mercato apud Witham. (l) c. 1153-4.

Stephanus Rex Anglie Ricauo (sic) de Lucy salutem. Precipio tibi quod facias dominum Ostenem magistrum et fratres de Templo tenere mercatus suum (2) de Witham Ita bene et plenarie et quiete sicud illud melius ibi fuit tempore Regis Henrici et in eo postea nec paciaris quod Baldewinus de Rouescestria (3) vel alius aliquis eis inde forisfaciat. Teste. Fulcone de Oilli apud Londoniam.

[Stephen king of England [sends] greeting to Ricauo de Lacy. I order you to allow the master Ostonem and the brothers of the Temple to hold their market of Witham, and that well, fully and peaceably just as it was their better in the time of King Henry and that afterwards' you do not allow (*pac* - must be a misprint for *fac*) Baldwin of Rochester or anyone else to exact forfeiture therefrom. Witness: Fulco d'Oilli at London.] Translation Essex County Record Office.

Notes:

1. Witham, Essex. In *MS. Cotton Nero,* E.VI, this charter immediately follows Stephen's confirmation of Matilda's grant of Cressing Manor to the Templars.

2. This market, established by Henry I, seems to have been one of the earliest, if not quite the earliest, in Essex after the Norman Conquest.

3. Baldwin of Rochester witnesses a charter of Thomas de Boklandia given in MS. Cotton Nero, E.VI, folio 130, under Dynnesley. This family held a barony of five and a half fees of the honour of Boulogne in the 12th century, consisting of Barkway and Newsells (Herts) Rivenhall and Lawford (Essex), and Eriswell and Cocclesworth (Suffolk). The family name was Merk, but several members of it were styled de Rouecestria. Of these, Baldwin may have been the father of the better-known Ralph of Rochester (*V.C.H. Herts.* iv. 27, and 66n. 44).

LOST CHARTERS

It should be noted that Newsells came into the honour of Boulogne and both Henry I and Matilda gave property to the Templars, including some at Rivenhall. Could they also have given a small portion of the Newsells' estate to the Templars? This should surely be considered. Not to be forgotten is the problem of 'lost charters' and information not included in the Templar *Inquest.*

At the close of 1140, the revolt of the half-brothers, earl Rannulf of Chester and William de Roumare earl of Lincoln, led onto the disastrous battle of Lincoln in the February of 1141, and to the defeat and capture of the king. It was probably in the summer of 1141 when Queen Matilda was in London, straining every nerve to help her husband, that she granted a charter to Gervase of Cornhill, which is of historical interest for its attestation by Richard of Boulogne, possibly a brother of Faramus, and by a witness from the Boulonnais, Simon de Girardmolendino. This latter person seems to have been attached to the English court, as he is found attesting royal charters both in England and in Flanders between 1141 and 1148. To the aforementioned date may also belong, not only Matilda's 'lost charter' to Geoffrey de Mandeville, but another 'lost charter of the queen'; her grant of Uphall in Essex to the

Templars (Terra de Luppehalla, part of the manor of Great Tey, Lexden hundred, Essex. This place, unidentified by D'Albon, is Uphall (Le Uppehalla) (*Archaeologia* xii, 25-40). It is the Huphal' of the *Inquest,* fo. 3 vo (p. 9), the Huppehall (al Huppehall) of the 13th century Rivenhall Extent, P.R.O. D. of Lanc. Rent and Surv. 14/1 (Rivenhall) (D.L. 45, 14/1) cf. p. 154. Though Uphall is in Essex, it is entered in the Hospitallers' *Register* under the page heading of Dynnesley [Temple Dinsley] Hertfordshire) - a grant confirmed by Stephen after his release in a charter issued at Westminster.

The original gift was made to 'Hugoni de Argent' et aliis fratribus de Templo.' This Hugh of Argentein seems to have been the provincial Master of the Temple in England, though his claim rests on rather slender foundations (q.v.). His name occurs again in a charter which may have been issued by Stephen during the siege of Oxford Castle in 1142. This latter Hertfordshire charter, a grant of land and mills at Dynnesley, as pointed out before, was witnessed by earl Geoffrey of Essex and by the Constable Robert de Vere. Here, too, the gift is made 'Deo et fratribus milicie Templi Jerusalem et Hugoni de Argent'. Though in the 12th century donations to the Templars are usually granted to the Order in general, viz:

> - Deo et militibus fratribus de Templo Jerusalem; fratribus de Templo Salomonis; Deo et beate Marie et fratribus Templi Salomonis, etc. -
>
> [To God and to the soldier brothers of the Temple Jerusalem; to the brothers of the Temple of Solomon; to God and blessed Mary and the brothers of the Temple of Solomon...]

Instances of the coupling of an individual name, or of several names, with the more comprehensive formula are not infrequent. These names are, as a rule, those of the Grand Master, of the provincial Masters, and of the local officials, who are often also the actual recipients of the gift.

Argentein was a well-known Hertfordshire name, see below. The family held the manor of Great Wymondley by grand serjeanty, and Stephen confirmed this tenure to John, son of Reginald de Argentein, in a charter attested by Simon de Girardimolendino, which was probably issued in 1142. A house of such distinction might suitably provide a Master for the English province, and the form of both the charters in which Hugo de Argentein appears suggests that he was regarded as the head of all the brethren of the Temple in England, not merely as a local preceptor, but as a procurator, or business agent. (Lees, 1935, xlii, xliii, xlv, 148)

There appears to have been various discrepancies in the past which have caused considerable confusion. For example, it can be seen above that Uphall of Essex is under Temple Dynnesley, Hertfordshire in the Hospitallers' *Register,* and yet Temple Dynnesley is itself included under Essex in the listing from the *Cartulaire du Temple LXII.* (See Appendix C)

Note. *It is likely that 'Roffa' should read as 'Rossa' as inscribed in the Church at Rivenhall; the alteration has come about due to the old English manner of writing the letter 's' resembling an 'f' in some documents.*

ARGENTINE (ARGENTEIN)

ARGENTEIN. *Gules three covered cups argent.*

Argentine Manor, Melbourn, Cambridgeshire

The whole parish was divided into four great fields. The parish extended from Ashwell Street near Kneesworth to opposite Royston's Town Hall, and then along the Newmarket Road to Branditch.

Lordship Farm, Melbourn

Before the Norman Conquest in the 11th century it belonged to an Anglo-Saxon thane named Edric the plain. The Argentine family were in possession in 1166 and probably even 80 years earlier. The last male Argentine died in the 14th century and the heiress married an Alington of Horseheath, whose descendant sold it to the Hitch family of Melbourn about 1700, and that was the first time the Lordship Farm had been sold. (Palmer, W. M. *Argentine's Manor, Melbourn* in *Cambridge Antiquarian Society Proceedings, with Communications and Report,* vol. XXVIII 1925-6, 1-153, et seq.) [The farmhouse still survives in private hands.]

Whether the family came over with William the Conqueror is not proved, but they possessed large estates within a century afterwards. The chief seat of the Argentine family was that at Great Wymondley in Hertfordshire, but the manor house at Melbourn was certainly used as a residence, even perhaps until the end of the 12th century when Reginald Argentine married the Fitz Teck heiress and brought Wymondley into the family, the Lordship Farm may have been their chief seat then. What is known of this Argentine manor house building, is that it consisted of a hall and a thatched chamber, an outside staircase, which was also thatched, a chapel, kitchen, granary and brewhouse. There must have been more rooms than the hall and chamber, because of the number of the Lord's household.

In the attic of the manor house, at either side were cambered beams of 14 inches [0.36 m] deep and 10 inches [0.25 m] thick. The edges carefully bevelled, were not intended to be hidden in the attic. In the centre of one beam was the place where a king-post had been chopped. At this point, I will make a slight digression. King-posts are rare in this district, but whilst alterations were being made, in 1971, to Bedwells hardware shop [Thomas Morris Estate Agents 2009] in Melbourn Street, adjacent to the present Cave entrance, a very fine example of a king-post was discovered in the roof and thought to be of the medieval period. From the carpentry details it presumably cannot be dated later than the early 1400s when that particular method of construction ceased. This suggests that the building is likely to be one of the oldest still standing in Royston. Of course, I realise it is only conjectural to assume there might be some building connection between these two properties.

Reginald de Argentein died in 1130, from which year the descent is certain. The earliest record linking the family with Melbourn is dated 1203. Members of this family had a full share in the Government of the country. The Reginald de Argentein, who died in 1223, was sheriff of several counties, sat in Westminster Hall as a judge, also rebelled against King John. There appears to have been another 'Reginald d'Argenton' who was standard bearer on the day of the battle near Damietta, Palestine in June 1237, and was slain. He unwearedly defended the standard till his arms and legs were cut off (Matthew Paris - *Chronicle of English History from the year 1235-1273*. Translation from Latin by the Rev. J. A. Gibbs, vol. I (1852) Henry G. Bohn, London). Whether he was an elder son of the former Reginald is not known but his son Richard, born about 1200, was a sheriff of several counties too, Governor of Hertford Castle and one of the stewards of the king's household. He went on a pilgrimage to the Holy Land, and owing to his prowess in war was known as 'David's Tower'. He was killed in 1246 in the battle with the Saracens before Antioch. He was thought to have been a Templar (*V.C.H.* III, 183; Clutterbuck II, 541) but as he was married could only have been a 'confrère' knight. It is this man who was first identified with Melbourn, for in the year 1227 he obtained the papal licence to build a chapel in his manor there. It was finished in 1229 when a list of rules to be observed by the Chaplain was promulgated by the Bishop of Ely. It seemed to be necessary to assign a reason for getting the chapel built. It was an expensive business, for besides the cost of the papal sanction he gave to the church a plot of land, probably that on which the vicarage now stands. On his departure to the Holy Land, it is more than likely, he gave up Wymondley to his eldest son and settled Melbourn on his wife, as a dower house. This seems to be confirmed by the fact that his wife in 1257, when a widow, executed a deed concerning her messuage and land in Melbourn. It may be that as Melbourn was much nearer to Cambridge than Wymondley, and Cambridge was of greater strategic importance in the 13th century, the Argentines found it convenient to have a complete establishment at Melbourn.

Richard was succeeded by Giles, a knight of great valour who took part with the rebellious barons. He was one of the Council formed to govern the realm after the king was taken prisoner at the Battle of Lewes in 1264, and his name was appended to all its decrees.

He had four sons, the eldest Reginald received a summons to the House of Lords as a baron. The youngest Giles was a Knight Hospitaller and won fame in battles with the Saracens in Palestine, where Robert Bruce was his companion. Sir Giles was killed at the Battle of Bannockburn, 1314.

Giles de Argentine was an adherent of Simon de Montfort and immediately after the battle of Evesham 1265, Warin de Bassingbourn, a king's man seized the Lordship Farm at Melbourn. No other Argentine was called Giles after his death, but when the Argentines' heiress was secured by the Allingtons, they revived the name Giles in honour of the crusader, and generation after generation was called by this name.

In 1307 Reginald de Argentine died. He was 'a knight of St. Mary', and is buried in Baldock Church, Hertfordshire in a chapel built by himself (q.v.). He left a son and heir aged over 30 years, named John.

The historian Weever, gives the interpretation 'Knight of St. Mary' which is doubtless correct. The expressions probably implied that he was a Knights Templar, for the Templars adopted the Rule of the Cistercians whose patron saint was the Blessed Virgin Mary, and some of the Templar Churches were dedicated to St. Mary. (See Baldock section for further information.)

The family held a curious hereditary post. The function was to serve the king at his coronation with a covered silver gilt cup of wine. The king paid for the cup, but the server claimed it as a perquisite, and some later members of the family mention these cups in their wills. The Argentines were so proud of this service, that they put the covered cups on their coat of arms. This service was known as 'sergeanty' and had no connection with the manor of Melbourn but was attached to the manor of Great Wymondly, the owner of which continued to exercise it, until the banquet was abandoned after the coronation of King George IV.

DE CLARE

There is considerable confusion over the de Clare family and their earldoms.

CLARE. *Or three cheverons gules.*

King Stephen made Gilbert fitz Gilbert earl of Pembroke in 1138. His elder brother, Richard fitz Gilbert, had been killed during the Welsh rising of 1136: another brother, Baldwin fitz Gilbert, who had subsequently been despatched to restore the situation, had failed to advance beyond Brecon. Gilbert fitz Gilbert's promotion presumably indicates that he was now to take control of the Welsh in that part of Wales, and in fact he captured or built Carmarthen Castle c. 1144. During the Civil War, over the contention for the Crown, he went over to the Empress' side for a short while in the summer of 1141. He was otherwise loyal to Stephen until 1147 when he revolted against him once more. However he became reconciled to Stephen before his death in 1148. He was also called Gilbert de Clare.

MARSHAL. *Party or and vert a lion gules.*

Regarding the earldom of Hertford, Gilbert fitz Richard de Clare witnessed as Comes Gisl' de Heorford [Hertford] at Christmas 1141, but it is generally believed that he got his earldom soon after 1138. This may well be correct, but it cannot be proved since it is often impossible to distinguish between the different earls Gilbert. He seems to have revolted as well in 1147 but subsequently made his peace with Stephen, witnessing documents between 1148 and 1153. He does not seem to have ever witnessed for the Empress. He died c. 1151-3 (Davis, 1967, 12, 13). It is difficult to sort out all the relationships, and dates do not always tally.

A couple of points remain to be noticed that later members of this family became linked with Royston. In the records under Bottisham, Staine Hundred, it is seen that in 1262 Richard de Clare, earl of Gloucester and Hertford, held at his death 1 fee in Botekesham held by William son of Martin and John de Darlee, and £12.0s.5d. rent of assize; in Bodekesham and Croyroys pleas etc. of courts 40s.; he had lately acquired the advowson of the Priory of Croyroys, of which Peter de Roph' (Peter de Rochester) was patron; *Cal. Inq.* 1., 160.

Also in the year 1296 Gilbert de Clare, earl of Gloucester and Hertford, held at his death in Bodekisham £12.2s.11d. of year rent of the honor of Buckingham; a court at La Croys Roys for his tenants, held of the honor of Gloucester; *Cal. Inq.* III, 236. (Farrer, 1925, III, 132) (See also information under Hertfordshire, Weston)

12. MAN-MADE SUBTERRANEAN STRUCTURES or SOUTERRAINS

The word 'souterrains', or more correctly 'souterrains amenages', are used by the French to describe man-made and man-used underground structures. It is a generic term used for excavated underground dwellings, for example: rock-cut houses, churches, catacombs, fortresses, quarries, marl-pits (dene-holes/chalkwells), including tunnels leading down from castles, churches and other structures etc. (Fig. 59). Natural caves which have been altered or 'arranged' can also be described in this way. The English language does not have a comparable word. 'Souterrain' in our language is specific to Iron-Age subterranean structures (one or two even above ground) found in Cornwall, others attached to *raths* in Ireland and *brochs* in Scotland. 'Souterrain' in German is a cellar in a house, and similarly in Dutch it is a basement to a shop.

Fig. 59. An example of splendid carving in the Dénezé-sous-Doué, France souterrain dated to 16th century. The souterrain was probably the meeting place of clandestine stone-masons during the times of religious persecution in the French Renaissance period, Photo Alan Beamon, 1985

EARLY RELIGIOUS EXPRESSION

In respect of early forms of religion, we principally depend upon rock pictures, in caves or gallery tombs; additionally, ethnographic models are drawn upon, inevitably with a lot of guesswork. Paintings and engravings were addressed to the divinities worshipped; they marked places where sacrifices were offered to ancestors and spirits, also where some cult ceremonies were performed. They were the expression of men's dialogue with eternal values. Examples can be seen from the primitive Aboriginal paintings in Australia, and the early Buddhist mural paintings of Ajanta in India, to those of comparatively recent times (1970s) in the catacombs of Naples, Italy.

Through the centuries succeeding religious thought, promoted by the leading protagonists of their particular time, was always threatened by that revered by those around them. In France, members of the Council of Arles (in AD 452) were moved to make pronouncements, not only against tree-cults and the cult of springs and wells, but also against that of the 'stones' - that is to say - the megalithic tombs or stone circles. Members of the Council of Tours (AD 567) forbade priests, on pain of excommunication, to perform cult-ceremonies at trees, springs or 'stones'. It was a common occurrence then for Christian ecclesiastics to officiate at heathen cult-sites. Comparable injunctions were made at the Councils of Nantes (AD 658) and Toledo, Spain (AD 681 and 682), and by Charlemagne himself in AD 789 [these edicts probably were the reason why several large stones have been found buried at some prehistoric sites].

Later still, Pope Calixtus III (died 1458) prohibited the Spaniards to carry out rites in caves that had pictures of horses in them, no-one now appears to know why: it is thought that they were possibly looked upon as being 'figures of devils'!

Another, and probably more efficient, way of combating surviving heathen customs was to exorcise the demons and to transform the areas and graves into Christian cult-sites. The exorcism was effected by the addition of a crucifix or by the engraving of Christian signs and symbols. As early as the 12th, or even the 11th century, the gallery-grave at Saint-Germain-de-Confôlens (in the Charente Department, France) was turned into a Christian chapel. One of the megalithic tombs of Plouaret (Côtes-du-Nord Department) was consecrated as the Chapelle des Sept-Saints. And Lourdes, the greatest place of pilgrimage in France, is built around a cult cavern dating back to ice age times. (Kuhn, 1956, xxiv, xxv)

Miraculous powers are still ascribed to images and paintings. In churches there are sacred pictures, in pilgrimage shrines there are sacred statues, or objects that are still attributed to work wonders. One saint's image will cure the sick, a portrait of Christ will heal wounds or save the supplicant in time of need. The Holy picture worn as an amulet, a medal or a talisman is thought by some people to protect its wearer all his life. St. Christopher the patron saint of travellers, although demoted by the Pope and Catholic Church several years ago, is still worn by many: often car drivers hold a replica with their driving licence. Some native people will not allow themselves to be photographed for they believe the possessor of the photograph can wrought, by magic, secret power over the man himself, or that the photographer actually takes an 'essence', that cannot be replaced, from the individual.

It seems that underground deities were revered in the far distant past. In England, Neolithic and Bronze Age long term dating [10,000-2000 BC] is agreed for the Grimes Graves, Norfolk flint mines where a female chalk figurine was found, which it is suggested may have represented a deity. Both in Essex and in Kent, there are subterranean passages and chambers excavated in the chalk, very similar to those of Picardy and Aquitaine, France. They are called 'dene-holes', formerly 'Danes' Pits', of which there are many in Darenth Wood and near Chislehurst, at East Tilbury, Crayford and Little Thurrock. Originally they were small chalk quarries - some very ancient - for British coins have been found in them. Chalk was largely exported in early times via the Thames to Zealand: from there, it was passed through the low countries and used in dressing the fields [marling]. Altars to the Roman Nethalennia, the patroness of the chalk quarries, have been found in the sand on the coast of Zealand and some bear votive inscriptions from dealers in British chalk. (Baring-Gould, 1911, 97).

SUBTERRANEAN CHAPELS IN EUROPE

Early Christians, particularly in Rome, became accustomed in times of danger to resort to subterranean chapels in the catacombs. The cult of the martyrs had grown to a passion, and it became customary to commemorate their 'nativities', as it was called, i.e. the anniversaries of their deaths, at their tombs in the catacombs. The faithful habitually prayed, near the bones of the saints where it was believed special sanctity dwelt. They believed prayers were most effectually answered through the intercession of the saints; and it was there, in the dark damp depths and akin to martyrs, that they themselves expected to be laid in anticipation of the Resurrection. The same fervour spread and underground chapels sprang up. Once the hermits, abbots, bishops, devout women, and confessors of all descriptions, were added to the recognised martyr sites their underground tombs became extraordinarily numerous, and were resorted to with great devotion. Such was the origin of the crypts found in profusion in France, not just under cathedrals, but under parish and monastic churches as well. The population having become predominantly Christian, the practice of visiting these subterranean chapels became so great as to cause inconvenience. The bishops then proceeded to 'elevate' and remove the bones of saints from their original resting places to the 'basilicas' [above ground church buildings]. With this change, the crypts lost most of their attraction and instead, the worshippers gathered about the altars in the upper churches to which the bones had been transferred. Throughout the rest of Northern Europe, Germany and Britain there were few early martyrs, or crypts used for the acceptance of their bones. A rare example being the excavated Anglo-Saxon crypt below St. Wystan's church, Repton, Derbyshire believed to be possibly the shrine of St. Wystan, who was murdered in AD 850 and 'was buried in the mausoleum of his grandfather Wiglaf' (King of Mercia, AD 827-840). It may, however, only have been a reliquary-crypt. (Taylor, H. M. (1979) *Repton Studies* 2, *The Anglo-Saxon Crypt and Church,* Printed by Fengraphic, Cambridge, 12-13)

There is a good example of a decorated rock cavern Monastery, Abbey of Brantôme (Dordogne) in France (Fig. 60), which was later abandoned for a stately structural monastery. The Romanesque tower of the church stands on top of a rock that is honeycombed with their cells. The old monolithic chapel below still survives but was turned into a 'pigeonry'. There are two pieces of sculpture on a very large scale, one represents the Crucifixion with the Virgin

Mary and Apostle John; the other has been variously explained as the Last Judgment or the Triumph of Death, but it was never completed. Beneath the figure of Christ is Death, figured by a head surmounted by a crown of bones, and a crest representing a spectre armed with a club. On each side is an angel blowing a trumpet. Below are ranged a dozen heads of popes, bishops, princes, knights, and ladies, in boxes to represent graves. [The idea of heads in boxes has connotations of the Italian cult (q.v.)] The sculptures are thought not to be earlier than 16th century, therefore the early uniqueness of Royston Cave still stands. Close by is another grotto called 'La Babayou' [of the statue] and probably at one time enshrined an image of a saint. Relics of St. Sicarius were a great draw to Brantôme in the Middle Ages. (Baring-Gould, 1911, 238-39).

Fig. 60. The Underground Chapel at Brantôme, France. The figure of Christ was never completed. Below is a head crowned with bones, representing Death, with Time as a crest. Below again, in boxes are the dead of various degrees. (After Baring-Gould, 1911)

The Holy Mysteries, first of all, were celebrated in private houses and churches on wooden tables, sometimes square, but often round supported by three legs. According to the historical writer William of Malmesbury, St. Wulstan, Bishop of Worcester (1062-1095) destroyed the wooden altars in his diocese that had been universal in England. From then onwards altars were transformed into a tomb (sepulchre), no doubt following the Roman pontifical and liturgical instructions. The change from a table to a tomb involved a change of material from wood to stone. The Bishops were to exact that if, at the time of an altar's dedication, it did not contain the whole body of a saint, then the slab should have a hole cut in it to receive a box containing relics. (Baring-Gould, 1911, 173-77)

The reason why the writer has gone into quite a lot of detail on early Christian practices is to show that the chances of Royston Cave being used as an underground chapel before the 12th century is indeed exceptionally remote. Although a human head and one or twe bones were recovered from the infill, it is not proven that a body was buried there (q.v.).

GROTTOS AND CAVE-CHURCHES OF THE MIDDLE EAST

Dean Stanley, writing in 1856, said: 'The moment that the religion of Palestine fell into the hands of the Europeans, it is hardly too much to say that as far as sacred traditions are concerned, it became 'a religion of caves', of those very caves which in earlier times had been unhallowed by any religious influence whatever. Wherever a sacred association had to be fixed, a cave was immediately selected or found as its home. First in antiquity is the Grotto of Bethlehem, as the scene of the Nativity. Next comes the grotto on Mount Olivet [Olives], selected as the scene of our Lord's last conversation before the Ascension. These two caves, Eusebius emphatically asserts, were the first seats of the worship established by the Empress Helena, to which was shortly afterwards added a third - the sacred cave of the Sepulchre. To these were rapidly added the cave of the Invention of the Cross, the cave of the Annunciation at Nazareth, the cave of the Agony at Gethsemane, the cave of the Baptism in the Wilderness of St. John and the cave of the Shepherds of Bethlehem.' (Stanley, 1856, 150)

At Mount Tabor, on the south-east part, near the highest point among the ruins, there is a small vault, where Latin monks from Nazareth still celebrated in the 19th century, an annual mass in memory of the Transfiguration. The spot is merely a rude cellar with an altar, and a small side vault with three niches or altars. (Robinson & Smith, 1838 & 1852, II, 353)

In Egypt, in the Levant, cave-churches are common. The Chapel of Agios Niketos, in Crete, is merely a smoke begrimed grotto beneath a huge mass of rock on the mountain side. The roof is elaborately ornamented with paintings representing incidents in the Gospel story, and the legend of St. Nicholas.

The rock-hewn church of Dayn Aboo Hannes, 'the convent of Father John', near Antinoe, also in Egypt, had its walls painted with subjects from the New Testament, and this church is thought to date back to the time of Constantine. (Baring-Gould, 1911, 193)

The last two examples illustrate that decorating with religious scenes was carried out in caves as well as in above-ground churches.

CAVE-DWELLING HERMITS

Perhaps, partly because of the constancy of the religious cause, and partly the effect of the actual consecration of grottos, began the occupation of caves by the hermits. One example being, the remarkable cells hewn or found in the precipices of the Quarrantania or Mount of the Temptation above Jericho. In some instances, the original selection of grottos would coincide with the events which were intended to be perpetuated as noted by, 'the hiding places of the prophets on Carmel, and the sepulchres of the patriarchs and of Our Lord... ' (Baring-Gould, 1911, 195)

There were a number of rock-cut hermitages in this country, some as early as the Saxon period, but the one, at Warkworth in Northumberland, dated to the late Middle Ages, was quite an elaborate affair. It contained a chapel dedicated to the Holy Trinity with three bays carved in Gothic style. Its altar was correctly aligned to the east. Another hermitage at Knaresborough in Yorkshire, was scooped out of the rock by the side of the river Nidd, and dignified by the name of St. Gile's chapel. (Baring-Gould, 1911, 219-20)

CRUSADER CHURCHES

To the east of the village of Ain Karim, is the Franciscan Church of the Magnificat in a convent. It has a domed roof which is a conspicuous object and the church has a grotto beneath, where St. John the Baptist is supposed to have been born. The church of St. John or the Magnificat is mentioned in AD 1113, and is of Crusading origin but rebuilt in 1621. On the southern hill west of the spring (Ain Sitti Miriam) and close to the new Russian hospice, when building the new chapel of the Summer-House of Zacharias in 1861, ruins were discovered by the Latins. The grounds were excavated to a depth of 15-20 feet [4.5-6 m], and the lower story 'of the old church (mentioned by John Poloner (1422) as having a subterranean and an upper chapel) was found.

In the valley of Kidron, that separates the city from the Mount of Olives, the church of the Tomb of the Virgin still has its 12th century entrance doorway, although set in a facade that has lost its upper storey. Within, a flight of stairs leads down to a cruciform crypt, covered with a groined vault and built in well-cut stone. Here is the sarcophagus known as the Virgin's tomb, whose emptiness played a part in the 12th century debates as to the corporeal assumption. The church belonged to the Abbey of St. Mary of Jehoshaphat founded by Godfrey de Bouillon and much patronised by Queen Melisende, whose tomb was in a niche half way down the staircase to the crypt.

The monastery had also in its charge the grotto of the Agony and the Church of Gethsemane, or of the Saviour. Built above Byzantine ruins, the latter was a typical crusading church with a nave and two aisles ending in three apses, now only known from an excavated ground plan.

Regarding Bireh, this village is the ancient Beeroth of Benjamin (*Joshua* ix 17). In the middle ages the place was called La Grande Mahomerie (*Cart. de* S. *Sep.*). It is mentioned under this name by William of Tyre. Outside the village on the south-west is a good spring, with a sacred place built over it and a trough on the east side. Towards the north-east are the Ruins of a

Crusading Church. The church, with a hospice attached, was completed by the Templars (to whom the place belonged in 1146 AD. (*Cart. de S. Sep.*). (Conder & Kitchener, 1881-3, III, 9 & 19)

The last paragraph shows, although just by one example, that the Templars also built churches outside of the City of Jerusalem, and even though they did not have a grotto beneath in this instance, it is obvious that they must have been well aware of the use of such structures for religious purposes by others.

CRUSADER CAVE FORTRESSES

Strangest of all may be, or alternatively, most sensible to those who are familiar with such sites, is the crusaders' use of natural defences in the form of cave fortresses as at Tyron (Shaquif Tirun) in the hills above one of the routes from Damascus to Sidon, and at Habis, above the Yarmuk to the south-east of the lake of Tiberias. The latter was an advanced post, in a country where a castle built by Baldwin I had been almost immediately destroyed. The caves, reached by narrow paths in the rock face, partially natural, partially cut, required little expenditure and were almost impregnable. Tyron was lost to the Franks in 1165, but reoccupied for a time in 1250. Furnished with grain stores, cisterns and a water supply brought in pipes from a nearby spring, it was not easily starved out, and its path of access was in places a matter of crawling on hands and knees under shelving rocks to reach entrances in the overhanging cliff. (Boase, 1967, 21 & 44)

CRUSADERS' RETURN TO THEIR OWN COUNTRIES

After the pilgrims, including members the Crusading Orders, who in their thousands had visited the Holy sites returned to their native lands, they were deeply impressed with the association of caves with everything that was held sacred. Their sense of reverence for places underground, consecrated to Holy purposes, promoted the multiplication of subterranean churches, of which quite a number occurred in France. Many of the caves had springs of water in them, some held to be invested with miraculous properties. Was Royston Cave one such subterranean chapel?

However, are there any examples of the Templars actually being associated with a chapel underground? According to the *Dossier Secrets,* the Templar commandery at Gisors, France, dated from 1306, was situated in the rue de Vienne. From here it supposedly communicated, via an underground passageway with the local cemetery and with the subterranean chapel of Sainte-Catherine located beneath the fortress. An excavation took place in 1962. It is still not known if the chapel was ever found but it was mentioned in two old manuscripts dated 1375, and 1696. (Baigent, Leigh & Lincoln, 1982, 134)

13. CONCLUSIONS

At this stage of drawing together the threads woven throughout the text, what can be established? What can be discounted? And what is conjecture or deduction?

WHEN WAS ROYSTON CAVE EXCAVATED OUT OF THE CHALK? WHAT WAS THE PURPOSE?

In all honesty, this is anyone's guess. It is rare in the study of underground man-made and man-used structures to be able to ascertain an exact date of construction (except in the case of mining records). Once a structure has had a function, other than for its extracted material, it can be used over and over again, concurrently or subsequently throughout centuries. As the founder of Subterranea Britannica, which is in association with most of the continental countries, the writer was grateful to her many contacts here and abroad who were able to suggest various research routes. The following are the evaluated alternatives to its use as an oratory used by the Knights Templar.

BURIAL PIT/BONE SHAFT
Evidence is slim. It is possible that a quantity of bones could have been removed and that the skull and one or two human bones remained, but I think this is unlikely. Either these were part of a Templar ritual or were random finds from the infilled soil removed in 1742.

COLUMBARIUM
Most unlikely as there are not sufficient numbers of niches for cinerary urns (q.v.).

DENE-HOLE
The bell or bottle shape of the Cave indicates that it could have been excavated primarily as a 'dene-hole' for the purpose of extracting chalk for marling fields (to give alkalinity to acid soils and/or breakup claggy soils, e.g. clay). Against this argument is the fact that chalk is liberally strewn throughout all the surrounding fields, and bedrock lies just 'two spits' below the surface of the ground. Nevertheless, it is possible that the chalk could have been carried by road to outlying areas for marling. Such quarried chalk might have been used for improving roads, giving a firm bed and assisting in drainage. Crushed chalk mixed with water and straw and/or animal hair could have been used also in wattle and daub building practices.

If the structure had been dug as a 'dene-hole', then the excavators must have commenced externally, working from the top downwards to form this belled chamber; and the tiled dome would have been created later when the cavern was altered for a different function. Both shafts could have been constructed later, although the Eastern shaft is believed to be the earlier as evidenced by the archaeological finds found at its original base (q.v.). The removal of chalk, in a sense for commercial purposes, by burrowing upwards from the Eastern shaft and carrying it aloft up narrow shafts is possible but would have been certainly time-consuming, and hardly practicable, unless the idea was to keep the structure relatively obscure.

FLINT MINE
Strategically, the Cave is sited on two main roads (Ashwell Street/Icknield Way and Ermine Street) across Britain. It was possibly started as a shaft dug by prehistoric man, maybe of the Neolithic or Bronze Age, perhaps in search of flint. The bedrock in Royston is Middle-horizon chalk containing only the occasional, very small flint nodule completely unsuitable for flint axes and other such tools. Grimes Graves, in Norfolk, early man's 'flint factory' is sited on the Icknield Way too.

GRANARY PIT
Granaries or silos were not as deep as the Cave, and were generally approximately 5 ft [1.5 m] in diameter and 6-10 ft [1.8-3 m] deep. Another serious reason to discount this suggestion is that water percolates within which would have rotted the grain.

HERMITAGE
A strong possibility at sometime but not necessarily associated with the hermit which died at Royston's crossroads in 1506 (q.v.).

ICE-WELL/ICE-PIT
For the same reason as for the granary, water would have been the problem, and, in this instance, cause the dissolution of the mass of ice. Not only that, but the storing of ice in general was a late introduction into this country - late 16th century: except that at least Richard I knew of the storage of ice in the 12th century for he sent Saladin an iced sherbert whilst in the Holy Land (Beamon & Roaf, 1990). The Cave is presumed to have been filled-in around the time of the Dissolution 1540, although it is strange that the carvings do not appear to have been desecrated in any way.

MITHRAS TEMPLE
One lady visitor claimed the Cave was a Temple to Mithras. From John Yarker's book, *The Arcane Schools* on p. 79, I give a few details which I think discounts this suggestion.

'The European Temples of Mithras were an oblong square reached by a Pronas on the level from which a few steps led to the actual Temple. On either side of the entrance was a human figure, one of which holds a raised torch, and the other a torch reversed. Benches occupied the two sides, and at the further end was an altar, and beyond a statue of Mythras Tauroticus with the sun at the God's left hand and the moon at his right hand...'

OUBLIETTE/PRISON
A vague possibility, except that prisoners are not usually given access to implements to carve walls, and even more exceptional would have been the gift of paint. Templars were imprisoned in Royston and held in the Priory. There is an example of an oubliette at St. Andrew's Castle, Fife, Scotland. It is alleged that Cardinal Beaton imprisoned Protestants in this bottle-shaped dungeon beneath the castle. Prisoners went mad in the darkness, then when their screams could be heard, they were murdered.

SACRED SHAFT
Of Pagan origin. The geomantic position of the Cave is supposedly correct for an entrance to the underworld, centred at the crossing-point of two major Roman routes. Pennick (1981, 136) claims, amongst other things, that the crowned woman is not St. Katherine but that of

Persephone, Queen of the Underworld; and that the carving of St. Christopher, 'sporting an uncharacteristic phallus' is in the guise of the Christianised Hermes. Dowsers, including Hamish Miller and Paul Broadhurst who wrote *The Sun and the Serpent* (1989), maintain that two earth energy forces, also called ley lines, the Michael and Mary currents, cross within the structure (p.189). It is interesting that in 1975 a member of Subterranea Britannica Mrs. Greta Maxwell-Comfort, who was a dowser, asked to dowse in the Cave and was puzzled to find two lines crossing. At that time the search was for a cavity below the floor.

WATER CISTERN

A minor possibility at some time. Royston has little natural water, but the bottom, and the walls of cisterns are usually cemented to stop natural drainage. They measured between 8-12 ft [2.5-3.65m] deep (exceptions being in the Middle East and elsewhere in arid areas). In Israel it was quite normal to have conduits running into a cistern. I have wondered whether, behind the remaining unbroken 'masonry' sealing the base of the Eastern shaft and above the depression a likely sump for water, there is a conduit. A few yards away from the entrance to the Cave is a 'surface water' well in St. Katherine's yard (formerly known as Bedwell's yard) which, when measured in June 1972, was 11 ft 9 ins [3.6m] deep and still containing 18 ins [0.46m] of murky water. Perhaps the well and the Cave were linked at some time but only by excavation could this be credited or discounted. (See also under Denny Abbey where there was an arrangement for collecting water.) [2008 – two cavities, one containing water, on an eastern alignment with the Cave were confirmed by ground penetrating radar. Not excavated.]

WAYSIDE ORATORY/CHAPEL

Beldam suggested the Cave was associated with a crusader returning from the Holy Land who wished to perpetuate what he had seen (q.v.). It was his suggestion which stimulated the writer to go even further and promote the idea that it was associated with the Templars.

THE CRUSADING ORDER OF THE KNIGHTS TEMPLAR

There will always be controversy over this Order's Christian values, or otherwise. Did they, as a complete group, become anti-Christ? Was there an inner circle - an élite? If so, did they become anti-Christ? If it is true that some became anti-Christ, why? What changed their views? Was it mixing with the infidel, particularly between warring campaigns, when, as lay men, they farmed and socialised together in Palestine?

In general, there are the two schools of thought: those who feel the 'Templars were suppressed at trumped-up trials, primarily out of greed by Philippe Ie Bel, the French king, for their wealth; that they were 'whiter than white', never dabbled in the occult, never gave each other obscene kisses in ritualistic ceremonies, and all the confessions, whether extorted under torture or not, were false. Others on the opposing side, believe they were haughty, decadent and cabbalists to their own ends. To assume that an all male institution did not have some homosexual activity would be naive; however, in my opinion the real answer lies somewhere in between the two theories.

I have studied this Order's behaviour from literature for over twenty years, listened to the views of the French experts and others, and tried to think myself back to Medieval times. I have carefully considered what was important to them as a group. The way in which the Christian religion rose and succoured the needs of the time. The rush to take up the cross, the final goal to gain the Holy City of Jerusalem for the whole of Christendom: in feeling, probably not a lot different to those fervent young men who signed up in the early days of World War I, with absolutely no idea of what war was about, but got carried away, full of enthusiasm for 'the cause'. The Templars were a dichotomy, temporal and spiritual. They were both warriors and monks. Spiritually, the Templars sought the Holy Grail, not the physical object of the search upon which it would be easier to focus the mind, but the embodiment of that which most individuals seek throughout their lives, some semblance of reason for 'the meaning of life'. I am not too bigoted to appreciate that with 20th century values it is virtually impossible to get back into the minds of the Medievalists, nevertheless, it has been worth a try.

Although academically speaking, 'I am putting my head on the block' I am of the opinion that from the 14th century, and perpetuated through the centuries, the true reason for the destruction of Templar ideology has been obscured by the prejudices of the times, and doctrines of the church which were rarely questioned through fear of the Inquisition together with the atrocious penalties meted out to unfortunates who dared to raise their voices.

During the 12th and 13th centuries the Christian faith had to all intents and purposes successfully ousted the old religions, and with great vigour and fanaticism many of the crusaders joined the ranks of the military cum monastic Orders. They zealously believed they were going to conquer the Holy Land through Jesus Christ and their Christian faith. All went well initially, for the Templars gained stature and prowess in warfare. They were given many lands and became rich, but when things began to go against them, what then? Did some members begin to doubt their faith and looked to themselves to find the reason why? For God always gave the victory to Christians unless they displeased Him, just as He had done with the people of Israel - or so they believed. If God and Jesus Christ were forsaking them, and it was for this very reason they were losing battles to the infidels, what then, could or should they do to get back into God's favour?

The Christians had been taught that you can only reach God through Jesus Christ. However, the seeds of doubt were sown. The Templars traded and mixed with not only the Assasins but with many people. Also various nationalities were allowed to join as 'confrère' knights, perhaps just for a short while or for a particular campaign. Maybe it was in this way alien ideas together with superstitious rituals gained ground when the tide turned and battles began to be lost. Few can intercommunicate and not absorb some aspects of the society in which they find themselves.

Supposing they had been misled? Suppose Jesus Christ was a false prophet? They still believed that God was omnipotent. Perhaps they felt if they were to propitiate Jesus Christ or Satan as believed by the Bogomils they could reach God again and win the day. Personally, I think quite a number of the Order did carry out various secret rituals but in their own estimation they did not do anything wrong. It was through their love of God that they did 'spit upon the cross' etc. so that

God would know they believed in him ONLY, that is to say, they became Anti-Christ but not Anti - God.

There are several cases where Templars apostasised and took the faith of Islam: again this action, in all likelihood, was not considered to be such a disgrace by most of them for the Islamists believe too, that 'There is no God but God.'

Clearly, it is unwise to be pedantic in these matters, and with the close of this last chapter in mind, assuredly there are certain questions which will never be answered.

One summary on the importance of the Knights Templar, set in the historical context, and written by Walter Phillips probably cannot be improved upon:

> 'A word must be added as to the significance of the work of the Templars 'and of the manner of their fall in the history of the world. Two great things the Order had done for European civilisation: in the east and in Spain it had successfully checked the advance of Islam; it had deepened and given a religious sanction to the idea of the chivalrous man, the HOMO LEGALIS [biding by his law], and so opened up, to a class of people who for centuries to come were to exercise enormous influence, spheres of activity the beneficient effect of which are still recognisable in the world. On the other hand, the destruction of the Templars had three consequences fateful for Christian civilization:
>
> 1) It facilitated the conquests of the Turks by preventing the Templars from playing in Cyprus the part which the Knights of St. John played in Malta.
>
> 2) It partly set a precedent for, partly confirmed, the cruel criminal procedure of France [Inquisition], which lasted to the Revolution.
>
> 3) It set the seal of the highest authority on the popular belief in witchcraft and personal intercourse with the devil, sanctioned the expedient of wringing confessions of such intercourse from the accused by unspeakable tortures, and so made possible the hideous witch-persecution which darkened the later middle ages and, even in Protestant countries, long survived the Reformation. 'If I were to name a day in the whole history of the world,' said Dollinger at the conclusion of his last public lecture, 'which appears to me in the truest sense as DIES NEFASTUS [Day of Doom - unlucky day], I should be able to name no other than the 13th October, 1307".
>
> Phillips, W.A., (1911) 'Templars' in *Encyclopaedia Britannica,* Eleventh Edition.

LOCAL FAMILY ASSOCIATION WITH THE CRUSADING ORDERS

Why did not any member of the Mandeville family appear to make a donation to the Knights Templar in reparation for Templar aid? The brethren placed upon Geoffrey's body, after he had died, the habit of their Order with the red cross, and then carried it to their Temple Church in London encased in lead, for he had been excommunicated by the orthodox church and could not be buried in consecrated ground. This act by the Templars was a great honour. Donations were made by the family to the Knights Hospitaller both at Chippenham and Shepreth as shown in the body of the essay.

Consider too, the Argentines, a member of their family was at one time Grand Master of the Order of the Knights Templar for England, another rebuilt Baldock church, and several were connected with the Crusades. No local gifts are recorded from them.

And the de Rochesters, what of this household? Two members signed Templar charters and Peter de Rochester who inherited Newsells estate became a Templar shortly before his death in 1255. He donated 100 acres of his land at Rivenhall, Essex to the Templars, why not at Royston as well? He also stipulated that his heirs Alice de Scales and her son Robert were to found a chantry for his soul's benefit. Did they do so? Or did they donate money for prayers to be said in a Templar chapel already in existence in Royston?

The Argentines and members of the family at Newsells jointly were connected with the hospitals sited in Royston. Did they also give land and support the Templars in the town? Or on the other hand, as the chances are quite high that the chapel was sometimes used for dubious activities, omitted the evidence from any records.

Not to be forgotten are the de Clares who were benefactors to this Order. There is an obscure reference in Kingston (1906, 121) that Lord Pembroke after the death of Charles I in 1649, claimed the eastern part of the Royston Court House property not far from the Cave. Why? Did the family think it had some claim to the land from long ago? Possibly this is a 'red herring' but it was a Countess of Pembroke who had claimed Denny Abbey, Cambridgeshire and Strood in Kent, both formerly Templar properties in the 14th century (q.v.).

RE-USE OF THE CAVE?

Who actually altered, carved, and painted the Cave? The author thinks the most likely explanation is as follows:

The Knights Templar of Baldock were primarily made up of ordinary artisans, who farmed and looked after the local estates. They would have worn the brown garments with the red cross and were not the fighting Knights clad in white exhibiting the red cross. Each week the marketing men would bring their goods to sell in the market which straddled around the crossroads at Royston. The present day A505 road undulates quite steeply, and in the past this track, particularly in wet and icy conditions, would have been difficult to pass along. The distance of 9 miles [14.4 km] by cart or even walking doubtless took quite some time. In summertime, the butter and cheese would spoil on such journeys back and forth. A sensible solution would have been to have a cellar so that the goods could be stored in a cool atmosphere, such as the Cave, which has a temperature of between 48 - 52° F.

When the disputes with the Prior of Royston commenced, it presumably caused the Templar marketeers problems. Where could they make their regular obligatory prayers? This is when the writer thinks the Cave was most probably altered. May be, initially, it was no more than a simple cellar, with the two shafts covered by trapdoors at ground level within a 'shop' or temporary superstructure, that opened into one small chamber (the top portion), with elongated cavities in the walling useful for storing cheeses. The northern shaft, although narrow, allowed the men to go up and down at will, and the eastern shaft assumed to have been used for lifting and lowering market goods. Whether the Cave was excavated by them to a lower level then to form an oratory, cannot be determined but the suggestion has some merit in view of the fact that the base was cut on the square, then to an octagon (q.v.). If the chamber was going to be used only for market goods, why elaborate the bottom in this way? The plan would not have aided the diggers constructionally.

Once the decision to formulate a chapel was made, a design needed to be followed, what is more natural than to emulate that which was known to the Order already? Even if some of the local men had not seen such a structure for themselves, the awareness was there from their companions. The 'arranging' of the chapel followed, niches and the decoration. Who carved the figures? Some visitors view them as being completely random, however, the main figures are large, as in Eastern artwork, and cut into the frieze. I think these were carved first, and as mentioned in Chapter 6, Harold Perrett, an artist, is certain that the same person executed several figures and had an understanding of the human muscle formation. St. Christopher is sited in his correct position, as would be expected in a church, on a north wall by an entrance.

Next, came the painting, some figures were enhanced by a darker pigment - to make them stand out. I think with our sophisticated eyes they appear primitive, but how we see them today is similar to seeing a rag doll left out in the rain when the painted face has been washed away. They may have seemed quite splendid when originally painted.

There is no reason why this small chapel could not have been used by the Templars from about 1199 when they first appear in the records as coming to Royston from Baldock for marketing, until the demise of the Order in 1308. Because of the distance from Baldock to Royston, the Templar marketeers - probably no more than two or three visiting weekly - possibly stayed overnight in the Cave before returning the next day. This would have given many of them the opportunity of embellishing further what was already there.

There is also the possibility that the chamber was used for initiations of some sort for the Cave was central to several groups of Templars in the surrounding area. Certainly, there are quite a number of cult symbols and the suggestion should not be discarded completely, although more research is necessary before it can be categorically sustained. Members of the fraternity engaged in any form of ceremony were not likely to be disturbed at this site. Another reason for the secrecy of the Cave is that it would have made a good depository for money and valuables entrusted to the Templars as certain members traversed the countryside distributing this wealth for their customers.

SUMMARY

Finally to summarise my findings:

The difficulties encountered in trying to prove the Cave's connection with the Templars have been enormous, lack of documents, many being scattered between several counties. No early maps, the centre of the Town like Buntingford was not titheable. Whether records were perhaps lost in the fires experienced in Royston in 1324, and again in 1405 on the feast of the Translation of St. Martin (Page, 1912, 259), is not known.

Factually, there is the recorded historical evidence that Templars were in Royston every week, at least from 1199 until 1254. They also owned property here but exactly where has not been established by documentation. This market town is only four miles [6.4 km] away from Wendy, eight miles [13 km] from Duxford (where they had a preceptory), and also nine miles [14.4 km] from Baldock. They had their respective churches at Baldock, Wendy and Whittlesford (Duxford). When the men were not on active duty they were obliged to make their devotions regularly throughout the day, including forty obits to their dead brethren. As mentioned, this devotion to prayer was not likely to have been possible in Royston's Priory church for any length of time, in view of the confrontations members of the Order had with the Prior of Royston, who was not averse to imprisoning some of the Baldock Templars in his Priory on occasions. He also extracted stallage of 37s. from them over quite a long period that had to be returned after a serious dispute which was finally settled at crown level. A Templar Chapel probably became more of a necessity than anything else, giving a haven overnight for the Templar marketeers, and from a practical point of view, if not already established, a warehouse for market goods - a welcome addition. This assumption presuming that the Cave was not being already reused.

I would like to hypothesise that: from the shape of the Cave with octagonal step, tiling in the dome, a frieze above the carvings, the altar on the west, cult symbols, evidence of Knights Templar in the town of Royston and district, this was deliberately a copy of the Holy Sepulchre Church (even if a rather amateurish attempt). Of course, there have been other examples, in the Italian church of San Stefano at Bologna and in Spain at Segovia the church of La Vera.

I rest my case.

ADDENDUM

If I am correct and the Cave was decorated by the Knights Templar, then this is the most remarkable surviving artwork of this Order. But, if I am wrong, then this Cave still remains the most unique structure of its kind both in this country and Europe and should be conserved at all costs for future generations. The site is a Scheduled Grade I monument, which unfortunately is suffering rapid deterioration. Since 1975 various experts have put forward suggestions but to date (1992) all have been abortive. Amongst the proposals were:

1) To keep rain water from 'melting away' some of the engravings (see Chapter 3) and to prevent a recurrence of past flooding. The problem has abated during the last three years as currently the area is in a drought condition.

2) To obtain 1 : 1 copies of photographs already taken by the Courtauld Institute of Art, enlarged to this size so that when portions fall from the wall they can be drawn on the photographs for record purposes.

3) To have a multi-disciplinary team to carry out scientific research into various factors, e.g. a review of what fungi is present and has it caused the intensified discolouration to the carvings (as reported by a representative of English Heritage)? Or does it also destroy the chalk surfaces and assist crumbling?

4) To have a plaster cast model made, perhaps followed by copies in fibreglass, similar to that constructed of the Lascaux Cave in the Dordogne, France and the facade at Petra, in Jordan.

It is obvious to the writer that, unless the deterioration can be stemmed within a relatively short time span, posterity will be left merely with a man-made hole in the ground and the carvings will be gone. If this is inevitable then the best visual record of this unique structure must be made in the very near future so as to ensure knowledge of the carvings in the round for later generations. [2008/9 – One step forward, English Heritage has now electronically digitised the Cave – fifteen years later after this book was originally published. SPB.]

APPENDICES

I - X

Scientific reports
Crusader information
Kings of the relevant times
Baldock and Temple Dinsley documentation
Original Cave sketches by Rev. Wm. Stukeley

A - E

Charters
Templar information extracted from D'Albon's manuscripts, Bibliothèque Nationale, Paris
Legends of Saints and Martyrs

APPENDIX I

Report on the Geology of Royston Cave, 1973

1. STRATA

The site is about in the middle of the Middle Chalk outcrop. This division of the Chalk is rather over 200 ft [60.1 m] thick hereabouts (Geol, Survey one-inch New Series Sheet No. 2049). The walls of the cave are seen to be composed of white chalk, as is appropriate to this horizon. There are [virtually] no flints.

Chalk of this sort is uniformly permeable to water. It is seen right to the top of the cave, just below topsoil and brickwork, and is no doubt present for some tens of feet below the floor. There is nothing to support a 'perched water table' (Mr. Rippon's letter of May 1972.)

2. PRESENT-DAY WATER-TABLE

As shown by Mr. Rippon's letter, water-level at the Queen's Road pumping station was at 127 ft [38.7 m] O.D. in April 1970 and at 110 ft [33.5 m] in November, 1970. 1970 was about an average year for ground-water in this district, so that in an extreme wet spring, following a wet winter, I would think the water-table might rise to about 140 ft [42.8 m] O.D. under the cave.

Cave floor level is about 200 ft [60.1 m] O.D. so it is evident that the water-table cannot now come anywhere near high enough to provide a supply to the cave. Moreover, seasonal fluctuation of water-table amounts to some tens of feet so that a shallow depression in the cave floor such as the 'grave', would never have been an appropriate supply expedient.

3. FORMER WATER-TABLE

For water-table to come as high as cave floor level, rainfall would have to be about double the present annual rate. History would certainly have shown trace or record of such a wet climatic spell, had it ever occurred. The principal evidence available locally, is in the siting of villages. Spring line villages such as Kneesworth and Bassingbourn show no indication of the migration which would have had to take place to higher ground if the present sites had become waterlogged.

Mrs. Beamon's letter of 24th May, 1972 with enclosures, shows that old wells in Royston are 80-110 ft [24-33.5 m] deep in accordance with expectation for more or less stable climate since the (unknown) dates of their construction.

4. SEEPAGE OF SURFACE WATER

As mentioned in Mr. Rippon's letter a likely source of water in the cave would be by seepage down from ground surface after rain. Although the chalk is uniformly permeable, percolation is often localised due to concentration of runoff along road verges, in the low corner of a market place or in similar positions adjacent to impermeable hard surfacing. Such percolation might well be sufficiently copious to constitute a nuisance in the cave and would not immediately soak down through the earth floor. The 'grave' is in my opinion quite possibly a drainage sump, cut down through the compact floor to permit percolation into the permeable chalk below.

5. NATURE OF THE CAVE FLOOR

The fairly smooth dark-coloured earth surface is deceptively uniform in appearance. The electrical resistivity survey of 26th June, 1972 provides evidence of underlying irregularities. Two areas of moderately high resistivity were investigated on 30th May, 1973 by striking with a small mattock. In each case, solid undisturbed white chalk was found an inch or two below the floor. Excavation has been minimal owing to the chance of there being depressions containing archaeological material demanding deliberate excavation. However, the sizes of the 'lows' and their relationship to the proved solid chalk indicates that such depressions will not be more than a foot or two [0.32-0.6 m] deep. It may be that some resistivity features are not indications of depressions, but only of local fissures emphasized by, for instance, salt derived from seepage of road runoff. A small excavation at the foot of the peripheral step, directly opposite the usual entrance to the cave, demonstrated that the solid chalk of the step is continuous with solid chalk close below floor surface.

Striking the floor with the head of the mattock handle gave different sounds in different places; the resistivity 'high' co-ordinates 7, 9 on the plan emits a hollow sound when struck as do a few other parts of the floor, whereas elsewhere a hard ringing sound is obtained indicating the presence of solid chalk.

Colin L. Forbes, M.A.. Ph.D. Curator - Sedgwick Museum of Geology Cambridge University, Cambridge (5.1.73).

APPENDIX II

i) PAINTED FIGURES

There is no mention at all of any pigmentation in the original communication sent by the Rev. George North dated 28.9.1742 to the Society of Antiquaries of London and minuted in vol. 4. However:

> '...Almost the whole circle between the podium and the cornice has been sculptured in low relief, as described by Stukeley, with crucifixes, saints, martyrs, and historical pieces; and many of these, if not all, have been coloured. Vestiges of red, blue, and yellow are visible in various places; and the relief of the figures has been assisted by a darker pigment...' Beldam, 1877, 15.

Unfortunately, Stukeley (1743) only makes one specific reference to colouring on p. 37 of his *Palaeographia Britannica:* No.1, thus:

> '...The mitred person is the cardinal Octavian, the other carrying the crucifix is Hugh de Nunant. Assuredly these are evident confirmation of the histories of these times, as are recorded in our authors.
>
> William Lilly, who lives in the house just over the oratory, and was very assistant in drawing out the earth, says these two figures at first appeared painted over of a red colour, and I myself saw the remains...'

Parkin only makes one specific comment, based on Stukeley's remarks on the two figures, which he thinks represent the patron saints of the Priory, but are one and the same as mentioned above: 'painted over a red colour'. He does mention that he thinks all the figures were painted and decorated, but time and rubbish that covered them has defaced their embellishments. The reader is reminded that Parkin may never have stepped inside the Cave, therefore his evidence is of some doubt.

To return to Beldam (p. 29):

> '...next to St. Christopher is the legend of St. Katherine of Alexandria. It is related of this virgin and martyr, that being imprisoned by a cruel tyrant, for twelve days without food, a dove was sent down by Providence to administer to her necessities. Her prison is here represented by a recess cut into the wall, and painted of a dark blue colour, which still remains. She first appears at the entrance, in a disconsolate position, and in a dress of yellowish hue. At the farther end of the prison, she again appears, lying on her back, her head placed on a pillow marked with a heart, and her whole person resting on a colossal arm and hand, painted in red, and engraved with a heart...'

> 'Above the prison, appears the same outstretched arm and hand, in the act of letting fly a dove, which hovers over the prisoner, with a wallet in its bill. The latter emblems have been likewise painted red...'

[This actual scene is considered by Parkin and myself to represent the Holy Sepulchre and the rolling away of the stone, see Chapter 6.]

> '...Immediately beyond the projecting shoulder of the eastern shaft, appears a group, consisting of two half-length personages above:" one of them female and the other a male clad in a toga or pallium: a large figure is seen kneeling on one knee beneath them, as if in the act of receiving a burden; and a small figure almost effaced is bestriding his neck. [Good enlarged photographs have failed to show up this scenario]. These figures have been painted red and appear to represent Joseph and Mary placing the infant Saviour on the neck of St. Christopher, who is preparing to cross a river...' Beldam, p. 28.

There is one other area which was coloured other than the engravings, that is, the blocking beneath the eastern shaft. Beldam, p. 15, states:

> '...Immediately above the grave, at the height of about 17 feet, appears the masonry, supposed by Stukeley and North to have concealed the original entrance. The two lower courses only of this masonry now remain formed of blocks of chalk neatly chiselled, and coloured red, giving them the appearance of brickwork...' [this colour was not sampled].

ii) PAINT SCRAPINGS FOR SPECTOGRAPHIC ANALYSIS

In the spring of 1974, Dr. H. K. Cameron of Cambridge University and the Monumental Brass Society, took small scrapings of the Cave walls for examination to determine whether the figures had been painted, and if so, whether any evidence might be produced to assist in dating the period in which the engravings were cut. Mr. Sturton of the Metallurgy Department, Cambridge University, did a spectroscopic analysis on these samples but little conclusion could be drawn. They were then passed to the Fine Arts Department in that same University.

Dr. Cameron wrote in September, 1976:

> 'I am really very sorry that I have not written to you before, but I have never felt happy or confident that the analytical information we obtained from the specimens from Royston Cave were capable of useful diagnosis. For what they are worth, here they are:
>
> Sample 1 Colour: grey (near Holy Sepulchre, North wall) Traces of Ag., Al, Fe, Mn, Pb.
>
> Sample 2 Colour: yellow (between the two figures close to the depression). North-east. Traces of Cd, Fe.
>
> Sample 3 Colour: ochre taken from over depression (grave) East. Traces of Al, Fe, Mn, P, Pb.
>
> Sample 4 From sword of the figure holding it upright (South-east). Traces Fe (strong), Al, Mn, P, Pb.

Sample 5 Colour: red (now dark) from above and left of pattée cross (South). Traces of Pb.

Sample 6 Colour: white from wall near entrance (East) as control, presumably chalk. Traces of Ag, Fe, Mn, Pb, (Al ?)

Sample 7 Above and to the left of St. Lawrence (West wall). Strong trace of Pb. Traces of Fe, Mn, P. Slight trace of Al.

You will see that the control specimen taken near the entrance, where there seemed no evidence of engraving or colouring, contains most of the elements found in the other samples. As cinnabar, or mercuric sulphide, is commonly used as a red pigment on Medieval monumental brasses we looked particularly for this element, especially in specimen 5. None was found, but the specimen was small and the sensitivity of the test not very great. The most interesting result is the presence of cadmium in sample 2, presumably from a cadmium sulphide yellow pigment. I have not yet found at what date this compound was first used as a pigment. I am sorry that the results have not proved more positive…'

It was suggested that the British Museum should be approached regarding the possible use of cadmium in colouring matter in the Medieval period but they answered that the National Gallery might be of more assistance.

A reply from Dr. Ashok Roy of the Scientific Department, National Gallery stated:

'Your letter concerning the history of the use of cadmium pigments was passed on to me by Dr. Mills of this Department. Unfortunately, I can't give you a definite answer to the question you ask, as the literature does not agree on the point.

In the context of artists' pigments, synthetic cadmium colours are associated with· yellows and oranges, through to reds and maroons. The yellow/orange varieties are physical modifications of cadmium sulphide (CdS), the colour being dictated principally by particle size. The red shades are composed of cadmium sulphoselenide, and here the colour depends on the sulphur/selenium relative proportions.

Artificial cadmium sulphide was first prepared by Stromeyer, the discoverer of metallic cadmium, in 1817 and it was introduced as a pigment by Melandri in 1829, although cadmium yellow was not commercially available until 1848 (I). The reds followed about fifty years later, at the beginning of this century.

However, although synthetic cadmium pigments are ruled-out before the early part of the nineteenth century, there is some possibility that natural (mineral) cadmium sulphide might have found use as a pigment. The natural material, Greenockite, is rather sparsely distributed, and usually found in close association with zinc mineral deposits. Its use as a pigment is cited in Gettens and Stout (1), Harley (2) or Cennino Cennini (3), although Patton (4) says, "for nearly 2000 years the natural cadmium sulphide was used by artists and painters before being replaced by the synthetic pigment in the early 1800s". The last probably refers to isolated and local use in North America. One reference in *Art and Archaeology Technical Abstracts* (5) records the presence of a cadmium-containing yellow in Medieval Bulgarian church paintings (11th-14th centuries), but the original paper is not accessible and it would be unwise to base any firm conclusion about general use in this period on such slim evidence.

During the period which interests you, three yellow pigments were in use - lead-tin yellow (basically Pb_2Sn0_4, but variable in composition); yellow ochre (hydrated ferric oxide); and orpiment (arsenic III sulphide). Of these, the first two dominate European easel painting between 1300 and 1600, whereas orpiment was used quite rarely. On balance, I think there is quite a low probability that natural cadmium sulphide would be used as a yellow pigment in a Medieval wall-painting, unless there was a local source for the mineral. The more likely explanation is a post 1850s restoration effort, using cadmium yellow. If you could show that the pigment was contemporary with the engravings, I think it would be an interesting and significant discovery...' (23rd August, 1977).

1) GETTENS, R. J. & STOUT, G. L. (1966) *Painting Materials:* Dover.

2) HARLEY, R. D. (1970) *Artists' Pigments c.1600-1835:* Butterworths.

3) HERRIDGHAM, C. (trans.) (1899) *The Book of the Art of Cennino Cennini:* George Allen.

4) PATON, T. C. (ed.) (1973) *Pigment Handbook:* Wiley-Interscience.

5) *Art and Archaeology Technical Abstracts.* vol. II, No. 657.

Details of Dr. Cameron's September letter were forwarded to Dr. Roy who wrote a further comprehensive reply (16.11.77) and made the following comments:

'...I've thought about the analytical results derived from Royston Cave, supplied to you by Dr. Cameron, and I think I have to agree with his cautious opening remark. I don't think the analyses as they stand are very meaningful, if only because of Dr. Cameron's point about the presence of most of the elements found in the colour samples also being found in the control (sample 6). Of course, I don't know your researcher's analytical method, but I assume it is not a fully quantitative one. Quantitative analyses of samples of this kind would, I think, be rather difficult to carry out and it is by no means certain that they would yield much more information on the pigments used than you already have.

Let me comment on the results as best I can. First, I wouldn't be unduly worried by the presence of iron, manganese and aluminium in the 'control' sample of chalk, although silver and lead are more difficult to explain. If the concentration of, say, iron in a painted area was markedly greater than in the control sample, it would be fairly safe to assume that an iron-containing pigment had been used. That is provided of course, that microscopic observation of the pigment indicated this as well. All the elements which were found in the colour samples, with the possible exception of silver in the context of wall-paintings can be identified with one or more pigments, but I must stress that on the information you have, it is not really possible to give a list of the pigments which have been used. However, the answer to your question as to whether 'these components are usual in colouring matter' is, yes.

I am sure you will appreciate that wall-paintings require particularly stable painting materials for the colour to survive over any length of time. The pigments used are required to stand up to a fairly harsh atmospheric environment and damp. This excludes a number of pigments, especially those of organic origin which are generally too sensitive for such exposed conditions. Also, wall-paintings often cover relatively large areas and the need for very brilliant colours was less felt than for panel painting or manuscript illumination.

One might expect wall-paintings of the period to have been produced from a fairly limited palette, most of the colours being derived from naturally occurring earths such as the ochres, siennas and umbers. White would probably have been supplied by lead white (or the uncovered chalk ground) and black by one or another form of carbon. The earth colours provide just the right kind of properties for wall-painting - they are chemically very stable and are not too garish for large areas of work. Moreover, these earths have been used as pigments from earliest times, although the numbers may not have been in general use in Europe before the end of the XV century.

Chemically, the ochres, siennas and umbers depend for their colour on varying proportions and forms of more or less hydrated ferric oxide and the siennas and umbers contain manganese dioxide in addition. The manganese content of the umbers is much greater than that of the siennas. All these earth colours contain mineral impurities such as silica, calcite and alumina mixed with the principal component, iron oxide. A very wide range of colours ranging from bright yellow and red, through russet to dark brown are available from these natural sources; the opacity of the pigments is also quite variable.

Turning back to the analyses of the Royston Cave samples, the presence of iron in most of the samples suggests the possible use of ochres etc. Those samples which contain lead may indicate the presence of lead white, but I can't explain the presence of lead in the 'red' sample. There is a red, lead-containing colour (minium - lead tetroxide) which has been known as a pigment since classical times, but Thompson's book, *The Materials of Medieval Painting,* states that it was not used for walls. However, it does darken with time as has been suggested for sample 5. I'm at a loss to explain the presence of silver in two of the samples. The phosphorus content in samples 3 and 7 is also mysterious - the only possible pigment of the period which contains this element is bone white (partly calcium phosphate), but I'm not convinced this is a likely explanation...'

iii) CONTAMINATION OF SAMPLES?

The correspondence continued and in January, 1978 I wrote to Dr. Ashok Roy again:

> '...The Cave is situated under the crossroads in Royston and the air vent in the dome is no more than a metre from the kerb. The A505 road in particular, is heavily used by traffic, predominantly with large long-distance lorries which are frequently halted near the vent because of traffic lights. Is it possible that some trace elements from the atmosphere could have permeated the chalk walls, for example, lead from exhaust fumes. Or would it be that each sample would have had an overall quantity from any pollution ...'

He replied in February:

> '...Your point about the possible contamination of samples by lead from petrol exhausts is a good one, and there is no reason to suppose that any such pollution 'fall-out' would produce an even distribution of lead traces in the cave. I would expect, as I'm sure you would, that the greatest contamination would be closest to the vent you mention, although I suspect the culprits to be cars rather than lorries. It is the lead tetraethyl 'anti-knock' additive in petrol which produces this kind of lead pollution and since most large commercial vehicles use lead-free diesel fuel, they would probably not be responsible. I'm not saying that they don't produce other kinds of pollution...'

Ashok Roy kindly volunteered to look at any residual material from the samples and I wrote to Dr. Cameron to find out and he advised me that as we only took small samples to avoid damage to the pictures there was none of the samples left. He commented that to his way of thinking, the only curious sample was the presence of cadmium in specimen 2. The presence of phosphorus in 3 and 7 he thought could possibly derive from surface contact with the large quantity of infill in the cave with local concentrations of animal bones. This latter point was considered to be highly plausible by Ashok Roy as there is no obvious reason to use bone white as a pigment with so much chalk available close to hand. [The quantity of any animal bone was not specified when the infill was removed in 1742].

The author would also like to make the observation that local industry in Royston includes Johnson Matthey, a metal refinery company, dealing in lead, silver, gold, platinum, cadmium etc. and that the Fertilizer Co. processed coprolites, bone-meal and other such chemical components.

Finally, Beldam qualified his first remark:

> 'that most, if not all the engravings had been coloured' by adding the comment later in his work 'though perhaps at a later period.'

This latter phrase is probably the key one, we just do not know whether the Cave has been embellished more since its rediscovery in 1742. It is possible that it was 'trigged-up' prior to Mr. Thomas Watson opening the Cave to the public in 1790 after he had gone to the expense of cutting the 'new passage' in that same year.

APPENDIX III

i) THE CRUSADES

In very simple terms, the Crusades began when Alexius Comnenus, Emperor of Byzantium, appealed for help to bolster his crumbling frontier in Asia Minor. This appeal was taken up by Pope Urban II, anxious to tame the bellicose spirit of the times and to direct what he could not exorcise. The Crusades were proclaimed at Clermont in 1095, and the 'whole weight of heaven and hell' gave momentum to the emblem of the Cross. (Crellin, 6 et seq.)

ii) THE GREAT SCHISM IN CHRISTENDOM

As opposed to 'Byzantine' or 'Greek' and in place of 'Frankish' (which is not quite French or Norman), 'Latin' is related to the Roman side of the Great Schism in Christendom between Pope and Patriarch: each side later came to be known as Roman Catholic or Greek Orthodox. The lands held by Crusaders are referred to as 'Frankish' or 'Latin' depending on whether the understanding relates to the predominant people or the predominant faith. Neither term is entirely satisfactory but 'Christian' is hardly acceptable, and 'European' had not been coined.

APPENDIX IV

i) KNIGHTS TEMPLAR ORGANISATION

TITLE OF THE ORDER: Pauperes Commilitones Christi Templique Salomonici (Pauperes Commilitiones Christi et Templi Salomonis) - The Poor Knights of Christ and the Temple of Solomon.

The organisation was based on the Cistercian Order with a similar hierarchy:

GRAND MASTER: He was chosen by a complicated election and for life. Although his powers were extreme, he was limited by a Council of Order in which he had only one vote.

SENESCHAL: He was the Grand Master's immediate subordinate in administration.

MARSHALL: He was the Grand Master's immediate subordinate on campaigns.

COMMANDER: For example, of the Realm of Jerusalem. He was Master of the province of Jerusalem and Grand Treasurer of the whole Order.

COMMANDER: Of the City of Jerusalem. He had ten knights assigned specially to safeguard the relics of the True Cross.

COMMANDERS: Elsewhere they were called - Provincial Master, Grand Preceptor, or Grand Prior. (Tripoli, Antioch, France, England, Poitou, Portugal, Apulis, Hungary etc.)

PRECEPTOR: Head of a local preceptory.

ESTATE STEWARD: Sometimes a secular person but often the duties were the responsibility of the preceptor.

The officers had graduated perquisites: e.g. the Grand Master had four horses for his personal use as well as a detailed household. The ensigns of his presence on campaign were the large tent and the *gonfanon baucent (beauceant)* the black and white pennant flying in the breeze. As other principal officers did, he made use of a Saracen secretary and a Turk to be in charge of his special 'turcoman' horses used in war. Other menials included farriers, drapers, footmen and servants.

Hair was to be worn short and a rough beard became one of the distinguishing marks of the Order.

ii) RULE 70

The Rule has been dealt with in the body of the work, but Rule 70 reads:

> "Périllous chose est compaignie de feme que le deable ancien par compaignie de feme a degete pluisors dou droit sentier de paradis."
>
> Which translated reads: 'A dangerous thing is the company of women [female company] because the devil of old, by the company of women, has turned many from the right path of Paradise.'

Of a secret Rule, in spite of the most diligent research no trace has ever been found. (Crellin, 9).

iii) MASTERS OF THE TEMPLE IN ENGLAND (known as Grand Preceptors of the Order):

Hugh de Argentein c. 1140
Otto (Ostro) c. 1150
Richard de Hastings 1155-64
Geoffrey Fitz-Stephen 1180-85
William New c. 1186
Aymaric de St. Maur 1200-18
Alan Martel 1218-28
Robert de Sandford 1229-48
Roscelin de Fos 1251-53
Amadeus de Morestello 1259-60
Ambesard 1264
Himbert Peraut 1271
Guy de Foresta 1273-74
Robert de Turvill 1276-90
Jacques de Molay 1295*
Brian de Jay 1296-98
William de la Mare 1298-1312

* He was to become the last Grand Master of the Order, imprisoned with other members of the Order in the Tour du Coudray, Châteaux de Chinon, France, and eventually put to death by burning in Paris (see p. 58). It seems for at least a year he was Grand Master of both England and France.

iv) MASTERS OF THE TEMPLE IN FRANCE

Hugues de Payns, 1118-36
Robert de Craon, 1136-49
Éverard des Barres, 1149-50
Bernard de Tremelay, 1150-53
André de Montbar, 1153-56
Bertrand de Blancfort, 1156-69
Philippe de Milly, 1169-70
Odon de Saint-Amand, 1170-80
Arnaud de Torroges, 1180-84
Gérard de Ridfort, 1184-89
Robert de Sablé, 1191-93
Gilbert Érail, 1193-1201
Philippe de Plaissiez, 1201-09?
Guillaume de Charizes, 1209?-19
Pierre de Montaigu, 1219-32?
Armand de Périgord, 1232?-44?
(disappeared at the battle of Gaza)
Guillaume de Sonnac, 1246?-50
Renaud de Vichiers, 1250-56 or 52?
Thomas Bérard, 1256 (52?)-73
Guillaume de Beaujeu, 1273-91
Thibaud Gardin, 1291-94
Jacques de Molay, 1294-1314 * (see above)

In the documents that emanated from the Temple, the chief of the Order carried the simple title of 'Maître' [Master] but under the *Rule* he is referred to as 'Notre Maître, frère un tel' [Our Master, brother as such]. The title of 'Grand Maître' [Grand Master] appeared in the pontifical bulls, where the entry in the documents was used to distinguish the head of the Order from his subordinates. (Melville, Marion (1974) *La Vie des Templiers,* Gallimard, 329)

APPENDIX V

Other Crusading Orders:

i) KNIGHTS HOSPITALLERS

The Order of the Hospital of St. John of Jerusalem was founded by a group of Italian merchants - 11th century reformers - to tend sick pilgrims. This body came into existence soon after the First Crusade, when the administrators of a pilgrim-hospice in Jerusalem, run by the abbey of St. Mary of the Latins, broke away from their parent body. They were recognized by the papacy in 1113 as belonging to an independent institution. At first they were just a normal monastic order, but then they changed Patron Saints and became military, though the work of their hospitals was continued alongside that of warfare. The fortress, Krak des Chevaliers in Palestine, is probably the most impressive monument to their military might. They survived by moving their headquarters and activities to Malta in the 16th century and continued there until they were dislodged by Napoleon in 1798. They were suppressed earlier in England at the Dissolution (1540).

ii) OTHER NOT SO WELL-KNOWN ORDERS:

The Order of the Holy Sepulchre of Jerusalem; The Order of St. Lazarus; The Order of Teutonic Knights [a German branch of the Templars]; Spanish military orders engaged along the Iberian boundaries of Christendom. Some orders were founded after the demise of the Templars for example, l'Ordre aux cinq croix rouges [Order of the Five Red Crosses]. Names of former defunct groups were changed, in a sense they were being reborn or reactivated in later centuries but carrying similar aims, not unlike some of the Masonic movements. (Personal notes of V. H. Crellin c. 1977; Riley-Smith, 1987, Press, 57; *Les Chevaliers Teutoniques, Les Chevaliers de Malte, les Ordres militaires et hospitaliers* in *Historia Special,* No. 403 bis, Librairie Jules Tallandier, 1980).

APPENDIX VI

Chinon (Indre-et-Loire), France

Chinon is a picturesque old town situated on the river Vienne, 26 miles [41.6 km] south-west of Tours. It lies below a rock, fortified since Roman times, on which stood the ruins of a castle that has been recently restored. In the Middle Ages, this immense stronghold belonged to the Plantagenets. It was originally three separate castles, Château du Coudray, Château du Milieu and Fort of Saint George, each with its own defences, and due in the main to Henry II of England.

Henry II spent much of his reign in France struggling against the French King and his subjects. Just three weeks before his death, in 1189, in the Fort Saint George, he was defeated by an army commanded by Philippe Augustus and his own son and heir Richard Coeur de Lion. It is alleged that as the body of Henry II was being carried from the Castle, his son Richard met the cortège on the road as he rode in. Also by tradition it is held that Richard I, expired in the baker's shop in the little village. Joan of Arc is also associated with Chinon, and it was in a room in the Château de Milieu that when newly arrived from Domrèmy, she revealed her mission to the Dauphin in 1429.

Today this town, not only a tourist attraction, is the site of a nuclear power station.

APPENDIX VII

English and French Kings of the Relevant Period

ENGLAND:

William the Conqueror	1066-1087
William Rufus	1087-1100
Henry I	1100-1135
Stephen	1135-1154
Henry II	1154-1189
Richard I (Lion Heart)	1189-1199
John	1199-1216
Henry III	1216-1272
Edward I	1272-1307
Edward II	1307-1327

FRANCE:

Philippe I	1060-1108
Louis VI	1108-1137
Louis VII	1137-1180
Philippe II (Augustus)	1180-1223
Louis VIII	1223-1226
Louis IX (Saint Louis)	1226-1270
Philippe III	1270-1285
Philippe IV (Le Bel 'The Fair')	1285-1314

APPENDIX VIII

Baldock:

i) DISPUTED NAME OF BALDOCK

The name of the town is under dispute. Its early spellings include Baldoce, Baldok, Baldac*, Baldak, Baldache, Baudac, Baudak, Baudach, Baudake, Baudok, Balddok, Bawdoake, Bawldoake. Some historians consider it is very unlikely that the town was named after Baghdad** by the Templars. Another assumption is that it was named after Baalbeck but there is no evidence.

There is another claim that it was named after a Templar holding in France, but again there is no evidence. A connection with the Norse God, Balder, is thought not to be impossible.

The more plausible connection seems to be that Baldock is a contraction of 'Bald Oak'. The oak tree does not grow well in the town, and those that do are normally poor specimens. But 'Bald Oak' or 'at the Bald Oak' is the sort of boundary name that appears in early travellers' writings or peregrinations. The crossroad site is a boundary; geographical, manorial, and milestone. This derivation from old English would have led naturally to the forms of 'Baldock' that occur.

In the opinion of V. H. Crellin, the former Headmaster of the Knights Templar School at Baldock, the most authoritative derivation is given by G. L. Evans, in *Hertfordshire Past and Present* No. 8, 1968, Hertfordshire Local History Council. Mr. Evans gives credit to the earlier independent conclusion of H. C. Andrews, *Remarks on the Place Names of Baldock,* in *East Herts. Archaeological Society Transactions,* vol. II, No. 9, 1945. These writers suggest that the Templars named their settlement by the nearest natural feature that had a name in a largely featureless and uninhabited woodland, and this feature was a notable 'round oak'. It is further supposed that this boundary mark was not just on a parish manorial boundary, but was a mark on the North Road as it passed through a dip in the chalk hills meeting:

The Strong Oak ...	Stevenache ...	Stevenage	- in the south
The Tall Oak ...	Langenache ...	Lannock	- in the middle
The Round Oak ...	Baldache ...	Baldock	- at the end

Crellin, c. 1977, 1.

ii) BALDOCK CHARTERS:

Other charters which are relevant to Baldock are held in the British Museum:

Add. Ch. No. 35436 - Grant for land exchange and mill lease by Robert de Dinesleia filius Everarum to Walter de Neuvill:

Add. Ch. No. 35543 - Covenant for a mill lease between Dom. Baldwin de Var and Robert clericus de Dineslee:

Add. Ch. No. 28823 - Grant of land from Luke Rayson of Walden Abbatis [St. Paul's Walden] and Christina his wife, with licence of the Priory of Wymondele [Little Wymondley] to Walter Poydras of Polytes [Ippollitts]

* Note: *Baldac is the Old French form for Baghdad (Italian - Baldacco).*

** *'Baghdad' representing Baldock is noted in Matthew Paris' book 'Angli Historia Major' of 1640 published by Richard Hodgkinson, p. 147.*

Temple Dinsley/Hitchin Area:

i) EXTRACT OF KING HENRY III'S CHARTER 9TH FEBRUARY IN THE 11TH YEAR OF HIS REIGN [1227]

...confirmed to them [Knights Templar] all the donations of his predecessors and of their other benefactors, with soc and sac [a jurisdiction claimed by lords as part of their manorial tenure: it included the right to hold a court, and to receive manorial profit and services], tol and theam, Infangenthef [right of taking and fining a thief], and Unfangenethef, and Hamsoca, and Grithbrich, and Blodwite, and Flictwite, and Hengewite, and Leirwite, and Flemenfrith, murder, robbery, forestall, ordel, and oreste. And acquitted them from the Royal and Sheriffs aids, and from hidage [tax assessed on every hide of land], carucage [tax on carucate - as much land as a team of oxen could plough in a season], danegeld [tax based upon the amount of land in each shire] and hornegeld [tax or service on number of horned cattle], and from military and wapentake [denotes a Hundred] services, scutages ['shield money' fixed amount so tenants could commute the obligation for military support for the crown], tallages [tax exacted by the manorial lord, or Crown on towns and boroughs on ancient demesne] lastages [duties for the right to carry goods], stallages [rents for liberty of erecting a stall in a market or fair], from shires and hundreds, and pleas and quarrels, from ward and ward-penny, and averpeni, and hundredespeni and borethalpeni, and thethingepeni, and from the works of castles, parks, bridges, the building of royal houses, and all other works. And also from waste regard and view of foresters. And from toll in all markets and fairs, and all bridges throughout the kingdom. And he also gave to them the chattels of fellons and fugitives, and all waifs within their fee...
(Clutterbuck, 1815-7, vol. III, 26)

ii) TEMPLE DINSLEY LEASE OF LAND, c. 1241

Omnibus Christi fidelibus ad quos presens scriptum pervenerit **Frater Robertus de Samford Milicie Templi in Anglia** minister humilis salutem in Domino Noveritis quod nos de communi consilio et assensu capiti nostri ad Pascha apud Dinesle (1) concessimus et presenti carta nostra confirmavimus Hugoni filio Petri de Brantona et heredibus suis totam terram quam habemus de dono Hugonis filii Ingeram in villa Brancona (2) habendam eo tenendam sibi etheredibus suis cum omnibus pertinenciis Libere integre et quiete reddend. inde Annuatim domui nostre tresdecem denarios ad duos terminos anni scilieet medietatem ad Pulchra Florida [Palm Sunday] et elteram medietatem ad festum Sancti Michaelis pro omni servicio et exactione solari salva domui nostre in obtitu suo et heredium suorum dimidia marca argenta. et nos totem praedictam terram cum pertinenciis praedicto Hugoni et heredibus suis contra omnes homines Warancitabimus quandiu carta donatoris eam nobis poterit Warancitare. Hiis testibus Fr. Mauricius capellanus. Fr. Roger de Scamelesby, Fr. Ada de Linton, Fr. Walt. le Blund, **Fr. Tho. le Sauvage**, Fr. Steph. Brito, Fr. Tho. de Gosebec, tunc preceptor of Eycle (Eagle, Lincs.)

1. The manuscript catalogue of the Charters and Rolls at the British Museum has been altered to ascribe the charter to Dingley, Northamptonshire, but the Knights Templars never had a Preceptory there; on the contrary, it was the property of the Knights Hospitallers from the days of King Stephen. (See Dugdales's *Mon.* VI, 802) But the printed *Index Locorum* locates it correctly at Temple Dinsley.

2. The same manuscript catalogue and the *Index Locorum* both describe this as Brampton in Derbyshire. The only likely confirmation seems to be in the *Inquisitio Terrarum* of 1185 printed by Dugdale (*Mon.,* VI, 827) where, in listing the rents arising from the Templars' baillewick of Lincolnshire, the document records rent of 15s arising "exfeudo Roberti Britonis et de feudo Ingelrami de Bratum", one of 7s "ex feodo Roberti Britonis" and another 3s paid by Ric. de Brantune from the same fief. Brampton in Cumberland has some claim for consideration too, as it lay in the district where activities of Thomas Le Sauvage and his family are recorded. (*Victoria County History, Yorkshire and North Riding,* 1, 135; *Harl.* MS., 83G)

(Information extracted from typewritten notes (undated pre-1918? held in NHDC Hitchin Museum), by H. C. Andrews, FSA entitled *Some Relics of the Knights Templars at Temple Dinsley.*)

APPENDIX IX

Prior to the re-opening of the Cave to the general public in 1966-7, two members of the newly formed local Royston and District History Society, F. John Smith and his brother Philip, together with John Moss-Eccardt [died 1991], Curator of the Letchworth Museum carried out, with the permission of the Ministry of Works, an exploratory 'dig' in the 'grave' area of the Cave. The lower steps were to be made good. In the course of the investigation half of a bedser millstone was uncovered, the striations of which can be seen underfoot at the base of the brick steps.

The unstratified material extracted from the depression was placed in three boxes in order of size and not washed until November 1973 when the writer took possession of most of it in order to have it examined, and where possible dated. It was assumed that the material was from 1790 when the 'new passage' was dug, however, some of the following items from this infill resembles that mentioned by Joseph Beldam in his book (1852, 17) - perhaps he put it back into situ!

BOX I	BOX II	BOX III
Pipe stems, pieces of bowl	Tiles & bricking - see Beldam, 1852, 17 Stukeley, 1743, 43 & Parkin, 1744, 19 - 20	Tiles, some showing signs of cremation
Oyster shells	Curved tile left unwashed	Bricking, some showing signs of cremation
Lots of animal bones, assorted	Pieces of limestone?	Pieces of clunch flooring? possibly hearth showing blackened patches
Small skull	Several pieces of unknown material, possibly some form of mortar?	Large flint and other stones including sandstone
Seven small spherical stones		
Seven large stones		
Clout-headed nails		
Various lumps of iron		
Glass, all broken - some medieval		
Glass stem		
Pottery - all broken		
Coke, clinker, charcoal		
Lump of light material probably wattle and daub?		
Old brush in pieces		
Flints, stones, fossils, clunch		
Teeth		
Button, backing of a button?		
Small metal object with chain - silver?		
Clay stem or handle		

A visit was made to the Department of Archaeology and Ethnology, Cambridge University on 5th December 1973 and a further visit on 18th March 1974. A representative selection was examined by Peter Danks, MA and Tony Legge, MA, besides all the glass and pottery.

POTTERY:

Lead glazed earthenware - Victorian modern (19th century)

Creamware; salt glaze; cobalt underglaze on cream ware body; Chinese porcelain; brown salt glaze; Delft (18th century)

Nottinghamware, salt glaze brown (mid 17th-18th century)

Mottled brown salt glaze (could be 17th century)

One very small piece of Delft (possibly just into the 17th century)

Of the medieval period several pieces appeared to be of a cooking pot (just shading into the 14th century) [one small piece was lost during investigation at Colchester Museum.]

Largest quantity of pieces of a browny/orange coloured shallow bowl, glazed and decorated with yellow (l4th-15th century). [There has been a lot of controversy over the dating of these pieces of bowl. It was suggested to the writer she should try several museums with a view to finding a closer date. The British Museum thought it could be Metropolitan ware, but try Harlow. According to Harlow museum it did not fit in with their examples either by fabric or colour, although similar with presumed cow-horn decoration. Colchester museum were also puzzled, they did not think it was Metropolitan ware but were unable to establish anything closer.]

Fig. 61a. Pottery - pieces of a shallow bowl, browny / orange in colour with yellow spots; and a cooking pot. These are thought to be the earliest sherds found in the Cave dated between 14th to 16th (?) *century. From material excavated in* 1966. *Photo R. H. Clark, 1974*

ANIMAL BONES:

Tibia – sheep
Scapula (left) – sheep, eaten by dog? (Teeth marks noted)
Humerus – sheep or goat
Femur, distal - sheep/goat, juvenile
Metacarpal – goat
Tausal back foot bone - cattle (bos)
Terminal phalange (three) – cattle
Second phalange (two) – cattle
Metatausal fragment, distal – cattle
Proximal, as above
Pelvis? – cattle, metal saw used to cut it

TEETH AND SMALL ANIMAL BONES

Molar, upper third left – cow (largest tooth in the collection)
Molar, lower, fragmentary – pig
Maxilla, right jaw – sheep or goat
Maxilla, right jaw – sheep or goat
Phalange, first – juvenile sheep or goat
Cat bones (two), juvenile
Piglet (four)
Rat bones – various
Frog (two)
Various rib fragments, pelvis, vertebrae, etc. of sheep or goat, cattle, plus 3 other teeth of no note

BIRD BONES

Pelvis and sacrum – small bird, possibly a wren or goldcrest, or at least a bird of that size.

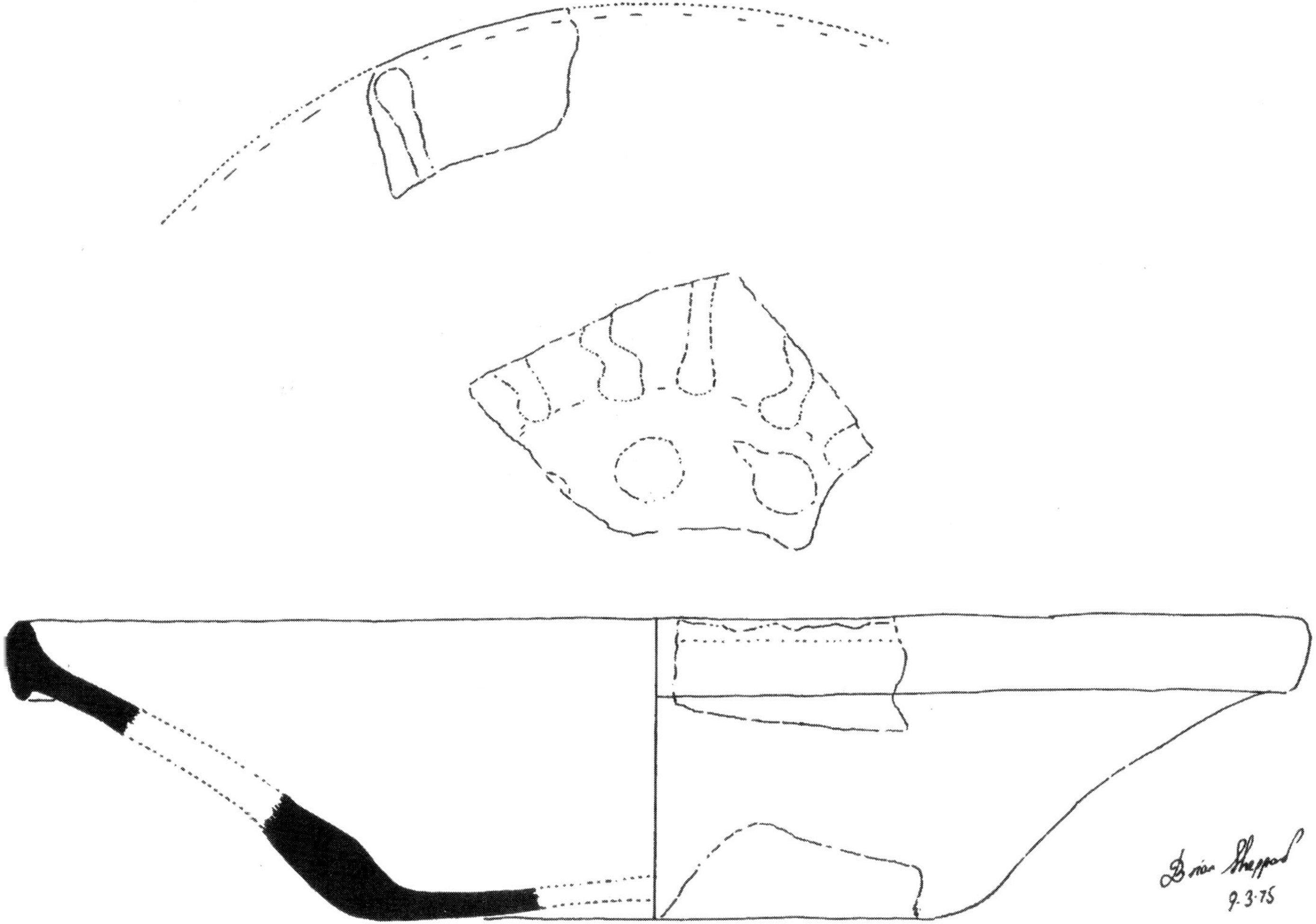

Fig. 61b. Red earthenware dish with trailed yellow slip decoration on a glazed interior. Diameter c. 30 cm drawn-up by Brian Sheppard, 1975.

Visit to Dr. C. L. Forbes, MA, Ph.D., Curator, Sedgwick Museum of Geology (known as Earth Sciences today), Cambridge University, Downing Street, Cambridge on 20 December, 1973.

Geological material - all specimens numbered

1) Sandstone - probably local pebble, possibly a honestone
2) Lime mortar or plaster
3) Natural stone, sandstone (not mortar too much sand) - crumbles because it has possibly been left in a damp condition for many years. Local - perhaps millstone
4) Lower horizon chalk, probably Totternhoe stone (Burwell Rock - hard variety of chalk used for building, carving, statuary (probably). Highly calcareous. [Mr. Moss-Eccardt pointed out that Melbourn, a village 3 miles [4.8 km] to the north-east of Royston, also has some of this lower horizon chalk.]
5) Flint from gravel or boulder clay, most probably gravel, presumably local
6) Rhaxella chert - common eratic of the local boulder clays and gravel
7) Brown sandstone - common in the local boulder clays and gravels
8) Fine grained lustre-mottled sandstone - local boulder clay and gravel (found about a mile [1.6 km] south and north of Royston)
9) Igneous greenstone, also common from local boulder clay
10) Round white flints direct from the chalk. Similar flints, not seen in the Cave, but in the neighbourhood uphill of the Town
11) Round flints similar to above, the brown colour indicates derivation from a gravel and not from the chalk
12) Flint probably been exposed to fire
13) Hard sandstone - local gravel
14) Spherical stones, grey marble, artificially rounded [although they were thought to be originally medieval, and still could be, Dr. Forbes later found out that marbles were manufactured up until 1903]. All seven are marbles: measuring in circumference 1 15/16 ins, 1 7/8 ins, 2 ins, 2 1/8 ins (3 of them, the brown one has been probably discoloured by smoke) and 2 1/4 ins. Similar ones have been found at Guilden Morden which are kept in Letchworth Museum.
15) Brown sandstone has formed part of a roadway or ploughed field as evidence by the brown rust stains
16) Eleven bits of flint, one piece of chert, natural shape
17) Two fossilised oyster shells gryphae
18) Piece of chalk
19) Two pieces of sandstone

Note: *The group 5-9 are consistent with the likelihood of their being included in a cobblestone pavement [see Chapter I].*

Note: *Numbers 16-19 – all items are natural shapes and origin could be found within a mile or so of the Cave, maybe road-metal.*

All the archaeological material is deposited in the Royston and District Museum.

APPENDIX X

William Stukeley's sketches 1742 - 46

The drawing-up of the Cave must have been a difficult undertaking by Stukeley without the aid of good lighting or the benefit of photography. From his sketches held in the Bodleian Library, Oxford it seems he made several attempts at accuracy and the variations are self evident to the reader if comparison is made with the current photographs illustrated in the text.

Of special note is the lengthening of the floriat cross and the omission completely of the figure to the left of St. Christopher in Fig. 62c. The notation in Fig. 62f shows he had latterly then decided on the genealogy of the row of figures below St. Christopher on the north walling, similarly as did Beldam a hundred years later.

There is also a. variation in the design of the fleur-de-lis on the seal in his published drawing (Book No. II) from that in his sketch Fig. 62a which is rather disturbing and causes doubt on any possible dating.

Fig. 62a.

Shown below are four of the many variations of the fleur-de-lis

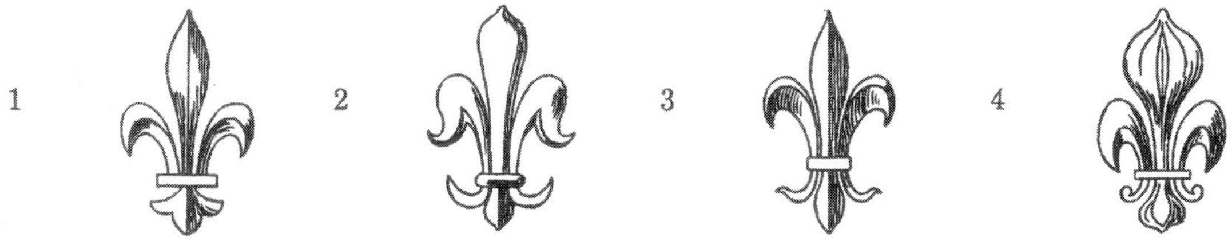

1. First appeared in the Middle Ages
2. Appeared in the late 15th century
3. Early 17th century
4. Time of the late Bourbon kings

The south side of Lady ROISIA'S Oratory at Royston. 19 oct. 1742.

Fig. 62b.

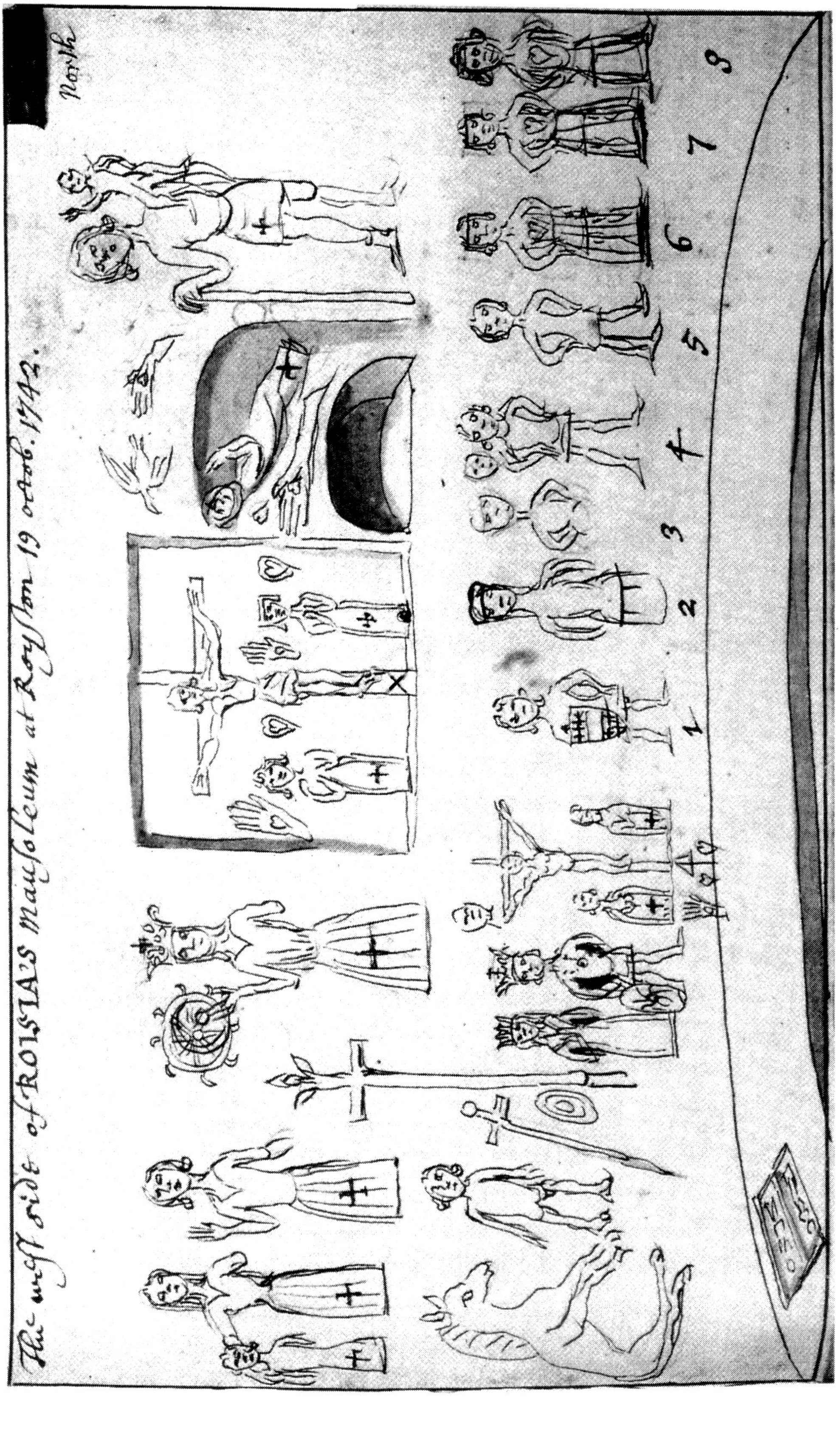
The west side of ROISIA'S mausoleum at Royston 19 octob. 1742.
North
1
2
3
4
5
6
7
8

Fig. 62c.

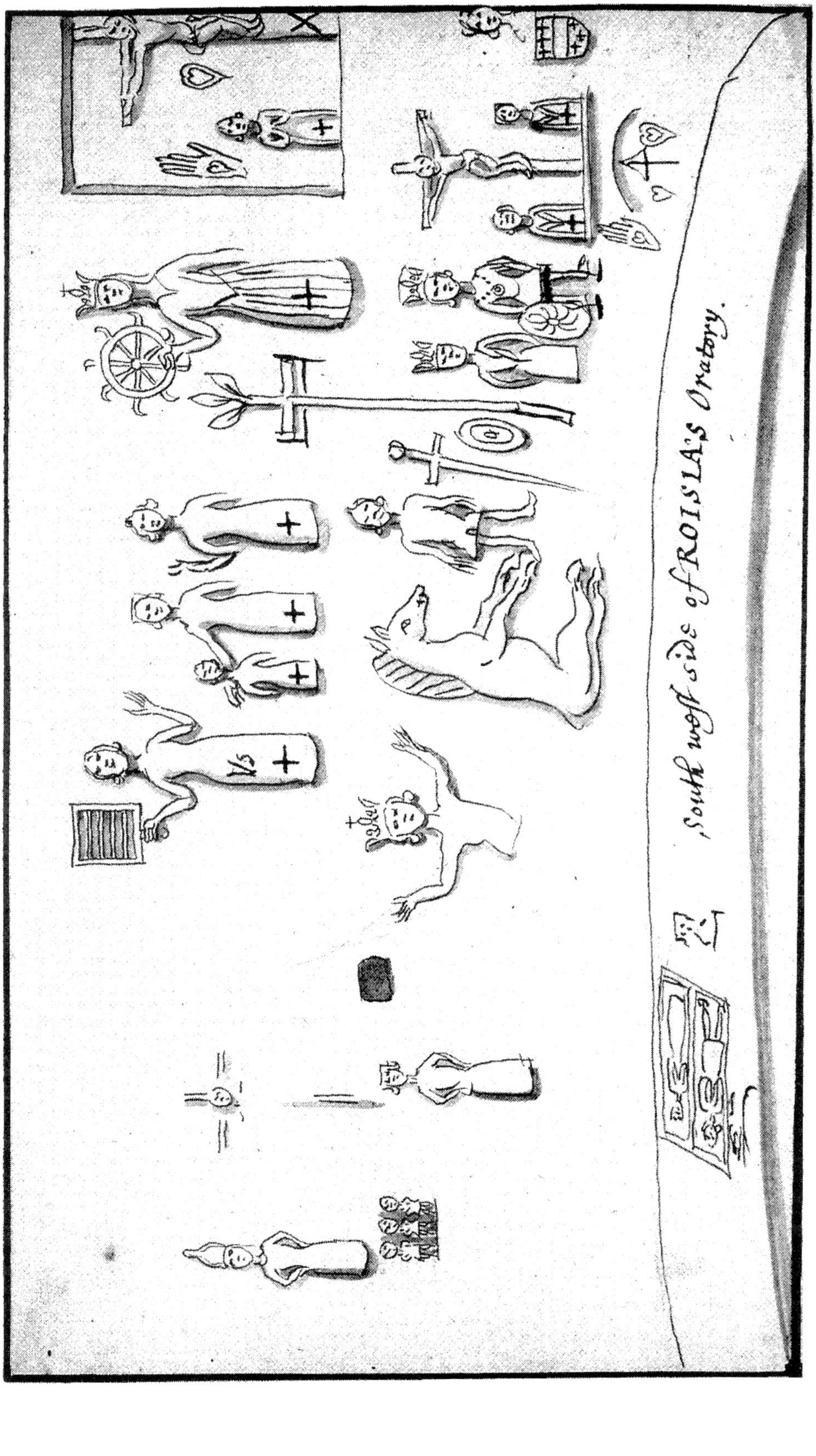

Fig. 62d.

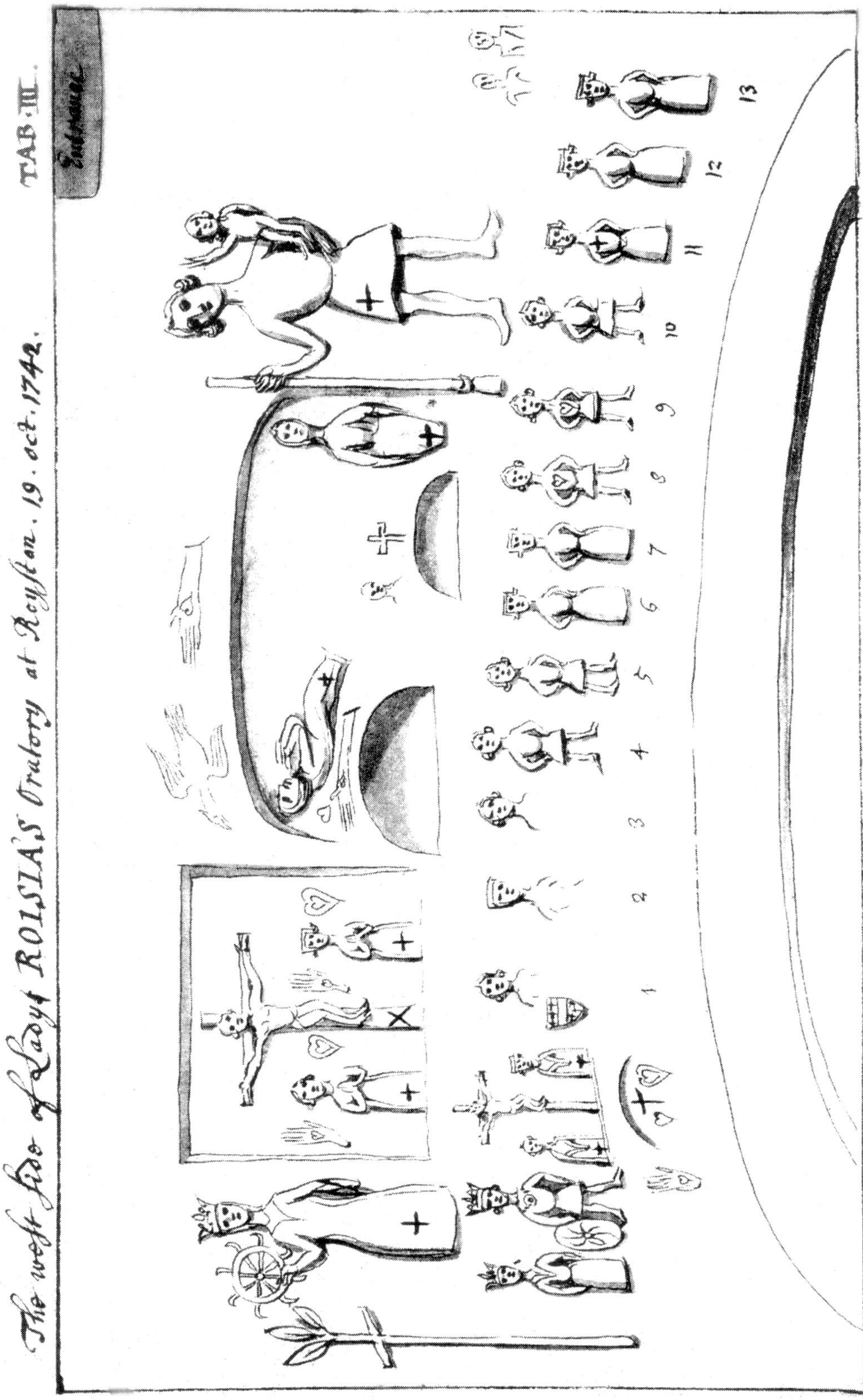

Fig. 62e.

Stukeley del.

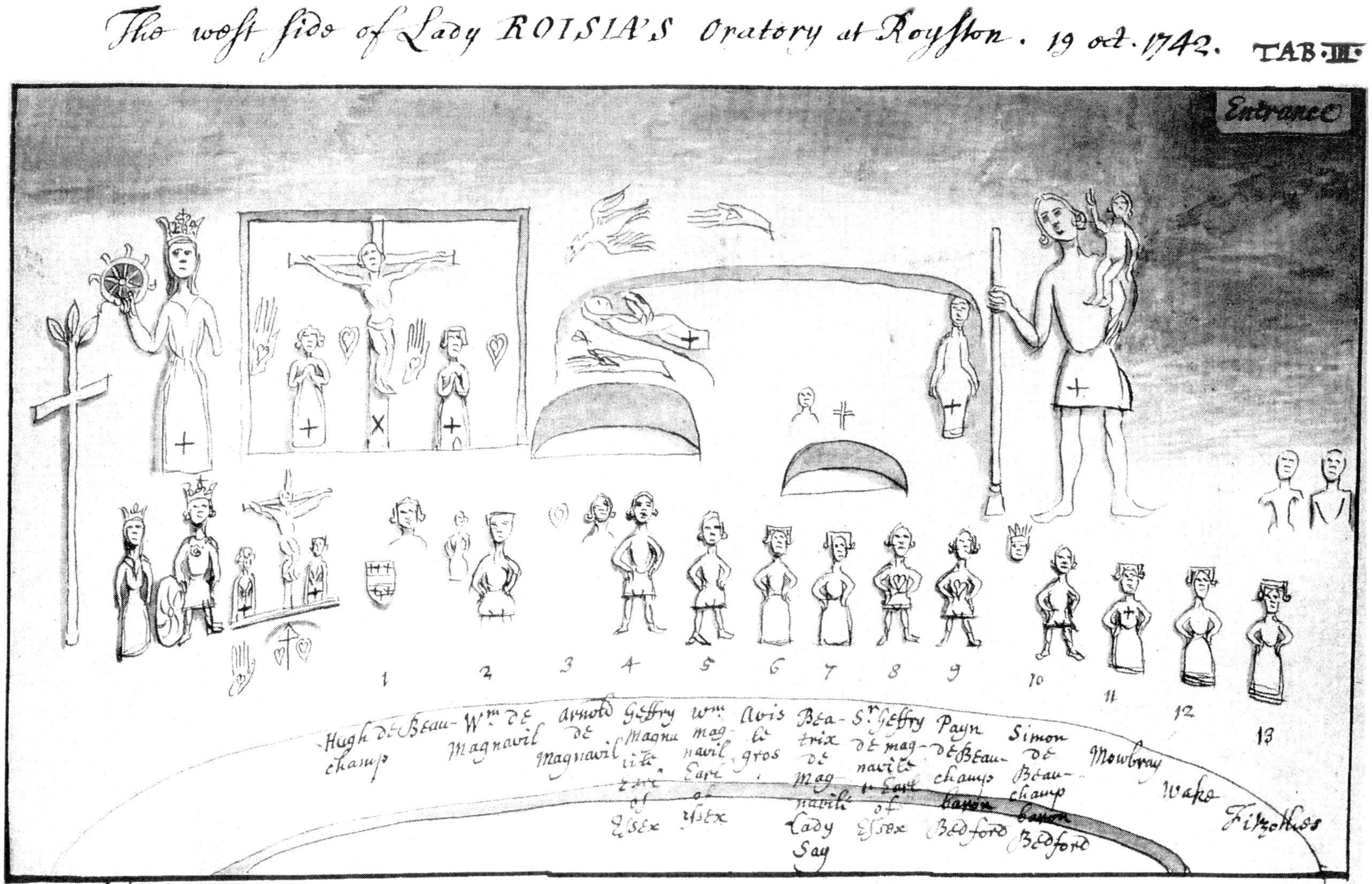

W. Stukeley del.

Fig. 62f.

APPENDIX A

THE FIRST CHARTER OF KING STEPHEN FOR GEOFFREY DE MANDEVILLE, PROBABLY DATED BETWEEN JUNE - DECEMBER 1140 (Round, 1892, 49, 51-3).

S. Rex Ang[lorum] Archiepiscopis Episcopis Abbatibus Comitibus Justiciis Baronibus Vicecomitibus et Omnibus Ministris et fidelibus suis francis et Anglis totius Angliae salutem. Sciatis me fecisse Comitem de Gaufr[ido] de Magnauilla de Comitatu Essex[e] hereditarie. Quare uolo et concedo et firmiter precipio quod ipse et heredes sui post eum hereditario jure teneant de me et de heredibus meis bene et in pace et libere et quiete et honorifice sicut alii Comites mei de terrâ meâ melius vel liberius vel honorificentius tenent Comitatus suos unde Comites sunt cum omnibus dignitatibus et libertatibus et consuetudinibus cum quibus alii Comites mei prefati dignius vel liberius tenent.

'I'[estibus] Will[elm]o de Iprâ et Henr[ico] de Essexâ **[This is the well-known Henry de Essex, son of Robert and grandson of Swegen of Essex (*Domesday*). He witnessed several of King Stephen's charters, probably later in his reign, but was also a witness to the Empress's charters to the Earls of Oxford and of Essex]** et Joh[ann]e fil[io] Rob[erti] fi l[ii] Walt[eri] **[John, son of Robert fitz Walter (sheriff of East Anglia, temp. Hen. I.) occurs in *Ramsey Cartulary*, i. 149]** et Rob[erto] de Nouo burgo (Robert de Neufbourg) et Mainfen[ino] Britoñ (Maenfininus Brito) et 'I'urg[esio] de Abrinc[is] (Turgis d'Avranches) et Will[elm]o de S[an]c[t]o Claro (William de St. Clare) et Will[elm]o de Dammart[in] et Ric[ardo] fil[io] Ursi **[Richard fitz Urse - he was the father of Reginald fitz Urse, one of Becket's murderers]** et Will[elm]o de Auco (William de Eu appears as a tenant of four knight's fees *de veteri feoffamento* under Mandeville in the *Liber Niger*) et Ric[ardo fil[io] Osb[erti] (Richard fitz Osbert similarly figures in the *Liber Niger* as a tenant of four knights' fees *de veteri feoffamento*. He also held a knight's fee of the Bishop of Ely in Cambridgeshire. **An Osbert fitz Richard, probably his son, attests a charter of Geoffrey's son, Earl William, to Walden Abbey)** et Radulfo de Wiret (sic) (Ralph de Worcester) et Eglin[o] et Will[elm]o fil[io] Alur[edi] **(William fitz Alfred, he also attests the earl's foundation charter of Walden Abbey)** et Will[elm]o filio Ernald[i] (William fitz Ernald). Apud Westmonasterium.

It was in this charter that Geoffrey received his earldom. Round states that he believes this is our earliest charter of creation extant or even known; the chief point is its intensely hereditary character plus the brevity and vagueness of the grant compared with the charters which followed.

CHARTER OF THE EMPRESS TO GEOFFREY DE MANDEVILLE (Midsummer, 1141)

M. Imperatrix regis Henrici filia Archiepscopis Episcopis Abbatibus (Comitibus Baronibus Justiciariis Vicecomitibus et ministris et omnibus baronibus et fidelibus) suis Francis et Anglis totius Angliae et Normanniae salutem. (Sciatis omnes tam praesentes quam futuri quod Ego Matildis regis Henrici filia et Anglor[um] domina) do et concedo Gaufrido de Magnavillâ (pro servitio suo et heredibus suis post eum hereditabiliter ut sit comes de Essex[iâ] et habeat tertium denarium Vicecomitatus de placitis sicut comes habere debet in comitatu suo in omnibus rebus, et praeter hoc reddo illi in feodo et hereditate de me et heredibus meis totam terram quam) tenuit (Gaufridus de Magnavilla avus suus et Serlo de Matom in Angliâ et Normanniâ ita libere et) bene et quiete sicut aliquis antecessorum suorum illam unquam melius (et liberius tenuit, vel ipsemet) postea (aliquo in tempore, sibi dico) et heredibus suis (post eum), et concedo illi et heredibus suis Custodiam turris Londonie (cum parvo Castello quod) fuit Ravengeri in feodo et hereditate de me (et heredibus) meis cum terris et liberationibus et omnibus Consuetudinibus quae ad (eandern terram) pertinerent, et ut inforciet illa secundum voluntatem suam. (Et similiter) do ei et concedo et heredibus suis C libratas terrae de me et de (heredibus) meis in dominio, videlicet Niweport **[Newport was an ancient demesne of the Crown. It lays about 3 miles SW of Saffron Walden]** pro tanto quantum reddere solebat die qua rex H[enricus] pater meus fuit vivus et mortuus, et ad rem[ovend'] mercatum de Niweport in Castellum suum de Waldena cum omnibus Consuetudinibus que prius mercato illi melius pertinuerunt in (Thelon[eo] et passag[io]) **[there was still a toll bridge there in the last century]** et aliis consuetudinibus, (et) ut vie de Niweport quae sunt juxta littus aquae **[Apparently, the high road on the left bank, and the way on the right bank, of the Cam]** dirigantur ex consuetudine ad Waledenam (sup[er] foris) facturam meam et Mercatum de Waldenâ sit ad diem dominicam et ad diem Jovis et ut feria **[Neither this market nor this fair are, it would seem, to be traced afterwards]** habeatur apud Waledenam et incipiat in (Vigiliâ Pentecost) et duret per totam hebdomadam pentecostes Et Meldonam [This was presumably a grant of the borough of Maldon (i.e, the royal rights in that borough), though Peverel's fee in Maldon was an escheat at the time.] ad perficiendum predictas C librates terrae pro tanto quantum inde reddi solebat die quâ (Rex Henricus fuit) vivus et mortuus cum omnibus Appendiciis et rebus qua adjacebant in terrra et mari ad Burgum illud predicto die mortis Regis Henrici, et (Deopedenam) [Depden, three miles south of Walden. It had formed part, at the Survey, of the fief of Randulf Peverel] similiter pro tanto quantum inde reddi solebat die qua rex Henricus fuit vivus et mortuus cum omnibus Appendiciis suis et Boscum de chatel egâ (Catlidge, according to Morant) cum (hominibus pro) xx solidis, et terram de Banhunta [Bonhunt, now part of Wickham Bonhunt, adjoining Newport] pro xl solidis, et si quid defuerit ad C libratas perficiendas perficiam ei in loco competenti in Essexa (aut in Hert(fordescirâ) aut in Cantebriggscirâ tali tenore quod si (reddi)dero Comiti Theobaldo totam terram quam (tenebat) in An(gliâ) dabo Gaufrido Comiti Essex[ie] escambium suum ad valentiam in his praedictis tribus Comitatibus antequam de) predictis terris dissais(iatur; si etiam reddidero totum honorem et totam terram) heredibus Willelmi peur[elli] de Lond[onia] [This apparently refers to Depden, as forming part of Peverel's fief, which had been an escheat, in the king's hands, as early as 1130 (Rot. Pip., 31 Hen. 1.)] dabo similiter ei escambium ad valens antequam dissaisiatur de illâ quae fuit peurelli et illud (escambium erit) de terrâ que remanebit illi hereditabiliter. Et preter hoc do et concedo ei et heredibus suis de me et heredibus meis tenendum feodum (et servicium) xx militum et infra servicium istorum xx militum do ei feodum et servicium terre quam Hasculf[us] de tania [Hasculf de Tany was ancestor of the Essex family of Tany, of Stapleford-Tany, Theydon Bois, Elmstead, Great Stambridge, Latton, etc. He appears repeatedly in the *Pipe Roll of 31 Hen. I.*] tenuit in Anglia die qua fuit (vivus et) mortuus, quam tenet Graelenglus] (Graelengus is proved to be identical with 'Graelandus de Thania', the Essex tenant-in-capite of 1166, by Stephen's second charter (Christmas, 1141), which gives his holding as 7 1/2 fees, the very amount at which he returns it in his *Carta*. But his contemporary, Graeland 'fitz Gilbert' de Tany, on the *Pipe Rolls of Henry II*, was probably so styled for distinction, being a son of Gilbert de Tany who figures on the *Essex Pipe Roll of 1158*) et mater sua pro tanto servicii quantum de feodo illo debent et totum superplus istorum xx militum ei perficiam in (prenomina)tis tribus comitatibus. Et servicium istorum xx militum faciet mihi separatim preter aliud servicium alterius feodi sui. Et preterea concedo (illi ut) castella sua que habet stent et ei remaneant (ad) inforcia(nd[um]) ad voluntatem suam Et ut ille et omnes homines sui teneant terras (et tenaturas) suas omnes de quocunque teneant sicut tenuerunt die qua ipse homo meus effectus est salvo servitio dominorum Et ut ipse et homines sui (sint quieti) de omnibus debitis que debuerunt regi Henrico aut regi Stephano et ut ipse et omnes homines sui per totam Angliam sint quieti de Wastis foresttariis et) assartis que facta sunt in feodo ipsius Gaufredi usque ad (diem quo) homo meus devenit Et ut a die illo in antea omnia illa ess(arta sint amodo excultibilia et arrabilia sine forisfacto et ut habeat mercatum die Jovis apud Bisseiam **[Bushey in Hertfordshire. Part of Mandeville's Domesday fief]** et feriam similiter ibidem quoque anno; et incipiat vigilia Sancti Jacobi et duret tres dies. Et [preterea] do et concedo ei et heredibus suis in feodoet hereditate ad tenendum de me et heredibus meis vicecomitatum Essex[ie] reddendo inde rectam firmam que inde reddi solebat die qua rex Henricus pater meus fuit vivus et mortuus, ita quod auferat de summâ firmâ (vice)comitatus quantum pertinuerit (ad) Meldonam et Niweport que ei (donavi et) quantum (pertinuerit ad tertium) denarium de placitis Vicecomitatus unde eum feci Comitem, et ut teneat omnia excidamenta mea que mihi exciderint (in com)itatu Essexe reddendo inde firmam rectam quamdiu erunt in Dominio meo Et ut sit capitalis Justicia in Essexa hereditabiliter mea (et hered[um]) meorum de placitis et forisfactis que pertinuerint ad Coronam meam ita quod non mittam aliam Justiciam super eum in Comitatu illo nisi (ita sit quod ali)quando mittam aliquem de paribus suis qui audiat cum illo quod placita mea juste tractentur Et ut ipse et omnes homines sui sint(quieti versus) me et versus heredes meos de omni forisfacto et omni malivolentiâ preteritâ ante diem quo meus homo devenit Et ei firmiter concedo et (heredibus suis) quod bene et in pace et libere et sine placito habeat et teneat hereditabiliter, sicut haec carta confirmat, omnia tenementa sua (que ei concessi, in terns) et tenaturis et in feodis et firmis et Castellis et libertatibus et in omnibus Conventionibus inter nos factis (sicut aliquis Comes) terre mee melius et quieti us et liberius tenet ad modum Comitis in omnibus rebus ita quod ipse vel aliquis hominum suorum non (ponantur in ullo modo) in placitum de ali quo forisfacto quod fecissent antequam homo meus factus esset, nec pro ali quo forisfacto quod facturus sit in (anteaponatur in) placitluml de feodo vel Castello vel terra vel tenura quam ei concesserim quamdiu se defendere potuerit de scelere sive (traditione) ad corpus meum pertinente per se aut per unum militem si quis coram venerit qui eum appellare inde voluerit.

(T[estibus] H[enrico] Ep[iscop]o Winton[ensi]) et A[lexandro] Ep[iscop]o Lincoln[ensi] et R[oberto] Ep[iscop]o Heref[ordensi] et N[igello] Ep[iscop]o Ely[ensi] (et B[ernardo] Ep[iscop]o de S[ancto] David et W[illelmo] Cancellario et Com[ite] R[oberto] de Glocestr[ia] et Com[ite] B[aldewino]) (possibly of Devonie) et Com[ite] W[illelmo] de Moion et B[riano] fil[io] Com[itis] (et M[ilone] Glocestr[ie] et R[oberto] Arundell et R[oberto] Malet (A west-country baron, sometimes styled 'Dapifer' and was the predecessor of William Malet, dapifer to Henry II.) et Rad[ulfo] Lovell et Rad[ulfo] Painell) et W[alkelino] Maminot et Rob[erto] fil[io] R[egis] (natural son of Henry I by Edith) et Rob[erto] fil[io] Martin et Rob[ert]o fil[io] Heldebrand[i] Apud Westmonaster[ium]).

The above is the result of how the scholar, J. H. Round, in his book Geoffrey de Mandeville (pp. 88-95) took two transcripts which are copies respectively found in the Dugdale MSS (L. fol. 81) and the Ashmole MSS. (841, fol. 3) and amalgamated them. (There are some variations in the witnesses not stated above.) Round maintains he has reason to believe that this charter was among those duly recorded in the missing volume of the Great Coucher.

The closing clauses of this charter suggest that Geoffrey was even then guarding himself against the consequences of future treason. Shortly afterwards, he was again to change his allegiance from Queen Matilda to King Stephen once more, see below.

SECOND CHARTER OF THE KING TO GEOFFREY DE MANDEVILLE (Christmas, 1141) (Round, 1892, 140-44)

S. rex Angl[orum] Archiepiscopis Episcopis Abbatibus Comitibus Justic[iariis] Vicecomitibus Baronibus et Omnibus Ministris et fidelibus suis francis et Anglis totius Anglie salutem. Sciatis me reddidisse et firmiter concesisse Gaufr[ido] Comiti de Essexa omnia sua tenementa que tenuit, de quocunque illa tenuerit, die qua impeditus fui apud Linc[olniam] et captus. Et praeter hoc dedi ei et concessi ccc libratas terrae scilicet Meldonam [this manor, and those which follow are the same, with the addition of 'Inga' and 'Phingria' as had been granted Geoffrey by the Empress to make up his £100 a year] et Neweport et Depedenam et Banhunte et Ingam et Phingriam (the 'Phenge' and 'Inga' of Domesday were part of the fief of Randulf Peverel (of London) et Chateleam cum omnibus suis Appendiciis pro c libris. Et Writelam (Writtle was an ancient demesne of the Crown (*Pipe Roll, 31 Hen. 1.*) pro vi. xx libris. Et Hadfeld (Hatfield Broadoak, alias Hatfield Regis. This was also ancient demesne) pro quater.xx libris cum omnibus appendiciis illorum Maneriorum. Et praeter hec dedi ei et concessi in feodo et hereditate de me et de meis haeredibus sibi et suis heredibus c libratas terrae de terris excaatis, scilicet totam terram Roberti de Baentona (Lord of Bampton, Devon.) quam tenuit in Essexâ, videlicet Reneham (Rainham, on the Thames, in south Essex.) et Hoilandam (Great Holland, in Essex) et Amb[er]denam (Amberden, in Depden) et Wodeham (Woodham Mortimer, Essex.) et Eistan, (Easton, Essex. Geoffrey de Mandeville had held land at the Survey in (Little) Easton) quam Picardus de Danfront (Picard de Dombront occurs in the *Pipe Roll of 31 Hen. I* as a landowner in Wiltshire and Essex) tenuit. Et Ichilintonam [Ickleton, Cambridgeshire on the borders of Essex, it appears as part of the honour of Boulogne] cum omnibus eorum appendiciis pro c libris. Et praeterea dedi ei et firmiter concessi in feodo et hereditate c libratas terrae ad opus Ernulfi de Mannavilla **(eldest son of Geoffrey de**

Mandeville and Lady Roisia de Vere) de ipso Comite Gaufredo tenendas, scilicet Anastiam, **[Anstey, Herts., the 'Anestige' of Domesday, part of the honour of Boulogne]** et Braching [Braughing, Herts., the 'Brachinges' of Domesday, also part of the honour of Boulogne] et Hamam [possibly that portion of Ham (East and West Ham), Essex, which formed part of the fief of Randulf Peverel] cum omnibus eorum appendiciis. Et c solidatas terrae in Hadfeld ad praefatas c libratas terrae perficiend[um], Et praeterea dedi ei et concessi custodiam turns Lond[onice] cum Castello quod ei subest habend[um] et tenendum sibi et suis haeredibus de me et de meis heredibus cum omnibus rebus et libertatibus et consuetudinibus prefate turn pertinentibus. Et Justicias et Vicecomitat' de Lond[onia] et de Middlesexâ in feodo et hereditate eadem firma qua Gaufridus de Mannavilla avus suus eas tenuit, scilicet pro ccc libris. Et Justitias et Vicecomitat' de Essexâ et de Heortfordiscirâ eadem firmâ quâ avus ejus eas tenuit, ita tamen quod dominica que de praedictis Comitatibus data sunt ipsi Comiti Gaufredo aut alicui alii a firmâ praefatâ subtrahantur et illi et haeredibus suis ad scaccarium combutabuntur. Et praeterea firmiter ei concessi ut possit firrnare quoddam castellum ubicunque voluerit in terrâ suâ et quod stare possit. Et praeterea dedi eidem Comiti Gaufr[edo] et firmiter concessi in feodo et hereditate sibi et haeredibus suis de me et de meis heredibus lx milites feudatos, de quibus Ernulfus de Mannavillâ tenebit x in feodo et hereditate de patre suo, scilicet servicium Graalondi de Tania pro vii militibus et dimidio Et servicium Willelmi filii Roberti pro vii militibus Et servicium Brient[ii] filii Radulfi pro v militibus Et servicium Roberti filii Geroldi pro xi militibus Et servicium Radulfi filii Geroldi pro i milite Et servicium Willelmi de Tresgoz (Landowner in Essex) pro vi militibus Et servicium Mauricii de Chic[he] pro v militibus et servicium Radulfi Maled[octi] pro ii militibus Et servicium Goisb[erti] de Ing[â] pro i milite Et servicium Willelmi filii Heru[ei] pro iii militibus Et servicium Willelmi de Auco pro j milite et dimidio Et servicium Willelmi de Bosevilla (Landowner in Essex, and or, a tenant of the Earl of Essex) pro ii militibus Et servicium Mathei Peur[elli] Mathew Peverel holding lands in Essex and Norfolk) pro iij militibus Et servicum Ade de Sum[er]i de feodo de Elmedonâ (Elmdon, Essex) pro iij militibus Et servicium Rann[ulfi] Briton[is] pro i milite. Et praeterea quicquid Carta Regine testatur ei dedi et concessi. Omnia autem hec praedicta tenementa, scilicet in terns et dominiis et serviciis militum et in Custodia turns Lon[doniae] de Castelli quod turri subest et in Justiciis et Vicecomitatibus et omnibus prae dictis rebus et consuetudinibus et libertatibus, dedi ei et firrniter concessi Comiti Gaufredo in feodo et hereditate de me et de meis heredibus sibi et heredibus suis pro servicio suo. Quare volo et firmiter praecipio quod ipse et heredes sui post eum habeant et teneant omnia illa tenementa et concessi ones adeo libere et quiete et honorifice sicut aliquis omnium Comitum totius Angliae aliquod suum tenementum tenet vel tenuit liberius et honorificentius et quietius et plenius.

T[estibus] M. Regina et H[enrico] Ep[iscop]o Wint[onensi] et W[illelmo] Com[ite] Warenn[a] et Com[ite] Gisl[eberto] de Pembroc et Com[ito] Gisl[eberto] de heortford et W[illelmo] Com[ite] de Albarm[arla] et Com(ite) Sim[one] et Comite Will[elmo] de Sudexâ et Com[ite] Alan[o] et Com[ite] Rob[erto] de Ferrers et Will[elmo] de Ip[ra] et Will[elmo] Martell et Bald[wino] fil[io] Gisl[eberti] **[he was the younger son of Gilbert de Clare, a brother of Gilbert, afterwards Earl of Pembroke, and uncle of Gilbert, Earl of Hertford]** et Rob[erto] de V[er] **[a relation of Lady Roisia, most likely to be the younger brother of Aubrey de Vere, the chamberlain, slain in 1141: or, he is Robert (fitz Bernard) de Vere, who is presumably the "Robert de Vere" who figures as an Essex landowner, in the *Pipe Roll of 1130*]** et Pharam[o] et Ric[ardo] de Luci et Turg[isio] de Abrincis et Ada de Belum. Apud Cantuar[iam] (Canterbury)

SECOND CHARTER OF EMPRESS MATILDA TO GEOFFREY DE MANDEVILLE

This charter represents another change of front by Geoffrey de Mandeville. The Empress describes it not as a charter, but as a "convencio et donatio" which virtually denotes it as a treaty between two contracting powers. The original has been lost and its exact date is in doubt, but it is likely to have been drawn-up between 1st April and June 7th 1142. This edition has been collated by Round (1892, 166) from the Dugdale transcript, among his MSS at Oxford (L. 19) and that of the Dodsworth MSS (xxx, 113) made in 1649. The slight variants are not shown hereunder:

"Carta M. Imperatricis facta Com Gaufredo Essexiae de pluribus terris et libertatibus.

M. Imperatrix. H. regis filia et Anglorum Domina Archiepiscopis. Episcopis, Abbatibus. Comitibus. Baronibus. Justiciariis. Vicecomitibus. Ministris, et omnibus fedelibus suis Francis et Anglis totius Angliae et Normanniae Salutem. Sciatis me reddidisse et concessisse Comiti Gaufr[edo] Essexe omnia tenementa sua, sicut Gaufredus avus suus, aut Willelmus pater suus, aut ipsemet postea unquam melius vel liberius tenuerit aliquo tempore in feodo et haereditate sibi et haeredibus suis, ad tenendum de me et de haeredibus meis. Videlicet in terris et turribus in Castellis et Bailliis. Et nominatim Turrim Lund[oniae] cum Castello quod subtus est, ad firmandum et efforciandum ad voluntatem suam. Et Vicecomitatum Lund[oniae] et Middelsex per CCC lib[ras] sicut Gaufredus auus eius tenuit. Et vicecomitatus Essex per CCC lib[ras] sicut idem Gaufredus auus eius tenuit. Et vicecomitatum de Heortfordscirâ per LX libras sicut avus ejus tenuit. Et praeter hoc do et concedo eidem Gaufredo quod habeat haereditabiliter Justiciã Lund[oniae] et Middelsex et Essex et de Hertfordscirâ, ita quod nulla alia justicia placitet in hiis supradictis vicecomitatibus nisi per eis [sic]. Et concedo illi ut habeat illas C libratas terrae quas dedi illi, et servicium illorum XX militum sicut illud ei dedi et per aliam cartam meam confirmavi. Et illas CC libratas terrae quas Rex Stephanus et Matildis regina ei dederunt. Et illas C libratas terrae de terris Eschaetis quas idem Rex et Regina ei dederunt, et servicium militum quod ei dederunt, sicut habet inde cartas illorum. Et do ei **totam terram quae fuit Eudonis Dapiferi [Eudo Dapifer] in Normannia et Dapiferatum ipsius**. Et haec reddo ei ut Rectum suum ut habeat et teneat haereditabiliter, ita ne ponatur inde in placitum versus aliquem. Et si dominus meus Comes Andegaviae et ego voluerimus, Comes Gaufredus accipiet pro dominiis et terris quas habet Eschaetis et pro servicio militum quod habet **totam terram quae fuit Eudonis Dapiferi in Anglia** sicut tenuit ea die qua fuit et vivus et mortuus, quia hoc est Rectum suum, Praeter illas libratas terrae quas ego dedi ei Et praeter seruicium XX militum quod ei dedi. Et praeter terram **Ernulfi de Mannavill** sicut eam tenet de Comite Gaufredo ex servicio X militum Et si potero perquirere erga Episcopum Lund[oniae] et erga ecclesiam Sancti Pauli Castellum de Storteford per Escambium ad Gratum suum tunc do et concedo illud ei et haeredibus suis in feodo et hereditate tenendum de me et haeredibus meis. Quod si facere non potero, tunc ei convenciono quod faciam illud prosternere et ex toto cadere. Et concedo quod **Ernulf[us] de Mannavill teneat illas C libratas terrae quas ei dedi, et servicium X militum de Comite Gaufredo patre suo**. Et praeter hoc do et concedo eidem Ernulfo C libratas terrae de terris Eschaetis Et servicium X militum ad tenendum de domino meo Comite Andegau[ie] et de me in capite haereditarie sibi et haeredibus suis de nobis et de haeredibus nostris videlicet Cristeshalam **[formerly Chreshall, Christhall, and today Chrisall, Essex. Part of the honour of Boulogne, Was held by Count Eustace, at the Survey in demesne. Stephen granted it to his own son William, who gave it to Richard de Luci]** et Benedis (Bendish Hall, in Radwinter, Essex. Part of the honour of Boulogne. It was given by Stephen's son William to Faversham Abbey, Kent) pro quanto valent. Et superplus perficiam ei per considerationem Comitis Gaufredi. Et convenciono eidem Gaufredo Comiti Essex quod dominus meus Comes Andegauie vel ego vel filii nostri nullam pacem aut concordiam cum Burgensibus Lund[oniae] faciemus, nisi concessu et assensu praedicti Comitis Gaufredi quia inimici eius sunt mortales. Concedo etiam eidem Gaufredo quod novum castellum quod firmavit super Lviam (River Lea) stet etremaneat ad efforciandum ad voluntatem suam. Concedo etiam ei quod firmet unum Castellum ubicunque voluerit in terrâ suâ sicut ei per aliam cartam meam concessi, et quod stet et remaneat. Concedo etiam eidem Gaufredo quod ipse et omnes homines sui habeant et lucrentur omnia essarta sua libera et quieta de omnibus placitis facta usque ad diem qua servicio domini me Comitis

Andegavie ac meo adhesit. Haec autem omnia supradicta tenementa in omnibus rebus concedo ei tenenda haereditarie sibi et haeredibus suis de me et haeredibus meis. Quare volo et firrniter praecipio quod ipse Gaufredus comes et haeredes sui teneant haec omnia supradicta tenementa ita bene et in pace et libere et quiete et honorifice et plenarie sicut unquam aliquis Comitum meorum totius Angliae melius vel liberius tenuit vel tenet Et praeter hoc dedi Willelmo filio Otuel **(William fitz Otwell Earl Geoffrey's 'brother' is referred to by Earl William (Geoffrey's son) as his uncle (avunculus) in a charter confirming his grant of lands (33 acres) in "Abi et Toresbi" to Greenfield Nunnery, Lincolnshire (*Harl, Cart.,* 53 C, 50). He is also witness as ('patruus meus' to a charter of Earl Geoffrey the younger (*Sloane Cart.,* xxxii 64) early in the reign of Henry II. He was clearly a 'uterine' brother of Earl Geoffrey the elder, so that his father must have married William de Mandeville's widow - a fact unknown to genealogists)** fratri ejusdem Comitis Gaufredi C libratas terrae de terris Escaetis tenendis de me et de haeredibus meis in feudo et haereditate pro seruicio suo, et pro amore fratris sui Comitis Gaufredi. Concedo etiam quod Willelmus de Sai **(William de Say married Beatrice, sister (and in her issue heiress) of the earl, by whom he was ancestor of the second line of Mandeville, Earl of Essex. In the following year he joined the earl in his furious revolt against the king)** habeat omnes terras et tenementa quae fuerunt patris sui, et ipse et haeredes sui, et quod Willelmus Cap' **(William Capra (Chevre) whose family gave its name to the manor of 'Chevers' in Mountnessing, Essex. He was probably another brother-in-law of the earl)** habeat terram patris sui sine placito et ipse et haeredes sui. Concedo etiam eidem Comiti Gaufredo quod Willelmus filius Walteri et haeredes sui habeant custodiam Castelli de Windesh (Windsor) et omnia sua tenementa sicut ipse Willelmus et antecessores sui earn habuerunt de Rege H. patre meo et antecessoribus ipsius. Et quod Matheus de Rumilli (son of Robert de Romeli, lord of Skipton.) habeat terram patris sui quam Gaufridus de Turevill (Tourville) tenet. Et Willelmus de Auco (William de Ou (Auco) or Eu is returned in the carta of the Earl of Essex (1166) as holding four fees of him.) habeat Lauendonam sicut Rectum suum haereditarie. Concedo etiam eidem Comiti Gaufredo quod omnes homines sui teneant terras et tenementa sua de quocunque teneant sine placito et sine pecuniae donatione et ut Rectum eis teneatur de eorum Calumpnijs sine pecuniae donatione Et quod Osb[ertus] Octod[enarii] habeat illas XX libratas terrae quas ei dedi et confirrnaui per cartam meam.

"Hanc autem convencionem et donationem tenendam affidavi manu mea propria in manu ipsius Comitis Gaufredi. Et hujus fiduciae sunt obsides per fidem et Testes Robertus Comes Gloec': et Milo Com' Heref' (Herefordiae): et Brianus filius Comitis: et Rob' fil' Reg' (Robertus filius Reginaldi) et Rob' de Cure' Dap. (Robert de Courci of Stoke (Courcy) Somerset. He was slain at Counsylth, 1157) et Joh'es filius Gisleberti: (John Fitz Gilbert, marshal to the Empress and brother of William her chancellor) et Milo de Belloc': **(Miles de Beauchamp, son of Robert de Beauchamp, and nephew to Simon de Beauchamp, hereditary castellan of Bedford, brother of Payn de Beauchamp who afterwards married Rohaise [Roisia] widow of Geoffrey de Mandeville)** et Rad' Paganell: et Rob' de Oilli Conest: et Rob' fil' Heldebrande.

Et convencionavi eidem Comiti Gaufredo pro posse meâ quod Comes Andegavie dominus meus assecurabit ei manu sua propria illud idem tenendum et Henricus filius me us similiter. Et quod rex Franciae erit inde obses si facere potero. Et si non potero, faciam quod ipse Rex capiet in manu illud tenendum. Et de hoc debent esse obsides per fidem: Juhel de Moduana, et Robertus de Sabloill et Wido de Sabloill (Guy de Sable) et Pagan de Clarevall (Payn de Clairvaux) et Andreas de Aluia, et Pipinus de Turon: et Absalon Rumarch et Reginaldus comes Cornubiae et Balduinus Comes Devon': **et Gislebertus Comes de Penbr' (Penbroke): et Comes Hugo de Norff': et Comes Albericus (Aubrey de Vere, Lady Roisia's brother): et Henricus de Essex: et Petrus de Valon': (Valoniis' - Valoines)** et alii Barones mei quos habere voluerit et ego habere potero, erunt inde obsides similiter. Et quod x'rianitas Angliae quae est in potestate mea capiet in manu istam supradictam conventionem tenendam eidem Comite Gaufredo et haeredibus suis de me et de haeredibus meis. Apud Oxineford. (Oxford)

Sub magno sigillo dictae Matildis Imperatricis."

NOTES:

Aubrey de Vere married Beatrice, who was the heiress of Guisnes at the death of her grandfather Count Manasses (?1139). Aubrey became Count of Guines for only a short while because he and his wife divorced, and Beatrice remarried between 1144 and 1146 Baldwin d'Ardres, the claimant of Guisnes. He was Earl of Oxford by at least 1147. Earl Gilbert of Pembroke was the maternal uncle of Aubrey and of course, Roisia.

William de Say, brother-in-law of Geoffrey, actively took up the cause of the warring in the fens against King Stephen, and was to die in 1144, in the same skirmish at Burwell which killed Geoffrey.'

Ernulf, eldest son and heir of Geoffrey, who was supporting his father, was taken prisoner before the year was out. He was disinherited and banished from the realm. Chroniclers and genealogists subsequently ignored Ernulf but he reappears, early in the following reign, as a witness to a royal charter (prior to 1158) and was in contact with other members of his family. He held lands in Wiltshire and Yorkshire. Ernulf occurs as principal witness in a family charter c. 1157-8. This document, which is addressed to Earl Geoffrey (his brother) "baronibus suis" is a confirmation of a grant of lands in Sawbridgeworth, by his tenant Warine fitz Gerold and his brother Henry, to Robert Blund of London, who is to hold them. Amongst the witnesses are: "Roesia Comlitissa] matre mea (widow of Geoffrey and his mother), Eustlachia] Com [iti ssal, Ernulfo de Mannavilla fratre meo ... Waltero de Mannavilla"

When William de Mandeville became Earl (1166) he confirmed a gift of land at Kingham in Oxford to his disinherited brother which included the witness Alberic de Vere, uncle of the granter and grantee; Simone de Bellocampo (Simon de Beauchamp) uterine brother by his mother and Payn de Beauchamp her second husband; Geoffrey de Say, their first cousin.

Ernulf married Aaliz and they had at least two sons, Geoffrey and Ralph. Geoffrey had issue, a son, named yet again Geoffrey. It is possible that Ernulf had a third son, also named Ernulf, for an 'Ernulf de Magneville' was among the Crusaders that reached Acre in June 1191 (assuming his father was dead). An Ernulf de Mandeville is found among the witnesses to a star of Abraham fitz Muriel (1214), granting a house in Westcheap to Geoffrey 'de Mandeville' Earl fo Essex and Gloucester. (Round, 1892, 227-35).

APPENDIX B

From vol. LXI of the Marquis D'Albon's unindexed manuscripts held in the Bibliothèque Nationale, Paris, France.

Chancery Inquisitions Post Mortem Henry III File 19 (2) (Calendar (p. 100) No. 367)

Inquisituo facta apud Wautham coram Rogero de Thurkelby et Henrico de Mara die Mercurin proxima post festum Sancti Andree Apostoli de Manerio de Rewehal in Comitatu Essex et de Manerio de Neweseles in Comitatu Hertfordie anuo Regia Henrici regis filii regis Johannes XIO (sic) [XI year of his reign].

Preceptum fuit Vicecomite ie et Hertfordie quod venire faceret Essex (Essex) coram predictis Rogero et Henrico at diem et loco quos ... facerent (Hertford) tot et tales probos et legales hommus ... tam illos qui fuerunt in inquiitione prius facto de Manerius de Rewenhal et Neweseles quam alios per quos rei veritas melius et pleinus innesticar possit et inquiri de proffamentis perquod dominus Robertus de Scales clamat predictum Manorium de Rewenhale in Comitatu Essex de dono patri (sic) [Petri] de Roffa annunculi ipsius Roberti et per quod Alicia de Scales claat predictum Manerium de Neweseles in Comitatu Hertfordie de dono ejusden Petri et quod inquisitio prius inde factori insufficienter facta fuit. Et per quos rei veritas melius sciri poterit quando et quibus presentibus et in quo statu predictus Petrus fuit quando predicta feoffamenta facta fuerunt et ubinium ipso Petro volenti et scienta vel non. Que Maneria dominum rex corpi fecit in mannum suam tanquam pertinencia ... Eo quod predictus Petrus tempore quo predicta feoffamenta fieri debuerunt in extremis ajebat et tabiter se habuint per quod predicta feoffamenta valere non debent, rot dicitur.

Et Henricus de Bathomia dicit pro regi quod predictus **Petrus non potuit feoffare predictaitum Robertum de Manerius de Rewenhal eo quod idem Petrus prius demisit predictum Manerium Magistro Milicie Templi in Anglia att terminum sex annorum onde tres annio venturi erant quando predictus Petrus obit. Et dicit quod predictus Magister Milicie Templi tunc non fuit in partibus illis.** Ita quod eidem Petro reddidase protuit predictum Mannerium. Dicit ecian quod predicta Alicia ... in vito ipsius Petro ipso scienti habuit seisman de Manerio de Neweseles immo sine assensu et vol un tate ipsuis Petri, intrusit se in predictum Manerium et dicit quod predictus Petrus quando predicta feoffamenta fieri debuerunt, non finit talis memo re quod cos feoffare potuit de predictus maneris et quod in extremis agebat quando ipsiposuerunt se in predicta maneria.

Et Gibertus Manduzt, Johannes de Boksted, Radulphus Marcel, Ricardus filius Johannes de Teye, juratores de prima inquiscione et Petrus de Radley, Adam de Loges, Alexander de Beynflat, Thomas Burdun, Gibertus Chippenmere, Johannes de Broke, Johannes Adgar, Willelmus de Chemino, Robertus de Hebrugge, Thomas de Thopingho et Johannes le Marzun de Torbinges juratores de Comitatu Essexe venerunt. **Et Petrus de Radlegh et alii juratores qui mon fuerunt in prima inquisicione dicunt super sacramentum suum quod predictus Petrus per tres annos et amjilius ante mortem suam demiserat predicto Magistro Milicie Templi in Anglia Manerium de Rewenhal cum pertinecus. Tenendum ad terminum sex annorum pro viginti duabus libris per annum de quibus idem Magister paianit eidem Petro pre manibus sexaginta et sex libras pro tribus annis. Et ad paseham in quartoanno proximo ante mortem ipsius Petri reddidit predictus Magister predicto Petro vindicum Iibras,** Et post paxham sensit idem Petrus se debilem et mandarint predictus Roberto et Alicie quod venient ad eum.

Et dicent quod die sabbatti proxima ante Ascensione domim anna xxxix inter horam primam et terciam venerunt frater Willelmus del Estre preceptor de Kersing et Wyham et frater Radulphus de Bedeford et frater Willelmus de Wyham fratres predicto Milicie Templi ex voluntate ipsius Magistri et credunt, eo quod predictus frater Radulphus propter hoc venit de Londonia et reddiderunt predicto Petro pre dictum

Manerium cum pertinenciis et cartam de convencione quam habuerunt depredicto Manerio et similiter confirmaccionen domini regis quam inde perquisinerunt. Et idem Petrus eodem die dedit fratribus predicti Milicie Templi circiter centum aeras terre in predicto Manerio in perpetuam elemosinam. Et eodem die anti horam nonam venerunt predicta Robertus et Alicia ad ipsum Petrum apsud Rewenhale ad domas pertinentes ad ecclesian de Rewenhale eo quod ipse fuit persona ejusdem et die illo concessit predicto Roberto Manerium de Rewenhale et predicte Alicie Manerium de Neweseles et die dominica sequenti fieri fecit cartas ipsorum de feoffamento de predictus Manerius circa horam priman et propria manu sua sigillamit cartam predicti Roberti et Ricardus Capellanus ipsius Petri coram eo et per precepitum ejus sigillavit cartam predicto Alicie pro debilitate ipsius Petri et idem Petrus ceput homagium ipsorum de predictus Manerius set dicunt quod carts illas eis noluit deliberare, quousque uterque ipsominum affidant quod inneret ei verum cajellanum inperpetuum, joro arima ejus divina celebrantem.

Et quod predictus Robertus daret et Manerium suum de Hoo in Comitatu Norffolkie, si ipse conualesceret de infirmitate quo tune granatus erat tenendum tota vita sua. Et quod predicta Alicia daret ei Manerium de Hicelingfeld in Comitatu Cantebrigie eodem modo tenendum et statim post quam hie affidauerunt liberavit eis predictis cartas propria mam sua et precepit Alfredo servienti suo quod poneret ipsum Robertum in seisinam de predicto Manerio de Rewenhal qui ipsum in seisinam suam posiuit die lune proxima sequente ante horam primam. Ita quod idem Robertus ... die cepit homagium liberorum hominu et fidelitatu villanorium de eodem Manerio et succident fraxinos et dedit et ... fregit vinarium et piscarian fecit in eodem et fuit in pacifica seisinia usque advigiliam Pentecoste quod Vicecomes et exactrones Comitatu Essexe ipsam inde ejecerunt. Et eodem die dominica precepit idem Petrus, Willelmus Martel serviente suo quod viet cum predicta Alicia cum litteris suid patentibus quas ei fieri fecit apud Neweseles et poneret ipsam in seisina de predicto Manerio. Im ibidem venerunt die Martis proxima ante Ascensionem domini, et predictus Willelmus simul cum Johanne serviente ipsius Petri de eodem Manerioin plena curia tunc ibidem summonita fecit legi litterus patentes ipsius Petri de seisima eiden Alicie ... faciende quas modo profet et posiuit ipsam circa horam primam in seisina de predicto Manerio. Et ipsa capit homagialiberorum hominum et fidelitatem villanorum de predicto Manerio. Et die Mercurii in vigilia Ascensious domini cepit verum damum in parco ejudem Manerii et vendidit et dedit arbories in eodem et prosterni fecit. Et sicremansit in seisina usque ad diem veneris in septimana Penticoste quod exaetores domini regis ipsam inde ejecermunt et dicunt quod predictus **Petrus obiit die Ascenionis domini proximo sequentis posthoram monam et paululum ante mortem suam eodem die habitum Templariorum suscepit. Et dicunt quod finit hone memo ire die quo eos feoffarut et semper prostea usque ad mortem suam.** Et predicti juratores qui fuerunt in prima inquisitione de Comitatu Essexe et similiter Robertus de la Rohele, Stephanus Camerarius et Johannes filius Gilberti juratories de Comitatu Hertfordie qui fuerunt in prima inquisicione. Et Alanus de Wadlington, Walterus Hacun, Willelmus Basset, Johannes filius Johannes, Brianus de Trokkinge, Willelmus filius Bernardi, Robertus de la Dene, Willelmus de Hodenho, Theobaldus de Mora et Ricardus Dignon super sacramentum suum hoc idem in omnibus testantur. Et Johannes de Coggeshal et Radulphus de Wyrham testes nominati in cartis vtrius que ipsorum Roberti et Alicie super sacramentum suum hoc idem testantur. Et similiter Mjellus Trot, Albredus de Haselingfield, Johannes de Camera et Willelmus Marcel servientus ipsius Petri et qui presentes fuerunt quando eos feoffauit de predictis Manerius jurati et separatim examinati hoc idem dicunt super sacramentum suum. Et Alicie ponit loco suo Robertum de Scales, vel Radulphum de Wyrham vel Willebruum de Wytewell.

Sur le revers [on the reverse]: Domino regi de inquisitione de Rewenhal in Comitatu Essexe et de Neweselelsl in Comitatu Herefordia (sic) [should be Hertfordshire - Marquis D'Albon confused Herefordshire with Hertfordshire several times in his documentation.]

APPENDIX C

Extract from pp. 127-8 ofthe Marquis D'Albon's, *Cartulaire du Temple,* vol. LXII, Angleterre III

CANTEBRIGG - (Cambridge)

Frater Willelmus Thorp	Frater apud Wilburham
Frater Willelmus Ravei	Frater ibidem per Vannos
Frater Willelmus et Le Fronde	Preceptor apud Deney
Frater Willelmus de Scottho	Frater apud Deney
Frater Hugo de Tadcaste	Frater ibidem
Frater Johannen de Newent	Frater ibidem
Frater Alexander de Bulbeck	Frater ibidem
Frater Rogerus de Daltune	Frater ibidem per VII canos
Frater Willelmus de Cestertone	Frater apud Deney
Frater Willelmus de Welles	Frater apud Deney
Frater Rogerus de Lodelarve	
Frater Robertus Scot	Frater apud Deney
Frater Johannes de Moune,	Preceptor apud Dokeswosche (Duxford)
Frater Johannes de Hauwile	Frater apud Deney Demens

ESSEX

Frater Rogerus le Norreys	Preceptor apud Cressingy
Frater N'cusdus Paytefyn	Frater apud Dynesle*
Frater Huricus et Pawell	Frater Ibidem Per iii - et Diuidienne
Frater Robutus et la Wolde	
Frater Johannes et Suttone	Frater apud Suttone
Frater Johannes Cofyn	Frater apud Cressing

NOTES: The information above was hand-written, then copied again by hand on my visit to Paris. It is more than likely that some mistakes have occurred, for example, Willelmus et Le Fronde is likely to be William de la Forde; Willelmus Ravei, William Raven; Johannes de Moune, John Mohun. Frater N'cusdus Peytefyn is interesting too, could he be 'Ricardus' Richard Petevyn, preceptor, who in 1308 was arrested at Dynnesley? (See Chapter 9)

* It will be seen that Dynnesley (Hertfordshire) is included in the above list under Essex.

Extract from vol. LXI - D'Albon's manuscripts held at the Bibliothèque Nationale in Paris

POMMIOND [sic] DE TEMPLI EN ANGLETERRE

Compton	Sussex
Cressing	Essex
Dartford	Kent
Dokesworth	Cambridgeshire
Dunwich	Sussex (*sic*) [Suffolk]
Dynnesley	Hertfordshire
Ewill	[Kent]
Garway	Herefordshire
Langenok	Hertfordshire
Shipley	Sussex
Walthan	Kent
Great Wilburgham	Cambridgeshire

COMMANDERIE DE TEMPLI QUI EX (...unreadable) - PAR IL' HOPITAL

Sadlecomb	Sussex
Deneye	Cambridgeshire
Flaxflete	[Yorkshire]

APPENDIX D

Carta Com Rogeri

In nomine sancte et in-dividue Trinitatis, Notum esse cupimus quod Rogerus de Montgomery, Comes de Scosberiensi tam pro animabus dulcissimi domini sui ducis Normanorum et regis Anglorum Willelmi et regine Matilde quam pro sua et uxoris sue Mabilie omnium antecessorum et successorum suorum comedentibus et laudantibus filiis et filiabusque suis dedit atque perpetualitur in elemosina concessit deo, et Sancto Martino de Sagii et monachis ibedem deo servientibus vel servituris Fissaburnam et Wath, et Kantonam et quicquid ad eam pertinet in Arintonam * et decimas Senegaie et Orwelle, et Herlingtone, et eccesiam Hertingis pro quodam fratre Mabilie comtisse qui in predicto monasterio factus est monachus. Robertus vicecomes filius Tetbaldi dedit in obitu suo eidem sancto concedente Rogero et filiis suis Tintonam. Norwanus venator omnium supradictorum consensu dedit eidem sancto decimam omnium terrarum suarum. Eudo filius Huberti dedit predicto Sancto decimam Neisellis. Hec omnia data sunt et ab eis firmiter concessa tempore procellentissimi ducis Normanorum et Regis Anglorum Wilelmi et Matilde Regine, Comes Rogerus, concedente Hugo filio suo, dedit Sancto Martino Sagii ecclesiam Dodelbrie cum omnibus forisfacturis. Testantibus Domino abbate de Gloucestro et Serlon, Bernardo de Novo mercato, Rogero Venator, Fulcone fratre Alcheri, Gisleberto de Condovere, Wodeboldo Sacerdote, Herberto Archdiacono, et subscribur confirmatio. Will'i Regis et signum ejus. Sign Rogeri Comitis Scrob. Sign Alan Comitis, Sign Hugo Comitis Cestren. Sign Walchelini. Sign Roberti Filii Hamonis. Sign Ethon' Senescall. Sign Hugonis de Montgomeri. Testibus Hamone Piperell, et Ricardo filio Corbellini, et Constabulario et Roberto filio Corbellini and Ricardo Belhomisio. (*Liber Albus St. Martin fo. 4.* In the town library at Seez),

(*) Arrington

(There are some differences from the above account in *Newsells Deeds* to that found in Round's edition of 1899)

APPENDIX E

Legends of the Saints and Martyrs in History and Art

THE FORTY MARTYRS

Died at Sebastea, 320 AD. Feast day 9 or 10 March.

In 320, Emperor Licinius suddenly commanded all Christians in the East to cast off their religion on pain of death. Amongst those who refused, were forty soldiers of the 12th, 'Thunder-struck' legion, which was made up of several nationalities, and at the time stationed at Sebatea in Armenia [now Sivas in Turkey]. Efforts to win them over by persuasion failed. Orders were then given that they should be stripped naked, herded onto a frozen pond, and kept there. To help break down their resistance a fire was kindled and warm baths prepared where they could see them.

By the next day most of them were dead; those who were not were then killed, including the youngest, Melito, whose widowed mother had encouraged him to the last. Only one of the forty failed in the atrocious ordeal, and his place was supposedly taken by another soldier, who was moved by his comrades' example, and by a dream of angels, to declare himself a Christian. Doubts are cast on this story. [A mosque dedicated to The Forty Martyrs is encompassed by the El Aksa Mosque in Jerusalem (q.v.).]

(The term 'The Forty Martyrs' is also used for an unspecified group, or number, of the many English and Welsh Roman Catholics who suffered death for conscience sake during the 16th and 17th centuries and were canonised in 1970.) (Attwater, 1974, 134-5)

MARY MAGDALEN(E) - Patroness of Marseilles, and of Penitent Women

Died in the 1st century AD. Feast day 22 July.

Mary of Magdala, whom Jesus had healed of 'seven devils', was one of the women who followed and ministered to him in Galilee. She was present at his crucifixion and with two others went to his tomb and found it empty. St. Mark states that it was to her that the risen Christ first appeared, to which St. John adds in his account that the Master gave her a message to deliver to the brethren.

In western art no distinction is made between the three women mentioned in the gospels - Mary Magdalen; Mary of Bethany sister of Martha and Lazarus; "the woman which was a sinner". In the east they are treated as three distinct individuals.

In the west, traditionally, Mary Magdalen is looked upon as an outstanding type of penitent and the contemplative. Later medieval stories of the saint owed much to romantic legends, and that she had been betrothed to St. John the Apostle. Amongst other legends it is alleged that after the Ascension, together with her brother and sister accompanied by the two saints Maximin and Marcella, they set out in a boat, without sails, oars or rudder and came to Marseilles where they preached and converted the heathens. Her emblem is an ointment jar. (Attwater, 1974, 237; Tabor, 1924, 82)

ST. CHRISTOPHER, Martyr

Date of death unknown. Feast day 25 July.

There are two different versions of the legend: one that is of Greek origin and the second which is normally told in the west. The name Christophoros in Greek means 'one who carries Christ', and its original connotation was spiritual, not physical.

The western story is that Christopher, a native of Canaan, was a man of gigantic stature and proud of his size and strength, who wished to serve the mightiest of masters. He went to the Court of King Maximus renowned for riches and power, but even the king made a sign of the cross at the mention of the devil. Christopher left to seek Satan as a more powerful ruler but Satan trembled at a wayside cross. Having been disappointed by both the king and the devil, he sought Christ, the king whose emblem was a cross. In the course of his wanderings he found a hermit who instructed him in Christianity but Christopher refused to be bound by prayers and fasting. The hermit told him he could still serve Christ by living alone by a ford where many travellers passed; he further directed him to use his great strength in carrying travellers across a certain river, thereby atoning for his former sins. Christopher rooted up a palm-tree for a staff and day and night carried over all who came to the ford.

One night Christopher heard a voice calling him from across the river. Upon going out he found a little child waiting to be carried across. He took the child in his arms and began to wade through the river and as he did so he felt the child growing heavier and heavier until it was almost more than the giant could bear. The waters rose, waves and wind roared. On reaching the other side he exclaimed to the child, 'You seem to weigh as heavy as the whole world'. 'No wonder!' said the child, 'You have been carrying the whole world. I am Jesus Christ, the king you seek.' [A variation, probably of Greek descent: 'You seem to weigh as heavy as the whole world.' 'Well said, Christopher, I created the world, I redeemed the world, I bear the sins of the world,' ... It was after this that the heathen giant was named Christopherus, or the Christ-bearer]. On the other side, the child said Christopher's service was accepted and that, as a token, if he planted his staff in the ground, in the morning it would bear leaves and fruit, then the child vanished. In the morning all was as foretold and he went forth and preached Christianity. In due course he was put to death for his faith.

A church was built in St. Christopher's honour at Chalcedon, [at the entrance to the Black sea opposite Byzantium] as early as 450 AD and it is surmised he was a martyr in Asian Minor, perhaps in the 3rd century.

In medieval times it was a common belief that 'he who looked on the image of St. Christopher would suffer no harm that day', which led to the painting of large pictures of him on church walls, e.g. St. John the Baptist Church, Cottred, Herts. where there is a 15th century wall painting. He is the patron saint of wayfarers and now of motorists.

In art he is represented as very tall and strong, generally fording a river with a huge staff in his hand, and carrying the Christ Child on his shoulders. (Attwater, 1974, 85; Tabor, 1924, 29-30; *The Golden Legend*)

ST. JOHN, THE APOSTLE AND EVANGELIST, called 'the Divine', the Theologian

Died at Ephesus (?) c. 100 AD. Feast day 27 December.

John, and his brother James, sons of Zebedee, were Galilean fisherman and were 'called' from mending their nets to follow Christ. The brothers could be quick-tempered and excitable so Jesus nicknamed them 'sons of thunder', however, Christ chose them, together with Peter, to be with him on the momentous occasions such as his transfiguration and agony in Gethsemane. Tradition has identified John with the unnamed 'disciple whom Jesus loved' and was entrusted with the care of his mother, the Virgin Mary. It was John who ran ahead of Peter to the tomb on the morning of the resurrection and seeing it empty, believed; he also first recognised the risen Lord by the Sea of Tiberias. [St. Paul names John together with Peter and James as pillars of the church in Jerusalem.]

Tradition maintains that John was sent to Rome in the reign of Domitian, and cast into a cauldron of boiling oil, but was miraculously preserved. Another legend relates that whilst in this city an attempt was made to poison him with the sacramental cup - some say by the order of Domitian - but the poison issued miraculously from the cup in the form of a serpent, at the same time his enemies fell dead at his feet, and he and the communicants were saved. A cup, often shown in the hand of St. John, may refer to this, or to Christ's words to him: "Ye shall indeed drink of My cup." Other legends exist but are not related here.

He was exiled later to the island of Patmos, where he wrote the Apocalypse, returning afterwards to Ephesus. It was at Ephesus that he died at the great age of nearly a hundred years. He was variously represented in art:

1) As an Apostle; generally young, beardless, sometimes with book or pen, sometimes with a cup (and serpent) as mentioned above
2) As an evangelist; with an eagle
3) As the writer of the Apocalypse; an old man, on th Isle of Patmos, with the sea in the distance

The fourth gospel, three biblical epistles, and the book of *Revelation* (*The Apocalypse*) traditionally bear the name of John as their author. The authorship and historical value of these works have been the subject of serious debate among biblical scholars of recent years, some of whom feel it is impossible to know who actually wrote them. (Tabor, 1924, 65-6; Attwater, 1974, 189-90)

Many lecterns in churches have an engraved eagle, on the front representing the four books *Matthew, Mark, Luke* and *John.*

ST. JOHN THE BAPTIST (Ital. Giovanni Battista)

Died c. 29 AD. Feast days 24 June (his birth) and 29 August (his death).

The Patron Saint of Florence, and a frequent subject in Florentine pictures. The whole of his life being comprised in the Gospel narrative, few legends have grown around his name.

He was the forerunner and herald of Christ, his cousin. His father was Zachary, a priest of Jerusalem and his mother Elizabeth, a kinswoman of the Virgin Mary. John appeared as an itinerant preacher, c. 27 AD, announcing: "Repent, for the Kingdom of Heaven is at hand," and those who confessed their sins he washed in the river Jordan. He gained many followers, including several who were to be chosen apostles of Christ, and Jesus himself came to be baptized by him. From then onwards, John pointed Jesus out as "the Lamb of God who takes away the sin of the world." Shortly afterwards, John was thrown into prison as he had rebuked Herod Antipas for taking Herodias, his half-brother's wife. From prison John was able to follow Jesus's ministry, and sent messengers to ask him questions. But Herod, in a moment of folly promised to give Herodias's daughter, Salome, whatever she wanted, and Herodias told the girl to ask for John the Baptist's head. It was duly given to her on a platter. Contrary to usual custom the principal feast of St. John the Baptist is kept on his birthday.

There is a possibility that John spent some time with the community whose documents and buildings were discovered at Qumran, near the Dead Sea in 1947.

In pictures of the Holy Family he is represented as a child; then as a boy, generally with a lamb, and as a young man in raiment of camel's hair, sometimes holding a book or a scroll with the words:

"Behold the Lamb of God." However, almost invariably his attribute is the cross. (Tabor, 1924, 64; Attwater, 1974, 191)

ST. KATHERINE (CATHERINE) OF ALEXANDRIA

No exact date is known of her death, it was sometime during the early-mid 4th century AD. Feast day 25 November.

According to legend, Katherine was the daughter of Costis, a brother of Constantine the Great, and of Sabinella, daughter of the King of Egypt. At a very early age she supposedly showed signs of an extraordinary virtue and had the remarkable ability to absorb learned works so that by the time she was fifteen years old she had surpassed her masters, who were the seven wisest men of the day. Her father died at this time, and she became queen [this is also why she is depicted wearing a crown], but continued her life of study, and refused to marry much to the chagrin of her people. A vision appeared to an old hermit, in the desert near Alexandria, in which the Virgin told him to go to Katherine and comfort her, telling her that the Saviour of the world would be her bridegroom. She asked what she should do to become worthy of Him, and learnt the Christian faith from the hermit, and was baptised, together with her mother. That same night, the Son of God appeared to Katherine, in a vision, and put a ring on her finger. When she saw it she was determined to give up the world, and live entirely for the service of the Church.

Maximin (Maxentius), the tyrant, now began his persecutions of the Christians at Alexandria, and Katherine's opportunity came to prove her worth. She argued so forcibly with Maximin against the worship of idols that he called together fifty of the most learned philosophers of the empire, promising them great rewards if they could get the better of her. But she disputed so wisely by demolishing their arguments that, one after another, they acknowledged themselves vanquished and accepted Christianity. Maximin consigned them all to the flames; but struck by her beauty, had Katherine brought to his palace. Failing utterly in all his attempts to seduce her and win her over from her faith, he ordered her to be scourged and thrown into a dungeon where she was allegedly fed by a dove and Christ which appeared to her in a vision. Her virtue and her miraculous preservation in prison was of such influence that the Empress, and Porphyry a minion of Maximin, together with their attendants, were converted during an absence from home of the tyrant. When Maximin learnt of this subterfuge he grew more furious than ever. He had his wife, Porphyry, and the other converts put to death. Upon Katherine, who refused with scorn to become his Empress, he ordered her to be bound on the sharp points of four revolving wheels, and torn to death. Katherine went out gladly to die, but an angel came and broke the wheels, the fragments of which killed thousands of the onlookers [Many reports claim it was only one wheel and 'some' spectators were killed by flying splinters]. She was unhurt, but was then carried outside the city, tortured, and finally beheaded as she called down blessings on all who should remember her. From her severed veins there flowed not blood but milk. The angels came and carried her body away to the top of Mount Sinai, where the Orthodox monastery is now called St. Katherine's and her shrine acknowledged.

Legends were most popular in Europe in the Middle Ages, and St. Katherine is a universal favourite in the world of art. She is represented as young, beautiful, and crowned, with a palm, book, or sword in her hand; but her distinguishing attribute is a spiked wheel, often broken. (Tabor, 1924, 25-6; Attwater, 1974, 209-210)

ST. LAWRENCE (Laurence; Ital. San Lorenzo; Fr. St. Laurent)

Died at Rome 258 AD. Feast day 10 August.

Tradition says he was a native of Aragon; one of seven deacons to Pope Sixtus II. He was afterwards chosen as the first archdeacon, and given charge of the vessels and embroideries of the altar, and of its services. When Sixtus was led away to martyrdom, Lawrence requested that he might go with him, and wept; but Sixtus said that he should follow in three days time to a much more painful death. Meanwhile, he told him to take all the possessions of the Church, and distribute them to the poor, which St. Lawrence did, visiting from house to house. On his rounds he came to the house of a devout widow, Cyriaca, on the Coelian Hill, who concealed and ministered to the Christians. She was sick, and he healed her by laying on of hands, and washed the feet of the Christians in the house. When the Prefect heard that St. Lawrence had the treasures of the Church, he threw him into prison, under the charge of a certain Hippolytus, who was converted and baptised, with all his family. The Prefect then asked where the treasures were, and St. Lawrence said he would show him three days later. He called together the poor and sick, and at the allotted time said to the Prefect: "Here are the treasures of Christ's Church." The Prefect, in a rage, ordered St. Lawrence to be bound on a gridiron, and roasted over fires. In the midst of the torture he uttered his famous taunt: "Seest thou not that I am roast on one side? Turn me on the other." So he died. [Some scholars are not wholly in agreement about how much credence can be given to such particulars and think he may have been beheaded]. Hippolytus came in the night, took the body, and buried it. When the Prefect heard of Hippolytus' action, he had him seized then commanded he should be tied to the tail of a wild horse - he too suffered martyrdom in death.

St. Lawrence is represented young, as a deacon. Sometimes he holds a dish or bag of gold (the treasure of the Church), perhaps a censer, a cross; but his distinguishing attribute is a gridiron. His life is represented in Fra Angelico's frescoes in the Chapel of Nicholas V in the Vatican. From the 4th century he was venerated as one of the most famous martyrs of Rome and with St. Sixtus is named in the canon of the Roman Mass. (Tabor, 1924, 71-2; Attwater, 1974, 214)

ST. MICHAEL, THE ARCHANGEL (Ital. San Michele or Sammichele)

Feast day 29 September. This date originated in the annual commemoration of the dedication before the 7th century AD of a church in his honour near Rome.

He is the chief of the Celestial Host, and victor over the powers of evil, therefore he represents the triumph of the spiritual over the material. He is the Lord and Arbiter of souls, the Guardian Angel of the Hebrews and also venerated by Christians. The well-known passage in *The Apocalypse* (*Rev.* xii, 7-9) concerning the 'war in heaven' contributed to his being honoured in the West as the 'captain of the heavenly host' and protector of Christians in general and of soldiers in particular. In the East he is looked on as a special guardian of the sick. He appears in *Old Testament* scenes as the messenger angel. To the Virgin Mary he also announced her death.

He is represented winged, with spear and shield, overcoming the dragon; also with a banner and cross, sometimes with a sceptre, or weighing the souls of men in a balance. (Tabor, 1924, 88)

Both the angels Gabriel and Raphael are now commemorated with Michael on his feast day. (Attwater, 1974, 245; Tabor, 1924, 88)

ST. THOMAS À BECKET, THOMAS OF CANTERBURY.

Died at Canterbury, 1170. Feast day 29 December.

He was born in Cheapside, London, of well-to-do Norman parentage, and given a good education prior to entering the service of Archbishop Theobald of Canterbury c. 1142. Theobald sent Thomas abroad to study canon law and in 1154 gave him Deacon's Orders and the Archdeaconry of Canterbury. King Henry II chose Becket to be the royal chancellor in 1155 and for seven years he served as a friend, statesman, diplomat and soldier, and appeared outwardly to the court as an ecclesiastic of extravagant worldly tastes.

When Thomas was appointed to the vacant see of Canterbury, in 1162, he obviously 'saw the light', and changed from being "a patron of play-actors and a follower of hounds, to being a shepherd of souls." - his description of himself. He then threw himself into his duties with great zeal, was profuse in alms giving whilst living very austerely himself and soon came into conflict with the king. The situation deteriorated, a crucial point of issue concerned the respective jurisdictions of church and state over clergymen convicted of crimes. Bishops became divided in their views and after a stormy royal council at Northampton in 1164, Becket fled secretly to France. It took six years before the archbishop and king were reconciled, but immediately Thomas arrived back in England (1 December 1170), the quarrel broke out yet again, over certain bishops whom Becket had disciplined for infringing his see's prerogatives at the king's instigation. Henry, who was in Normandy when he received the news, became enraged and uttered reckless words against his adversary, probably not intentionally, but which were Thomas's death-warrant. Four knights [who later took up service with the Knights Templar] hastened across the Channel and, in the early evening of 29 December, killed the archbishop in a side chapel of his cathedral. His last words were reported to be: "Willingly I die for the name of Jesus and in defence of the church." Christendom was aghast; all over western Europe Thomas was spontaneously acclaimed as a martyr, and in 1173 Pope Alexander III formally canonized him. (Attwater, 1974, 325-6)

SELECT BIBLIOGRAPHY

ADDISON, C. G. (1852) *The History of the Knights Templar* : Longman & Co, London.

D'ALBON, Marquis Andre (1913) *Cartulaire Générale de L'Ordre du Temple 1119? – 1150*: Librairie Ancienne, Imprimerie Valentinoise, Valence, Paris.

– *Cartulaire Générale de L'Ordre du Temple 1119? – 1150 – Recueil des chartes et des bulles relatives a L'Ordre du Temple* – vols. LX, LXI, LXII, LXIII: unpublished (fische catalogue générale) held at the Bibliothèque Nationale, Paris.

ALLEN, J. Romilly (1887) *Early Christian Symbolism in Great Britain and Ireland before the thirteenth century.* (Rhind Lectures in Archaeology for 1885), 8 vols. : Whiting & Co., London.

ANDERSON, M. D. (1971) *History and Imagery in British Churches*: J. Murray, Edinburgh.

ANDREWS, W. (1969) *Bygone Essex*, Colchester 1892 (County History Reprints) East Ardsley, Yorks.

APPLEBY, John T. (1965) *England without Richard, 1189-1199* : G. Bell & Sons, London.

ARGYLE, R. (1958) *Religious Behaviour*: International Library of Sociology & Social Reconstruction, London.

ASHDOWN, Charles H. (1988 Reprint) *Armour and Weapons in the Middle Ages*: The Holland Press, London.

ATTWATER, Donald (1974) *The Penguin Dictionary of Saints*: Penguin Books Ltd., London.

BAIGENT, M., LEIGH, R. and LINCOLN, H. (1982) *The Holy Blood and the Holy Grail*: Book Club Associates, by arrangement with Jonathan Cape, Beccles & London.

BAIGENT, M. and LEIGH, R. (1989) *The Temple and The Lodge*: Jonathan Cape Ltd. one of the publishers in the Random Century Group, London.

BAKER, G. (1822-1830) *History & Antiquities of the County of Northampton,* vol. I : John Bowyer, Nichols & Son, London.

BARBER, Richard (1974) *The Knight and Chivalry*: Cardinal, London.

BARING-GOULD, S. (1911) *Cliff Castles and Cave-dwellings of Europe*: Seeley, London.

BEAMON, Sylvia P. and ROAF, Susan (1990) *The Ice-houses of Britain*: Routledge, Chapman Hall, London.

BELDAM, Joseph (1884 3rd ed) *The Origin and Use of the Royston Cave being the substance of a report some time since presented to the Royal Society of Antiquaries*: J. Warren, Royston.

BERESFORD, M. W. & ST. JOSEPH, J. K. S. (1958) *Medieval England, an Aerial Survey*: Cambridge Air Surveys 2 : CUP, Cambridge.

BESSY, Maurice (1968) *A Pictorial History of Magic and the Supernatural* (Translated by M. CROSLAND and A. DAVENTRY): Pragre pr., Feltham, Middx.

BLAAUW, W. H. (1857) *Saddlescombe & Shipley Preceptories, Sussex* reprinted from *Sussex Archaeological Collections*, vol. IX: J. R. Smith, London, pp. 227 et seq.

BOASE, T. S. R. (1953) *English Art 1100-1216* (Oxford History of English Art): Clarendon Press, Oxford.

– (1967) *Castles and Churches of the Crusading Kingdom:* OUP, printed by Olten Press, London.

BRANSTON, B. (1974) *The Lost Gods of England*: Book Club Associates by arrangement with Thames & Hudson, London.

BROOKE, Iris (1935) *English Costume of the Later Middle Ages...* : A. & C. Black Ltd., London.

BUCK, J. D. (1967) *Symbolism of Freemasonry or Mystic Masonry...* 3 ed : The Charles T. Powner Co., Chicago.

BURMAN, Edward (1986) *The Templars Knights of God* : Crucible.

BUSSELL, F. W. (1918) *Religious Thought & Heresy in the Middle Ages*: Robert Scott, London.

CARTWRIGHT, E. (1815-27) *The Parochial Topography of the Rape of Bramber* in *A History of the Western Division of the County of Sussex* vols. I & II : J. B. Nichols & Son, London.

CHAPLIN, Dorothea (1935) *Matter, Myth & Spirit...* : Simpkin Marshall, London.

CLARK, Evelyn (1961) *Cornish Fogous* : Methuen & Co., London.

CHARPENTIER, Louis (1974) *Les Mystères Templiers* : Robert Laffont, Paris.

CLUTTERBUCK, R. (1815-17) *History and Antiquities of the County of Hertfordshire,* vol. III : Nichols, Son & Bentley, London.

CONDER, Capt. C. R. and KITCHENER, Capt. H. H. (1881-3) *Survey of Western Palestine. Memoirs of the Topography, orography, hydrography and archaeology,* vols. I, II, and III. Ed. with additions by E. H. PALMER and W. BESANT : Palestine Exploration Fund, London.

COOPER-OAKLEY, Isabel (1977 2nd ed) *Masonry & Medieval Mysticism: Traces of a Hidden Tradition* : Theosophical Publishing House, London.

COPE, S. (1948) *Heraldry, Flags, and Seals*: Assocn. of Special Libraries & Information Bureaux, London.

DARBY, H. C. (1971) *Domesday Geography of Eastern England*: CUP, Cambridge.

DAVIS, R. H. C. (1967) King Stephen, 1135-1154 : Longmans, Green & Co. Ltd., London.

DE SEDE, Gérard (1962) *Les Templiers sont parmi nous* (*l'énigme de Gisors*) : Edition J'ai Lu, Paris.

DOUBLEDAY, H. Arthur and PAGE, William (Eds) (1903) *Victoria County History of Essex* vols. I & II: Archibald Constable & Co., London.

DOUGLAS-IRVINE, Helen (1914) *East Herts.* in *Victoria County History*, vol. IV.12. (see Wm. PAGE. 1912).

ELLIS, H. (Ed) (1783-1816) *Inquisitio Eliensis, Survey of estates of the Abbey of Ely in the counties of Cambridge, Essex, Herts. etc. contained in Domesday book*, vol. IV : Record Commission, London.

EKWALL, Eilert (1985 4th ed.) *The Concise Oxford Dictionary of English Place Names* : Clarendon Press, Oxford.

FARRER, William (1920) *Feudal Cambridgeshire*: CUP, Cambridge.

– (1923-5) *Honors and Knight Fees*, vol. I & III: Printed for the author, London.

FFOULKES, C. J. (1909) *Armour and Weapons*: Clarendon Press, Oxford.

– (1912) *European Arms and Armour in the University of Oxford* (principally in the Ashmolean and Pitt-Rivers Museums): Clarendon Press, Oxford.

– (1912) *The Armourer & his Craft from the XI to the XVI century*: Methuen & Co., London.

– (1927) *Bible.* A book of Old Testament illustrations of the Middle of the Thirteenth century sent by Cardinal B. Maciejowski to Shah Abbas the Great, King of Persia held in the Pierpoint Morgan Library in New York; described by S. C. COCKERELL with an introduction by M. R. JAMES, and notes on Armour by C. J. FFOULKES, Roxburghe Club, Cambridge.

FINCHAM, H. W. (1933 2nd ed) *Order of the Hospital of St. John of Jerusalem and its Grand Priory of England:* (held in the Archives of the Library at St. John's Gate, Clerkenwell) : First ed. published by W. H. & L. Collingridge, London.

FISHER, John L. (1946) *Cartularium de Colne*: Essex Archaeological Soc., Occasional Publication 1, Colchester.

FOURNIER, P. F. (1922) *Fascicule Complémentaire* (additional documents from D'Albon) : Paris.

FOX, H. S. A. (June 1970) *Going to Town in 13th Century England* in *The Geographical Magazine*, 658, 660-1

GARDNER, Gerald B. (1968) *Witchcraft Today*, introduction by M. Murray: Arrow Books, London.

GIBBS, The Hon. Vicary (Ed) (1926) *Complete Peerage of England, Scotland and Ireland*, vol. V with assistance of H. Arthur DOUBLEDAY: London.

GOVER, J. E. B., MAWER, A., STENTON, F. M. (1933) *The Place-names of Northamptonshire*: University Press, Cambridge.

– (1938) *The Place-names of Hertfordshire*: University Press, Cambridge.

HAMILTON, N. E. S. A. (1876) *Inquisitio Comitatus, Cantabrigiensis*: Royal Society of Literature, London.

HASTINGS, J. (Ed) (1908) *Encyclopaedia of Religion & Ethics*, vols. 1 & 12 : T. & T. Clark, Edinburgh.

HIBBERT, Christopher (1970) *The Search for King Arthur* by the Editors of 'Horizon Magazine', Consultant C. THOMAS: Cassell, London; U.S.A. pr.

HINE, Reginald (1927-9) *History of Hitchin*, vols. I & II : G. Allen & Unwin, London.

JAMESON, Mrs. A. (1850) *Legends of the Monastic Orders* : Longman, Green & Co., London.

– (1857) *Sacred and Legendry Art*, vols. I and II : Longmans & Co., London.

JAMESON, Mrs. A. and Lady EASTLAKE (1864) *History of our Lord, as exemplified in Works of Art*, vols. I & II : Longman, Green, Longman, Roberts & Green, London.

JARVIS, C. S. (1931) *Yesterday and Today in Sinai* : W. Blackwood & Sons, Edinburgh.

KINGSTON, Alfred (1893) *Fragments of Two Centuries* : Warren Bros., Royston.

- (1912) *History of Royston* : Elliot Stock, London. Warren Bros., Royston.

KNOOP, D. & JONES, G. P. (1942) *Freemasonry and the Idea of Natural Religion* : privately printed.

- (1943) *Second Thoughts on Masonic History Old and New* : privately printed.

KNOWLES, D. & HADCOCK, R. N. (1953) *Medieval Religious Houses: in England and Wales* : Longman, Green, London.

KUHN, Herbert (1956) *The Rock Pictures of Europe*. First published in Germany, 1952. Translated by Alan HOUGHTON Broderick Sidgwick & Jackson, London.

LAKING, G. F. (1920-2) *A Record of European Armour and Arms through Seven Centuries* 5 vols. : Bell, London.

LAMBERT, Elie. (1955) *L'Architecture des Templiers* : Paris.

LANDAY, Jerry M. (1972) *Dome of the Rock: three faiths of Jerusalem* : Reader's Digest Assoc. Ltd., London in assoc. with Newsweek, New York.

LARKING, Lambert B. (Ed) (1857) *The Knights Hospitaller; being the report of Prior Philip de Thame to the Grand Master Elyan de Villanove for AD 1338* : Camden Soc. Publications vol. LXV, London.

LEES, Beatrice A. (1935) *Records of the Templars in England in the Twelfth Century: The Inquest of 1185 with illustrative charters and documents*. British Academy Records of the Social and Economic History, of England and Wales : Oxford University Press, London.

LEONARD, Emile. G. (1930) *Introduction au Cartulaire Manuscrit du Temple du Marquis D'Albon* : Paris.

LETHBRIDGE, T. (1975) *Gogmagog: The Buried Gods* : Book Club Associates by arrangement with Routledge & Kegan Paul Ltd. London.

LEYS, Agnes (1938-41) *Sandford Cartulary*, 2 vols. : Oxford Record Series 19 & 22, Oxford.

LYSONS, Daniel & Samuel (1808) *Magna Britannia...* vol. 2 pt. 1 containing, *History of Cambridgeshire* : Printed by T. Cadell, W. Davies, London.

MACKEY, Albert G. (1860) *A Lexicon of Freemasonry.* Revised by Donald CAMPBELL : Richard Griffin & Co., London.

MALE, Emile (1961) *Religious Art in France XIII century* : Translated by Dora NUSSEY, Collins, London.

MATTHEWS, J. & GREEN, M. (1986) *The Grail Seeker's Companion: A Guide to the Grail Quest in the Aquarian Age* : Guild Publishing, London.

MELVILLE, Marion (1974 2nd ed) *La Vie des Templiers* : Gallimard, Paris.

MILLER, Hamish and BROADHURST, Paul (1989) *The Sun and the Serpent* : Pendragon Press, Launceston, Cornwall.

MORANT, Philip (1768) *The History & Antiquities of the County of Essex*, vol. II : London.

MORRIS, John (Ed) (1976) *Domesday Book, Hertfordshire*, 12 : Phillimore, Chichester.

NEILSON, Nellie (1941) *Medieval Agrarian Society in its Prime in Cambridge Economic History of Europe*, vol. I; *the Agrarian Life of the Middle Ages*, Ed. CLAPHAM, J. H. & POWER, Eileen : CUP, Cambridge.

O'DEA, T. F. (1966) *The Sociology of Religion* : Prentice-Hall Foundations of modern sociology series, Engelwood Cliffs, New Jersey.

OLIVER, G. (1826) *Signs and Symbols, illustrated and explained in a course of 12 Lectures on Freemasonry* : Printed for the author, Grimsby.

OWEN, Dorothy M. (1971) *Church and Society in Medieval Lincolnshire in vol. V of the History of Lincolnshire.* Series ed. by Joan THIRSK : Lincolnshire Local History Society, History of Lincolnshire Committee, Lincoln.

PAGE, William (1907) *Victoria County History of Suffolk* : Reprint (1975) : Dawson for University of London Institute of Historical Research, London.

– (1912) A *History of Hertfordshire*, *Odsey Hundred*, vol. III (Victoria County History); vol. IV : Constable & Co., London.

PARKER, Thomas W. (1963) *The Knight Templars of England* : Uni. of Arizona Press, Tucson.

PARKIN, Rev. Charles (1744) *An Answer to, or Remarks upon Dr. Stukeley's Origines Roystonianae. The Antiquity and Imagery of the Oratory, lately discovered at Royston in Hertfordshire, are truly stated and accounted for* : J. Hoyles, London.

– (1748) *A Reply to the weak, peevish and malevolent objections brought by Dr. Stukeley in his Origines Roystonianae no. II against an Answer to or Remarks upon his Origines Roystonianae no. I* : T. Trye, Norwich.

PARTNER, Peter (1982) *The Murdered Magicians: The Templars and their Myth* : Oxford University Press, Oxford.

PENNICK, Nigel (1981) *The Subterranean Kingdom. A Survey of Man-made Structures beneath the Earth* : Turnstone Press Ltd., Wellingborough, Northamptonshire.

PIGGOTT, Stuart (1985) *William Stukeley An Eighteenth-Century Antiquary* : Thames & Hudson, London.

PRESTON, William, (1861) *Illustrations of Masonry* with additions by G. OLIVER : A. Spencer, London.

PRITCHARD, Violet (1967) *English Medieval Graffiti* : Cambridge University Press, Cambridge.

RICE, David T. (1963) *Art of the Byzantine Era* : Thames and Hudson, London.

– (1965) *Islamic Art* : Thames & Hudson, London.

RICHARDSON, E. (1843) *The Monumental Effigies of the Temple Church...* : Longman, Brown, Green & Longmans, London.

RICHARDSON, John (1989 rev.edn.) *The Local Historian's Encyclopaedia* : Historical Publications, New Barnet, Herts.

RILEY-SMITH, Jonathan (1967) *Knights of St. John of Jerusalem and Cyprus c. 1050-1310* : Macmillan & Co., London.

– (1987) *The Crusades: A Short History* : The Athlone Press, London.

ROBINSON, E. and SMITH, E. (1841) *Biblical Researches in Palestine, Mount Sinai & Arabia Petraea*, vol. II : John Murray, London.

ROBINSON, John J. (1989) *Born in Blood: The Lost Secrets of Freemasonry* : Guild Publishing, London.

ROE, Frederick (1929) *Essex Survivals* : Methuen & Co., London.

ROUND, J. H. (1892) *Geoffrey de Mandeville - A Study of the Anarchy* : Longmans, Green, & Co., London & New York.

– (1899) *Calendar of Documents preserved in France, Illustrative of the History of Great Britain and Ireland*, vol. I : Her Majesty's Stationery Office, London.

RUNCIMAN, S. (1951-54) *A History of the Crusades*, vols. I, II, III : Cambridge University Press, Cambridge.

SALMON, Nathanial (1728) *History of Hertford describing the County and its Ancient Monuments, particularly the Roman with the character of those that have been the processors of the land, and an account of the most memorable occurrences* : London.

SALTZMAN, L. F. (1948) *Victoria History of Cambridgeshire and Isle of Ely*, vol. II : Oxford University Press for Institute of Historical Research, London.

SEWARD, Desmond (1972) *The Monks of War – The Military Religious Orders* : Eyre Methuen, London.

SIMON, Edith (1959) *The Piebald Standard. A Biography of the Knights Templar* : Cassell, London.

SMAIL, R. C. (1956) *Crusading Warfare (1097-1193)* : Cambridge University Press, Cambridge.

– (1973) *The Crusaders in Syria and the Holy Land* : Thames and Hudson, London.

STUKELEY, W. (1743) *Palaeographia Britannica or discourses on Antiquities in Britain no. I, Origines Roystonianae, or an account of the Oratory of Lady Roisia, Foundress of Royston discovered in Royston in August 1742* : R. Manby, London.

– (1746) *Palaeographia Britannica or discourses on Antiquities in Britain no. II, or defence of Lady de Vere Foundress of Roiston; against the Calumny of Mr. Parkin, rector of Oxburgh wherein his pretended answer is fully refuted: the former opinion further confirm'd and illustrated. To which occasionally are added, many curious matters in antiquity: and six copper plates* : Francis Howgrave, Stamford.

TABOR, Margaret E. (1924) *The Saints in Art* : Methuen & Co. Ltd., London.

TWINING, L. (1855) *Types and Figures of the Bible, Illustrated by the Art of the Early and Middle Ages* : Longman, Brown, Green & Longmans, London.

– (1885) *Christian Symbols and Emblems of Early and Medieval Christian Art* : John Murray, London.

VALIENTE, D. (1973) *An ABC of Witchcraft Past and Present* : Robert Hale & Co., London.

WAGNER, A. R. (1939) *Heralds & Heraldry in the Middle Ages* : Oxford University Press, Oxford.

– (1939) *Historic Heraldry of Britain* : Oxford University Press, Oxford.

– (1960) *English Genealogy* : Clarendon Press, Oxford.

WEBSTER, Nesta H. (1955 7th ed) *Secret Societies & Subversive Movements* : Britons Publishing Society, London.

WEIR, Anthony & JERMAN, James (1986) *Images of Lust - Sexual Carvings on Medieval Churches* : B. T. Batsford Ltd., London.

WHALLEY, Rev. Peter (1791) *The History and Antiquities of Northamptonshire compiled from the Manuscript Collection of John BRIDGES*, vol. I : Sold by T. Payne, London, D. Prince & J. Cook, Oxford & Mr. Lacy, Northants.

WILLIAMS, Jay & FREEMAN, Margaret B. (Eds of *Horizon Magazine*) (1962) *Knights of the Crusades* : Cassell, London.

WOOD-LEGH, K. (1965) *Perpetual Chantries in England* : CUP, Cambridge.

WRIGHT, Wm. (1884) *The Empire of the Hittites, with decipherment of Hittite inscriptions by Prof. A H. SAYCE and complete set of Hittite inscriptions by W. H. RYLANDS* : James Nisbet & Co., London.

YARKER, John (1909) *The Arcane Schools. A review of their origin and antiquity: with a general History of Freemasonry and its relation to the theosophic, scientific and philosophic mysteries* : William Tait, Belfast.

JOURNALS, TRANSACTIONS, PROCEEDINGS, LEAFLETS, GUIDES

BEAMON, Sylvia P. (1973) *Énigmatique Sculptures de Royston Cave* in *Archeologia*, Document no. 2 : Paris.

BEAMON, Sylvia P. and DONEL, Lisa G. (1978) *An Investigation of Royston Cave* in *Procs. of the Cambridge Antiquarian Soc.*, vol. LXVIII : Imray Laurie Norie and Wilson, St. Ives, Huntingdon, pp. 47-58.

Bedfordshire Historical Record Soc., vol. XIV. Published by the Society at the Old House in Apsley Guise, MCMXXXI.

BELDAM, Joseph (1852) *The Icenhilde Road* in *Archaeological Journal*, vol. XXV, p. 26 et seq. : Royal Archaeological Institute, London.

BISHKO, Herbert (1973 3rd ed) *This is Jerusalem* : Heritage Publishing Ltd., Tel Aviv.

CARNY, Lucien (1972) *Les Sceaux de l'Ordre du Temple* in *Atlantis* no. 268, 336-48. Vincennes.

CASTLE, E. J. (1890) *Proceedings against the Templars in France and England for Heresy* in *Ars Quartor Coronatorum*, vol. III (1890) and vol. XX (1906-7), Margate.

Chislehurst Caves (undated pre 1974) : Official Guide.

CHRISTIE, Patricia M. & COAD, J. G. (1981 for 1980) *Excavations at Denny Abbey* in *The Archaeological Journal*, vol. 137, London, pp. 138-279.

CLARKE, George E. (undated after 1960) *The Margate Caves*, Clifton ville : (Guide).

COULTON, G. G. (1914-15) *Medieval Graffiti, especially in the Eastern Counties* in *Procs. Cambridge Antiquarian Soc.*, vol. XIX with Comm. no. LXVII : Printed by John Clay at the Uni. Press, Cambridge, pp. 53-63.

CRELLIN, V. H. (unpublished) *Notes on Baldock and the Knights Templar* c. 1976.

FRY, K. (1878) *Fragments concerning Eudo Dapifer* in *Trans. Essex Archaeological Soc.* N.S. i, pp 33-4.

GRAY, H. J. (c. 1960) – *St. Mary the Virgin Church, Baldock, Herts.* (Guide) : The British Publishing Co. Ltd., Gloucester.

– Personal unpublished notes.

Inspeximus of Temple Dinsley, 1280 from a seventeenth century copy of the original : (Hertford County Record Office).

Leaflets of Local Lore – The Hermits Cave at Royston from *Mems and Gems of Cambridgeshire*, 1897.

LE COUR, Paul (Mai/Juin 1972) *Les Graffiti du Château de Chinon* in *Atlantis* no. 268, pp. 289-294. Vincennes.

LETHBRIDGE, T. C. (1934-5) *Excavations at Burwell Castle, Cambridgeshire* in *Procs. Cambridge Antiquarian Soc.* vol. XVI with Report pp. 1-171.

– (1949) *Byzantine Influence in Late Saxon England* in *Procs. Cambridge Antiquarian Soc.* vol. XLIII with Report, pp. 1-51.

LEWER, David (1964) *The Temple Church*, no. 1 Pitkin Pictorials English Churches Series, London (Guide)

Little Wymondley Cartulary – British Museum ADD.MS. 43972

LUKIS, Rev. W. C. (Ed) (1883-1) *The Family Memoirs of the Rev. William Stukeley, MD and the Antiquarian and other correspondence of William Stukeley, Roger and Samuel Gale etc.* in *The Surtees Society* vol. II *Stukeley's Diaries and Letters.*

MAUNY, Raymond (Mai/Juin 1969) *Les Graffiti du Donjon de Chinon attribués aux Templiers* in *Archeologia* no. 28, pp. 78-81. Paris.

MILBOURN, Thomas (1886) *Notes on the History of Royston in the Counties of Hertford and Cambridge* : Reprinted from the *Trans. of the Evening Meetings of the London and Middlesex Archaeological Soc.*

MOULE, A. C. (1921-2) *Some Trumpington Inscriptions with special reference to the Base of the Old Village Cross* in *Procs. Cambridge Antiquarian Soc.*, vol. XXIV with Comm. & Report, no. LXXII, pp.112.

Newsells Park Estate Ownership Calendar, 1929 and maps held in the Estate Office, Newsells.

Newsells Park Estate maps for 1788 and 1791 held in the County Record Office, Hertford (Ref: D/ERy P3 and P5).

Origines Roystonianae – An Account of the Cave or Oratory at Royston in Hertfordshire with an Appendix – printed and published by J. Warren, Royston 1825.

PALMER, W. M. (1904) *Notes on the Early History of Shingay, Co. Cambridge* in *Trans. of the Cambridgeshire & Huntingdon Archaeological Soc.* vol. I, part II : Pub. at Ely by the Society. Printed by G. H. Tyndall, Minster Press, Ely, pp. 126-141.

– (1925-6) *Argentine's manor, Melbourn* in *Procs. Cambridge Antiquarian Soc.*, vol. XXVIII with Comm. & Report. pp. 1-153.

– (1935) *John Layer (1586-1640) of Shepreth, Cambridgeshire. A seventeenth-century local historian.* Cambridge Antiquarian Soc. Octavo Publications, no. LIII : Bowes & Bowes, Cambridge.

PARSONS, Catherine E. (1914-5) *Cambridgeshire Witchcraft* in *Procs. Cambridge Antiquarian Soc.* vol. XIX, Michaelmas, Lent & Easter Terms. With Comm. no. LXVII.

PREVITE-ORTON, C. W. (1931) *Eudo Dapifer's Honour of Walbrook* in *English Historical Review* vol. XLVI, London, pp. 622 et sec.

RAINBIRD CLARK, R. (1970) *Grimes Graves*, Norfolk : (Min. of Public Buildings & Works Guide).

RALEGH-RADFORD, C. A. & DONALDSON, G. (1953) *Whithorn & Kirkmadrine, Wigtownshire (St. Ninian's Cave & Chapel)* : (Official Guide) Edinburgh.

RIGOLD, S. E. (1962) *Temple Manor, Strood, Rochester, Kent*: DoE., HMSO., London.

Royston Notes, published and unpublished prepared for the *Victoria County History of Hertford* : County Record Office, Hertford.

RUSTON, Rev. Mark (undated) *Holy Sepulchre Church, Cambridge*. No 2 in Pitkin Pictorials English Churches Series : (Guide).

ST. JOHN HOPE (1908) *The Round Church of the Knights Templar at Temple Bruer* in *Archaeologia* vol. LXI, pp. 177-98, pls. XIX-XXI : Society of Antiquaries of London.

– (1918) *Round-naved Churches in England and their Connexion with the Orders of the Temple and of the Hospital of St. John of Jerusalem* in *Archaeologia Cantiana* (Trans. of the Kent Arch. Soc.) vol. XXXIII : pub. for the Soc. by Mitchell, Hughes & Clarke, London.

Saturday Magazine (1842) *The Round Churches of England,* in July, no. 646; August no. 651; September nos. 654 & 656; October no. 659.

Shell Temple of Margate known as The Grotto (undated pre 1973) : (Guide).

SMITH, John (1965) *The Royston Cave* (Official Guide) : Royston Town Hall, Royston.

STOKES, Rev. H. P. (1915-6) *Wayside Crosses in Cambridge* in *Procs. Cambridge Antiquarian Soc.*, vol. XX, with Comm. no. LXVIII p. 173. Plates I – XXIV and other illust.

TEVERSHAM, T. F. (undated pre-1970) *A History of the Hospice – Priory Chapel in the hamlet of Whittlesford-Bridge* : Printed by Crampton & Sons Ltd. Sawston, Cambridge.

Trans. of the Cave Research Group of Great Britain, 1 – 12.

VOLTZ, Eugene (March 1973) *La Chapelle des Templiers de Metz* in *Archeologia* no. 56, Paris.

Archeologia, Tresors des Ages, Paris, France:
– No. 11 juillet – août, 1966;
– No. 27 mars – avril and no. 28 mai - june 1969;
– No. 32 janvier – février 1970;
– No. 43 novembre – décembre 1971;
– No. 56 mars 1973.

Atlantis, no. 268, mai – juin 1972 – Chinon et L'Énigme Templiers : Vincennes, France.

STATE AND OTHER OFFICIAL PAPERS CONSULTED

Feet of Fines and Rolls Series are published by the Pipe Roll Society of London.

Cartae Antiquae Rolls 1-10 – edited by Lionel LANDON.

Cartae Antiquae Rolls 11-20 – edited by J. Conway DAVIES.

Rotuli Dominabus 1185.

Rolls of the King's Court in the reign of King Richard I 1194-1195.

Ancient Charters, Royal and Private part I, prior to AD 1200.

Feet of Fines for the first seven years of the reign of King Richard I 1182-96.

Feet of Fines of the 7th and 8th year of the reign of King Richard I 1196-7.

Feet of Fines in the Public Record Office of the 9th year of the reign of King Richard I 1197-8.

Feet of Fines for Lincolnshire for the reign of King John 1199-1216 – edited by Margaret S. WALKER.

Feet of Fines for Norfolk in the 10th year of the reign of King Richard I 1198-1199 and the first four years of the reign of King John 1199-1202 – edited by Barbara DODWELL.

Feet of Fines for Norfolk and Suffolk, 1201-1215 for the reign of King John, and for Suffolk etc. 1199-1213 – edited by Barbara DODWELL.

Early Medieval Miscellany, Pipe Roll Soc. – edited by Doris M. STANTON.

Regesta Regum Anglo-Normannorum, 1066-1154 – edited by H. E. CRONNE.

Memorandum Roll of King John (1199-1200) for Michaelmas Term of first year of his reign.

Memorandum Roll of King John (1207-8) together with Curia Regis Rolls of Hilary, Richard I (1196) and Easter Richard I (1198) – edited by R. Allen BROWN.

Memorandum Roll of Kings Remembrances, Michaelmas 1230 – Trinity 1231, edited by Chalfont ROBINSON : Pipe Roll Society, London.

The Great Roll of the Pipe for the 7th year of the reign of King John, Michaelmas 1205 – edited by Sidney SMITH.

The Great Roll of the Pipe for the 8th year of the reign of King John, Michaelmas 1206 – edited by Doris M. STENTON.

The Great Roll of the Pipe for the 9th year of the reign of King John, Michaelmas 1207 – edited by A. Mary KIRKUS.

The Great Roll of the Pipe for the 10th year of the reign of King John, Michaelmas 1208 – edited by Doris M. STENTON.

The Great Roll of the Pipe for the 11th year of the reign of King John, Michaelmas 1209 – edited by Doris M. STENTON.

The Great Roll of the Pipe for the 12th year of the reign of King John, Michaelmas 1210 – edited by C. F. SLADE.

The Great Roll of the Pipe for the 13th year of the reign of King John, Michaelmas 1211 – edited by Doris M. STENTON.

The Great Roll of the Pipe for the 14th year of the reign of King John, Michaelmas 1212 – edited by Patricia M. BARNES.

The Great roll of the Pipe for the 16th year of the reign of King John, Michaelmas 1214 – edited by Patricia M. BARNES.

Pipe Roll 17 John and Praestita Roll 14 -18 John – edited by R. A. BROWN and J. C. HOLT.

The Great Roll of the Pipe for the 14 years of the reign of King Henry III Michaelmas 1230 – edited by Chalfont ROBINSON.

Statutes of the Realm, vol. III. Reprinted 1963 by Dawsons of London.

Letters and Papers of Henry VIII, vol. 15, 1540.

Index

The Temple Publications' Books

Over the course of human history there have been many men who have stood out amongst the rest. Whether writers of fiction, great physicians or even politicians, these men may in fact share a common purpose, regardless of the age they lived in. *What Wise Men Do* analyses various great men such as:

Paracelsus

Grand Master Pinto of the Knights of Malta

Sir Arthur Conan Doyle

Jules Verne

H. G. Wells

Bram Stoker

Bob Kane (creator of Batman)

In this series of investigations a thread of truth is discovered, revealing an inner yearning linked to our own evolutionary path and shared by each and every one of the individuals in question.

What Wise Men Do, investigates concepts of magic as seen in each age and questions the truth of the statements against modern science and even theoretical science. In each case some new and startling discovery is made, making this compelling book a revelation from chapter to chapter.

What Wise Men Do.

Philip Gardiner
ISBN 978-0-9555970-9-1
Paperback

£ 11.99

Following on from *The God-Kings of Europe, The God-Kings of England,* continues the Saga of the great Ulvungar Dynasty. It shows that there was a plan to counter the hegemony of Roman Christianity, by counter attacking, first with Viking raids and later by conquest and settlement. This is the tale of the Ulvungars and their attempt to conquer England, under the leadership of Danish Kings such as Sweyn Forkbeard and Canute. They were opposed by their Odonic Anglo-Saxon cousins such as Alfred and Aethelred. The Ulvungars would take control by force of arms. One branch would take England; another would take control of Normandy. Ultimately, they would combine after the Battle of Hastings in the Anglo-Norman Dynasty that would found the Angevin Empire.

This book shows the web of marriages and alliances and the detailed planning that went into the final push that culminated at the Battle of Hastings. It shows how the Davidic line of Jesus was protected by the Odonic Kings of England and Dukes of Normandy.

In the appendices the author traces and explains who William the Conqueror's real ancestors were and shows detailed genealogies.

The God Kings of England – The Viking and Norman Dynasties and their Conquest of England (983-1066).

Hugh Montgomery
ISBN 978-0-9555970-4-6
Paperback, 166 pages

£ 11.99

Countless myths and legends attest to the ancient sanctity of the Isle of Avalon. Yet archaeologists have long been puzzled by the absence of material evidence for prehistoric activity upon the hills of Glastonbury. This book provides decisive proof of the island's especial importance to our distant ancestors, by showing how its unique conjunction of landscape with key celestial movements would have indicated its extraordinary sanctity to Neolithic peoples, even to their Mesolithic forebears. Because of the intimate relationship between its holy hills and the pathways of sun, moon and stars, Avalon would have been understood as an exceptionally potent spiritual sanctuary, a place of otherworldly power.

Nicholas Mann and Philippa Glasson reveal the site of an ancient astronomical observatory at the heart of the Avalonian landscape. They show how prehistoric sky-watchers appear to have modelled key parts of the island, including the Tor and the summit of St Edmund's Hill, to refine their celestial observations. The Isle of Avalon was truly an ancient "temple of the stars".

The Star Temple of Avalon – Glastonbury's Ancient Observatory Revealed.

Nicholas Mann & Philippa Glasson
ISBN 978-0-9555970-8-4
Paperback, 127 pages

£ 11.99

ISBN 978-0-9555970-5-3
Hardback, 500 limited signed edition

£ 14.99

GWYN – **Ancient god of Glastonbury and key to the Glastonbury Zodiac**, is the debut book written and illustrated by Glastonbury based artist and researcher, Yuri Leitch. Adorned with many of his own beautiful illustrations, and quotes from arcane medieval Welsh manuscripts, the author hopes that this book will educate, uplift and inspire the reader's imagination.

'Gwyn' is the culmination of six years of contemplation, historical research and investigation into the sacred landscape of Somerset's unique landmark, Glastonbury Tor to the ancient Britons, this isle in the marshes, later named 'Glastonbury' by the Saxons, was known as Ynys Witrin or (The Glass Isle). This was their beloved sacred ground, the threshold of 'Annwn' - (their 'Otherworld' paradise.) Gwyn was the protective warrior god of Ynys Witrin and the British Lord of Paradise.

The book takes the reader back to the beginning of the 1st century - to the tribal society of the Native Britons specific to this area; the tribe that are known to us as the Durotriges. We glimpse their spiritual world by looking at The Children of Don; the Durotriges' pantheon of gods, goddesses and specifically Gwyn ap Nudd, the ancient god of Glastonbury. By doing this, we begin to understand Ynys Witrin as their most sacred ground

The author deals with the Roman invasion of Britain, and of how these ancient Britons adapted to their new Romano-British lifestyle. Despite their cultural changes the Durotriges continued to use Ynys Witrin as their sacred island at least up until the 5th century.

Controversially, this view challenges the popular legend that Jesus' kinsman, Joseph of Arimathea, founded a Christian church at Glastonbury in the 1st century - Yuri explains that whist Christians were the enemies of Rome well into the 3rd century, and that the lack of any archaeological remains indicating Christian presence until the 5th century shows how Glastonbury probably functioned as a sacred burial ground until the Dark Ages.

Gwyn also accounts for the first Christian missionaries of the 5th century who made very deliberate attempts to banish the old god from Glastonbury Tor.

By taking the reader step by step through medieval Welsh literature, Yuri Leitch explains how Gwyn has an intimate link with many of Glastonbury's unusual characteristics. The Tor's it's placement on the St. Michael Line alignment with the Mid Winter sun-roll up the Tor and most curiously, with the landscape enigma of the Glastonbury Zodiac.

This is the tale of the Saxon invasion of Britain and the mass exodus of the native Britons from their homeland and their sacred isle. It tells the evocative tale of Centwine, the Saxon king of Wessex, who 'pushed the Britons to the sea' in the 7th century and the forced retreat into Wales, Cornwall and Brittany and beyond.

Here is some of the history, giving rise to the legendary tales of Avalon and the sacred Otherworld and- related faerie-realm mythology. Gwyn, the Lord of Paradise, is diminished by time and the newly imported traditions to become the 'King of the Fairies'. And then finally debased into the 'Demon King' of the Celtic Hades by ignorance; in this book you will discover the true god of Glastonbury.

Gwyn – Ancient god of Glastonbury and key to the Glastonbury Zodiac.

Yuri Leitch
ISBN 978-0-9555970-1-5
Paperback, 106 pages
£ 11.99
ISBN 978-0-9555970-8-4
Hardback, 500 limited signed edition

£ 14.99

E-Books

What is Living? Tradition of the Islands of Britain? What is the Keltic inheritance? How can it be known when so much has been lost? How can we, by drawing on the roots of our Native Land, the Spiritual Unfoldment of Ourselves and our Planet at this time? By Substantive means of the Pictish Symbol Stones, and consideration of the Nature of the Keltic Gods and Goddesses, the Author brings forward a Key for the relevance of some of the Mysteries of the Keltic Root Race.

The Keltic Power Symbols – Native Traditions,
The Keltic Goddess and God. The Serpent,
The Power Animals and The Pictish Symbol Stones.

Nicholas R. Mann
ISBN 978-0-9557400-3-9
48 pages

3.95 (on line)

Underground Mythology, edited by Sylvia P. Beamon is a unique study by experts in subterranean lore from the UK and Central Europe.

Chapters:

1. *The Shell Grotto at Margate* – Ruby M. Haslam

2. *Exploring Water in Underground Mythology* – Dr. Bruce E. Osborne

Introduction to the Czech Republic contributors – Editor

Post-Mesolithic finds from Bohemian Karst Region and the Exploitation of Caves in the Post-Mesolithic Development of Central Europe – a summary of this unpublished paper, 1987 – Dr. Vaclav Matousek

3. *The Motif of the Cave in Folk Culture* – Dr. Vaclac Matousek

4. *Cave of Nymphs, Archaic Mind, and the Symbol of the Cave* – Dr. Vaclav Cilek

5. *Who and What were the Knockers or the Knackers?* – Sylvia P. Beamon

6. *Mithraism, A 'Subterranean' Religion* – M. C. Black

Underground Mythology.

Edited by Sylvia P. Beamon
ISBN 978-0-9557400-2-2
123 pages

£ 6.95 (on line)

Original print also available
£15.99 from The Temple Publications

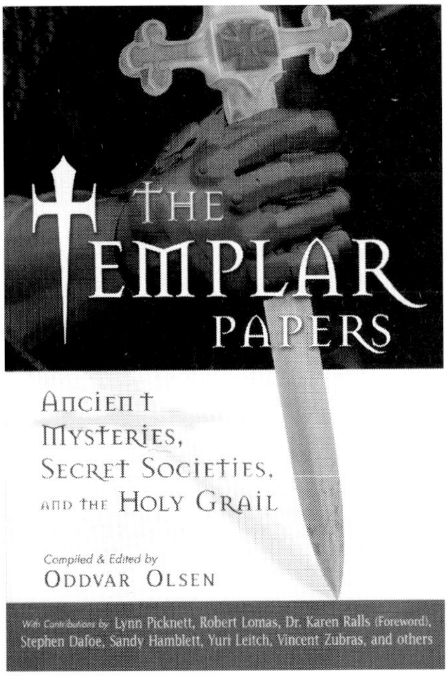

"A broad range of key issues by various contributors relating to the Knights Templar today, a valuable compendium ...both historical and speculative."

Dr Karen Ralls, Oxford based medieval historian and author of the best-selling *The Templars and the Grail.*

Much has been written about the group of 14th-century warrior monks known as the Knights Templar. Some authors, such as Dan Brown in *The Da Vinci Code,* portray them as folk heroes wrongly accused. Others disagree, saying the Templar story is ultimately one of greed, deception, and idolatry.

Just who were the Knights Templar? And what is their legacy? In **The Templar Papers**, author and historian Oddvar Olsen has assembled a veritable Who's Who of experts to unravel the mystery, You'll hear answers to some intriguing questions.

1. Were the Templars devil worshippers who venerated a mysterious head, supposedly that of John the Baptist?

2. What exactly did they find in Solomon's Temple?

3. Did they keep, and later hide, the Holy Grail and the Ark of the Covenant?

You'll also learn about the Templar link to Mary Magdalene and the Freemasons and other mysteries of the ages.

The Templar Papers offers the inquisitive reader lifetimes of research and insight. This is a distinctive and truly unique compilation.

Oddvar Olsen has studied mystery traditions and mythology since the late 1980's, when he decided to specilalize in the Knights Templar. In 2002, Olsen started The Temple, a successful periodical on the Knights Templar and related subjects. He lives in Somerset, England.

Lynn Picknett wrote Mary Magdalene - Christianity's Hidden Goddess and co-wrote the International bestseller, *The Templar Revelation.* **Robert Lomas** is the co-author of the first four books in the Hiram Key series and author of *Turning the Hiram Key.* **Stephen Dafoe,** the Canadian authority on the Templars and Freemasonry, co-wrote *The Templar Continuum.* **Sandy**

Hamblett edits and publishes *The Journal of the Rennes Alchemist.* **Vincent Zubras** is the Grand Master of OPCCTS, a group claiming direct lineage from the Knights Templar.

The Templar Papers - Ancient Mysteries, Secret Societies, and the Holy Grail

Compiled and Edited by Oddvar Olsen. Foreword by Dr Karen Ralls with Contributions by Lynn Picknett, Robert Lomas, Stephen Dafoe, Sandy Hamblett, Yuri Leitch, Vincent Zubras, and others.
Publisher: New Page Books, US,
ISBN: 1-56414-863-7
Paperback, 256 pages. Illustrated

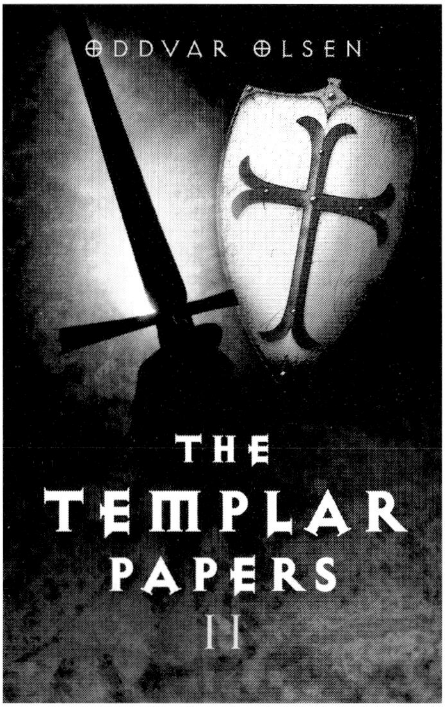

The Templar Papers II is the follow up to the best selling *The Templar Papers*. The second compilation represents a selection of articles from issues 7-12 of *The Temple*.

To further the students knowledge of the grand order of the Knights Templar; *The Templar Papers II* deals not only with the two hundred years of the orders existence but also studies relating to the Templars both before and after 1118 -1307. In error many authors see the Templars as an isolated order; however in this compilation the editor has compiled substantial material to give the reader a broader understanding of the Templar Knights, related subjects and the formation of society, as one knows it today. Renowned authors like Evelyn Lord, Sylvia Beamon, Philip Gardiner, Oddvar Olsen, Yuri Leitch and Paul Broadhurst are represented as well as a selection of aspiring authors. Topics discussed in this compilation includes King Arthur, early Christianity, the St Clairs, sacred geometry, Royston Cave, ancient British history, star lore and of course the Knights Templar.

ISBN: 978-1-84694-325-6
Size (mm): 216/140
Publisher: O-Books
Publishing date: Summer 2010
Email Thetemplebooklet@yahoo.co.uk to pre-order

Periodicals

The Temple was created in August 2002 with an aim to encourage research into the Knights Templar – their related and interrelated subjects, such as; the Grail Legends, Arthurian Mythos, the Rosicrucians, Masonic Lore, Early Christianity, Cathars, Gnostic Theology, Alchemy, Folklore, Rennes Le Chateau, Geomancy, the Occult, Mythology and Symbolism etc.

*The Templ*e started as a periodical with articles written by a few friends in Glastonbury, Somerset, England. Over the years it has published extensively research on relevant subjects by a varied selection of researchers. In *The Temple* publication and on its website you can read the latest discoveries written by the 'coffee table' student as well as by renowned authors. As *The Temple* deal with so many subjects, ranging from the shadowy past, legends and myths, as well as the latest historical data, all are well represented. In early 2006, a compilation of issues 1 - 6 of *The Temple* called *The Templar Papers* was published by New Page Books, US, and is now obtainable in various languages (see advertisement on previous page).

See www.thetemplebooklet.co.uk for further details.

The Temple Publications Ltd.
PO Box 47
Watchet,
Somerset
TA23 0WT
United Kingdom
www.thetemplepublications.com